FROM ANNA'S KITCHEN

Anna Thomas wrote her first cookbook, *The Vegetarian Epicure*, while she was a graduate student in film at the University of California at Los Angeles. Widely acknowledged as the book that brought pleasure to vegetarian cooking, it became a phenomenal success and remains a classic.

Since that time, Anna Thomas has expanded her culinary horizons through much travel, and the tasting and testing of new foods. Her second book, *The Vegetarian Epicure, Book Two*, was completed in 1979 and published by Penguin as *The New Vegetarian Epicure* in 1991.

When she is not cooking, Anna Thomas writes screenplays and produces films. Her screen credits include *My Family, Mi Familia* and *El Norte*, for which she was nominated for an Academy award. She is married to film director Gregory Nava and they live with their two young sons in the orange-growing valley of Ojai, California.

Also by Anna Thomas

The Vegetarian Epicure
The Vegetarian Epicure, Book Two

FROM ANNA'S KITCHEN

Plain and Fancy Vegetarian Menus

ANNA THOMAS

PENGUIN BOOKS

PENGUIN BOOKS

Published by the Penguin Group
Penguin Books Ltd, 27 Wrights Lane, London w8 5tz, England
Penguin Books USA Inc., 375 Hudson Street, New York, New York 10014, USA
Penguin Books Australia Ltd, Ringwood, Victoria, Australia
Penguin Books Canada Ltd, 10 Alcorn Avenue, Toronto, Ontario, Canada m4v 3b2
Penguin Books (NZ) Ltd, 182–190 Wairau Road, Auckland 10, New Zealand

Penguin Books Ltd, Registered Offices: Harmondsworth, Middlesex, England

First published in the USA as *The New Vegetarian Epicure* by Alfred A. Knopf 1996

First published in Penguin Books 1996
1 3 5 7 9 10 8 6 4 2

Set in 12/13.5pt Monotype Perpetua
Typeset by Rowland Phototypesetting Ltd, Bury St Edmunds, Suffolk
Printed in England by Clays Ltd, St Ives plc

CONTENTS

INTRODUCTION

I wrote the original *Vegetarian Epicure* when I was barely out of my teens, in a rush of enthusiasm for the great-tasting food I wanted to enjoy but could not find in the cookbooks I saw then. In the late sixties and early seventies, when I was a college student, vegetarianism was a popular idea, but most vegetarian food was pretty awful. I wanted food made from fresh ingredients, not a substitute for anything but true to its own bright flavours and, above all, delicious to eat. I wanted to enjoy myself, not deny myself. The book I wrote seemed to fill that need for me and, to my great delight, for a great many others.

That first *Vegetarian Epicure*, and its sequel, *The Vegetarian Epicure, Book Two*, captured the *geist* of a certain time – it was a guilt-free era, when butter and cream were used without a care and when cheese ruled. Today, of course, our attitudes are different. And while some may say, 'Alas, things are so different now,' I say thank goodness they are. We are all finding healthier ways to eat and enjoying lighter food, and I, for one, have never enjoyed it more.

But this is not the only change that inspired me to work on a new book. The years roll by, crowded with living, and so many things have changed since then. I have lived and cooked in many different situations. I have travelled and worked. I've started raising two wonderful children. I've grown older. My food now is a product of those years. It's full of souvenirs of life abroad and things learned from friends.

As a country, too, we've grown more sophisticated about cooking. Ethnic and cultural influences keep surfacing, and the availability of good raw materials continues to expand. Ingredients that were unheard of twenty years ago are now common on supermarket shelves, and farmers' markets are sprouting up everywhere, providing the freshest seasonal produce in greater abundance than ever. American food is not just healthier but infinitely more interesting and varied than it was when I first started to cook. Still, above all, this is a personal book, about the flavours I love, the places I've been, and the way I cook now. Because I adore Italy and Provence, because I've spent time in many Mediterranean regions and live in a similar climate, virgin olive oil, sweet basil, ripe tomatoes, and peppery green leaves are essential to me. Because I live in southern California and I'm crazy about chillies, the flavours of Mexican and southwestern foods have become a part of me, too. And because I'm Polish, I learned to make Easter Baba from my mother, and the taste of wild forest mushrooms runs in my veins.

I decided to organize this book around menus for two reasons. First, because I so much enjoy putting things together in interesting ways and also because I like planning a menu to suit the season and the moment. For me, it's another recipe — the big recipe for the whole experience of the meal. But I've also found that many people who want to eat well in new ways are baffled when it comes to devising a menu without meat as a main course. I hope that these menus, arranged loosely according to seasons, will be used as guides and will give rise to many creative variations.

Some of what I cook now is fancier, like the big multi-course dinners I've done for events and celebrations. A lot of it is simpler than ever: the plain, rustic foods that kids love, and I do too. And, of course, my cooking is lighter and leaner now than it once was — with a few indulgent exceptions. And yet, the really important things don't change. Food is part of our lives every day. We eat to live, and why not live well? Fresh food, prepared with pleasure, is a wonderful thing — whether it is a piece of home-baked country bread with a thick slice of ripe tomato from the garden eaten at the kitchen table, or a dinner party served with crystal and silver, to guests in their elegant clothes. Good food brings sustenance and joy. Friendships are formed over it, wounds are healed, milestones are celebrated, and children raised on it. Good food is more than a recipe; it's part of everything else.

I'm flattered when people tell me they've used one of my recipes — and what a delicious dish it made. And then I'm amused when they add, apologetically, 'But I changed it a little — I didn't do it exactly the way it's written . . .' Well, of course not. Why should you? You're cooking, not slavishly following a formula. You're participating in something that's part of nature, and nature is always alive, always changing. Moreover, cooking is a fusion of nature with culture. Food binds us to our roots as strongly as any song or poem. Many of us have learned more about our ancestors in the kitchen than we ever will from a book. The mother who stirs the soup and says to her children, 'Eat your vegetables,' might also say, 'Eat your history.' And no recipe from a book will ever have the meaning of the food we learn to make at someone's side, hands in the dough together, watching, kneading, tasting, smelling, learning, and holding dear.

Early on in my cooking days, I realized that I have as much fun preparing food as I do eating it. I know we live in an age of fast food, but I admit to a strong bias for slow food. I talk frequently about the importance of using good ingredients, but the truly essential ingredient of all my food is the pleasure I take in preparing it. Yes, there are times when the various demands of life collide, and food must be prepared and eaten on the run. I have children who have soccer schedules, play rehearsals, piano recitals, and important dates with friends. I have jobs, meetings, and deadlines. I know that life cannot always be an ideal of relaxed gourmet cooking in a sunlit kitchen, wine with dinner, dishes washed by helpful children, and no weight gain from dessert. I live with reality like everyone else, and there are times when I will gladly settle just for the sight of my kids eating a green vegetable. I myself have eaten a fast sandwich for lunch. I've eaten it in the car, on my way to work, between phone calls.

It's too easy to get caught up in the rush of things and lose the enjoyment of them. For me, a day spent at the farmers' market, in the kitchen, and at the table with my family is a beautiful day well spent. I love to choose the nicest produce, see the changes of the season in the market stalls, take my time preparing food, and enjoy it at leisure with congenial company. Now I have a new enjoyment: a few days ago, my eleven-year-old son, Christopher, said to me, 'Mom, tonight I want to fix dinner.' He measured my curious stare for a moment and then added, 'And I want you to show me how.' What a real source of pleasure we lose when we think of cooking as a mere chore! Food is not a chore; it's a gift. Food shared with others repays you many times over. And cooking is mythology – a story told over and over, passed on again and again, always with the same meaning but expressed in endlessly different ways.

Perhaps I love cooking even more because it has never been my profession. I am a dedicated and ardent amateur. I was not trained for restaurant cooking, and the foods in this book are all things I've cooked at home and eaten with my family or friends. They are the foods I love. Their tastes, their vivid colours, and fragrant aromas are part of my life. This is my telling of the story, and I hope you like it, change it, and make it part of yours.

SPRING AND SUMMER

AN EARLY SPRING DINNER

Spa Salad with Bitter Leaves, Asparagus,
and Mint

Risotto di Zucca

Strawberries with Honey-sweetened
Yogurt Cheese

This is a delightful meal for early spring or even late winter, when you can still find good winter squashes and when asparagus is arriving in the markets.

If it's too early to find slender, crunchy asparagus to slice raw into the salad, something else could be sneaked in — sugar peas, or even the tender stalks of broccoli, peeled and thinly sliced. The important thing is the sparkling combination of tastes in the salad, followed by the richness of the risotto, which is so satisfying, yet amazingly low in fat.

Bright red juicy strawberries for dessert, with a dollop of Honey-sweetened Yogurt Cheese, are perfect for the season and in keeping with the very low-fat style of this meal. If you are watching your fat intake diligently, use yogurt cheese made from non-fat yogurt. And if you don't care, a wedge of Gorgonzola cheese and a ripe pear would also make a fabulous ending.

SPA SALAD WITH BITTER LEAVES, ASPARAGUS, AND MINT

I made up this salad once when I gave a talk about 'spa cuisine', of all things. I wanted to give an example of why good salads did not need much oil or heavy dressing. If the salad is made of good things to begin with, things that are full of intense flavour, it stands to reason that you don't have to douse them with a lot of sauce. This combination of green, red, white and gold tastes as explosively bright as it looks – it is tart and sweet, pungent and mild, and a teaspoon of good olive oil per serving feels like plenty to me.

225 g (8 oz) fresh young rocket, watercress, radicchio or a mixture of leaves

3–4 heads Belgian endive

3 tablespoons mint leaves

1 large red pepper

225 g (8 oz) slender green asparagus

125 g (4 oz) inoki or button mushrooms

75 g (3 oz) aduki or small black beans or lentils, cooked

6 spring onions, thinly sliced

2–3 tablespoons sultanas

2 tablespoons fruity green olive oil

a splash of balsamic vinegar

a few drops of soy sauce

freshly ground pepper to taste

Wash the rocket, watercress, or radicchio leaves and spin them dry, then tear them into manageable pieces, discarding any tough stems. Wash and slice crosswise the Belgian endive, discarding the woody core in the centre. Slice the clean mint leaves into strips if they are large, or just cut them in half if they are smaller.

Quarter the red pepper lengthwise, core it, and slice the quarters crosswise very thinly. Slice off the asparagus tips, then continue slicing thinly on a slant, using only the tender part of the stalk, and put the tips and slices into a large, shallow bowl. Raw asparagus is delightful in a salad, but you must stop short of the tough, fibrous bottom.

Trim off the bottoms of the mushrooms. Wash them, and dry

them gently on a tea towel. Rinse and drain the cooked beans or lentils.

Toss the prepared ingredients together in the bowl with the asparagus, sprinkle in the sultanas, and add the oil, vinegar, soy sauce and pepper at the end, just before serving.

This serves 6–8 people generously as a first-course salad. It is also interesting enough to be the centrepiece of a spring lunch for 4; just add a soup and some good bread.

RISOTTO DI ZUCCA

My version of this Italian winter classic is a squash risotto in which some of the dense golden squash falls apart into a sauce, and some stays in chunks among the rice. The nutty taste of Marsala and the caramelized onions support the sweet flavour of the squash. A touch of balsamic vinegar offsets it. The result is a rich and beautiful flavour with a hint of acid to enliven it. Use acorn squash if you can't get Kabocha.

2–3 medium onions
1 medium Kabocha squash
  (1 kg / 2¼ lb)
1½ tablespoons olive oil
1 tablespoon butter
1 clove garlic, chopped
1 teaspoon salt
1 teaspoon crumbled dried
  sage leaves

about 1.2 litres (2 pints) Basic
  Light Vegetable Stock (see
  page 460) or water plus
  good-quality stock cube
350 g (12 oz) Arborio rice
60 ml (2 fl oz) Marsala
175 ml (6 fl oz) white wine
1 tablespoon balsamic vinegar
freshly ground black pepper

garnishes: freshly grated Parmesan cheese
  basil leaves, cut in thin slivers

Peel the onions and cut them in quarters, then slice them crosswise. Peel the squashes, cutting away any dark green parts, seed them, and cut the flesh into 1 cm (½ inch) cubes.

Heat the oil and butter in a large, preferably non-stick sauté pan.

Add the onions and chopped garlic and stir over high heat for 3–4 minutes, then add the cubed squash, salt, and crumbled sage. Continue cooking on medium-high heat, stirring often, until the vegetables are spotted with golden brown and the squash is becoming tender – about 15 minutes. Meanwhile, heat the vegetable stock to a simmer.

Add the rice to the squash mixture and stir constantly for 2 minutes. Add the Marsala, stir quickly as it cooks away, then add the white wine.

When the wine has all been absorbed, add about 250 ml (8 fl oz) of the hot stock, along with the balsamic vinegar. Lower the heat to a simmer and stir the risotto gently with a wooden spoon. As the stock is absorbed, add another ladle, and then another, always keeping the rice moist, and stirring constantly or at least very often. Some of the squash will fall apart into a purée.

Use as much stock as you need to achieve rice that is *al dente*, tender but firm, with a creamy sauce around it. It will take about 30 minutes, but start tasting after 20 minutes.

At that point, correct the seasoning with a touch more salt and some pepper if needed, and stir in about 25 g (1 oz) of grated Parmesan cheese. Add another ½ ladle of stock, stir well, and serve at once in warmed, shallow bowls. Garnish each serving with slivers of fresh basil, and pass more Parmesan cheese separately.

Serves 6.

STRAWBERRIES WITH HONEY-SWEETENED
YOGURT CHEESE

450 g (1 lb) Yogurt Cheese　　**900 g (2 lb) ripe**
　(see page 85)　　　　　　**strawberries, sliced**
6–8 tablespoons honey　　　**1–3 teaspoons balsamic**
　　　　　　　　　　　　　　　vinegar

optional garnish: mint sprigs

Combine the Yogurt Cheese with 5 tablespoons of honey and whisk together until smooth. In a separate bowl, sprinkle the strawberries with a little balsamic vinegar, then drizzle them with 1 – 3 tablespoons of honey. How much vinegar and how much honey you use will be determined by how sweet or tart the berries are. Stir the berries gently with a large spoon, making sure not to bruise them.

　　Spoon the berries and their juice into 8 sorbet glasses, and top each serving with some of the sweetened Yogurt Cheese. Garnish with mint sprigs if desired.

Serves 8.

A SOUTHWESTERN SUPPER

❧

Black Bean Chili
with *queso fresco and salsa*

Corn and Jalapeño Muffins
or Fresh Corn Tamales

Mango Sorbet

Here are the principal foods of pre-Columbian America: corn, beans, chillies, fruit. The flavours are straightforward and delicious, and the other beauty of this meal is that almost everything can be prepared ahead, and the muffins take only moments, so it makes an easy family meal or can be dressed up for company.

In California, I like to make this supper with the Fresh Corn Tamales. Their flavour is pure corn, the most simple of tamales, with no filling. I serve them hot from the steamer with a favourite salsa and a cold beer, either before the chili, after it or alongside.

The Black Bean Chili is a hearty dish, and not terribly spicy, so even the tamest palates can enjoy it – but you could certainly crank up the heat by adding more chillies. And if you cannot find the makings of tamales, the delicate muffins, with a touch of fresh corn, are a beautiful accompaniment. Afterwards, Mango Sorbet is the clean, sweet, tropical taste you want.

Any seasonal salad would also go well with this, but if this is a party, and not just a Tuesday night dinner, you could add guacamole and fresh tortilla chips with margaritas at the start, or a ceviche if you eat fish. Then decorate the sorbet with bitter-sweet chocolate bark for a fancy dessert.

BLACK BEAN CHILI

I make this chili with dried ancho and chipotle chilli pods. They are not yet commonly available in many areas, but if you are willing to mail-order them or can otherwise lay your hands on them, don't hesitate to try them.* Simply use five ancho pods and two or three chipotles in place of the sweet red peppers and the dried red chillies. Follow the instructions given for the dried red chillies to simmer and purée them. The chipotle especially will add a subtle and gorgeous flavour to this dish.

450 g (1 lb) dried black beans
1 whole onion, peeled
2 whole cloves garlic
5–6 branches coriander
1 teaspoon salt, more to taste
(1·4 kg (3 lb) canned black beans could be used in place of the first five ingredients)
2 large red peppers
4–5 dried red chilli pods (about 25 g (1 oz))
4 teaspoons cumin seeds
4 teaspoons dried oregano leaves

4 teaspoons paprika
2–3 tablespoons corn oil or olive oil
3 onions, chopped
5 cloves garlic, minced
1 bay leaf
425 g (15 oz) canned chopped tomatoes
½–1 teaspoon salt
1–2 tablespoons wine vinegar
3–4 fresh green chillies, seeded and chopped
6 tablespoons chopped coriander

optional: mild Mexican chilli powder
garnishes: sour cream
    Salsa Cruda (see page 272), or any fresh chilli salsa
    crumbled fresh white cheese
    coriander leaves

If you're starting with dried beans, soak them overnight in cool water to cover, then change the water and simmer them with the

* Ancho and chipotle chillies can be ordered from the Cool Chile Company (see page 470).

whole onion, whole garlic cloves, and coriander branches until almost tender. Cooking time will vary with the age of the beans, and could be anywhere from 1 hour to 3–4 hours. Stir in the salt and continue simmering until the beans are perfectly tender, adding water if needed to keep them covered with liquid. Discard the onion, garlic and coriander when the beans are done.

Meanwhile, put the red peppers under a hot grill, turning them from time to time, until they are blistered and charred all over. Put them in a small paper bag for a few minutes to sweat, then peel the blistered skins off under cool running water. Remove and discard the stems and seeds.

While the peppers are under the grill, rinse the dried red chillies, then put them in a very hot cast-iron pan for a minute or two on each side, pressing them down a little, until they are darkening in colour. They may develop a few black spots – no matter. Put the scorched chillies in a small pot with enough water just to cover them and simmer them for about 10 minutes, or until they are soft. Under running water, pull out and discard their stems and seeds.

Combine the red peppers, the chillies and their simmering water in a blender, and purée. You can put the purée through a strainer to remove any bits of skin or seed if you like, but it's not necessary.

Toast the cumin seeds in a small pan until they begin to release their aroma. Add the dried oregano and the paprika, remove from the heat, and stir together in the hot pan for about a minute. Then pour the spice mixture into a mortar and grind it to a coarse powder. Add the spices to the chilli purée.

Heat the oil in a large sauté pan and sauté the onions and minced garlic in it, with a bay leaf, until they just begin to colour. Stir in the chilli purée, the chopped tomatoes with their juices, the salt, the vinegar and the chopped green chillies. Add the beans, with their liquid, and simmer the mixture over low heat, stirring occasionally, until it has the consistency you like. Stir in the 6 tablespoons of chopped coriander leaves. Taste, then add a little Mexican chilli powder if you want a spicier chili.

Serve hot, with any or all of the garnishes, accompanied by corn muffins, tamales, or any good bread.

Serves 8–10 generously.

CORN AND JALAPEÑO MUFFINS

150 g (5 oz) white flour
175 g (6 oz) yellow cornmeal
3 tablespoons sugar
1 tablespoon baking powder
1 teaspoon salt
4 tablespoons butter
½ onion, chopped
3 tablespoons finely chopped
  jalapeños, or other fresh
  green chillies
kernels from 1 ear of
  sweetcorn, or 125 g (4 oz)
  frozen corn kernels
2 tablespoons chopped
  coriander
1 egg
250 ml (8 fl oz) milk
butter or oil for muffin pan

Sift together the flour, cornmeal, sugar, baking powder and salt.

Melt 1 tablespoon of butter in a pan and sauté the onion in it for a few minutes, just until it barely begins to colour. Add the remaining butter, the corn kernels, and the coriander. When all the butter is melted, remove from the heat.

Beat together the egg and milk, and stir it into the dry mixture. Then fold the butter and onion mixture into the batter thoroughly but gently.

Spoon the batter into 12 buttered muffin cups, preferably in a non-stick muffin pan. Bake the muffins at 200°C/400°F/Gas 6 for about 15–18 minutes, or until they are golden brown on top and a toothpick inserted in the centre of a muffin comes out clean. Serve the muffins hot or warm.

Makes 12 muffins. This recipe can easily be doubled for hearty appetites.

FRESH CORN TAMALES

When I want a plain tamale, buttery and full of the taste of fresh corn, this is it. It can be served with a raw or cooked salsa, any soft white cheese, and some sliced fruit – a combination that works for breakfast, lunch, or dinner.

Dried corn husks and masa harina can be obtained from specialist shops and suppliers (see p. 470). Use frozen corn when fresh is unavailable.

450 g (1 lb) roasted or steamed
   fresh corn kernels (about 4
   large ears of corn)
16–20 large dried corn husks
350 ml (12 fl oz) milk, or
   slightly more if needed

300 g (10 oz) masa harina (see
   page 38)
2 teaspoons baking powder
1 teaspoon salt
225 g (8 oz) + 2 tablespoons
   butter, softened

To roast corn: put the ears of corn, still in their husks, on a baking sheet, and roast them in a 200°C/400°F/Gas 6 oven for about 40 minutes. Allow them to cool a bit, then husk them and clean off the silk. (If you have to use frozen corn, it will take 10–15 minutes.)

To prepare the dried corn husks: start with at least twice as many as you will need (they usually come in packages of a few dozen). Soak them in hot water for about 30 minutes. When they're soft, rinse them under running water as you separate them, discarding the very small or torn ones. Lay them flat on a plate and keep them covered with a damp tea towel until you need them. The longer torn ones can be torn further, into 1 cm (½ inch) strips, and used for ties.

To prepare the masa: slice the kernels off the roasted or steamed corn and scrape the cobs well. Simmer the corn in the milk for about 10 minutes, or until it is quite soft. Purée the mixture in a blender. Sometimes at this point I reserve a few spoonfuls of the corn kernels, and then stir them into the finished masa for more texture.

Sift together the dry masa harina, baking powder, and salt. In a large bowl, whip the softened butter with an electric mixer until it is fluffy. Alternately add spoonfuls of the sweetcorn purée and the dry mixture, beating each time, until everything is well combined. The masa should be light, fluffy, but firm enough to hold a stiff shape. If it seems too sticky, add a bit more dry masa harina. Fold in the whole corn kernels if you have reserved them.

To form the tamales: lay a prepared corn husk flat on your work surface. Put about 4 tablespoons of masa in the centre of it and spread the masa slightly. Be sure to leave a 4 cm (1½ inch) border on each side and a couple of inches at each end.

Fold one side of the husk gently over the masa, then fold the narrow, pointy end in, and then finish rolling up the whole husk, loosely. If you have extra-long husks, you can fold the wide end in as well, envelope style, before you finish rolling, but this is not absolutely necessary.

Tie a thin strip of corn husk around the middle to hold everything together, but not too tightly, as the tamale will expand in cooking. If you have trouble tying strips of corn husk, use plain brown twine, or any other kind of tie that won't react with the food in steaming.

Forming tamales is tricky the first time, but soon gets much easier, and then becomes a lot of fun.

To steam the tamales: arrange them loosely in a roomy vegetable steamer. If you left the wide end unfolded, be sure open end up. Steam the tamales for 35–45 minutes, then serve.

Tamales can be prepared a few hours ahead of time and held in the refrigerator, covered, until it's time to steam them — just add a few minutes to the cooking time to take the chill off. They can also be resteamed briefly a day or two later.

This makes 16 fairly large tamales.

MANGO SORBET

Treat yourself to this exceptional sorbet if you can get some ripe mangoes.

500 ml (16 fl oz) water
225 g (8 oz) sugar
2–3 ripe mangoes, peeled and sliced
120–175 ml (4–6 fl oz) fresh lemon juice

1 teaspoon finely grated lemon zest
2 tablespoons Triple Sec or Grand Marnier

Put the water and sugar in an enamelled pot and heat gently, stirring occasionally, until the sugar is completely dissolved. Wash down any sugar crystals from the sides with a brush or by swirling the liquid. Simmer the syrup for a few minutes, then allow it to cool completely.

Add the peeled, sliced mangoes to the syrup, along with 120 ml (4 fl oz) of lemon juice, the lemon zest, and the Triple Sec or Grand Marnier. Purée it all in a blender until perfectly smooth. Taste, and add more lemon juice as needed to balance the sweetness of the mangoes and achieve the greatest intensity of flavour.

Freeze in an ice cream freezer, according to manufacturer's instructions.

Makes a little more than 1.2 litres (2 pints).

A PICNIC

❧

Pan Bagnia

Artichoke Frittata

Lentil Salad

Gorgonzola cheese
baguettes
honeydew melon, cantaloupe, fresh berries

Chocolate-dipped Macaroons

These are foods that travel well. All of them can be packed up in a cooler and taken somewhere beautiful without suffering. All taste wonderful in the open air with a fresh, light-hearted wine.

Pan Bagnia is the definition of picnic food – a tasty salad packed within a loaf of French bread. It's hard to explain how great this can taste after some walking or rowing. Artichoke Frittata and Lentil Salad are both substantial dishes, ready to satisfy hearty appetites, because we always eat more in the open air than we do at home. Together, these make a sumptuous plate.

A good piece of cheese is simply a requirement on a picnic, so I've included Gorgonzola, one of my personal favourites, but take any cheese you like. Bring along fresh baguettes to go with it.

The best fruits to take on a picnic are whole melons, which are ideally protected for travel by their own skins – cut them up on the spot. A basket of berries is also great, as long as you take care not to let anything land on top of it.

For a sweet, take along a tin of Chocolate-dipped Macaroons.

They're not likely to crumble or flatten or break — I still remember the time my two-year-old son sat on the birthday cake at a picnic — and they can be grabbed and eaten on the run, which makes them popular with children. And they're delicious.

Don't forget the sharp knife and the corkscrew.

PAN BAGNIA

This is a Provençal sandwich, of which there are many variations. The basic idea is to cut a long crusty loaf of French bread in half lengthwise, fill it with a terrific Mediterranean salad, drizzle oil and vinegar on it, then let it cure for a few hours in the refrigerator. It is one of the best picnic foods ever invented. Here is my variation:

1 long loaf French bread
1 clove garlic
2–3 tablespoons olive oil, more to taste
10 black olives, pitted and chopped
3 ripe tomatoes, sliced
about 3 tablespoons coarsely chopped basil leaves
about 3 tablespoons coarsely chopped parsley leaves

½ onion, thinly sliced
1 small bunch rocket or watercress
2–3 red peppers, roasted (see page 17), peeled, and sliced (roasted peppers from a jar are also fine)
a few drops wine vinegar (optional)
salt and pepper

optional: sliced fresh mozzarella
thinly sliced Parmesan or other cheese of choice

Split the bread in half lengthwise. Rub both halves very lightly with a cut clove of garlic and brush with a little olive oil. Spread most of the chopped black olives evenly over the bottom half, then layer on the sliced tomatoes, overlapping them. Salt the tomatoes delicately, sprinkle them with basil and parsley, then spread across them a few slices of onion — more or less, depending on the sharpness of the onion. On top of that, lay the rocket leaves, and then big strips of roasted red pepper. Drizzle a little more olive oil and, if desired, a few drops of wine vinegar over the vegetables. Scatter on the remaining chopped olives. Add a few grinds of black pepper and cover with the top of the loaf.

Press down hard on the loaf to squash everything together somewhat. Wrap it tightly and refrigerate, preferably with a weight on top of it, for at least 30 minutes.

Other ingredients can be added to this, of course. Capers, grilled vegetables, slices of soft mozzarella or thin slivers of Parmesan, anchovies or tuna, thin slices of radish . . .

Slice the loaf in 5 cm (2 inch) sections to serve. This is fabulous with a glass of cold, fruity wine.

Serves 6–8.

To roast peppers: Arrange the whole peppers on a baking sheet and put them under a hot grill. Check them every few minutes and turn them from time to time as they blister and char. When they are soft and blistered all over, remove them and put them in a paper bag or wrap them in a kitchen towel for 3–4 minutes to sweat. Then slip off the charred skins, core the peppers, and cut them in strips.

ARTICHOKE FRITTATA

A frittata is a flat, round omelette, in which herbs, vegetables, or other flavourings are mixed with beaten eggs and cooked into them. It is finished to a golden brown on both sides and cut into wedges to serve. Frittatas can be eaten hot, warm, or cool, and are sturdy enough to travel well.

I make this with marinated artichoke hearts, which are easily available in jars, and just drain them well to make sure they're not too oily. I like the slightly tart, lemony taste mixed with eggs – it reminds me a little of *avgolemono*. However, if you have an abundance of steamed artichokes and want to trim out the hearts and use those, by all means do.

2 medium onions
450 g (1 lb) small potatoes
2 tablespoons olive oil
1 large clove garlic, chopped
1 teaspoon salt, more to taste
2 × 175 g (6 oz) jars marinated artichoke hearts, well drained, or an equivalent amount of freshly cooked and trimmed artichoke hearts
10 eggs
3 tablespoons chopped flat-leaf parsley
40 g (1½ oz) grated Parmesan cheese
black pepper to taste

Peel, quarter, and slice the onions. Scrub the potatoes, and if they are very small, cut in 0.5 cm (¼ inch) slices; if they're larger, quarter them lengthwise, then slice them.

Heat 1½ tablespoons of olive oil in a large non-stick sauté pan. Cook the onions, potatoes, and garlic in the oil, with a little salt, stirring them often until they are tender.

Drain the marinated artichoke hearts well and trim off any tough, fibrous leaves. Quarter the artichoke hearts and add them to the pan; stir everything together, then remove the pan from the heat.

Beat the eggs in a large bowl with ½ teaspoon of salt, the chopped parsley, grated Parmesan cheese, and black pepper to taste. Add all the vegetables in the pan to the eggs, and stir it all together.

Clean the sauté pan to remove the starchy residue from the potatoes, wipe it dry, and then heat the remaining ½ tablespoon of olive oil in it. Pour in the egg and vegetable mixture, spreading it evenly, turn the heat very low, and cover the pan. Cook the frittata for 8–10 minutes, or until the eggs at the top are almost set.

Put the pan under a hot grill for a few minutes to finish the frittata. It should be just slightly golden brown on top. Loosen the frittata gently with a knife or spatula until it moves freely in the pan, then slide it out on to a platter or place a platter over the pan and invert. Cut the frittata in wedges to serve.

This is best eaten warm or at room temperature, so, if you are taking it to a picnic, pack it into the hamper rather than the cooler. If you must keep it longer than a few hours, refrigerate it but allow it to come to room temperature before serving for best flavour.

Serves 6–8.

LENTIL SALAD

450 g (1 lb) green, brown or
   Puy lentils
3–4 cloves garlic
salt to taste
350 g (12 oz) potatoes
1 large bunch spinach
4 tablespoons olive oil
3 tablespoons fruity wine
   vinegar

8–10 spring onions, thinly
   sliced
6 tablespoons chopped
   flat-leaf parsley
½ teaspoon hot red chilli
   flakes
freshly ground black pepper
   to taste

Pour boiling water over the lentils, covering them by at least 5 cm (2 inches), and leave them to soak for 30 minutes. Drain them, and put them in a pot with well-salted water to cover, and 2 whole cloves of peeled garlic. Bring the water to a boil, turn down the heat, and simmer the lentils for about 15–20 minutes, or until they are tender but not mushy. Drain them again, discarding the garlic.

Meanwhile, boil the potatoes in their skins in salted water until they are tender. Drain them and allow them to cool completely, then peel them and cut them in 1 cm (½ inch) dice.

Wash the spinach thoroughly, and discard the tough stems. Chop the spinach leaves coarsely, or cut them in thin strips. Chop the remaining garlic. Heat 1 tablespoon of olive oil in a sauté pan, stir the chopped garlic in it for a minute or two, then add the spinach. Toss the spinach over high heat until it wilts and all the excess liquid cooks away. Sprinkle it with a tablespoon of the vinegar and toss again.

In a large, wide bowl, combine the drained lentils with the diced potatoes, sautéed spinach and garlic, spring onions, parsley and chilli flakes. Drizzle the remaining 3 tablespoons of oil and 2 tablespoons of vinegar over it, add a little salt and pepper, and toss gently until everything is well mixed. Taste, and add more salt if needed. Let the salad sit for 30 minutes, then taste it again, and correct the seasoning.

This makes enough salad to serve 8–10 generously and still have leftovers for the next day's lunch.

CHOCOLATE-DIPPED MACAROONS

5 large egg whites
pinch of cream of tartar
175 g (6 oz) icing sugar
½ teaspoon almond extract
350 g (12 oz) ground almonds

175 g (6 oz) shredded,
    sweetened coconut
grated zest of 1 lemon
175–200 g (6–7 oz) best-
    quality dark chocolate

Allow the egg whites to come to room temperature, then beat them with the cream of tartar until they just begin to hold a stiff shape. Add the icing sugar and the almond extract, and beat again until smooth. Mix in the ground almonds, the coconut, and the lemon zest. You'll have a thick, sticky batter.

Line 2 baking sheets with parchment. Drop heaped teaspoons of the batter on to the parchment, nudging it into a nice shape with the tip of the spoon. Bake the macaroons in a preheated 150°C/ 300°F/Gas 2 oven for about 40 minutes, or until the macaroons are golden brown. Allow them to cool on wire racks.

Melt the chocolate. As it begins to cool, dip macaroons into it, coating one half and leaving the other half plain. Lay them on waxed paper to allow the chocolate to harden.

Apricot Variation: Add 50 g (2 oz) of chopped dried apricots to the batter. When shaping the macaroons, if pieces of apricot are sticking out on top, poke them in with a toothpick so that they are not so exposed. Apricots left on the surface will turn quite dark during baking, but still taste great. Dried cherries could be used the same way.

This recipe makes about 3 dozen exquisite macaroons.

RASPBERRY BORSCHT AND STUFFED CRÊPES

❦

Raspberry Borscht

Pumpernickel Parmesan Toasts

Crêpes with Swiss Chard

cantaloupe and honeydew slices

Walnut Tart

The foods in this meal are part of my culinary history. Borscht, pumpernickel, crêpes, fresh white cheese, a sweet made with walnuts – my taste for these things is genetically imprinted in my Polish blood. I was weaned on borscht, and cut my teeth on pumpernickel.

But some of these familiar tastes have new little twists. The beetroots are blended with raspberries in a cold, intensely flavourful soup that is the reddest red you'll ever see. The pumpernickel is made into Parmesan toasts. Crêpes stuffed with Swiss chard and cheese, on the other hand, are a nice, traditional dish, and the Walnut Tart, which reminds me of walnut tortes I ate as a child, is actually a variation on American pecan pie. It adds up to a great-tasting dinner, just different enough to be interesting, yet old-fashioned in the best sort of way.

RASPBERRY BORSCHT

The idea for this came from a recipe in *Eating Well* magazine, and whoever thought of pairing raspberries with beetroot is a genius. My version has quite a bit more lemon juice, enhancing the sweet-sour character, and an almost traditional spoonful of sour cream on top. It's an intensely flavoured soup with an amazing colour (don't wear white).

900 g (2 lb) beetroots
spring water
pinch of salt
300 g (10 oz) raspberries
50 g (2 oz) grated red onion

120 ml (4 fl oz) + 2 tablespoons
freshly squeezed lemon
juice, strained
3 tablespoons balsamic vinegar
40–50 g (1½–2 oz) sugar

garnish: reduced-fat sour cream (or the real thing if you like)

Cut the tops off the beetroots, scrub them thoroughly, and put them in a saucepan with enough spring water to cover them by 2.5 cm (1 inch) and a little pinch of salt. Simmer the beetroots, covered, for 30 minutes if they're small, closer to 45 minutes if large. They must be tender.

Drain the beetroots, reserving the cooking liquid, and allow them to cool. When you can handle them, peel them and cut them into quarters or eighths.

Combine the beetroots, raspberries, red onion, and 500 ml (16 fl oz) of the reserved cooking liquid, and purée it all in batches in a blender. Strain the purée through a sieve to remove the raspberry seeds. Stir in 120 ml (4 fl oz) of lemon juice, the balsamic vinegar, and 40 g (1½ oz) of sugar. Stir until the sugar is dissolved, and taste. Add more lemon juice and more sugar only if needed, until the right sweet-sour balance is achieved. You might need a teensy pinch of salt, but be careful.

Chill the soup in the refrigerator, and when it is completely cold, taste it again. Correct the seasoning if necessary. Serve in chilled bowls, with a spoonful of sour cream in the centre of each one.

Serves 8.

PUMPERNICKEL PARMESAN TOASTS

For these you need the dense, square pumpernickel bread that is cut in very thin slices.

2½ tablespoons butter, softened	8 thin square slices pumpernickel bread
75 g (3 oz) finely grated Parmesan cheese	

optional: finely chopped parsley

Mash the softened butter in a bowl with the Parmesan cheese, and a little chopped parsley if you like, until you have a thick, well-blended mass. Spread a rounded teaspoonful evenly over each slice of bread, taking it right out to the edges.

Cut the slices in half diagonally to make triangles, and arrange them on a baking sheet. Toast them under a hot grill for a couple of minutes, watching them all the time, until they are turning golden brown in spots. Serve at once.

Makes 8 servings.

CRÊPES WITH SWISS CHARD

for the crêpes
3 large eggs
575 ml (6 fl oz) milk
90 ml (3 fl oz) single cream
120 ml (4 fl oz) water
½ teaspoon salt
150 g (5 oz) plain flour
1 tablespoon melted butter
1 tablespoon sugar

optional: 2 tablespoons cognac

for the filling
575 g (1¼ lb) fresh ricotta
   cheese, drained
2 eggs, lightly beaten
50 g (2 oz) grated Parmesan
   cheese
700 g (1½ lb) Swiss chard (or
   spinach if chard is not
   available)
1 large onion
1–2 cloves garlic
2 tablespoons olive oil
2–3 teaspoons red wine
   vinegar
3 tablespoons chopped fresh
   basil leaves
salt and pepper to taste
butter for greasing baking
   sheet and for sautéing

garnishes: about 20–24 cantaloupe or honeydew melon slices
   sour cream or crème fraîche

To make the crêpe batter: beat the eggs, then beat in the milk, cream, water, and salt. When the mixture is well blended, add the flour gradually, whisking it in until the batter is perfectly smooth. Or combine all these things in a blender. Stir in the melted butter, sugar, and cognac, if using, and leave the batter to rest for at least 2 hours.

To make the filling: allow the ricotta cheese to drain in a colander lined with cheesecloth until it is quite solid and dense. Then whisk it together with the beaten eggs and the Parmesan cheese.

Wash the Swiss chard, remove the stems and tough inner ribs, and chop it coarsely. Chop the onion and garlic and sauté them in the olive oil until the onion begins to colour. Add the chopped chard and keep cooking over medium heat, stirring often, until the mixture is quite dry. Sprinkle it with the wine vinegar and toss over heat for another minute.

Combine the chard and onion mixture with the ricotta cheese mixture, stir in the chopped basil, and season to taste with salt and pepper.

To make the crêpes: heat a medium-sized (18−20 cm/7−8 inch bottom) non-stick pan and melt a small piece of butter in it. As soon as the foam subsides, pour a small ladle of batter, equivalent to about 4 tablespoons, into the pan, then quickly but gently tilt it around so that the batter spreads evenly over the bottom of the pan.

Cook the crêpe over medium heat for about a minute. Loosen the edge by running a knife or thin spatula under it, turn the crêpe over, and cook the other side for just under a minute. The crêpe should be light golden, with golden-brown spots here and there. Brush the pan lightly with butter between crêpes. Stack the crêpes and keep them covered with a slightly damp towel as you work. They can be made ahead and stored, tightly covered, in the refrigerator up to a day. (If you do refrigerate crêpes, allow them to return to room temperature before filling or rolling them.) This amount of batter makes 15−18 × 18 cm (7 inch) crepes, or a dozen larger ones.

To assemble and serve the crêpes: lightly butter a large baking sheet. Take 1 pliable crêpe at a time and mound 2 rounded table-spoons of filling down the centre of it, leaving plenty of room all around. Roll the crêpe over the filling, folding in the sides envelope style as you finish rolling it up. Fill and fold all the crêpes this way. Arrange the crêpes, seam side down, close together on the prepared baking sheet. Brush their tops lightly with softened or melted butter. Bake the crêpes for about 25 minutes at 180°C/350°F/Gas 4 —they will puff up like golden pillows.

Put 2 crêpes on each plate, and garnish with sliced fruit. A spoonful of sour cream or crème fraîche could be added if you like.

Serves 6−7.

WALNUT TART

for the pastry
215 g (7½ oz) plain flour
2 tablespoons sugar
pinch of salt
½ teaspoon baking powder
125 g (4 oz) cold butter
50 g (2 oz) Yogurt Cheese (see page 85), or cream cheese
1 egg
½ teaspoon vanilla extract

for the filling
3 eggs
pinch of salt
125 g (4 oz) dark brown sugar
175 ml (6 fl oz) golden syrup, diluted with 3 tablespoons water
2 tablespoons melted butter
½ teaspoon cinnamon
½ teaspoon vanilla extract
grated zest of 1 large orange
175 g (6 oz) coarsely chopped walnuts

Combine the flour, sugar, salt, and baking powder in the container of a food processor. Add the cold butter, cut up in pieces, and process until the mixture resembles coarse meal. Add the Yogurt Cheese or cream cheese and process again for a few seconds. Beat the egg with the vanilla, add it to the flour mixture, and process in several short pulses just until the pastry pulls itself together into a solid mass.

Remove the pastry from the processor and form it into a ball. Handling it as little as possible, lay the pastry on a well-floured board and roll it out into a circle about 36 cm (14 inches) across. Roll the circle of pastry loosely over the rolling pin, then unroll it over an 27 cm (11 inch) loose-bottomed flat tin. Fit the pastry into the pan, and trim the edges with a sharp knife about 1 cm (½ inch) above the rim. Press the edges down slightly, making sure they are evenly thick and extended above the rim of the pan. Chill the prepared tart shell while making the filling.

Beat the eggs with a pinch of salt, the brown sugar, and the diluted golden syrup. Let the melted butter cool slightly, then beat it into the egg mixture. Add the cinnamon, vanilla, grated orange zest (orange only, no white), and chopped walnuts, and stir everything together well.

Pour the filling into the tart shell, spreading the walnuts evenly. Bake the tart in the lower part of a preheated 180°C/350°F/Gas 4 oven for 50 minutes. The filling should tremble only slightly or not at all when the tart is moved.

Allow the tart to cool on a wire rack before serving.

Serves 8–10.

A PASTA DINNER FROM THE SUMMER GARDEN

❦

mixed salad of baby lettuces

Summer Vegetable Pasta

Fresh Peach Ice Cream

The menu is utter simplicity, formed around one fabulous pasta dish that combines aubergines, peppers, onions, basil and tomatoes, all full of the voluptuous flavours of midsummer.

A salad of your favourite leaves can be served as a first course; add a good chewy country loaf, and that's all that is needed of food. Open a bottle of Chianti or a spicy-fruity California Zinfandel, and relax with this simple meal in the lingering twilight of a hot summer day.

Finish with Fresh Peach Ice Cream, a taste straight from heaven. If you're watching your fat or cholesterol, serve a plate of ripe peaches instead, big and sweet, the kind you want to eat out of hand with the juice running down between your fingers – a taste straight from low-fat heaven.

SUMMER VEGETABLE PASTA

The delicious taste of this vegetable-rich dish comes from cooking the onions forever, the aubergines and peppers for a few minutes, and the tomatoes not at all – they're barely heated. Pungent olives and spicy red pepper flakes add a kick, and the result is just what you want on a summer evening with a bottle of red wine and a country loaf.

3 medium aubergines
salt
2 large onions
2 tablespoons olive oil
4 red and green peppers
6 cloves garlic
12 Kalamata olives

900 g (2 lb) ripest tomatoes
2–3 tablespoons coarsely
  chopped fresh basil
black pepper
½ teaspoon hot red chilli
  pepper flakes
450 g (1 lb) penne pasta

optional: big shavings of Parmesan cheese

Wash, trim, and cut the aubergines in 1 cm (½ inch) cubes. Sprinkle them with salt and leave in a colander to drain for about 30 minutes as you proceed with the rest.

Roughly chop the onions and cook them slowly in 1 tablespoon of the olive oil, with a dash of salt, stirring occasionally, until they are melted into a caramel-coloured marmalade.

Meanwhile, trim and seed the peppers and cut them into thin, 2.5 cm (1 inch) long strips. Chop the garlic, and slice the olives off their stones. Cut the tomatoes into chunks, keeping all their juice.

Press the aubergines gently to release excess water. Then heat the remaining olive oil in your largest non-stick pan and sauté the peppers, aubergines, and garlic in it, stirring frequently over high heat until the vegetables are just tender and beginning to spot, about 5–7 minutes. Add the caramelized onions and cook everything together for a couple more minutes. Stir in the olives, basil, additional salt if you need it, a few grinds of black pepper, and the chilli flakes. Now remove the mixture from the heat.

Cook the pasta in several quarts of boiling salted water until it is *al dente*. About 2 minutes before the pasta is ready to drain, replace the pan of vegetables on a high heat and stir in the chopped tomatoes and their juice. Stir over maximum heat just until everything is thoroughly hot. Drain the pasta, add it to the pan, toss everything together, and serve at once.

Big shavings of Parmesan cheese could be passed at the table, but aren't absolutely necessary. I love the taste of this just as it is — pure summer garden.

Serves 4–6. If you are serving appetizers, or a substantial salad, you will probably have 6–8 servings.

Variation: If you do not add the juicy tomatoes, the aubergine mixture could be cooled to room temperature and tossed with greens in a salad, or served as part of an antipasto.

FRESH PEACH ICE CREAM

The taste of fresh fruit ice creams made at home in the summer, when fruits are at the peak of ripeness, is incomparable. The fruit is never heated, and retains an orchard flavour and intensity that you can't get in the shops.

For this ice cream, use juicy, heavy, fully ripe peaches.

120 ml (4 fl oz) double cream	dash of grated nutmeg
350 ml (12 fl oz) low-fat milk	6 medium peaches
225 g (8 oz) sugar	2 tablespoons freshly
1 teaspoon vanilla extract	squeezed lemon juice

Combine the cream, milk, 175 g (6 oz) sugar, vanilla, and nutmeg in a heavy saucepan, and heat, stirring gently, until all the sugar is dissolved and the liquid is near boiling. Cover and allow the mixture to cool, then chill it in the refrigerator for about an hour.

Peel the peaches and cut away any bruised or soft spots. Slice them off their stones and chop them roughly. Stir in the remaining sugar and the lemon juice. Leave them for a few minutes to let the sugar dissolve, then process them briefly in a food processor or blender to make a rough purée.

Strain the chilled cream mixture through a sieve into the peach purée, stir together well, and freeze according to manufacturer's instructions in an ice cream freezer.

Makes a little over 1.2 litres (2 pints) of ice cream.

ABOUT NOPALITOS

In the spring, we eat cactus. While folks in the East are hunting for fiddleheads, we in the Southwest are watching our enormous nopal cacti with greedy eyes. Dry and sagging at the end of the long summer, they puff up firm and juicy with the winter rains. Then, in the sunny days of early spring, they sprout their new little paddles, bright green and tender – nopalitos.

Within a few weeks those little 'leaves' become big, thick grey-green paddles, destined to sprout their own nopalitos in another season, and no longer good to eat. They must be picked while still thin, and a bright, tropical green.

Around Easter, they turn up in the Mexican markets, at the farmers' market, and in all the Mexican restaurants, because traditional Mexican Easter dishes are made with them.

But nopalitos don't care about the calendar. They come up when they're ready. I remember one February, the sun blazed hot for a week after torrential winter rains. I had been working in my study, and wandered into the kitchen, hungry for lunch. At that moment, my friend and fellow cook Guillermina came in the back door, carefully holding a big brown paper bag, and shimmering with excitement.

'Your nopalitos aren't coming up yet, but I found these in another place!' She dumped the contents of the bag on to the kitchen counter – there they were, the season's first bright green little cactus paddles, bristling with needle-sharp spines. My mouth watered. Fleetingly I hoped that she hadn't invaded anyone's property too deeply to find them . . .

'We need guajillo salsa,' she said firmly. Who was I to argue? Guajillo chillies were soon in the iron pan, blistering and smoking. As she tended the sauce, and the tantalizing aroma of charred chillies and tomatillos filled the room, she quickly began slicing away the cactus spines. I watched, rapt, coffee cup in hand. Once I blinked, and when I looked again, the nopalitos were clean and sliced into thin strips.

As she ground the salsa in the big stone mortar, I was at her side, dipping into it with a spoon, eating it even before it was finished, even before the pungent coriander leaves and sharp spring onions were stirred in.

I wondered how she would cook the nopalitos. Here's how: she threw them in a very hot pan and turned them a few times as they sizzled and spat, until they were tender. That's it. No oil, no water, no anything – just nopalitos seared on hot metal. It keeps the juices in, she explained.

A few minutes later, the rich red-brown salsa and deep green nopalitos were on the table, Guillermina was at the stove patting out tortillas and laying them on the griddle, and I was on the phone, calling a friend who lived next door. 'Come at once,' I said. 'Don't ask questions. Drop what you're doing.'

The three of us spooned nopalitos and salsa into fresh, warm tortillas, and devoured them in a trance of pure pleasure. We ate them plain, and with refried beans. We washed them down with cold beer, suddenly not caring about the afternoon's work. We ate every last one of them and we ate all the salsa. Then we sighed with contentment, and I put on a fresh pot of coffee.

We had eaten the first nopalitos. A rite of spring had been celebrated.

FIRST NOPALITOS OF THE SPRING

❧

Pan-roasted Nopalitos

Guajillo Chilli Salsa

Refried Pinto Beans

Hot Corn Tortillas

sliced fruit
coffee

This is the exact lunch that Guillermina fixed that sunny day in February. It was one of the best meals I ever had, perfect in its simplicity and freshness. Part of what made it so fabulous was the unexpectedness of it, and if you can find fresh nopalitos, they will certainly be seasoned with that quality of happy surprise. I have heard of occasional nopalito sightings in street markets, so if you get lucky, here's what to do with them.

First, get all those sharp needles off without getting them into your skin. The ones you almost can't see are the worst.

Then either pan-roast the nopalitos or boil them. If you can get guajillo chillies,* snap them up, and make that delicious salsa. If you can't find them, a salsa made from the dried red chillies available in many shops will go very well.

Have a cold beer or ale, make some fresh corn tortillas, and savour spring.

* Guajillo chillies can be ordered from the Cool Chile Company (see page 470).

PAN-ROASTED NOPALITOS

This is a staggeringly simple dish – with one ingredient (unless you're picky, and count salt).

nopalitos – as many as you want
   (about 125 g (4 oz) per person)
salt

Take fresh nopalitos and trim away the sharp spines, using a thin, sharp knife and handling with care. I find it helps to wear a rubber glove on one hand, or hold the nopalito with a folded tea towel or a pot-holder. With your sharpest, thinnest knife, slice flat against the side of the nopalito, shaving away every last needle. Hold the nopalitos so that the spines point away from you, and slice in the same direction that the spines are pointing – away from you. Try not to cut too deeply into the paddle, but above all – get rid of all the needles! Then rinse the paddles well under running water. Now the work is done – the rest is nothing. Just slice them crosswise into strips about the thickness of green beans.

Heat a seasoned cast-iron or non-stick pan for several minutes on a high flame. Throw the nopalitos into the hot pan with a good sprinkling of salt – they should sizzle at once. Be sure not to overload the pan, as you want to sear them, not steam them.

Turn the nopalitos frequently for about 8 or 10 minutes, keeping the flame hot. They'll spit and hiss and start to blister and release some juice. When the juice has cooked away, and the nopalitos are tender and beginning to colour, they're ready.

Sprinkle on a little more salt, and serve the nopalitos at once, with lots of good home-made chilli salsa – guajillo salsa is perfect – and fresh, warm corn tortillas. Refried pinto beans or black beans go well with these, also some crumbly, dry white cheese.

BOILED NOPALITOS

Here is another way to prepare nopalitos.

700 g (1½ lb) trimmed, sliced   **4–5 large coriander branches**
** nopalitos**   **salt to taste**
½ medium onion

Slice away the spines of the nopalitos as described in the recipe above.

Cut the trimmed nopalitos crosswise in 0.5 cm (¼ inch) strips. Put them in a non-reactive pot with enough water to cover by 5 cm (2 inches). Add ½ a peeled onion, several branches of coriander, and some salt. Simmer for 20 minutes, or until the nopalitos are crunchy-tender. Cool and drain, discarding the onion and coriander. The water you drain away will have a viscous quality, as it might from okra. This is normal.

The nopalitos are now ready to use in salads, soups, tacos, tostadas, or as a garnish for Cornmeal Griddlecakes (see page 369).

Makes approximately 700 g (1½ lb).

GUAJILLO CHILLI SALSA

If you have guajillo chilli pods, but can't get tomatillos, try green tomatoes instead, and add a squeeze of lemon juice to the finished sauce.

50 g (2 oz) dried guajillo   **2 cloves garlic**
** chillies (about 6–8 pods)**   **1 teaspoon salt, more to taste**
** (see page 33) or other**   **6 spring onions, thinly sliced**
** mildly hot dried chillies**   **6 tablespoons chopped**
450 g (1 lb) fresh tomatillos   **coriander leaves**

Toast the chillies in a very hot cast-iron pan, pressing them down with a spatula so that they make good contact with the hot pan. In a few minutes, they will release the exquisite perfume of roasting chillies, and dark brown or blackish spots will develop on their red-brown skins. Put them in a dish with enough water just to cover, and let them soak for about 10 minutes.

If using tomatillos, peel off the dry husks and put them in the hot iron pan or under the grill. Turn them occasionally for about 15–20 minutes as they sizzle and spit, until they are soft, and well charred in most places. Under cool running water, peel away the skins where they are black and blistered.

Pull the stems out of the soaked chillies. Combine the soaked chilli pods, the charred, peeled tomatillos, and the garlic clove in the container of a food processor or blender, and process in brief bursts, scraping down as necessary, until you have a rough purée. Push it through a coarse sieve, and discard the pulp of skins that remain.

Stir in the salt, spring onions, and coriander. Taste, and add more salt to taste.

This makes about 600 ml (1 pint) of salsa.

REFRIED PINTO BEANS

I like refried beans, but don't want to eat a lot of fat, so I've worked out my own way with them, not too heavy, but still very flavourful. If you're in a hurry and don't want to start with dried beans, you can use canned pinto beans in place of the Boiled Pinto Beans.

1½ tablespoons olive oil
1 large onion, minced
1 recipe Boiled Pinto Beans
   (recipe follows)

salt if needed
350–500 ml (12–16 fl oz)
   liquid from cooking beans

optional: chopped coriander
   minced hot green chillies, or
   chopped mild green chillies

Heat the oil in a large non-stick sauté pan and stir the minced onion in it, over medium heat, until it colours. Add the beans in their liquid, and a little salt if it's needed, and let them simmer gently for a while, until the liquid is somewhat reduced and the beans are getting mushy. If you want drier beans, cook them longer. You can add some chopped coriander at this point, or any kind of chillies, but these are extras, and not required.

Now take a potato masher and mash the beans with the remaining liquid. You can mash as few or as many as you like. I usually mash about half and leave the rest whole.

This makes about 8 — 10 servings.

Suggestions: Scoop them up into a tortilla for a taco, add them to quesadillas, or serve them alongside Huevos Mexicanos (see page 343). If you purée them with some stock and a chilli salsa, you have a simple soup. Roll them up with anything you want in a big flour tortilla and you have a burrito.

Leftovers: I use refried beans to make one of my favourite breakfasts, Molletes (see page 344).

BOILED PINTO BEANS

450 g (1 lb) dried pinto beans
pinch of bicarbonate of soda
1 onion
5–6 cloves garlic

several branches coriander
1½ teaspoons salt, more as
    needed

Rinse the beans and put them in a pot with enough water to cover by 5 cm (2 inches), and the bicarbonate of soda. Bring the water to a boil, let it boil for 5 minutes, then turn off the heat, cover the pot, and let the beans soak for an hour.

Add the peeled onion, cut in half, the whole, peeled garlic cloves, and the coriander, and simmer the beans for at least an hour, or until they are completely tender. Cooking time will vary with the age of the beans. Add more water if needed to keep the beans covered. Near the end of the cooking time, add the salt.

When the beans are done, remove and discard the onion and coriander. The cooked garlic, now very soft, can be left to become part of the broth.

This yields about 1.2 litres (2 pints) of cooked beans in a savoury broth.

HOT CORN TORTILLAS

I am repeating here the technique for making fresh corn tortillas at home, which I gave in *The Vegetarian Epicure, Book Two*, because tortillas are so basic to all the foods of Mexico. If you're going to eat fresh nopalitos, you shouldn't miss the experience of eating them with fresh tortillas. (If you have nopalitos but simply cannot get masa harina to make the corn tortillas – well, just have flour tortillas instead, which are delicious in their own right.)

But corn tortillas are incredibly easy to make, and I want to encourage everyone to try it. I saw my eleven-year-old son come home from school one day, hungry for a snack. He mixed up some masa, rolled it into balls, pressed them, put them in a hot pan, and five minutes later he was having fresh, buttered tortillas, hot off the stove.

Here's how. First, it helps to have a tortilla press. This simple gadget is available in some specialist kitchen shops, and sometimes in Indian food shops. Practised tortilla makers slap out perfectly round, thin tortillas between their hands in seconds, but trust me on this one – get the tortilla press.

Masa harina is a finely ground meal from corn that has been treated with lime water. Do not confuse it with cornmeal, which is an entirely different thing, or cornflour, which is a different thing again. It is available in specialist shops, or you can order it by mail (see page 470).

300 g (10 oz) masa harina
250 ml (8 fl oz) water, more as needed

optional: about ½ teaspoon salt

Put the dry masa in a mixing bowl and stir in a cup of water. Add salt if you want to; I prefer corn tortillas made without salt. Mix with a spoon, then knead for a minute or so with your hand, until it comes together into a smooth, putty-like dough, stiff but moist. If it feels dry and crumbly, add a bit more water.

Heat a couple of good, big sauté pans, non-stick or seasoned cast iron. Pinch off pieces of masa and roll them into balls a little bigger than walnuts. Put the thin plastic liner on the bottom of the tortilla press, place a ball of masa in the middle of it, and fold the plastic over it, leaving room all around for the tortilla to spread. Now fold the top of the press over it and bring the handle down. Open the press and there you are — a tortilla. Peel back the plastic liner from the top, turn a over on to the flat of your hand, and gently peel back the plastic from the bottom. Drop the tortilla into the hot pan.

(If you don't have a tortilla press and just can't wait until you do, put the ball of dough on your counter between two sheets of wax paper, then place the flat bottom of a heavy pan on top of it and press down hard. It won't give you quite as thin a tortilla as the press, but it works pretty well.)

Remember, all this takes much longer to explain than to do.

Cook the tortilla in the hot pan for about 40 seconds, then slide a spatula under it and turn it. Cook it another 40–50 seconds on the other side. If it starts to puff up, just press it down gently with the flat spatula to keep the bubbles even. For a thicker tortilla, you may want to give it another turn, and another 30 seconds. The total cooking time will be about 1½–2 minutes, depending on thickness and the heat of the pan.

The tortilla is done when it is pale gold all over and freckled here and there with dark spots. Brush it with a little butter and eat it. Or put it in a basket lined with a thick, folded kitchen towel. Stack all the tortillas there, and keep them well covered to preserve their heat. Serve them as quickly as possible. If you need to keep them for a while, let them cool slightly, then put them in a plastic bag. Reheat them by throwing them on a very hot pan for a few seconds on each side, or heat them in the oven in packets of 6 or 8, tightly wrapped in foil.

This makes 12 – 18 tortillas, depending on size.

ARTICHOKES AND POLENTA DINNER

❧

Stuffed Artichokes

Polenta with Leeks and Gorgonzola, Garnished with Caramelized Fennel and Onions

Coffee Cream

This strikes me as a restrained but sophisticated meal, with flavours that are pleasantly familiar yet surprising in their combinations. If you were to poll the next twenty people you see, I'll bet that most of them would not have eaten Polenta with Leeks and Gorgonzola in the last week or so, if you see what I mean.

Yet none of these are new tastes.

The artichokes are an extravagant creation, only because of the way artichokes look. These are opened up to be the flowers they really are, and spill over with a garlicky filling that tastes like your favourite tomato bruschetta. If you have really giant artichokes, consider letting people share, or there won't be room for polenta.

In this polenta, the taste of melted leeks and Gorgonzola is subtle and seductive. Garnished with caramelized fennel and onions, it becomes truly great. The whole combination cries out for a big, marvellous Italian red wine, like a Barolo.

Having started with a flamboyant gesture, we can end with the most elegant simplicity. The cream, with a suggestion of coffee beans, is silky and beautiful.

There is no ingredient or technique in any of this that is strange or difficult, but the way it all comes together is exceptionally good.

STUFFED ARTICHOKES

Large artichokes are cooked, opened up into great blossoms and filled with tomatoes, garlic, olive oil, and Parmesan cheese. It's a spectacular first course or light lunch salad.

6 large artichokes
5–6 cloves garlic
2–3 tablespoons olive oil
1.4 kg (3 lb) tomatoes
3 tablespoons chopped fresh basil
3 tablespoons chopped flat-leaf parsley

salt to taste
125–175 g (4–6 oz) coarse breadcrumbs from a good country loaf
75 g (3 oz) freshly grated Parmesan cheese

optional: ½ tablespoon vinegar or lemon juice

Trim off and discard the stems of the artichokes, leaving about 1 cm (½ inch). Scrub the artichokes clean under running water. Using sharp scissors, cut 1 cm (½ inch) off the top of each leaf, and with a very sharp knife slice about 2.5 cm (1 inch) off the top of the artichoke.

To a large pan of boiling salted water, add 2 or 3 whole garlic cloves and a tablespoon of olive oil. Cook the artichokes, covered, for 45–55 minutes, or until tender. Remove them carefully with tongs or a big slotted spoon, and place them upside down on a rack to drain as they cool.

To make the filling, cut the tomatoes into 0.5 cm (¼ inch) dice and chop the remaining garlic. Mix the tomatoes and garlic with the chopped herbs, ½ teaspoon of salt, 1½ tablespoons of olive oil, and a touch of vinegar or lemon juice if you want it. Stir in most of the breadcrumbs, check the consistency, then stir in more as needed to make a fairly thick mixture. Finally, add the Parmesan cheese.

When the artichokes are cool enough to handle, turn them right side up and gently pull open the leaves from the centre of each one.

Pull out the thin leaves from the very centre and then scrape out the fibrous choke with a teaspoon.

Spoon some of the filling into the centre cavity of each artichoke, then spoon a bit more here and there between the leaves. Distribute it evenly between the 6 artichokes. A little bit more olive oil can be drizzled over the artichokes just before serving.

Serve these at room temperature or chilled, and don't hold them longer than 3 or 4 hours.

Serves 6.

POLENTA WITH LEEKS AND GORGONZOLA, GARNISHED WITH CARAMELIZED FENNEL AND ONIONS

2 large white fennel bulbs
3 large onions
5 tablespoons fruity green olive oil
salt and pepper to taste
175 ml (6 fl oz) dry red wine
2 very large leeks, white part only

1 teaspoon butter
1.5–1.7 litres (2½–3 pints) any low-salt vegetable stock (see page 459)
175 g (6 oz) coarse or regular polenta (see page 260)
75 g (3 oz) Gorgonzola cheese
chopped flat-leaf parsley

Trim the fennel bulbs, wash them well, cut them in half lengthwise, and then slice them about 0.5 cm (¼ inch) thick. Peel the onions and slice them the same way.

Heat 3 tablespoons of the olive oil in a large non-stick pan and cook the fennel and onions in it slowly, stirring often, adding a little salt and pepper to taste, until they are completely soft and golden brown. Stir in the wine, and continue cooking until it almost all simmers away, then set the pan aside.

Clean the leeks thoroughly, cut them in half lengthwise, then slice them quite thinly crosswise. Heat the remaining olive oil and the butter in a non-stick pan and sauté the leeks in it, stirring them often, until they are soft and beginning to colour. Add a little sprinkle of salt – but not too much.

Heat 1.5 litres (2½ pints) of stock in a medium-sized saucepan and whisk in the polenta. Lower the heat and simmer the polenta, stirring with a wooden spoon constantly, or at least very often, until it is thick and smooth, about 30 minutes. Stir in the sautéed leeks; break the Gorgonzola into chunks and stir it in. Keep stirring until the cheese is all melted into the cornmeal. The polenta should be thick and smooth, but not stiff. If it is holding a shape as you stir it, gradually mix in a bit more stock.

Meanwhile, warm up the caramelized fennel and onion mixture. This too could be moistened with a bit of vegetable stock if needed.

Ladle the polenta into warmed, shallow bowls or on to warmed plates, and spoon some of the fennel and onion mixture around the polenta. Scatter some fresh flat-leaf parsley across the top and serve at once with a good red wine.

Serves 6.

COFFEE CREAM

The subtle, alluring flavour of this cream is created by steeping whole coffee beans and cinnamon sticks in the scalded milk and cream. It creates a cream that seems bigger, richer, and more complete, somehow. The actual taste of the coffee only becomes apparent when you're told about it.

600 ml (1 pint) milk	225 g (8 oz) sugar
120 ml (4 fl oz) double cream	4 eggs
7.5 cm (3 inch) stick cinnamon	2 egg yolks
50 g (2 oz) whole coffee beans	½ teaspoon vanilla extract

Heat the milk and the cream with the cinnamon stick and coffee beans until the milk barely begins to simmer. Turn off the heat and leave it to steep for at least an hour, longer if possible. Bring it to a simmer again, then let it cool down just a little.

Select a 1.5 litre (2½ pint) baking dish, perhaps a soufflé dish or a casserole. Heat the dish in a 200°C/400° F/Gas 6 oven while you melt half the sugar in a heavy-bottomed pan over a medium flame.

When the sugar is entirely melted and a rich golden caramel colour, put on your thickest pot-holder gloves, take out the heated baking dish, and carefully pour the caramel into it, immediately tilting the dish around so that the caramel coats both the bottom and the sides. Set the prepared dish aside.

Beat the eggs and egg yolks with the remaining sugar and the vanilla until they are thick and smooth. Strain the milk, discarding the cinnamon and the coffee beans, and gradually beat the warm milk into the egg mixture.

Pour the custard into the caramelized baking dish, and place it in a larger baking pan in which there is at least 2.5 cm (1 inch) of hot water. Bake the cream, in its water bath, at 170°C/325°F/Gas 3 for about 50 minutes to an hour. The centre should tremble just a little when moved, and a thin knife inserted in the centre should come out clean.

Chill the coffee cream for several hours, then invert it on to a large, deep platter just before serving, letting the caramel sauce pool around it. Cut in wedges to serve, spooning some of the caramel over each serving.

Serves 6–8.

A MIDSUMMER DINNER

❧

Red Pepper Pesto

crostini

Salad of Rocket and Radicchio

Sweetcorn Risotto

Cassis Sorbet

Anise Biscuits

This is summer food at its most vibrant, full of colour and brilliant flavours.

The Red Pepper Pesto is rich-tasting without being heavy, with the sweetness of peppers and the pungency of olives and garlic. Serve it with a cool aperitif – a simple kir or one of the lovely champagne-based drinks.

The salad, dark green and red, is full of bite, preparing the way for a Sweetcorn Risotto, creamy and pale gold.

After that, an intense concentration of blackberries and crème de cassis in an icy purple sorbet, with delicate Anise Biscuits.

RED PEPPER PESTO

This is a pesto made of sweet red peppers – the garlic is the only thing that has any bite. You can roast fresh red peppers over hot coals and peel them, for superb results, or use the roasted and peeled red peppers that are available in cans or jars in good Italian delis and some supermarkets. Just don't buy the pickled ones.

This spread is fabulous on crostini (see page 75), served with a sweet, fruity aperitif. It's great with fresh white goat's cheese.

75 g (3 oz) sun-dried tomatoes
3–4 red peppers, roasted and
  chopped (see page 17)
125 g (4 oz) Kalamata
  olives, pitted and finely
  chopped
5 tablespoons finely chopped
  flat-leaf parsley

5 tablespoons finely chopped
  fresh basil
3–4 cloves garlic, minced
3 tablespoons olive oil
1 teaspoon balsamic vinegar
freshly ground black pepper
  to taste
salt if needed

Put the sun-dried tomatoes into a bowl and pour boiling water over them just to cover. Leave them to soak for 20–30 minutes.

If using canned peppers, rinse and drain them well, blot them on kitchen paper, then chop them pretty finely. Combine them with the chopped olives, the chopped fresh herbs, and the minced garlic.

Drain the sun-dried tomatoes, reserving the water, and press them gently in a colander. Pulse them in a food processor until they are finely chopped. (I don't use the food processor for the other ingredients, as it can too easily turn them into mush, and you want to keep a little texture in this spread.) Add the olive oil and vinegar and pulse again, scraping down as needed, until no large chunks of tomato are left.

If you do not have a food processor, just finely chop the soaked sun-dried tomatoes as you do all the other ingredients. It will only take a little longer.

Combine the tomato mixture with the other ingredients, mix well, and taste. Grind in some black pepper if you like, and add some salt if needed, though probably the olives provide enough. If the pesto is too thick for your taste, moisten it with a few drops of the reserved tomato water until it has the consistency you like. The texture should be somewhere between thick pesto and soft pâté.

Makes about 600 ml (1 pint) of intensely flavoured spread.

SALAD OF ROCKET AND RADICCHIO

This is a lively salad. The rocket or watercress gives it bite, the radicchio gives depth, peppers and raisins add sweetness, and altogether it's delicious.

225 g (8 oz) radicchio
225 g (8 oz) rocket or
   watercress
handful of fresh basil leaves
small handful of fresh mint
   leaves
1 large red pepper

75 g (3 oz) plump raisins
125–175 g (4–6 oz) crumbled
   goat's cheese or blue cheese
2 tablespoons walnut oil
2 tablespoons raspberry
   vinegar
salt and pepper to taste

Wash the radicchio and the rocket or watercress and spin it dry in a salad spinner. Trim off tough stems and tear everything into manageable pieces.

Cut the basil and mint leaves into thin slivers. Trim and core the pepper, quarter it lengthwise, and cut into very thin slices. If your raisins are not absolutely plump and soft, soak them briefly in a cup of scalding water with a dash of wine vinegar in it. Drain them well before adding them to the salad.

Toss everything together in a large mixing bowl, dress lightly with the walnut oil and raspberry vinegar, add a little salt and pepper if you like, and serve. A good olive oil can be used instead of walnut oil, and any vinegar with a slightly sweet overtone would be good with the sharp taste of rocket or watercress.

Serves 6–8.

SWEETCORN RISOTTO

If you haven't picked the corn yourself, it's a good idea to taste a bit of each ear and make sure it's fresh, sweet, and tender. Old corn tastes like wood, and if you ever chewed a pencil at school you know you wouldn't want to make a risotto with it. But with good, fresh corn, this is an ambrosial dish.

4 ears of freshly picked
  sweetcorn
2 onions, chopped
1 tablespoon olive oil
½ tablespoon butter
salt
1.5–2 litres (2½–3½ pints) any
  delicate vegetable stock (see
  page 459)

450 g (1 lb) Arborio rice
175 ml (6 fl oz) dry white wine
75 g (3 oz) grated Parmesan
  cheese
2 tablespoons chopped
  flat-leaf parsley
additional Parmesan cheese
  and parsley for the table

Husk and wash the corn and peel away all the silk, then slice the kernels off the cobs with a sharp knife. Spin about half the kernels in a food processor until they are roughly chopped and milky. Scrape out the chopped corn and return it to the remaining whole kernels.

In a large non-stick sauté pan, sauté the onion in the olive oil and butter with a pinch of salt until it is translucent and tender. Meanwhile, heat the vegetable stock and regulate the flame to keep it just below a simmer. Add the Arborio rice to the onions and stir it gently in the pan for about 2 minutes. Pour in the wine and stir until it is absorbed.

Add a soup ladle of the heated stock and all the corn kernels to the rice and stir, keeping it just at a simmer. Keep stirring until the stock is nearly all absorbed into the rice, then add another ladle. Continue this way, adding a little stock at a time and stirring constantly, or at least very frequently, with a wooden spoon for about 25 minutes, or until the rice is *al dente*. It should form a creamy sauce around grains that are no longer crunchy, but still firm.

When the rice is just achieving this perfection of tender-firmness, stir in a last ladle of stock, the grated Parmesan cheese, and 2 tablespoons of chopped parsley. Serve the risotto at once in warmed shallow bowls of generous size, and pass additional parsley and grated Parmesan cheese.

Serves 6–8.

CASSIS SORBET

This is simple, elegant, and divine. Perhaps the only drawback is that you want to make it in that season when you might be wearing white linen, so be very careful handling those blackberries.

225 g (8 oz) sugar	**700 g (1½ lb) blackberries**
250 ml (8 fl oz) water	**60 ml (2 fl oz) crème de cassis**

Stir the sugar and water together in a heavy-bottomed saucepan over low heat until the sugar is completely dissolved. Boil the syrup gently for 6–7 minutes, washing down the sides of the pan with a brush dipped in water to avoid forming crystals. Allow the syrup to cool.

Combine the syrup and the blackberries in a blender and purée. Force the purée through a sieve and discard the seeds. Stir in the crème de cassis, then chill the mixture well. Freeze according to manufacturer's instructions in an ice cream freezer.

Makes about 1.2 litres (2 pints) of intensely flavoured sorbet.

ANISE BISCUITS

175 g (6 oz) lightly salted butter	**2 teaspoons anise seeds, partly crushed**
225 g (8 oz) light brown sugar	**300 g (10 oz) flour + extra for rolling out**
1 egg	
½ teaspoon ground ginger	

Cream the butter in a bowl with the brown sugar until it is fluffy and light. Beat in the egg, ginger, and lightly crushed anise seeds. Stir in the flour, form the dough into a ball, wrap it in waxed paper or plastic wrap, and chill it for at least an hour, longer if possible.

On a floured board, roll out half the dough to a thickness of about 0.5 cm (¼ inch). Cut it with a sharp knife into 4 cm (1½ inch) squares or diamonds or cut out shapes with a biscuit cutter. If you have a butter-decorating press, you can press in little designs in the centre of each biscuit.

Arrange the biscuits on a buttered baking sheet and bake them in a preheated 180°C/350°F/Gas 4 oven for 12−15 minutes, or until they are just becoming golden.

Makes about 4 dozen biscuits.

Tomatoes are the elixir of summer. I love them, red and heavy, warm in my hand from the sun that ripened them. I never tire of them. I eat them in salads and pastas, soups and sandwiches, salsas and risottos. And the best way of all – standing in the garden, biting into a sun-baked tomato that I have just picked, letting the juice run between my fingers.

So, even when I don't have time for a true garden, and happily buy my vegetables at the farmers' market, I always feel I must at least put in a few tomato plants.

I really have no excuse not to, because I'm blessed with the benign climate of southern California and I have a plot of land. But even if you only have a patio or a sunlit balcony in a city, try growing some well-fertilized plants in tubs. If you have a windowbox, forget the geraniums one summer and put in a few tomato vines instead. Add a small pot of basil at either end, and see how your summer meals improve.

Luckily, tomatoes are hardy. Mine seem to thrive on neglect. I start by putting them in too late. I mean to put them in in February or early March, because we have such mild and sunny winters when we're not having floods, yet they sometimes don't go in until Mother's Day. But finally a fever takes me over. I drop everything and rush off to do what must be done.

I dig the soil, haul compost, clean out the tomato cages from last year, and buy new rolls of that green stuff to tie them up. I untangle the drip lines. Finally, I plant the baby plants, give them a good drink of water and tomato food.

After that, I forget them for a while, and by the time I check they are beginning to sprawl, and it's a big chore to get them into their cages. Over the next month or two, I go out occasionally, tie up branches, break off some suckers, and pull out a thousand weeds. My hands turn black, but they smell like tomatoes.

If a plant gets sick, I yank it out. My method is to put in about three times as many plants as I really need. Then I can afford to lose a few. And I only water my tomatoes once every few weeks, letting the water drip into the beds for twenty-four hours. The plants grow deep roots, and the flavour of the tomatoes is better if they are not overwatered.

In July, when the sun burns and everyone is complaining, I secretly rejoice. My tomatoes are ripening.

For the next few months, I revel. I pick baskets of tomatoes. I eat them for breakfast on toast. I have tomato salad for lunch. Tomato bruschetta for dinner.

In late August or maybe in September, we have a heat wave. The temperature hits 100 degrees, then 105, and one day a hundred pounds of tomatoes are ripe at the same time. That is when I make sauce for the winter, and if you have such an opportunity, do not resist the call.

And even if you haven't grown a single plant, you might drive to the nearest pick-your-own farm, buy a crate of the reddest tomatoes you can find, and indulge in this essential summer ritual, which will reward you all year long.

TOMATO SAUCE FOR THE WINTER

Like many other things, this is much more fun if you do it with a friend.

For 45 kg (100 lb) of tomatoes, you will want 4 or 5 heads of garlic, several big bunches of fresh basil, some salt, and only about 1.2 litres (2 pints) of good olive oil.

First the tomatoes must be peeled and cored and cut up, and that is the tedious part. Keep a large pot of water simmering. Cut crosses in the bottoms of all the tomatoes with a sharp knife. Put them into the hot water, ten or twelve at a time, and leave them in it for less than a minute, then fish them out and drop them into a bowl of cool water. Now you can easily slip off their skins.

Next, trim out the stem ends, and any hard cores. Cut larger tomatoes into quarters or halves. I usually run the tomatoes through the blender to make a rough purée, but you can leave them in big pieces if you prefer.

While you prepare the tomatoes, your friend peels and chops the garlic, rinses the basil and shakes it dry, and takes the leaves off the stems.

Canning jars, rings and lids (always get new lids) should be sterilized or at least run through the dishwasher and dried, then lined upside down on clean kitchen towels, ready for action. Have extra lids on hand, as some may be duds and then you have to reseal a jar with a fresh lid.

When your enormous piles of tomatoes have been tamed into several big bowls of purée or chunks, take out your biggest pots and sauté pans. Use only non-reactive pots. I personally like to use very large sauté pans, because they are so wide, and the sauce can cook down faster with greater air contact.

With the first batch of sauce, you will probably want to measure. For each litre (quart) or so of prepared tomatoes, heat a tablespoon of oil, add 2 cloves of chopped garlic, and stir for a minute, then pour in the tomatoes. Add ½ teaspoon of salt or a little more, to your taste, and some basil, chopped or whole leaf. Let this simmer until it feels thick enough to be sauce and turns a dark-red colour.

You will soon adjust your quantities to get the maximum use of your pots. Just remember, a gallon of tomatoes simmering in a giant pot will take longer to cook down to the right consistency than a quart, so be patient, watch, and stir. It's done when it looks and feels done.

At the end, you can combine all the finished batches of sauce in one very large pot, stir it up, and adjust the salt if you need to.

Now you are ready to ladle hot tomato sauce into clean, dry jars, and to seal them according to the instructions that come with the canning jars. Here are my tips. Remember to leave at least 1 cm (½ inch) of air space at the top of the jar. Wipe the rims of the jars until they are absolutely clean and dry. Check each lid to be sure that the little rubberized circle which forms the seal has no flaws in it. If you are using a boiling water bath, keep the jars completely submerged in boiling water for at least 20 minutes.

When you take your jars out of the boiling water, line them up on the counter to cool, and listen for the satisfying little 'ping' of each lid as the vacuum seal is formed. If a lid does not seal properly, you must take it off, wipe the rim of the jar again, put on a fresh lid, and reprocess. Or put that jar in the refrigerator for more immediate use.

Let the jars cool, then label them with a date. You think you will never forget when you did this, but you will. And it's fun to see that date, later. I've kept tomato sauce in jars for up to two years with no problems.

When you have a cool, dark pantry shelf lined with shiny jars full of sweet red sauce, you will be able to face the winter. Every time you open a jar, the concentrated flavour of summer is there. You can whip together a great-tasting dish in no time, and you do not have to wait eight months for the wonderful, wonderful taste of tomatoes.

But never will the sauce taste as good as it will that evening, when you enjoy your well-earned Tomato Harvest Dinner.

The next four menus feature tomatoes in pasta, in soup, in risotto, and in salad. This is a little sampler of the bounty of summer tomatoes.

TOMATO HARVEST DINNER

❦

Cream of Sweetcorn Soup

Fresh Pasta
with
Summer Tomato Sauce

sliced peaches and raspberries, with sweetened crème fraîche

One day in August, when tomatoes all ripen at once, I make my tomato sauce for the winter. As I stand over a hot stove on a hot day, tomato-mania gets hold of me, and I want to eat some of that sauce right away, with a good plate of pasta. This might be my favourite summer meal.

Greg makes the fresh pasta – or we open a package of good dried pasta if time is short. We save some of the last batch of tomato sauce. We call a few friends, open a good Italian wine, and set the table outside.

A fresh soup made of sweetcorn from the same garden is a very nice start, although a salad would do as well. Afterwards, nothing could be better than summer fruits, with crème fraîche, slightly sweetened.

CREAM OF SWEETCORN SOUP

This is one of the simplest soups, and one of the best, and it has no cream in it.

9–10 freshly picked ears of sweetcorn	**3 tablespoons butter**
1 large onion	**900 ml (1½ pints) milk**
1 large clove garlic	**1 teaspoon salt, more to taste**

garnish: chopped chives or coriander leaves

Husk and clean the corn, and slice the kernels off into a big bowl with a sharp knife. Scrape the cobs to release as much juice as you can.

Chop the onion and garlic and cook them in 2 tablespoons of the butter until they are soft and golden, about 10 minutes. Combine the corn kernels, the onions and garlic, and about 250 ml (8 fl oz) of the milk, and purée in batches in a blender.

Combine the purée with the rest of the milk in a soup pot, add the salt and the remaining butter, and simmer for 15–20 minutes. Taste and correct the seasoning if needed.

The soup can be run through the blender again at this point if the texture feels too rough for you. For an absolutely silky texture you can go a step further and press it all through a sieve, which will reduce the quantity a bit.

Serve the soup hot and sprinkle each serving with chopped chives or coriander.

Serves 6–8.

FRESH PASTA

We've used this recipe many, many times in the years since we've owned an electric pasta-cutting machine. It's been a foolproof formula. It makes the equivalent of about 450 g (1 lb) of dried pasta, enough for 4–5 generous servings (people always want to eat more when it's home-made pasta).

Pasta flour, sometimes labelled 'semolina', is available in delicatessens and Italian food shops, and in some supermarkets.

450 g (1 lb) pasta flour	120 ml (4 fl oz) water
1 teaspoon salt	additional pasta flour for
2 eggs	kneading

Mix the pasta flour and salt together in a large mixing bowl. In a small bowl, lightly whisk together the eggs and water. Make a well in the centre of the flour, pour in the egg and water mixture, and gradually stir in the flour until it is all absorbed into a dough.

Turn the dough out on to a board lightly sprinkled with a little more pasta flour, and knead it with your hands until it begins to spring back quickly.

Finish kneading the dough by passing it repeatedly between the rollers of a pasta machine, until it is absolutely smooth and very elastic. You can also complete the kneading process by hand, but be ready for a workout.

Divide the dough into 2 or 3 parts, and keep the others covered with plastic wrap as you begin rolling out the first.

Roll out long sheets of pasta by adjusting the rollers on the machine progressively closer together until you achieve the thinness you want, probably about 0.125 cm ($^1/_{16}$ inch) or less.

Cut the pasta manually for ravioli, manicotti, lasagne, papardelle, or wide fettucine. Cut it with the blades of the machine for tagliatelle, linguine, or fettucine.

The pasta can be cooked immediately, or you can drape it over something or lay it on towels to dry until you need it. I have found the backs of my kitchen chairs ideal for this. I put a kitchen towel over the back of each chair and I'm ready to hang enough pasta for ten people. In fact, I got so used to doing this that it became a unit of measure for me. 'How much pasta should I make?' – 'Oh, about eight chairs.'

When you're ready to eat, bring a very large pot of water to a rolling boil, salt it well, add a drop of olive oil (not absolutely required, but I like it), and cook the pasta in it for moments only, until it is *al dente*. I've found that about 30 seconds or a minute after the water returns to a boil is usually enough.

Drain the pasta at once and toss it with the sauce in a large, warmed bowl. Serve immediately.

Serves 4–5.

SUMMER TOMATO SAUCE

This is the formula I use when I prepare tomatoes to put up in jars for the winter, but reduced to an amount that is right for one dinner – in case this *isn't* the day you cook 100 lb of tomatoes. The important thing is to use absolutely vine-ripe tomatoes. It is the pure taste of the tomato that is wonderful. However, this sauce can be varied endlessly with the addition of herbs, scented vinegars, a bit of wine.

1.4 kg (3 lb) ripe tomatoes
1 tablespoon fruity green
  olive oil
2–3 cloves garlic, minced

2 tablespoons finely chopped
  fresh basil leaves
salt and pepper to taste

Scald the tomatoes in boiling water for about 45 seconds and slip off their skins. Trim their stems and process briefly to a somewhat rough texture in a blender or food processor.

Heat the olive oil in a saucepan and add the garlic. Stir it for about a minute, then pour in the tomatoes. Add the basil and a little salt and pepper, and cook the sauce on a medium flame for about 30 minutes, or a little longer if the tomatoes were very juicy, until reduced by about a third.

You can use the sauce at once or keep it in the refrigerator, covered, for several days. You can also double or triple or quadruple the recipe, just remembering that if you are cooking down a huge panful of sauce it will take longer. And you can vary the proportions; it's pretty foolproof if the tomatoes are good.

This makes about 600–750 ml (1–1¼ pints) of sauce.

TOMATO SOUP AND PASTA

❦

Summer Tomato Soup

Penne with Goat's Cheese and Ruby Chard

fresh fruit

You can just as easily make this dinner in the winter if you have put some garden tomatoes into jars. Then it's even easier, because the tomatoes are already peeled, and to have that true tomato flavour in a steaming bowl when it's cold and grey outside is a wonderful thing.

After the slight acidity of tomatoes, green or ruby chard in a sauce of creamy, melted goat's cheese is very pleasant. Because the cheese adds an element of richness to the pasta dish, ripe, fresh fruit of the season is the ideal dessert. In summer, serve berries or melons or ripe peaches. In winter, pears cut in thin slices.

SUMMER TOMATO SOUP

1.8 kg (4 lb) ripe tomatoes
2 tablespoons virgin olive oil
½ onion, finely chopped
3–4 cloves garlic, finely chopped
1 teaspoon salt, more to taste

handful of fresh basil leaves, chopped
500 ml (16 fl oz) vegetable stock (see page 459)
75–125 g (3–4 oz) rice (white or brown), cooked
freshly ground pepper to taste

Scald and peel the tomatoes, and trim off their stem ends. Cut them in halves or in quarters, and then process them briefly in a blender; they should be somewhere between chopped and puréed.

Heat the olive oil in a large, non-stick sauté pan and stir the chopped onion in it over a medium flame for about 3 minutes. Add the garlic and sauté for another 2–3 minutes.

Add the puréed tomatoes, a teaspoon of salt, and the basil. Simmer for about 30 minutes, until the tomatoes are reduced to a sauce and dark red. Add the vegetable stock and the rice, and bring back to a simmer. Taste, and correct the seasoning if necessary with a touch more salt or a little freshly ground pepper.

Serves 6–8.

PENNE WITH GOAT'S CHEESE AND RUBY CHARD

Chard and goat's cheese always go well together. In this dish, the slightly bitter taste of chard and the creamy goat's cheese melting into it make a superb pasta sauce. The pine-nuts add an essential crunch to the texture.

The more commonly found dark green Swiss chard can be substituted if ruby chard is unavailable.

450 g (1 lb) ruby or green
  Swiss chard
2 large onions, chopped
2 tablespoons olive oil
1 teaspoon butter
salt to taste
1–2 tablespoons balsamic
  vinegar (or 2 teaspoons red
  wine vinegar)

150 g (5 oz) creamy white
  goat's cheese
75–125 g (3–4 oz) pine-nuts
450 g (1 lb) penne pasta
120 ml (4 fl oz) white wine

Wash the chard thoroughly, cut off and discard the thick stems, and chop the leaves and thin inner stems coarsely.

Sauté the chopped onions in the olive oil and butter until they are soft and beginning to colour. Add the chard and toss it together with the onions until it wilts. Continue cooking, stirring occasionally, for a few more minutes, until the chard is tender. Toss the chard with a tiny bit of salt and the vinegar. Crumble the goat's cheese and set aside. Lightly toast the pine-nuts, stirring them in a small pan over medium heat until they begin to turn golden and fill the air with fragrance. (At this point, you could set everything aside and hold it for a few hours if necessary.)

Boil the penne in plenty of salted water until it is *al dente*. Just before it's ready, bring the chard back to high heat and add the white wine. Drain the pasta. Add the crumbled cheese to the hot chard mixture, along with the pasta, and mix it all together well. Serve at once on warmed plates, and sprinkle each serving with toasted pine-nuts.

Serves 6—8.

TOMATO RISOTTO FOR THE FAMILY

❧

Fresh Tomato Risotto

Roasted Summer Vegetables

Parmesan Cheese Toasts

fresh fruit plate

This was a dinner I never planned. I just looked in the larder at the end of the day, saw what's always there all summer – courgettes, tomatoes, basil, peppers – and put together something easy. You can do the same.

Walk into the kitchen about an hour before dinner and put a nice bottle of white wine in to chill, and it will be ready to drink just a little while before the food is ready to eat.

Start by cutting up the vegetables and putting them into the oven. While they roast, prepare the risotto, and then put your children to the task of stirring it while you make the Parmesan Cheese Toasts and open the wine. Life does not have to be too complicated.

FRESH TOMATO RISOTTO

I make this easy risotto in the summer, when tomatoes are abundant and sweet, or in the winter with tomatoes I've put up in jars.

1 medium onion, chopped
1 tablespoon olive oil
1 teaspoon butter
salt to taste
1.5 litres (2½ pints) vegetable stock (see page 459)
500 ml (16 fl oz) Summer Tomato Sauce (see page 60), or 900 g (2 lb) ripe tomatoes plus 1 additional tablespoon

olive oil and 2–3 cloves garlic, chopped
350 g (12 oz) Arborio rice
175 ml (6 fl oz) dry white wine
1–2 tablespoons chopped fresh parsley
1–2 tablespoons chopped fresh basil
50 g (2 oz) grated Parmesan cheese

garnishes: additional Parmesan cheese
slivered fresh basil
toasted pine-nuts

In a large non-stick sauté pan, sauté the onion in the olive oil and butter, with a dash of salt, until it begins to turn golden. In separate pans, heat the vegetable stock and the tomato sauce, and keep them both just below a simmer.

If you are starting with fresh tomatoes, scald and peel them, and chop them or process them in a blender for a few seconds. Heat a tablespoon of olive oil in a non-stick pan, sauté the chopped garlic in it for about 2 minutes, then add the tomatoes and cook them down for about 15 minutes.

Add the rice to the sautéd onion and stir it gently in the pan for about 2 minutes. Pour in the white wine and stir as it is absorbed.

Add a soup ladle of the heated stock and stir, keeping the mixture just at a simmer. Keep stirring until the stock is nearly all absorbed into the rice, then add a ladle of tomato sauce and the chopped herbs, and stir until that is nearly absorbed. Continue this way, alternating stock and sauce until the sauce is used up, then carry on with the stock until the rice is *al dente*. This process will take about 25 minutes, and at the end a creamy sauce will form around rice grains that are tender but firm.

At the moment the rice is no longer crunchy, stir in a last ladle of hot stock and the grated Parmesan cheese, and serve the risotto at once. Scatter slivered basil and toasted pine-nuts over each serving, and pass additional Parmesan.

Serves 6–8.

ROASTED SUMMER VEGETABLES

Beginning in late summer, we get beautiful, huge squashes, and the little bit of sweet squash added to the courgettes and peppers is so good in this. All the flavours sing when combined with the bright, fresh taste of tomatoes in a risotto (or in anything).

6 medium courgettes (about 575 g/1¼ lb)	225–300 g (8–10 oz) Kabocha or acorn squash
1 large red pepper	4 garlic cloves, chopped
1 large green pepper	2 tablespoons olive oil
1 large onion	salt and pepper to taste

Trim the courgettes and slice them into 1 cm (½ inch) rounds. Trim and core the peppers and cut them in pieces about 2.5 cm (1 inch) square. Cut the onion into large chunks. Cut the squash into 1 cm (½ inch) cubes.

In a large bowl, mix all these vegetables together with the chopped garlic, olive oil, and a liberal sprinkling of salt and pepper.

Spread the vegetables on 2 baking sheets and roast them in a 220°C/425°F/Gas 7 oven for 50 minutes to an hour, or until tender and spotted with dark golden brown here and there. You should turn the vegetables once or twice during the roasting time.

Serves 6.

PARMESAN CHEESE TOASTS

I have to ration these to my boys at dinner, or they simply will not eat anything else. They learned to make them perfectly, without my help, at an early age. Of course, you must use real aged Parmigiano from Parma.

12 thick slices excellent country bread or French bread	3½ tablespoons butter, softened 75 g (3 oz) freshly grated Parmesan cheese

Be sure to use a good fresh bread with some texture to it. Warm the butter gently until it is as soft as it can be without being completely melted – and even if a bit of it melts, no matter.

Stir the grated cheese into the butter to form a thick, soft paste. Spread this mixture evenly over the slices of bread, all the way out to the crusts to prevent burnt edges.

Arrange the slices on a baking sheet and put them under a hot grill for 2 minutes, moving their position once during that time if needed, until the cheese is golden brown and bubbling. Remove at once! It's a matter of seconds from perfectly browned to burnt, so watch them. Serve hot.

Serves 6.

A FRITTATA SUPPER

❧

Summer Tomato Salad

Garlic Bread

Green Herb Frittata

Berry Cobbler

Every part of this simple meal is saturated with flavour and colour: bright red salad, dark green frittata, and purple berries bubbling under a golden crust.

The salad and Garlic Bread take only a few minutes. Put the garlic into the oil to steep before you start doing other things. You can prepare the cobbler early in the day, or just a while before dinner – it's delicious hot or warm. Once the frittata is in the pan, the rest of the meal can be made while it is cooking.

If you need to keep your preparation time really short, replace the cobbler with berries and ice cream (but the delicious cobbler takes only about 15 minutes to prepare).

SUMMER TOMATO SALAD

In August, when you're carrying in those big, dark red tomatoes, heavy with juice, it's time for this salad.

This is one of those simple things – not really a recipe, just great food. I can eat a whole platter by myself for lunch and be ready for another by dinnertime.

1.4–1.8 kg (3–4 lb) juicy
  vine-ripened tomatoes
½ medium red onion
10–12 tablespoons flat-leaf
  parsley leaves

2 tablespoons fruity green
  olive oil
a few drops vinegar
salt and freshly ground black
  pepper to taste

Wash the tomatoes and slice them thickly crosswise. Arrange them in a single layer on a large platter. Slice the onion crosswise, thinly but not paper thin. Scatter the onion rings over the tomatoes.

Wash the parsley leaves and spin them in a salad spinner. Arrange them in a wreath around the tomatoes. Drizzle the tomatoes with the olive oil and sprinkle them with a few drops of your favourite vinegar. Add salt to your taste, and grind on some black pepper. Serve within the hour, accompanied by some crusty, chewy bread. Do not refrigerate!

This makes enough for 6–8 normal salad servings. Or add a wedge of pungent hard cheese, some olives, and a good loaf of bread and it's a meal for a couple of voracious tomato-eaters.

GARLIC BREAD

garlic
fruity green olive oil
coarse-textured country bread
salt

Slice or coarsely chop a few cloves of garlic and combine in a bowl with a few tablespoons of olive oil. I usually use 3–4 tablespoons of oil for an average loaf of French bread – but you might like a bit more. Crush the garlic into the oil a little and leave it to steep for at least 30 minutes, longer if you like.

Thickly slice as much bread as you think you'll need. Brush the bread slices lightly with the garlic-infused oil, and sprinkle them with a tiny bit of salt.

Toast the prepared bread slices on a rack under a hot grill for a minute or two, watching them like a hawk, and remove them when they start to turn golden brown.

That method makes a nice, subtle garlic bread. If you want garlic bread with a real kick, here's another way.

Peel a clove of garlic and cut it in half. Brush your bread slices with plain olive oil and toast them under a hot grill. Rub the toasted bread with the cut garlic and sprinkle lightly with salt. This second method retains the sharp, biting flavour of raw garlic.

GREEN HERB FRITTATA

Like any frittata, this also makes a wonderful picnic dish. It's very good at room temperature, and slices of frittata in a split baguette make a great sandwich.

350 g (12 oz) mixed leafy greens, such as spinach, chard, kale, frisée, etc.
2½ tablespoons fruity green olive oil
2 cloves garlic, chopped
½ teaspoon salt, more to taste
1–2 teaspoons wine vinegar
10 eggs
freshly ground pepper to taste

10–12 tablespoons chopped flat-leaf parsley
3 tablespoons chopped fresh basil or mint, or a combination
40 g (1½ oz) freshly grated Parmesan cheese
40–50 g (1½–2 oz) rice, cooked

Wash the greens and trim away any tough stems, then chop the leaves coarsely.

Heat 2 tablespoons of olive oil in a large non-stick sauté pan, add the chopped garlic, and stir over medium heat for 2 minutes. Add the chopped greens and a little salt, and sauté, stirring and tossing frequently, until all the greens are wilted and tender, about 5–7 minutes. Sprinkle the greens with a little wine vinegar to bring out their best flavour.

Beat the eggs lightly in a large bowl with ½ teaspoon of salt, some pepper, the chopped herbs, and the Parmesan cheese. Stir in the sautéd greens and the cooked rice.

Heat the remaining ½ tablespoon of olive oil in a 25 cm (10 inch) non-stick pan. Pour in the frittata mixture, spread it evenly, and lower the heat. Cover the pan and leave the frittata on a very low heat for about 10 minutes before checking it. If the top is still very runny, leave it a few minutes more.

When the top is only slightly runny, put the frittata under a hot grill for a couple of minutes to finish and brown the top. As soon as the surface is set, remove it from the heat – overcooked eggs get rubbery, so be careful.

Turn the frittata out on to a large plate and cut it in wedges to serve.

Serves 6–8.

BERRY COBBLER

This is a cobbler that I don't mind serving to my kids in any quantity, as it is not inordinately high in fat or in sugar – just enough to be very good. The topping is more like a buttermilk scone than a sweet pastry crust. Of course, when you add a scoop of vanilla ice cream, the healthful profile deteriorates, but does it ever taste great!

for the filling
125–175 g (4–6 oz) sugar
1 tablespoon cornflour
120 ml (4 fl oz) water
2 tablespoons lemon juice
900 g (2 lb) fresh blackberries,
   or other prepared fruit

for the topping
125 g (4 oz) flour
2 tablespoons sugar
½ teaspoon bicarbonate of
   soda
1 teaspoon baking powder
½ teaspoon salt
2–3 tablespoons butter
120 ml (4 fl oz) buttermilk

Preheat the oven to 200°C/400°F/Gas 6.

In a fairly large, non-reactive pan, combine 125 g (4 oz) of sugar, the cornflour, water, and lemon juice. Stir to dissolve the cornflour, then add the fruit. Bring this mixture to a boil over medium heat, then simmer for a minute, stirring gently. Taste it, and add a bit more sugar if needed. Pour the berry mixture into a 1.7 litre (3 pint) casserole or 20 cm (8 inch) square glass baking dish.

Combine the dry ingredients for the topping in a bowl. Melt the butter and whisk it into the buttermilk, then stir the liquid into the dry mixture, just until it is all combined. The dough will be sticky.

Drop the dough by spoonfuls on to the hot fruit. Bake the cobbler for 20–25 minutes, until the crust is golden. Serve it hot or warm, with vanilla ice cream.

Serves 6–8.

Note: If you are not using berries, the amount of sugar and lemon juice can vary with the type of fruit used – peaches or nectarines, for example, are much less acidic than berries and will need more lemon. Taste and correct as needed.

LITTLE DINNER PARTIES
FOR SPRING AND SUMMER

A RELAXED SUMMER
DINNER PARTY

❧

Garlic Crostini with Tapenade

Cold Melon Soup with Mint Cream

Risotto with Courgette Flowers

fresh blackberries

Crème Anglaise

This is a beautiful, easy dinner based on the foods that are available only in summertime. To make life comfortable on a hot day, everything except the risotto is prepared ahead, and there's not much work to it at all.

The pungent, salty taste of the Tapenade, wonderful with an aperitif, is the perfect foil for cool, sweet melon soup. Then a delicate and creamy risotto with flecks of green and gold flowers. If it's very hot, you could drink white wine throughout – or switch to a light red. Afterwards, ripe blackberries, one of the great tastes of summer – although any ripe summer berries would be fine.

Best eaten in a garden, with a slight sunburn on your shoulders . . .

GARLIC CROSTINI

1 or more baguettes, thinly   **olive oil**
    sliced   **salt**
garlic cloves

Slice as much bread as you want, and toast the slices in a medium oven or under a grill until they are golden on both sides. Rub the toasts very lightly on one side with a cut clove of garlic, then brush with olive oil. Sprinkle the toasts with salt if you like.

Another way to make Garlic Crostini, which I like a lot, is to drop 5–6 cloves of garlic, peeled and slightly bruised, into a cup of green olive oil and let it steep for a few hours. Then discard the garlic cloves and use the oil to brush the hot toasts, omitting the raw garlic rub. This method gives a more subtle garlic flavour.

TAPENADE

225 g (8 oz) Kalamata olives   **1 tablespoon capers**
2 medium cloves garlic   **1 teaspoon grated orange zest**
75 g (3 oz) chopped walnuts   **2 tablespoons lemon juice**
1 teaspoon chopped fresh   **black pepper to taste**
    rosemary leaves   **2–4 tablespoons olive oil**
½ teaspoon chopped fresh
    thyme leaves

Slice the olives off their stones, and combine them in a food processor with the garlic, walnuts, rosemary, thyme, capers, orange zest, and lemon juice. Process for a few seconds, then again, until you have a chunky paste. Add pepper to taste and trickle in the olive oil as you process again. Add only as much oil as you need to get the consistency you like. The Tapenade should be thick but not stiff.

Serve the Tapenade with crostini – little toasts of French or Italian bread.

Makes about 300 ml (10 fl oz), enough to serve 8 as an appetizer with crostini.

COLD MELON SOUP WITH MINT CREAM

This is a wonderful soup for a summer dinner party, refreshing, cool, and successful with many varieties of melon. However, don't attempt it if the melon is not absolutely ripe and sweet. The flavour of the melon is the essence of this.

Everybody has a way of choosing a really ripe melon. I believe in sniffing – a ripe melon will be sweetly fragrant. It should also give a little when gently pressed at the stem end.

750 ml (1¼ pints) water
225 g (8 oz) sugar
1–2 large, perfectly ripe
  melons (approx. 2.8 kg/
  6 lb) – honeydew or other
  juicy, sweet-fleshed variety
500 ml (16 fl oz) good dry
  white wine

juice of 2 large lemons,
  strained
3–4 tablespoons finely
  chopped fresh mint
250 ml (8 fl oz) double cream
additional 1–2 tablespoons
  sugar if desired

Put the water and sugar in a saucepan and bring it to a simmer, washing down any crystals from the sides of the pan with a brush. When the sugar is completely dissolved, continue simmering the syrup for 3–4 minutes, then allow it to cool completely.

Slice the melon, seed it, and scoop out all the soft, ripe flesh. Purée it in a blender. You should have about 1.2 litres (2 pints) of melon purée.

Stir the white wine into the melon purée, then start adding the sugar syrup gradually, a few tablespoons at a time at first, then even less. Stir and taste each time. You may use about 300 ml (10 fl oz) of the syrup, or a little more. When the sweet taste becomes pronounced, add 2 tablespoons of the strained lemon juice. Taste again. Now add a little more lemon juice or a little more sugar syrup, to achieve just the right tart-sweet balance, without overwhelming the melon flavour.

Remember – every melon is different, every lemon is different, every wine is different. That's why taste buds were invented.

Chill the soup thoroughly; you may want to put it in the freezer for the last 30 minutes before you serve it.

To make the mint cream, add the finely chopped fresh mint to the cream, along with a little sugar if you like, and beat the cream until it barely begins to thicken.

Serve the soup cold, in chilled bowls, with a spoonful of the soft mint cream in the centre of each one.

Serves 8.

RISOTTO WITH COURGETTE FLOWERS

Why is this so good? I don't know, but it's so much better with the flowers than it would be with just courgettes.

2 tablespoons butter
1½ tablespoons olive oil
125 g (4 oz) finely chopped
    shallots
125 g (4 oz) chopped mild
    onion
25–30 courgette flowers,
    chopped
225 g (8 oz) chopped baby
    courgettes
salt to taste
1.2–1.5 litres (2–2½ pints)
    vegetable stock (see
    page 459)

350 g (12 oz) Arborio rice
90 ml (3 fl oz) Marsala
175 ml (6 fl oz) white wine
1–2 teaspoons finely chopped
    fresh basil
3–4 tablespoons grated
    Parmesan cheese
pepper to taste
additional Parmesan cheese
    for the table

Heat the butter and olive oil in a large sauté pan and stir the shallots and onion in it until they are soft. Add the chopped courgette flowers and baby courgettes. Salt lightly and stir often over medium heat until the vegetables begin to colour. Meanwhile, heat the stock in a separate pan and keep it hot over a low flame.

Add the rice to the vegetables and stir constantly for 3–4 minutes, then add the Marsala. As soon as it is absorbed, add the white wine, and when that is almost absorbed, begin adding stock. Add about 250 ml (8 fl oz) of stock at a time, and lower the heat so that the liquid is just simmering. Stir occasionally. As soon as the stock is nearly absorbed, add another 250 ml (8 fl oz), stir again, and so on.

After about 20 minutes, have a taste. The rice texture you want is a grain that is creamy on the outside but still quite firm to the tooth inside. Not crunchy, not mushy. The rice should achieve this texture in about 25 minutes of simmering, give or take a bit. Add a final 120 ml (4 fl oz) or so of stock, stir in the chopped basil and a little cheese, and correct the seasoning with a touch of salt or pepper if needed. Then serve at once, passing more Parmesan cheese.

Serves 6–8.

CRÈME ANGLAISE

(Custard Sauce)

500 ml (16 fl oz) milk, or part milk, part cream	**6 tablespoons sugar**
4–5 egg yolks	**pinch of salt**
	½ teaspoon vanilla extract

Scald the milk and keep it hot. Beat the egg yolks with the sugar and salt until they are pale and thick. Still beating with a whisk, pour the hot milk into the egg yolks in a thin, slow stream.

Return the mixture to a very low heat, using a double boiler or a very heavy-bottomed saucepan. Stir until the mixture thickens enough to coat a spoon. Add the vanilla and strain. Cover.

Serve warm or cool with fruits and puddings.

Makes about 600 ml (1 pint).

A SLIGHTLY MIDDLE EASTERN
PILAF DINNER

❧

Minted Tomato Salad with Feta Cheese

Baba Ghanouj

toasted pitta triangles

*Wheat and Lentil Pilaf with Shiitake
Mushrooms*

Roasted Potatoes and Fennel

Yogurt Cheese with Honey and Fresh Figs

The pilaf in this dinner is not a Greek or Turkish recipe – it's just something I made up and liked. The various elements of this meal and the way they come together have a Middle Eastern feeling for me.

Tomatoes and mint, while not as familiar as tomatoes and basil, are a wonderful summertime combination. This salad combines ripe tomatoes with both those herbs and feta cheese. It pairs up well with the subtle, smoky flavour of charred aubergines in Baba Ghanouj, served with toasted pitta triangles.

The pilaf is not a heavy dish, but it's very satisfying, with the earthy tastes of lentils and mushrooms. With it, a simple dish of roasted vegetables, delicately scented with sweet fennel.

For dessert, Yogurt Cheese with Honey and Fresh Figs, a seductive combination of tastes and textures which requires almost no effort. It does take a little advance planning, though, to drain the yogurt. If you haven't done that, you could substitute mascarpone or crème fraîche.

MINTED TOMATO SALAD WITH FETA CHEESE

Of course you know that this should be made with ripe, red summer tomatoes, still warm from the vine.

1.2 kg (2½ lb) ripe tomatoes
1 tablespoon + 1 teaspoon
   olive oil
1 tablespoon balsamic vinegar
2 cloves garlic, minced
3–4 tablespoons chopped
   fresh mint

2 tablespoons chopped fresh
   basil
½ teaspoon salt
125 g (4 oz) feta cheese
½ medium red onion
slices of crusty French bread

Wash and trim the tomatoes and cut them in generous chunks – about 1–2.5 cm (½–1 inch). Combine them in a bowl with 1 tablespoon of olive oil, the vinegar, minced garlic, 2 tablespoons of chopped mint, and the chopped basil. Sprinkle on a little salt – but not too much, as the feta is likely to be salty.

Mound the tomatoes in the centre of a deep platter. Rinse the feta cheese if it's very salty, then break it into rough chunks and arrange them around the tomatoes. Slice the red onion very thinly and scatter the slices over the cheese.

Drizzle the remaining olive oil on the cheese and sprinkle on the rest of the chopped mint. Spoon the salad, with its juices, over slices of crusty French bread.

Serves 6–8 as a first course, or 10–15 as part of a buffet.

BABA GHANOUJ

This is a less rich but exquisitely tasty version of the traditional dish. Be sure you select firm young aubergines. Aubergines that have become overly mature get a bitter taste.

4–5 medium aubergines	1½ tablespoons tahini (sesame
2 medium onions	paste)
½ head garlic	3 tablespoons freshly
1 tablespoon olive oil	squeezed lemon juice
½ teaspoon salt, more to taste	pinch of cayenne

garnish: lots of fresh coriander leaves
   additional olive oil if desired
   pitta bread

Prick the aubergines here and there with a fork, put them on a big baking sheet and roast them in a 200°C/400°F/Gas 6 oven until they are charred and collapsed – at least an hour. Allow them to cool, then split them lengthwise with a sharp knife and scoop out the flesh, first pulling out and discarding any pockets of dark seeds.

While the aubergines are roasting, chop the onions and peel and mince the garlic. Heat the olive oil in a non-stick pan and cook the onion and garlic in it with ½ teaspoon of salt, stirring often, until they are a deep golden brown – probably at least 45 minutes. The flavour of the dish depends much on this slow caramelizing of the onion and garlic.

Stir the cooked onion and garlic into the aubergine flesh, along with the tahini, lemon juice, and cayenne. Now either chop everything finely until it has the texture you like, or process it a few seconds in a food processor for a smoother finish.

Let it rest 1 – 2 hours (refrigerate if longer), then taste it and correct the salt and lemon juice if needed. Serve the Baba Ghanouj in a shallow bowl surrounded by lots of coriander leaves, and pass toasted pitta triangles to dip into it. If you're not worried about fat content, you can drizzle more olive oil on top, but it certainly isn't necessary.

Serves 6–8 generously, more if part of a buffet.

WHEAT AND LENTIL PILAF WITH SHIITAKE MUSHROOMS

This is a delicious hot pilaf to serve with roasted vegetables or sautéd greens, or as an accompaniment to all sorts of things. It also makes a very nice salad when cooled and spooned over an interesting mix of fresh leaves, such as Chinese greens or a mix of curly endive and watercress. You may want to sprinkle on a touch more vinegar if using it as a salad. And one of my favourite pitta bread sandwiches was made with this, a spoonful of Baba Ghanouj and a drizzle of yogurt.

225 g (8 oz) wheatberries
salt
3 medium onions
2 tablespoons olive oil
175 g (6 oz) lentils
about 2 litres (3½ pints)
    spring water

225 g (8 oz) shiitake
    mushrooms (or mixed
    shiitake and cultivated
    mushrooms)
½ teaspoon dark sesame oil
½–1 teaspoon soy sauce
1 tablespoon rice vinegar

Simmer the wheatberries in about 2 litres (3½ pints) of water, with a pinch of salt, until they are tender; this could take about 2 hours. Drain the wheatberries, reserving the liquid, and add enough water to the liquid to make 600 ml (1 pint).

Meanwhile, chop the onions rather finely. They will seem like a lot but later will turn out to be just enough. Heat 1½ tablespoons of the olive oil in a large non-stick sauté pan and cook the onions slowly in it, with a sprinkle of salt, until they are caramel-coloured. This could take up to an hour.

Add the cooked wheat to the caramelized onions, along with the lentils, the 600 ml (1 pint) of reserved liquid, and ½ teaspoon of salt. Cover the pan tightly and simmer for 30–35 minutes or until the lentils are tender. Uncover, and if there is any remaining water, let it cook away.

Meanwhile, clean the mushrooms, trim away the tough stems and cut the caps in 0.5 cm (¼ inch) dice. In another non-stick pan, heat the remaining ½ tablespoon of olive oil with the sesame oil and sauté the mushrooms in it, stirring often, until they lose their water, dry out and sizzle. Sprinkle on some soy sauce, toss the mushrooms in it and cook them a couple minutes more.

Remove the mushrooms from the heat, toss them with the rice vinegar, then stir them into the wheat mixture when you remove the lid.

This is ready to serve as soon as all the liquid is absorbed or evaporated.

Makes 8 generous servings.

ROASTED POTATOES AND FENNEL

1.2 kg (2½ lb) red-skinned potatoes

2 large fennel bulbs, white only

2 large onions

2 large, ripe tomatoes

8–10 small carrots

1 large red or green pepper

½ head garlic

175 ml (6 fl oz) any home-made tomato sauce

salt and pepper to taste

2–3 tablespoons olive oil

optional: chopped fresh basil

Scrub, clean, and trim all the vegetables. The potatoes should be cut in approximately 2.5 cm (1 inch) cubes, the fennel, onions, and tomatoes about the same or slightly larger. Slender carrots can be cut to the size of your little finger, and the pepper sliced into strips or cut in squares. Slice the garlic or chop it coarsely.

Mix everything together in a big bowl with the tomato sauce, some salt and pepper, and the olive oil. Add chopped fresh basil if you like.

Spread the vegetables out on two baking sheets and roast them in a 220°C/425°F/Gas 7 oven, checking them every 7–8 minutes. Stir and turn the vegetables when you see brown or charred spots appearing on top. When all the vegetables are tender – probably about an hour – serve at once.

Serves 6–8.

YOGURT CHEESE WITH HONEY AND FRESH FIGS

With sweet, ripe figs, this is a dish from heaven. However, if fresh figs are unavailable, you could try sliced white peaches (slice them at the last moment) or big, juicy berries, both of which also have that voluptuous quality. Perfect ripeness is essential.

1 recipe Yogurt Cheese **8 tablespoons honey, more to**
(recipe follows) **taste**
  16 large ripe figs

optional garnish: mint sprigs

On each of 8 medium-sized dessert plates, put a nice big dollop of freshly stirred Yogurt Cheese. Drizzle at least a tablespoon of honey over it, more if you like.

Cut your figs in half with a sharp knife and split them open, keeping the halves connected at the stem if you want to. Put 2 figs on each plate next to the Yogurt Cheese. Garnish with mint sprigs if desired.

Serves 8.

YOGURT CHEESE

Yogurt Cheese is nothing more complicated than well-drained plain yogurt. It has a creamy, silky texture, and a flavour similar to cream cheese, though slightly more tangy. It can be spread on bagels, used to make fresh herbed cheese, or sweetened with sugar or honey and eaten with fruit for a wonderful dessert.

2.4 litres (4 pints) plain
non-fat yogurt, or a mixture
of non-fat and whole-milk
yogurt

Use plain yogurt that has no starch or gums added to it.

Line a colander with a triple thickness of damp cheesecloth. Put the yogurt into it and stand the colander in a bowl. Cover with clingfilm and refrigerate for about 18–20 hours. Drain the liquid from the bowl and discard it once or twice in the course of this process.

If you want an even thicker, denser cheese, pick up the 4 corners of the cheesecloth, twist them together, then put a weight on top of the cheese and let it drain another few hours.

2.4 litres (4 pints) of yogurt will yield about 575–700 g (1¼–1½ lb) of Yogurt Cheese, depending on how long you drain it.

Part of the fun of chillies, besides their addictive flavour and heat, is the fact that there are so many of them, and the same chilli often goes by different names in different places. Don't worry. If the worst thing that happens to you is that you use an Anaheim (not its real name) when you meant to use a guajillo (who knows?), then life is good. At least you're eating chillies.

These are the chillies I use most frequently. They are usually available where I live, and the dried pods can be ordered by mail. (See page 470 for information about mail order in Britain.)

Jalapeño – This is the best known and most commonly used pepper in Mexican food. It is always there, in fresh salsas, sliced on top of nachos, pickled, finding its way into everything. It has become so popular that fancy jellies are made from it, and it's turning up in sushi bars.

It is used in its fresh form. It is small, smooth, usually dark green, and has a cone-like shape about 5–7.5 cm (2–3 inches) long. It turns bright red when riper. Jalapeños are quite hot, and have a fantastic, distinctive flavour with their heat.

In America, jalapeños are widely available. In Britain, the small (about 2.5 cm (1 inch) long) fresh green chillies that are commonly found in supermarkets make a reasonable substitute. They are a bit milder, however, so increase quantity when substituting them for jalapeños.

Ancho, or **poblano** – When it is fresh and green, this pepper is called a poblano, and is frequently used to make *chiles rellenos*, or stuffed chillies. When it is fully ripened and dried, it becomes a dark reddish brown, and is called a *chile ancho*, or 'wide pepper', because the flat, dried pods are almost as wide as they are long. The dried anchos are an important ingredient of Mole Poblano.

Poblanos are about the size of smaller bell peppers, and are very mild.

New Mexican, or **New Mexico**, also still called **Anaheim** – This is the chilli that defines New Mexico. It is a staple food, served in some form in almost every restaurant, hanging in *ristras* from beams of adobes, perfuming the air during the autumn roasting season. It used to be called an Anaheim, but its name was formally changed to New Mexican recently.

The New Mexican chillies are 15–18 cm (6–7 inches) long, dark green, and later bright red as they fully ripen. They are medium hot, and are commonly used in both fresh and dried form.

Pasilla, sometimes also called **negro**, because of their very dark colour. I have only used them in their dried form. They have a nice, rich chilli flavour, with almost no bite.

Pasillas are usually about 12–15 cm (5–6 inches) long and fairly narrow, with very dark brown, wrinkled skin, and are mild.

Guajillo – It's possible that this long, narrow chilli is a variety of the New Mexican chilli, as they have a very similar look. Guajillos, however, are hotter, and have a terrific flavour.

The guajillo pods are a deep reddish brown when mature, and have a smooth texture. They are 15–18 cm (6–7 inches) long, little more than 2.5 cm (1 inch) wide, and medium hot.

Serrano – This is a hot little chilli, noticeably hotter than the familiar jalapeño. It is used fresh, and makes a delicious hot salsa.

Serranos are only 2.5–7.5 cm (1–3 inches) long and very narrow. They are dark green when young, and ripen to red, though some are orange or yellow. They are very hot.

Chipotle – I'm crazy about chipotles. They are smoke-dried jalapeños, hot and tasty, with a seductive combination of the unique jalapeño flavour and a deep, intriguing smokiness.

The dried pods are nut-brown, wrinkled and hard. They vary in size, like all jalapeños, but most are 5–7.5 cm (2–3 inches) long.

Chipotles are available dried, or canned in an *adobo* sauce. I prefer to use the dried pods and soak them, to get the purest flavour.

All dried chilli pods last a very long time if stored in a cool, dry place, safe from bugs. Once you know which ones you like, it makes sense to buy or order them in quantity.

In a chilli emergency, the dried red chillies sold in many shops – narrow pods about 7.5–12 cm (3–5 inches) long – can be made into a perfectly nice salsa (see page 98), and a green salsa can be made with the easily found, small, fresh green chillies (see page 272). But if you like fiery cuisine, I heartily recommend that you treat yourself to the distinctive, seductive flavours of my favourite chillies.

Note: When working with chillies, wear rubber gloves, or wash your hands very thoroughly afterwards. I find that rubbing my hands first with vegetable oil, and then washing them several times with soap and water, is very effective for removing chilli oil.

GUILLERMINA'S CHILLI SALSAS

A chilli salsa of some kind is the most common condiment in my house. Put a good salsa on your table, freshly made and fragrant in the air around you, and watch your ordinary, everyday food come alive and dance. It really is like turning up the music.

I'm not talking about *moles*, those complex symphonies of flavour involving dozens of ingredients and serious time over a hot stove. I'm talking about the easy salsas that you can throw together at the last minute, the daily salsas, raw or cooked, fiery, brash, dramatic, and refreshing.

One of my favourites is the easiest. Salsa Cruda (see page 272), also sometimes called *pico de gallo*, is just chopped tomatoes, green chillies, onion, and coriander, with a little salt. Everything is raw. This is freshness itself, and everyone loves it. Even the kids pile it on their tortilla chips. It is dynamite with guacamole, terrific in burritos or tacos and spooned into hot quesadillas. If you throw it into a hot pan, let it sizzle a moment, then stir in beaten eggs, you have a fast version of Huevos Mexicanos.

The easiest cooked salsas are made by putting dried chillies, onion, garlic, and maybe tomatoes into a pot with a little water and salt, simmering until everything is soft, then spinning it all in a blender for a moment. I sometimes add toasted cumin at the end, or chopped coriander. This method is almost effortless, and can be adapted to any kind of dried chilli pods. A fiery salsa can be made with dried serranos or pequins, a mild one from anchos, and a smoky-hot salsa from chipotles.

I'm also completely in love with salsas made from fresh chillies and tomatillos, scorched on a griddle or grill, and roughly ground up in a mortar. (See Guajillo Chilli Salsa, page 35.)

To make a good salsa of this type, it's best to have a cast-iron pan or griddle. You can use stainless steel, or one of the new non-stick finishes, but I recommend the cast-iron pan because after you char the tomatillos you will have to scrub some charcoal off that pan, and cast iron is indestructible.

It's also nice to have a big stone mortar for grinding the softened chillies. This is called a *molcajete* in Mexico, and I use mine almost daily. It's very practical for quickly grinding up a spoonful of cumin seed, it gives a nice rough texture to a salsa – and I like the way it looks on my kitchen counter. But this certainly is not essential; a normal blender will do the job very well.

I learned to make these salsas watching Guillermina, who is from Jalisco, Mexico. One day she threw some green chillies and whole tomatillos into a naked, hot cast-iron pan. For the next ten minutes she casually knocked the vegetables around, turning them over as they charred in big black blisters and sizzled on the hot iron. The smell of those scorching chillies and tomatillos, rising up through the house, made my tongue drip.

When they were well blackened, she peeled the chillies under running water, pulled out their stems, and tossed them in the *molcajete* with the tomatillos. A few brisk pushes with the stone pestle, and they were salsa. She threw in a big handful of sliced green onions and a bigger one of coriander, added a dash of salt, gave a few more turns with the stone, and put it on the table. It was sensational. Utterly irresistible. Wow! I thought. That's really cooking. The whole operation had taken less than half an hour.

We dipped our warm tortillas in that salsa and ate it up, and our taste buds danced.

CINCO DE MAYO DINNER

❦

Nopalito Salad
or Green and Black Bean Salad

Tamales with Courgette and Coriander Filling

Ancho Chilli Salsa — or Red Chilli Salsa

Garlic and Cumin Rice

white cheese

Caramel Custard with Pineapple

Café de Olla

This Mexican meal is authentically delicious and full of surprises. You may have to search a bit for the ingredients. Perhaps you will have to plan ahead and order some things. But you will have fun!

The nopalitos will probably be the hardest to find, but fresh nopalitos are occasionally seen in street markets. If you find them, revel in them. And if not, don't worry — the Green and Black Bean Salad is a delicious alternative.

To make tamales, the masa harina, corn husks, and various dried chillies are all available by mail order (see page 471) and probably will become more commonly available in shops as the popularity of Mexican food grows.

In Mexico and in the American Southwest, tamales are often prepared for holidays and festivals. Dozens or even hundreds of tamales are prepared in an afternoon. For these occasions, the preparation of the tamales becomes a party of its own, with friends sitting around a big table, gossiping and drinking as they wrap corn husks around the masa and filling. It's called a *tamalera*, and is likely to be as much fun as the fiesta itself.

But making tamales for six or eight people shouldn't take more than about an hour. If you have never made tamales before, allow yourself a little extra time. It's not difficult, but like all things it's easier when you're used to it. And you never know – once you get the hang of it, you may want to have a *tamalera* and make tamales for a crowd.

The Red Chilli Salsa can easily be prepared from the dried chillies commonly available in many shops. However, if you have ancho chillies, or the more flavourful guajillos or chipotles, by all means substitute your own favourite cooked salsa for a more exotic flavour.

After chillies, have a cool and silky custard, presented in its pool of caramelized pineapple sauce. Then serve strong, black Café de Olla, fragrant with cinnamon, for a complete experience.

NOPALITO SALAD

350 g (12 oz) cooked, diced nopalitos (for cooking instructions, see page 35)
2 medium ripe tomatoes
6–8 sliced spring onions or ½ large onion, finely chopped
1–2 tablespoons minced fresh green chillies

8–9 tablespoons coarsely chopped fresh coriander leaves
250 ml (8 fl oz) cooked pinto or black beans
1 tablespoon freshly squeezed lemon juice
salt and pepper to taste

garnishes: crumbled fresh white cheese, e.g. feta
sliced avocados
fresh chilli salsa

The nopalitos, cooked and cooled, can be cut in strips or in 1 cm (½ inch) dice. The tomatoes can be cut in chunks just a little larger than that.

Combine all the ingredients in an ample bowl and toss them together gently but thoroughly; taste and adjust the salt, lemon juice, and chilli if needed. The flavour of fresh jalapeños is delicious, but they are hot, so add a little at a time, tasting as you go, until you like the balance.

The salad is best served immediately, but can be kept covered in the refrigerator for 1–2 hours. Spoon the salad on to plates, and garnish each serving with a sprinkling of crumbled fresh white cheese. A mixture of white cheese and tangy goat cheese is also wonderful. Fresh avocado slices can be fanned alongside or on top. Then pass the salsa and a basket of fresh hot corn tortillas.

Serves 6.

GREEN AND BLACK BEAN SALAD

450 g (1 lb) tender green beans
350 g (12 oz) cooked black beans, drained
8 spring onions, sliced
3–4 tablespoons finely chopped fresh green chillies, or to taste
1 small bunch coriander, chopped leaves only

salt to taste
2 medium ripe tomatoes
1 avocado, ripe but not mushy
3–4 tablespoons freshly squeezed lemon juice
125–150 g (4–5 oz) crumbled fresh white cheese, e.g. feta

Wash and trim the green beans and slice them in 5 cm (2 inch) lengths. Steam them for a few minutes, just until they are tender-crisp, then let them cool.

Combine the green beans, black beans, sliced spring onions, chillies, and coriander leaves in a bowl and mix together gently. Add salt to taste.

Cut the tomatoes in 1 cm (½ inch) dice. Halve and peel and dice the avocado. Toss the avocado immediately in a bowl with 3 tablespoons fresh lemon juice.

Just before serving, add the diced tomatoes, avocado and lemon juice to the salad. Toss it gently again. Taste and correct the seasoning with more lemon juice, salt and green chilli as desired.

Mound the salad on a deep platter and scatter the crumbled white cheese over the top.

Serves 8.

TAMALES WITH COURGETTE AND CORIANDER FILLING

The masa for these tamales is somewhat denser than the one I make for fresh corn tamales. It will hold its texture well with a moist filling and has a nice, savoury flavour. It can also be used with any number of other fillings – goat's cheese and chipotle sauce, or a *mole*, for instance.

40 large dried corn husks (to yield 20) (see page 470)

for the filling
450 g (1 lb) tender young
  courgettes
1 teaspoon salt
1 large onion
4 cloves garlic
8 spring onions
1½ tablespoons olive oil
3–4 mild green chillies, diced
1 tablespoon lemon juice,
  more to taste
freshly ground pepper to taste
8 tablespoons chopped fresh
  coriander leaves

for the masa
175 g (6 oz) butter, softened
615 g (17½ oz) masa harina
  (see page 38)
½ teaspoon salt
2 teaspoons baking powder
120 ml (4 fl oz) milk
350 ml (12 fl oz) vegetable
  stock, cool or lukewarm
  (see page 459)

To prepare the dried corn husks: start with at least twice as many as you will need (they usually come in packages of a few dozen). Soak them in hot water for about 30 minutes. When they're soft, rinse them under running water as you separate them, discarding the very small or torn ones. Lay them flat on a plate and keep them covered with a damp tea towel until you need them. The longer torn ones can be torn further, into 1 cm (½ inch) strips, and used for ties.

To prepare the filling: wash and trim the courgettes and cut them into 0.5 cm (¼ inch) dice. Toss them with a teaspoon of salt and leave them to drain in a colander for about 30 minutes.

Meanwhile, chop the onion finely, mince the garlic, and trim and thinly slice the spring onions. Heat the olive oil in an ample non-stick pan and sauté all the onions and garlic in it until they begin to colour.

When the courgettes have released their water, press them gently in the colander, then add them to the onion mixture. Continue cooking the vegetables, stirring occasionally, until the courgettes are tender and the mixture is quite dry. It is essential to have no excess liquid here.

Stir in the green chillies, lemon juice, some pepper, and the chopped coriander. Taste, and correct the seasoning if needed.

This makes enough filling for at least 20 tamales. Any leftover filling is delicious in omelettes, quesadillas, or burritos, or stirred into a vegetable soup.

To prepare the masa: beat the softened butter in a mixing bowl until it is light and fluffy. Whisk the dry masa harina with the salt and baking powder until well blended. Beat some of the dry mixture into the butter, then the milk, then more of the dry mixture, then some of the stock, and so on until everything is combined.

The prepared masa should have the texture of a tender scone dough; it should hold its shape well, but not feel dry or crumbly. If it is too dry, add a few more drops of stock, and if too sticky, add a little more masa harina.

This makes enough masa for 18–20 tamales, using slightly less than 50 g (2 oz) per tamale.

To assemble the tamales: lay a prepared corn husk flat on your work surface. Put about 50 g (2 oz) of masa in the centre of it and spread it slightly. Be sure to leave at least a 4 cm (1½ inch) border on each side and a couple of inches at each end.

Put a rounded tablespoon of filling down the centre of the masa, then lift one side of the husk gently over the other until the edges of the masa meet around the filling. Pinch the masa together a little with your fingers, sealing in the filling. Fold the husk lengthwise over the tamale, then fold in the narrow end, then finish rolling up the whole husk, loosely. This makes a tamale that's open on one end. If you have extra-long husks, you can fold the wide end in as well, envelope style, before you finish rolling. Note: forming tamales is tricky the first time, but soon gets much easier, and then becomes a lot of fun.

Tie a thin strip of corn husk around the middle to hold everything together, but not too tightly, as the tamales will expand in cooking. If you have trouble tying strips of corn husk, use plain brown twine, or any other kind of tie that won't react with the food in steaming.

To steam the tamales: arrange them loosely in a roomy vegetable steamer. If you left the wide end unfolded, be sure to handle them carefully and fit them into the steamer with the open end up. Steam the tamales for 35–45 minutes, then test one. If the masa is cooked through and no longer sticky, they're done. Serve them hot.

Tamales can be prepared a few hours ahead of time and held in the refrigerator, covered, until it's time to steam them – just add a few minutes to the cooking time to take the chill off. They can also be resteamed briefly a day or two later.

This makes 18–20 tamales, enough for 6–8 servings.

ANCHO CHILLI SALSA

This is not a spicy salsa, but it is full of deep chilli flavour, and can be used in satisfying quantity.

3 large ancho chilli pods
   (about 50 g / 2 oz) (see
   page 87)
1 onion
175 g (6 oz) tomatillos*
3 cloves garlic

¾ teaspoon salt
6 tablespoons coriander
   leaves
1 tablespoon cumin seed
water or stock as needed
   (see page 459)

In a small pot, simmer the chillies in just enough water to cover until they are soft and their thin outer skins are curling away. Lift them out with a slotted spoon, pull away the skins, pull out the stems and cores, and return the trimmed pods to the water.

---

* If tomatillos cannot be found, green tomatoes can be used in their place, with a dash of fresh lemon juice added to the finished salsa for that essential zingy tart note.

Cut the onion into large chunks. Remove the dry husks from the tomatillos and cut them in halves or quarters. Peel the garlic cloves. Add the onion, tomatillos, garlic, salt, and coriander leaves to the chillies, add a little more water if needed, and simmer everything together for about 15 minutes.

Toast the cumin seeds lightly in a pan, grind them briefly in a mortar, and add them to the vegetables. When all the vegetables are completely soft, purée the salsa in a blender. It should be a coarse purée, thick enough to hold a soft shape in the spoon. This salsa can be thinned with a little water or stock if desired. It keeps well for about a week if tightly covered and refrigerated.

Makes about 750 ml (1¼ pints).

RED CHILLI SALSA

5–6 large dried red chilli pods (about 40 g (1½ oz))
450–500 g (1 lb) ripe tomatoes
1 large onion
5–6 garlic cloves
1 teaspoon salt
1½ tablespoons cumin seeds
6 tablespoons chopped fresh coriander

optional: mild or hot Mexican chilli powder
   a dash of fresh lemon juice

Rinse the dried chilli pods and throw them in a very hot cast-iron pan for a couple of minutes, pressing them down a bit and turning them over until their colour begins to darken. They may get a few black spots, which is fine. Put the scorched chillies in a small pot with enough water just to cover them and simmer them until they are soft, about 10 minutes. Under cool running water, remove and discard their stems and seeds. Return them to the cooking water.

Meanwhile, scorch the tomatoes in the same pan, rolling them around now and then until their skins are blistered and charred. Peel off the blistered skins and cut out the stems.

Peel and quarter the onion, and peel the garlic cloves. Add the tomatoes, onion, garlic and salt to the pot with the chilli pods, as well as a little more water if needed – just enough to keep it all barely covered. Simmer the vegetables for about 15 minutes, or until everything is mushy-soft, then purée it in a blender.

Toast the cumin seeds in a little pan over medium heat, stirring constantly, for a minute or two, just until they release a strong fragrance. Grind the seeds up in a mortar. Stir the ground cumin and the chopped coriander into the chilli purée and taste. Add salt if needed, and if you want a hotter sauce, add a dash of Mexican chilli powder. A little lemon juice can be added for a tart accent, and if you want a thicker sauce, just cook it down a little.

This makes about 600 ml (1 pint) of sauce.

GARLIC AND CUMIN RICE

1 medium Spanish onion, finely chopped	450 g (1 lb) long-grain white rice
3 cloves garlic, minced	1 teaspoon salt
1 tablespoon olive oil	450 g (1 lb) tomatoes, peeled and chopped
1 teaspoon butter	1 litre (1¾ pints) hot water
1 tablespoon whole cumin seeds	

In a medium-sized non-stick sauté pan, sauté the onions and garlic in the olive oil and butter until the onions are soft and just beginning to colour. Meanwhile, toast the cumin seeds in a small pan, over a medium flame, until they release their fragrance. Grind them lightly in a mortar.

Add the rice to the onions and garlic, stir it for 2–3 minutes, then add the cumin, salt, chopped tomatoes, and water. Bring the mixture to a simmer, lower the heat, cover the pan, and leave it to simmer for 20 minutes, longer if you like your rice softer. At the end of the cooking time, turn off the heat and allow to stand, covered, for another 5 minutes, then fluff with a fork before serving.

Makes 6–8 servings.

CARAMEL CUSTARD WITH PINEAPPLE

Flan is ever-present in Mexican and Spanish kitchens, and that's a good thing. A custard with a little caramel sauce, it is one of the simplest desserts, but when properly made it has a silky texture and purity of flavour that rightly make it a classic. This variation begins with a plain custard, prepared with slightly less sugar than usual, then finishes with a garnish of pineapple in a thin sauce of caramelized sugar and pineapple juice. I love the rich taste of burnt sugar mixed with the slight acidity of the fruit.

350 g (12 oz) sugar

750 ml (1¼ pints) low-fat or whole milk

4 large eggs

pinch of salt

½ teaspoon vanilla extract

250 ml (8 fl oz) pineapple juice

350 g (12 oz) crushed or chopped canned or fresh pineapple

Melt 125 g (4 oz) of sugar in a heavy-bottomed pan over a medium flame. When the sugar is entirely melted and a rich golden caramel colour, pour the caramel into a 1.7 litre (3 pint) baking dish, tilting it around so that the caramel lightly coats both the bottom and the sides.

Scald the milk and remove it from the heat before it boils. Beat the eggs with another 125 g (4 oz) of sugar, a pinch of salt, and the vanilla until they are smooth, then add the scalded milk in a small stream as you keep beating.

Strain the custard into the prepared baking dish. Place the dish inside a larger baking pan with about 2.5 cm (1 inch) of water in it, and bake in a preheated 180°C/350°F/Gas 4 oven for about an hour. If the top seems to be getting too brown, you can cover the custard loosely with a sheet of foil. It is done when a knife inserted near the centre comes out clean.

Remove the baking dish from its water bath and allow the custard to cool, then chill it in the refrigerator.

Meanwhile, melt the last of the sugar in a medium-sized pan, just as you did at the start. When it is a caramel syrup, remove it from the heat, add about half the pineapple juice, and stand back, as it will boil up and steam dramatically. Let it settle, return it to a low flame, and add the rest of the juice. Stir as it comes to a simmer and the caramel dissolves into the juice. Add the crushed or chopped pineapple and simmer the mixture for 2–3 minutes more, longer if it seems too thin. Then cover it and set aside until you are ready to serve the custard.

To unmould the custard, it helps to dip the bottom of the baking dish into a pan of hot water for a moment. Then run a knife around the edge of the custard to loosen the sides. Invert a large serving platter over the dish and, holding the two securely together, quickly turn them over. The custard will drop on to the serving platter, with a pool of caramel around it.

To serve, spoon the pineapple-caramel sauce around the custard on its platter, to mingle with the pure caramel, or spoon some on to each individual plate next to a slice of custard.

This makes 8 servings.

CAFÉ DE OLLA

cinnamon sticks　　　　**coffee beans**
spring water　　　　　　**lump cane sugar**

Café de Olla is a strong black coffee made with cinnamon water and sweetened with *piloncillo*, the cone-shaped solid brown cane sugar that is sold in every Mexican market.

Add several sticks of cinnamon to 3.4–4.8 litres (6–8 pints) of water, bring it to a boil, and then leave it to steep for several hours.

Grind your coffee beans and use the cinnamon water to make your coffee in the usual way. For an even stronger cinnamon flavour, add a few broken sticks of cinnamon to the ground beans in the filter.

When the coffee is brewed, add a little cane sugar and let it dissolve. This you must do to your own taste. Another way is to serve the cinnamon coffee unsweetened and pass a bowl of cane sugar, broken into small pieces, so everyone can sweeten to taste.

PICNIC FOR A SUMMER CONCERT

୫୫

assorted cured olives

Spinach and Feta Cheese Alligator

White Bean and Tomato Salad

Ratatouille

Panzanella

*cheese platter: Gorgonzola, marinated chèvre, thin-sliced
Parmesan*

olive bread, sourdough baguettes, breadsticks

fresh berries, peaches, apricots, and cherries

Chocolate-dipped Biscotti

coffee

This food is appealing and delicious, and tastes best at room temperature. And because it's virtually indestructible, it can easily be transported for a fancy picnic or a dinner in the park before an open-air concert.

This is also a menu that can be easily expanded for a more lavish buffet to serve at home, perhaps to a larger group. You can add some other favourite cold dishes, such as vermicelli with pesto, marinated peppers, a seafood salad, or something from the grill. It's summer food, and goes with everything that's in season.

The Spinach and Feta Cheese Alligator, a big hearty pastry, has a whimsical shape and a savoury, chewy filling. Take along a cutting board, and slice the alligator right at the picnic.

A trio of excellent salads go along: White Bean and Tomato Salad, Ratatouille, and Panzanella, a great Tuscan invention made of ripe vegetables and coarse bread. To complete the buffet, serve a little dish of assorted cured olives, a basket of great breads, and a platter of cheeses. I would include one ripe blue-veined cheese, a marinated goat's cheese, and one sharp, aged cheese such as Parmesan or Manchego.

With such good picnic food, you want a good picnic wine – not heavy or serious, but a younger wine with a taste of the fruit. A rosé from Provence, or an Italian white, such as a nice Vernaccia di San Gimignano, would be right. A light red wine would also be fine, especially for an evening picnic in cooler weather.

For dessert, bring along baskets of fresh, ripe summer fruit. You can line a flat wicker tray with vine leaves and fill it with berries, mixing raspberries, blueberries, and small strawberries. Keep blackberries separate, as they turn to sauce very easily. In another basket, pile up whole apricots, cherries, and peaches.

Serve chocolate-dipped biscotti with the fruit. Fill a thermos with strong, hot coffee, and you will have the perfect ending for a lovely *al fresco* experience, and also be able to stay awake for the concert.

SPINACH AND FETA CHEESE ALLIGATOR

This is similar to Chard and Fennel Pie (see page 134). It's a long, narrow pastry in which a filling of greens, potatoes, and herbs is wrapped in a soft bread crust. It's very low in fat and delicious warm or cool, and makes a good buffet or picnic dish when cut in thin slices. I called it an alligator because I made it in the shape of an alligator's head, but you don't have to.

for the crust
1½ teaspoon dried yeast
1 teaspoon sugar
60 ml (2 fl oz) warm water
425 g (15 oz) plain flour

1 teaspoon salt
1 egg
175 ml (6 fl oz) low-fat milk
1 tablespoon olive oil

for the filling
2 tablespoons olive oil
300 g (10 oz) chopped onion
3 cloves garlic, minced
1 large leek, white and
    light green only,
    chopped
6–8 spring onions, thinly
    sliced
450 g (1 lb) fresh spinach,
    washed and chopped
2 medium potatoes, peeled
    and cut in 0.5 cm (¼ inch)
    dice

3 tablespoons chopped fresh
    dill
1 tablespoon cider vinegar
4 eggs
120 ml (4 fl oz) low-fat
    milk
125 g (4 oz) feta
    cheese
3 tablespoons raw rice
50 g (2 oz) sliced Kalamata
    olives
freshly ground black pepper
salt, if needed

Start the dough first. Dissolve the yeast and sugar in the warm water and leave it a few minutes, until it starts to bubble and foam. Meanwhile, measure 325 g (11 oz) of the flour into a large bowl and stir in the salt. Beat together the egg, milk, and olive oil, stir in the yeast mixture, and then mix the liquid into the flour. Stir it with a big wooden spoon until it forms a dough.

When the stirring gets tough, spread the remaining flour on an ample board and turn the dough out on it. Knead it gently, turning often at first to keep it coated with flour, until it is smooth and becoming elastic. Form the dough into a ball and put it into a lightly oiled bowl. Cover the bowl with a towel and set it aside to rise in a warm place for about an hour, or until doubled.

While it rises, make the filling. Heat the olive oil in a large non-stick pan and sauté the chopped onions, garlic, and leek in it until the vegetables are soft and beginning to colour. Add the spring onions, chopped spinach, and potatoes, and toss everything together until the spinach wilts. Cover and keep cooking on low heat for about 10 minutes, or until the potatoes are tender. Uncover, raise the heat, and stir occasionally for a few minutes more, until the excess moisture completely cooks away. Stir in the dill and the cider vinegar, and remove from the heat.

Break the eggs into a bowl, reserving 1 yolk to use for a glaze. Beat the eggs with the milk. Crumble the feta cheese.

Transfer the hot vegetable mixture into a cool bowl, and stir in the feta cheese, the raw rice, and the sliced olives. Season with black pepper. Taste, and add salt only if it is needed – the salty cheese and olives may provide enough, so be careful. Finally, stir in the beaten eggs and milk. Let the prepared filling sit for about 15 minutes, to allow the rice and potatoes to soak up some moisture.

Punch down the dough and divide it in half. On a large, floured surface, pat one half of the dough into a rectangle, then gently roll it, turning it over and dusting with more flour to keep it from sticking, until you have an oval about 60 cm (24 inches) long and 20–25 cm (8–10 inches) across.

Fold the dough in half crosswise and lay it down on an oiled baking sheet. Unfold it, and spoon half the filling down the middle, from the fold line to within 2.5 cm (1 inch) of the end.

Beat the reserved egg yolk with a spoonful of water and brush the edges of the dough with it. Fold the other half of the dough over again, laying it evenly on top of the filling and pressing the edges together lightly. Then fold the edges up from underneath, curling the bottom crust over the edge of the top crust, and crimping or pleating it into a pattern. Pierce the dough here and there with a skewer or fork.

If you're feeling especially creative, you can stick on scraps of dough at the appropriate spots for the alligator's eyes. Brush the dough lightly with the egg yolk glaze.

Roll out and fill the second half of the dough, either into an alligator or else just a long, filled loaf. Bake the alligators or loaves at 180°C/350°F/Gas 4 for about 45 minutes. After 25 minutes, reverse their positions in the oven so that they brown evenly. Let them cool slightly before slicing.

Makes 2 alligators, enough to serve 15−20.

WHITE BEAN AND TOMATO SALAD

450 g (1 lb) small dried white beans
pinch of bicarbonate of soda
½ head garlic, separated into cloves and peeled
6−8 sage leaves
3 tablespoons fruity green olive oil
2 teaspoons salt
2 large stalks celery

½ medium mild onion
12 Kalamata olives
½ cucumber, peeled
6 tablespoons coarsely chopped flat-leaf parsley
3 tablespoons coarsely chopped fresh basil
freshly ground black pepper
3−4 medium vine-ripened tomatoes

Soak the beans overnight in plenty of water and a pinch of bicarbonate of soda. Drain them and put them in a large, heavy-bottomed pan with enough fresh water to cover them by 2.5 cm (1 inch). Add the peeled garlic cloves, cut in half if they are very large, the sage leaves, and 1 tablespoon of olive oil.

Bring the water to a gentle simmer and regulate the heat to keep it just simmering. After a while, skim some foam off the top. Simmer the beans for 2−3 hours, until they are tender, checking them occasionally to make sure they are still covered with water. Towards the end of the cooking time, gently stir in the salt. Don't overstir the beans or let them boil hard, as you want to maintain their shape.

Allow the beans to cool, then drain off the liquid and either discard it or reserve it for a soup.

Trim the celery, halve it lengthwise, and slice it thinly. Coarsely chop the onion. Slice the olives off their stones. Cut the cucumber in half lengthwise and slice thinly.

In a large bowl, combine the beans with the celery, onion, olives, cucumber, chopped herbs, 2 tablespoons of olive oil, and freshly ground black pepper to taste. Mix gently but thoroughly, being careful not to crush the beans.

Just before serving, mound the bean salad in the middle of a platter and surround with freshly cut tomato wedges.

Makes enough for 12–16 servings.

RATATOUILLE

Ratatouille is the quintessential dish of Provence. It is a dish for late summer, when aubergines and sweet peppers are abundant, and tomatoes at their sweetest. The vegetables are stewed in olive oil, and perfumed with herbs.

I used to make Ratatouille with much more oil, but I like this version better – made with just a little olive oil, and more tomatoes, which provide the liquid for stewing. The result is lighter, with fresh, pure flavours and the concentrated sweetness of the ripe tomatoes.

This recipe yields a big batch, enough for a party, or for several meals. I never seem to get tired of Ratatouille, and it's delicious cold, so this big recipe makes sense to me – this way you can stir over the hot stove once and eat at least twice. However, you can also cut the recipe in half.

4 young, firm aubergines
salt to taste
900 g (2 lb) courgettes
6 cloves garlic, chopped

700 g (1½ lb) red and green
peppers, seeded and cut in
1 cm (½ inch) dice
2 tablespoons olive oil

3 large onions, cut in 1 cm
  (½ inch) pieces
handful of chopped flat-leaf
  parsley
handful of chopped fresh basil
1 tablespoon balsamic vinegar

500 ml (16 fl oz) Summer
  Tomato Sauce (see page 60)
freshly ground black pepper
  to taste
3 large red tomatoes, cut in
  2.5 cm (1 inch) pieces

Peel the aubergines and cut them in 1 cm (½ inch) dice. Toss the cut aubergines with a generous amount of salt and put them in a colander, over a bowl, to drain for at least 45 minutes. Trim the courgettes and cut them into similar-sized pieces. Toss the courgettes with salt and put them in another colander to drain.

While the salted aubergines and courgettes drain, prepare the other vegetables, as well as the tomato sauce if you don't already have it on hand.

Heat the olive oil in your largest non-stick sauté pan — at least 30 cm (12 inches). Add the garlic and stir it for 1 minute. Add the chopped onion and a dash of salt and cook over medium heat, stirring frequently, until the onion is soft and just beginning to colour.

Briefly rinse the aubergines and courgettes in cold water, and press them gently against their colanders to squeeze out excess moisture. Add the aubergines and courgettes to the onions with a scant teaspoon of salt and sauté, stirring frequently, for 6–7 minutes. Stir in the peppers and the tomato sauce, cover, reduce the heat, and simmer for about 20 minutes.

Uncover the pan. If the Ratatouille looks too much like a soup, simmer it uncovered for a while, stirring often, until it is a thick stew. Add the chopped herbs, a little sprinkle of balsamic vinegar, more salt if needed, and a generous grind of black pepper. Finally, stir in the cut-up tomatoes and simmer for another 2 minutes or so, just to heat them through.

Served cold, this is a great salad. I also like Ratatouille hot over steamed rice, or with pasta. And it's wonderful wrapped in a crêpe with a bit of cheese.

Serves 12–15.

PANZANELLA

To make this, you need ripe, juicy tomatoes and really good bread
– a coarse, chewy, country loaf, about a day old.

Make this salad an hour or two before you're going to eat it.

1 large cucumber	1½ teaspoons capers
1 green pepper	1 teaspoon salt, more to taste
1 red pepper	black pepper to taste
½ small red onion	3 tablespoons fruity green
3 large red tomatoes	olive oil
1 clove garlic, minced	3 tablespoons balsamic
8–9 tablespoons flat-leaf	vinegar
parsley	225 g (8 oz) coarse country
5 tablespoons sliced fresh	bread, a day old
basil leaves	

Peel the cucumber, trim off the ends, cut it in half lengthwise,
scrape out the seeds, and slice the halves. Trim, core, and quarter
the peppers, and slice the quarters crosswise very thinly. Slice the
red onion lengthwise as thinly as you can.

Rinse the tomatoes and trim out their cores. Cut them into 2.5 cm
(1 inch) pieces, working on a plate so as not to lose a single drop
of their juice. This is important to the texture of the salad.

In a large bowl, combine the cucumber, peppers, onion, tomatoes
with all their juice, minced garlic, parsley leaves, sliced basil, and
capers. Sprinkle on about a teaspoon of salt, grind on some pepper,
add the oil and vinegar, and mix everything together gently. It will
look rather soupy at this point, and will become more so with the
salt and vinegar.

Slice the bread and cut the slices into 2.5 cm (1 inch) pieces, as
you would for a bread pudding or stuffing. You should have enough
bread chunks to fill a 1.2 litre (2 pint) measure. Add these to the
salad, and immediately start lifting and turning the salad ingredients
to mix in the bread thoroughly. The bread will start soaking up the
dressing and juices at once.

Taste, and correct the seasoning with more salt or pepper if needed. The salad should be moist throughout but not soggy. If it seems too dry, add a drop of oil, vinegar, or fresh tomato pulp. If it seems too wet, add a little more bread. The salad improves with a couple of hours' waiting, but by the next day it's too soggy.

Variations: Some nice things to add for a change are very thin slices of fennel bulb, leftover grilled aubergine, cut into pieces, or thinly sliced celery or radishes. Try replacing the capers with a few cured olives, pitted and chopped. Add hearts of romaine, sliced in wide ribbons, or torn radicchio.

Serves 6–8.

Chocolate-dipped Biscotti (see page 469)

MEZZE FOR TEN

❧

Dolmades
(Stuffed Vine Leaves)

Roasted Aubergine Dip

Charred Tomatoes with Garlic and Olives

Hummous

pitta bread

Mixed Greek Salad

Yogurt and Potatoes with Mint

figs, apricots, and almonds

Honey Pie

Mezze are the tasty little dishes that start any Middle Eastern meal. They are usually thought of as appetizers, but if you put a few of them together with the right combination of flavours and textures, they become a meal, and, what's more, a meal you will want to linger over, sitting on a shaded terrace and sipping a chilled wine or ice-cold ouzo.

The Roasted Aubergine Dip, Charred Tomatoes with Garlic and Olives, and Hummous are all ideal foods to be scooped up with warm pitta bread. You may want one or two other breads with the meal as well – a flatbread, and a big country loaf.

Dolmades – stuffed vine leaves – are also a finger food. The plate is really for the big, colourful salad and the cool yogurt and potato dish. These two go very well side by side: the salad is crunchy and pungent with marinated olives and salty cheese, the yogurt dish slightly creamy and mild.

Most of this food is best at room temperature, and it is served all at once, making it perfect for a long lunch, a late supper, or any other less structured occasion.

Lay a large table: cover it with a bright cloth and arrange all the food in the middle of it, on your most beautiful platters. Add a basket of breads, and a carafe of green olive oil.

Have the ice bucket nearby, with a good white Riesling or Chardonnay, or perhaps a dry rosé from Provence. Ouzo is great, too, although you probably won't want to drink it all evening. I like it frozen, served in very small glasses. It tastes particularly delicious with the stuffed vine leaves, the olives, and the feta cheese. For a refreshing non-alcoholic drink, try iced peppermint tea, sweetened with honey.

You almost have to have figs to end this meal. If fresh figs are not in season, serve dried figs, dried apricots, and almonds, along with a Honey Pie and sweet, hot tea or Turkish coffee.

Variations: This menu could be expanded to include grilled fish, chicken, or lamb, or a marinated seafood salad. The number of *mezze* could also be increased for a more elaborate table. Traditional Greek pastries such as *spanakopita* or *tiropita* would be good, as would steamed artichokes with oil and lemon, lentil salad, and tabbouleh.

DOLMADES (STUFFED VINE LEAVES)

50–60 large whole preserved vine leaves

2 tablespoons + 2 teaspoons olive oil

1 medium onion, chopped

1 clove garlic, minced

225 g (8 oz) long-grain white rice

3–4 tablespoons chopped fresh mint leaves

50 g (2 oz) chopped fresh dill

125 g (4 oz) raisins

125 g (4 oz) pine-nuts

3 tablespoons chopped Kalamata olives

½ teaspoon salt, more to taste
black pepper to taste
6–8 whole cloves garlic
500 ml (16 fl oz) vegetable
  stock (see page 459)

400 ml (14 fl oz) water
4–6 tablespoons freshly
  squeezed lemon juice

Remove the vine leaves from the jar or packet carefully, so as not to tear them. Lay them flat in a large bowl and cover them with boiling water. After a minute or two, drain them, then cover them with cold water, let them soak for about 5 minutes, and drain again.

Heat a tablespoon of the olive oil in a non-stick sauté pan and cook the chopped onion and garlic in it for a few minutes, stirring often, until the onion is soft. Put the rice in a bowl, cover it with boiling water, let it soak for 5 minutes, then drain.

In a large mixing bowl, combine the rice, onion and garlic, mint, dill, raisins, pine-nuts, olives, ½ teaspoon of salt, and some black pepper. Mix everything together thoroughly.

To wrap the vine leaves, take one at a time and lay it flat on a board, vein side up. Trim off the stem with a sharp knife. Place a heaped tablespoon of the filling almost in the centre of the leaf, near the stem end. Fold the bottom of the leaf up over the filling, then fold in the sides, and finish by rolling it up. The leaves should be wrapped neatly, but not very tightly, as the rice will expand when they cook.

When all the filling is used up, line the bottom of a large enamelled soup pan or casserole with the remaining leaves. Lay the stuffed vine leaves in the pot, close together and seam side down. Make 2 layers if you need to, fitting the Dolmades together compactly but without crowding. Slice the whole garlic cloves into 2 or 3 pieces each, and tuck them in among the Dolmades. Pour the vegetable stock and water over the Dolmades, then drizzle the remaining olive oil over them, as well as 2 teaspoons of the lemon juice. Place a flat, heavy plate directly on top of the Dolmades to hold them in place as they cook.

Bring the liquid to a boil, then lower the heat to a simmer, cover the pot tightly, and leave it simmering for about an hour. Almost all the liquid should be absorbed, and the Dolmades plumped up, with the vine leaves stretched tightly around the filling. Allow them to cool, covered, in the pot, then pour the remaining lemon juice over them before serving.

Makes about 50–60 stuffed vine leaves.

ROASTED AUBERGINE DIP

5–6 medium aubergines
salt to taste
3 medium onions
1½ tablespoons olive oil
1½ tablespoons butter

120 ml (4 fl oz) red wine
pepper to taste
chopped fresh oregano to taste
juice of 1 large lemon

Cut the aubergines in half lengthwise, make several incisions in the cut side with a sharp knife, and sprinkle with salt. Lay them cut side down on lightly oiled baking sheets.

Roast the aubergines in a 200°C/400°F/Gas 6 oven for 50–60 minutes, until they are completely soft. Allow them to cool, then scoop out the flesh, scraping out any pockets of dark seeds and discarding them. Chop the pale flesh coarsely.

Chop the onions and cook them slowly in the olive oil and butter until they are caramelized to a deep golden brown. Deglaze the pan with the red wine, let it simmer away, stirring often, and then season to taste with salt, pepper, and a touch of oregano.

Stir the soft brown onions into the chopped aubergines. Taste. Stir in lemon juice, a bit at a time, and keep tasting; correct with a little salt if necessary.

Serve this warm or at room temperature, with plain crackers or pitta bread.

This makes enough for an ample first course for 6–8 people.

CHARRED TOMATOES WITH GARLIC AND OLIVES

These slow-roasted tomatoes, allowed to char twice, have a terrific intensity of flavour. A bowl of these tomatoes, a bowl of Hummous, and some pitta bread make a great appetizer.

1.8 kg (4 lb) ripe red tomatoes   **1 teaspoon salt**
5 cloves garlic   **6–8 Kalamata olives**
2 tablespoons olive oil

Put the tomatoes on a baking sheet and put them directly under a hot grill. Watch them carefully – as they blister and the skins turn black, turn them over. When the skins are pretty well charred, remove the tomatoes from the grill, peel off the skins (they will almost fall off), and trim out their stem ends.

Cut the tomatoes into rather large pieces and put them back on the baking sheet. Peel the garlic cloves, cut them in half if they're very large, and scatter them among the tomatoes. Drizzle the tomatoes with 1 tablespoon of olive oil, and sprinkle them with salt. Preheat the oven to 200°C/400°F/Gas 6, and put the tomatoes in the middle. Check them every 30 minutes, and as they start to show little charred spots again, stir them up, mixing the blackened spots in.

In about 1½–2 hours, you should have a thickened mass of tomatoes, flecked with dark bits. Remove this from the oven, give it another stir, taste, and add salt only if needed.

Spoon the tomatoes into a shallow serving bowl, smooth the top, and drizzle the remaining tablespoon of olive oil on top. Remove the stones from the olives and chop the olives coarsely. Sprinkle the chopped olives over the tomatoes. Serve with wedges of pitta bread.

Makes about 600 ml (1 pint).

HUMMOUS

350 g (12 oz) dried chickpeas   **½ cup tahini (sesame paste)**
(or sprouted chickpeas if   **6–9 tablespoons freshly**
you can get them)   **squeezed lemon juice**
pinch of bicarbonate of soda   **4–5 cloves garlic, minced**
1–2 teaspoons salt

optional garnish: 1–2 teaspoons olive oil

Soak the dried chickpeas overnight in a large bowl of cool water with a pinch of bicarbonate of soda. Or put them in a pot with several quarts of water and a pinch of bicarbonate of soda, bring the water to a boil, let it boil for 5 minutes, then turn off the heat, cover the pot, and let the beans soak for an hour. Drain the soaked chickpeas and throw away the water.

If you are using sprouted chickpeas, you do not need to soak them at all.

Put the chickpeas in a pot with enough lightly salted water to cover them by about 1 cm (½ inch), and boil them gently, covered, until they are very soft. Add water from time to time to keep the chickpeas covered. For Hummous, you want your chickpeas very well cooked, and it may take 2 hours, or even longer. Drain the chickpeas, reserving the cooking water this time, and allow them to cool a little. After such long cooking, the water will have turned into a thick, almost gelatinous liquid. Set this aside.

Put the chickpeas into the container of a food processor with the tahini, about 5 tablespoons of lemon juice, and the minced garlic. Process in pulses of several seconds, scraping down the container with a spatula as needed, until the chickpeas are uniformly ground into a thick paste.

Add as much of the reserved cooking liquid as needed, a little at a time and processing with each addition, until the right texture is achieved. The Hummous should be thick enough to hold a soft shape, but soft enough to scoop up with a piece of pitta bread.

Taste, and add more salt and lemon juice as needed. The amount of lemon juice will depend on the acidity of your lemons.

Spoon the Hummous into a shallow bowl, smooth the top, and drizzle very lightly with olive oil if desired. Serve with wedges of pitta bread.

Makes about 750 ml (1¼ pints).

MIXED GREEK SALAD

1 large cucumber
1 large fennel bulb
1 large red pepper
1 large green pepper
½ medium red onion
2 × 175 g (6 oz) jars marinated
  artichoke hearts, well
  drained
15–20 Kalamata olives
15–20 cured green olives
2 tablespoons fruity green
  olive oil, more to taste

2 tablespoons wine vinegar
handful of dill sprigs
handful of fresh mint leaves
1–2 teaspoons chopped fresh
  oregano
freshly ground black pepper
350 g (12 oz) feta cheese,
  rinsed and patted dry
salt if needed
2 medium tomatoes, cut in
  thin wedges

Peel the cucumber, cut it in half lengthwise, and scrape out the seeds. Slice the cucumber thickly. Trim and quarter the fennel bulb and slice thinly. Trim and core the peppers, quarter lengthwise, and slice thickly. Slice the red onion.

Combine the cucumber, fennel, peppers, onion, artichoke hearts, and olives in a large bowl, together with the olive oil and vinegar. Add the dill sprigs and mint leaves – coarsely chopped or left whole, as you prefer – and the chopped oregano. Grind in some black pepper. Break the feta cheese into small chunks and add about two-thirds of it to the bowl. Toss all these things together gently until they are well combined.

Taste, and add some salt only if it is needed; this will depend on the saltiness of your feta cheese. Finally, at the last moment, add the tomato wedges and mix them in.

Pile the salad on to a large platter, and scatter the remaining feta cheese over the top. Garnish the platter with large mint sprigs if you wish.

Even though this salad has no lettuce, and looks as if it would hold up well, it should not be made too far in advance. If you need to work ahead, prepare all the vegetables and herbs, but do not mix them with the wine vinegar or salt until the last moment, as this will cause the cucumbers to weep and the salad will become watery.

Serves 8 – 10.

YOGURT AND POTATOES WITH MINT

1.4 kg (3 lb) red-skinned
  potatoes
1 teaspoon salt, more to taste
5 spring onions, thinly sliced
5 tablespoons sliced fresh
  mint leaves

2 tablespoons olive oil
freshly ground black pepper
1.2 litres (2 pints) plain
  yogurt, whole or low-fat
pinch of cayenne

Put the potatoes in a big pot with enough salted water to cover them by a couple of inches. Bring the water to a boil and cook the potatoes until they are completely tender; the time will vary with the size of the potatoes. Drain them and let them cool for about 30 minutes, until you can easily handle them.

Peel the skins off the potatoes; they should come off very easily, and don't worry about any little bits that cling. Pick up the still-warm potatoes two at a time, hold them over a large bowl, and crush them with your hands into rough chunks. (Your children will love this part.)

Sprinkle some salt over the potatoes, then add the spring onions and mint leaves. Drizzle the olive oil over the potatoes, grind on some black pepper, and mix them up well. Add about half the yogurt and a pinch of cayenne and stir. Now add more yogurt, a few tablespoons at a time, until the mixture has the consistency of a thick sauce or pudding. Taste, and correct the seasoning with more salt and pepper if needed.

Serves 8 – 10.

HONEY PIE

This is something like a cheesecake, though much lighter, and delightfully flavoured with honey.

Note: If you don't have Yogurt Cheese on hand, then, several hours before starting, put 500 ml (16 fl oz) of yogurt into a colander lined with 3 layers of cheesecloth, and let it drain for at least 3–4 hours. You should have about 300 ml (10 fl oz) of thickened yogurt.

for the pastry
185 g (6½ oz) plain flour
3 tablespoons sugar
½ teaspoon salt
½ teaspoon baking powder
125 g (4 oz) butter, chilled
1 egg
½ teaspoon vanilla extract

for the filling
4 eggs
225 g (8 oz) cream cheese
300 ml (10 fl oz) Yogurt Cheese (see page 85), or 500 ml (16 fl oz) yogurt drained for 3–4 hours
50 g (2 oz) honey
50 g (2 oz) sugar
30 g (1¼ oz) flour
grated zest of 1 orange

To make the pastry: put the flour, sugar, salt, and baking powder in the container of a food processor and process for a few seconds to combine. Cut in the butter and process until the mixture resembles coarse meal. Beat together the egg and the vanilla, and add it to the flour mixture. Process again, just until the dough holds together in one piece.

Lightly butter a 25 cm (10 inch) springform tin. Roll out two-thirds of the pastry to a 25 cm (10 inch) circle. Trim it to the exact size and fit it into the bottom of the cake tin. Roll the remainder of the pastry out into long strips about 4 cm (1½ inches) wide, and form the sides of the crust with them, pressing them together inside the tin, and sealing up the seam between the side and the bottom. Make sure the side of the crust is at least 4 cm (1½ inches) high, of even thickness, and well joined to the bottom part, or your filling could leak when you pour it in. Chill the dough while you prepare the filling.

To make the filling in a food processor: beat the eggs, then put them in the container of a food processor with the cream cheese, the drained yogurt, honey, and sugar. Process this mixture until it is completely smooth. Add the flour and the grated orange zest and process again, scraping down as necessary, until smooth.

To make the filling by hand: allow the cream cheese to soften at room temperature, and warm the honey. Beat the eggs. Cream together the cheese, drained yogurt, honey, and sugar until smooth. Beat in the eggs, flour, and orange zest.

Pour the filling into the prepared crust. It should fill this just short of the top. Bake the pie in a preheated 180°C/350°F/Gas 4 oven for 40 minutes, or until a sharp knife inserted near the middle comes out clean.

Place the tin on a rack to cool, and after a few minutes, remove the sides. Allow the pie to cool completely, then chill it.

Serves 10−12.

AUTUMN AND WINTER

PUMPKIN SOUP AND CORNBREAD

❧

Wild Rice Salad with Sesame Oil Dressing

Pumpkin, Potato, and Leek Soup

Honey-sweetened Buttermilk Cornbread

Warm Chunky Applesauce with cream

In the autumn and winter we have a lot of soup-based meals. They're satisfying, nutritious, and unfussy, which counts for a lot in our house. Soup is a very comforting food in wintertime, and when a fresh hot bread is added you don't need much more.

A salad with the earthy flavour of wild rice and a hint of soy sauce in the dressing complements the rich, golden soup and slightly sweet cornbread. Chunky Applesauce, served warm, is like having the best part of an apple pie – personally, I don't miss the crust. You can add more or less cream, for a richer or lighter dessert. I make the applesauce in big batches when the apple orchards in our area are being harvested and apples are at their plentiful best. I put a large bowlful in the refrigerator and it's gone in a few days.

This is all the kind of family food I like to make in larger quantities. When the kids bring friends home from school, or someone drops by, a generous pot of soup on the stove makes everything easy. And I like to have leftovers. Soup is always welcome, the rice salad makes a fine lunch, and even the cornbread is delicious the next morning, sliced and toasted for breakfast.

WILD RICE SALAD

750 ml (1¼ pints) water
1 teaspoon salt
175 g (6 oz) uncooked wild
  rice
125 g (4 oz) raisins
250 ml (8 fl oz) dry red wine
2 tablespoons sugar
2–3 small heads radicchio

225 g (8 oz) shredded rocket
225 g (8 oz) thinly sliced
  Belgian endive
5 or 6 fresh basil leaves, cut in
  thin slivers
125 g (4 oz) pine-nuts
Sesame Oil Dressing to taste
  (recipe follows)

Bring the water to a boil in a medium saucepan, add the salt and the wild rice, lower the heat to a simmer, and cover the saucepan. Simmer the rice, covered, for 45 minutes, then turn off the heat and let it stand for 10 more minutes. Check for texture – the rice should be tender-firm. Drain away any excess water and allow the rice to cool.

Combine the raisins, red wine, and sugar in a small stainless steel or enamelled saucepan and simmer for about 10 minutes, then leave to cool gradually. Drain off the excess wine syrup.

Wash the radicchio, reserve 8–10 of the largest nice leaves, and shred the rest. Combine the shredded radicchio with the other greens.

Toast the pine-nuts by stirring them in a dry pan over medium heat for 5–6 minutes, or until they just begin to colour and give off a fragrance.

Toss together the cooled rice, the poached raisins, all the greens, and the toasted pine-nuts. Shortly before serving, season to taste with Sesame Oil Dressing, then mound the salad in the reserved radicchio leaves to serve.

Serves 8–10.

SESAME OIL DRESSING

3 tablespoons peanut oil
1 tablespoon dark sesame oil
1½ tablespoons balsamic
  vinegar, or sweet rice
  vinegar

1 teaspoon soy sauce
freshly ground black pepper
  to taste

optional: chopped fresh chives

Combine all the ingredients in a bowl and whisk together briskly, or process in a blender for a few seconds. If using a blender, add the chopped chives after processing, and leave them out if you're not going to use the dressing the same day; they should be added at the last minute.

Makes 90 ml (3 fl oz) of dressing.

PUMPKIN, POTATO, AND LEEK SOUP

In general, smaller, denser-fleshed varieties of pumpkin have better flavour than the very large ones that are used for jack-o'-lanterns. If you cannot get a good, fresh pumpkin, you can use canned pumpkin, or substitute one of the nice winter squashes, such as butternut, Kabocha, or acorn.

900 g (2 lb) potatoes
500 ml (16 fl oz) water
1 teaspoon salt, more to
  taste
120 ml (4 fl oz) fruity white
  wine

700 g (1½ lb) peeled, cubed
  pumpkin, or 750 ml
  (1¼ pints) cooked
  pumpkin purée
3 large leeks, white part only
1½ tablespoons butter

500 ml (16 fl oz) vegetable   white pepper to taste
   stock (see page 459)   ¼-½ teaspoon grated nutmeg
2 tablespoons lemon juice   pinch of ground cinnamon
2 tablespoons sugar, more or less 120 ml (4 fl oz) cream

garnish: coarsely chopped fresh parsley, coriander, or chives

Peel and dice the potatoes and put them in a large soup pot with the water, salt, and wine. If you are using fresh, cubed pumpkin, add it now. If you are using purée, wait. Simmer until the vegetables are tender.

Meanwhile, trim, clean, and slice the leeks, and cook them in the butter over a medium flame, stirring often, until they are soft and beginning to colour. Add the leeks to the potato mixture, and continue simmering until the vegetables are all very soft – about 45 minutes total cooking time.

Add the vegetable stock, and the pumpkin purée if that's what you're using, and purée the mixture in batches in a blender or food processor until perfectly smooth. Return the purée to the soup pot and season to taste with the lemon juice, sugar, additional salt, and white pepper. How much sugar you need will depend on the variety of pumpkin or squash used – you may need none. When the sweet-sour balance is correct, add a touch of nutmeg and cinnamon, and stir in the cream. Heat thoroughly and serve, sprinkled with some chopped parsley, coriander, or chives.

Serves 8–10.

HONEY-SWEETENED BUTTERMILK CORNBREAD

150 g (5 oz) flour   ¾ teaspoon salt
250 g (9 oz) cornmeal   3 large eggs
½ teaspoon bicarbonate of   350 ml (12 fl oz) buttermilk
   soda   3 tablespoons honey
¾ teaspoon baking powder   2 tablespoons melted butter

Sift together the flour, cornmeal, soda, baking powder, and salt. Whisk together the eggs, buttermilk, honey, and melted butter.

Combine the wet and the dry mixtures, stirring gently just until the lumps are gone.

Pour the batter into a buttered 30 × 38 cm (12 × 15 inch) baking dish and bake in a preheated 180°C/350° F/Gas 4 oven for 30–35 minutes, or until a straw inserted in the centre of the cornbread comes out clean. Cut into squares and serve hot or warm.

Serves 8.

APPLESAUCE

The most important part is getting good apples. I use a mix of red, yellow, and green apples, whichever flavourful and juicy varieties are in season. I try always to include at least a few of the good baking apples, like Golden Delicious, which fall apart into a lovely sauce around chunks of the firmer varieties.

I like this applesauce warm, with a bit of cream, for dessert; cold, with a scoop of cottage cheese, for a light lunch.

2.2 kg (5 lb) fresh apples   **1 teaspoon grated nutmeg**
750 ml (1¼ pints) spring water   **2–4 tablespoons brown sugar**
2 teaspoons ground cinnamon

Wash the apples, quarter them, and core them, but do not peel. Put them in a large non-reactive pan with the spring water and the spices. Bring the water to a boil, then lower the heat and simmer, stirring often with a long-handled wooden spoon, for about 1½ hours, or until the apples have softened to the consistency you like. Sweeten to your taste with a little brown sugar – how much you use will depend on the varieties of apples.

If apple skins don't bother you, you're done. If you want a more refined applesauce, without the skins, take two or three batches and push it through an old-fashioned colander or vegetable mill with the big holes. Discard the skins.

This will make about 1.2 litres (2 pints) of a thick, coarse-textured applesauce with intense flavour.

Chunky Applesauce

If you want a chunkier applesauce, you cannot press it through a colander to remove the skins. Here is an alternative method that still gets the maximum flavour from the fruit.

Wash, quarter, core, and peel the apples. In a covered saucepan, simmer the peels and cores in the spring water for about 30 minutes, then strain. Discard the peels and cores, and add the peeled apples to the water. Proceed as above in the Applesauce recipe and stop when you have achieved the texture you like.

Makes about 1.2 litres (2 pints).

Variations: Applesauce can be varied endlessly. Honey can replace the sugar, or sweetener can be omitted entirely. For an even more intense apple flavour, use cider instead of spring water. To give a blander variety of apple some kick, add a tablespoon or two of cider vinegar. Another time, try a touch of cloves. For a fancy applesauce, throw a handful of raisins in towards the end of the cooking time.

AUTUMN LUNCH ON THE TERRACE

*Salad of Radicchio, Fuji Apples,
and Pistachio Nuts*

Cavatappi with Potatoes and Herbs

ripe pears, red grapes

Gorgonzola cheese

Biscotti

When the weather is warm, this is a beautiful lunch to have on the terrace on a sunny weekend. It's just as good for a dinner by the fireplace when evenings start darkening quickly and the air turns cold. The hearty, filling quality of the pasta dish, and the flavour of a new crop of apples mixed with the radicchio, are just what I want in the autumn.

For such a satisfying meal, it doesn't take an enormous effort, and that's the beauty of so many pasta and salad meals. The pasta sauce takes a little time but could be done ahead if you like, the salad is a matter of minutes, and the fruit, cheese, and biscotti can be bought. Because it's uncomplicated, and children will eat most of it (all you can really hope for, in my experience), it's a comfortable family meal as well as a lovely meal to share with company.

SALAD OF RADICCHIO, FUJI APPLES, AND
PISTACHIO NUTS

Yes, of course you can use another kind of apple. I'm just crazy about Fujis, with their dense texture and explosive tart-sweet flavour. But any variety that is crisp and has a tart edge will do well, complementing the taste and the colour of the radicchio.

1 large head radicchio, or 2 small (450 g/1 lb)	**2–3 tablespoons fruity green olive oil**
1 large or 2 medium Fuji apples (300–350 g/ 10–12 oz)	**aged wine vinegar**
	salt
3 stalks celery	**75 g (3 oz) lightly toasted shelled pistachio nuts**
¼ red onion	

optional: 25–50 g (1–2 oz) coarsely grated Gruyère or provolone cheese

Wash the radicchio, tear the leaves into bite-sized pieces, and spin them dry in a salad spinner. Quarter, core, and thinly slice the apple. Wash, trim, and thinly slice the celery. Thinly slice the red onion.

Combine the radicchio, apple, celery, onion, and optional cheese in a large salad bowl. Drizzle on a little olive oil and toss. Everything should glisten, but oil should not be dripping off. Sprinkle on a modest amount of vinegar and a little salt and toss again. Taste, and adjust the seasoning if needed.

Mound the salad on plates and sprinkle some pistachio nuts on top of each serving.

Serves 4–6.

CAVATAPPI WITH POTATOES AND HERBS

This is comfort food at its greatest, tasty, hearty, and absolutely good for you. Cavatappi are short spiral tubes, but any of the sturdy, interesting pasta shapes could be used for this – tubetti, rigatoni, etc.

1½ tablespoons olive oil
1 bay leaf
½ teaspoon crumbled dried
   sage leaves
pinch of dried thyme
2 medium carrots, finely
   chopped
1 thin inside stalk celery,
   finely chopped
1 medium onion, peeled and
   chopped
salt to taste
½ head garlic, peeled and
   thinly sliced
450 g (1 lb) medium potatoes,
   peeled and cut in 1 cm
   (½ inch) dice

500 ml (16 fl oz) vegetable
   stock (see page 459)
5 tablespoons chopped
   flat-leaf parsley
175 ml (6 fl oz) dry white wine
5–6 medium tomatoes, peeled
   and chopped, with their
   juice
freshly ground black pepper
450 g (1 lb) cavatappi, tubetti,
   or other sturdy pasta
Parmesan or Romano cheese,
   grated

Heat the olive oil in a large non-stick sauté pan and add the bay leaf, sage, thyme, chopped carrots, chopped celery, chopped onion, and a generous sprinkle of salt. Cook over medium heat, stirring frequently, until the vegetables just begin to colour. Add the garlic and stir for another 2 minutes.

Add the diced potatoes, vegetable stock and parsley to the vegetables in the pan, lower the heat to a simmer, and cook until the potatoes are tender, about 15 minutes.

Add the white wine and the chopped tomatoes, season with additional salt and some freshly ground black pepper, and continue simmering until the tomatoes are falling apart and the liquid is somewhat reduced.

Meanwhile, bring a very large pot of water to a boil and salt it generously. Cook the pasta in it until it is *al dente*, tender-firm. Drain the pasta and stir it into the potato sauce. Serve at once in warmed shallow pasta bowls, and pass the cheese separately.

Serves 6.

Biscotti (see page 468)

❦

Butternut Squash and Pear Soup

Chard and Fennel Pie

Brownies with strawberries and whipped cream

Think about an outdoor party at a football game or walking in autumn woods.

Fill your biggest and best thermos with steaming hot soup. This one is a velvety, sweet-savoury concoction perfumed with cinnamon. The soup makes a wonderful contrast to the robust Chard and Fennel Pie, redolent of garlic, greens, and salty feta cheese. It's a sturdy pie, made with bread dough rather than a crumbly shortcrust, so it travels very well, making it ideal for car trips or school lunches as well as for picnics.

Brownies and juicy strawberries, with some whipped cream for dipping, are a spectacular finish. However, any sweet-tart fruit could take their place – oranges or tangerines, for example, would be wonderful.

Of course, just because this food can be entirely prepared ahead of time and packed in a hamper doesn't mean it shouldn't be eaten at home, by the fireplace. The pie is delicious hot.

BUTTERNUT SQUASH AND PEAR SOUP

I worked out this recipe for my talk about 'spa cuisine' at a popular local spa because I wanted to give people something that was very low in fat but tasted luxuriously delicious. The pears add a natural sweetness and silky texture. For a really stripped-down version, you could substitute low-fat milk or yogurt for the single cream.

450 g (1 lb) butternut or acorn squash	¾ teaspoon salt
1 large yam (about 300 g/ 10 oz)	2 tablespoons butter
	2 medium onions, sliced
500 ml (16 fl oz) vegetable stock (see page 459)	3 large ripe smooth-textured pears
350 ml (12 fl oz) water	90 ml (3 fl oz) dry white wine
1 stick cinnamon	60 ml (2 fl oz) single cream
	white pepper to taste

optional garnish: chopped chives, or sprigs of coriander

Peel, seed, and dice the squash. Peel and dice the yam. Put them both in a pot with the vegetable stock, water, cinnamon stick, and salt, and simmer until tender, about 40 minutes. Discard the cinnamon stick.

Melt the butter and gently cook the onions in it, stirring occasionally, until they begin to caramelize. Peel, core, and thinly slice the pears, and add them to the onions. Continue cooking for about 5 minutes, stirring often. Add the wine, cover, and simmer for 10 minutes.

Add the pear mixture to the soup and purée everything in a blender in batches. Add the cream and some white pepper, and a bit more salt only if needed. Heat the soup again just to a simmer, but do not boil. Serve plain or garnished with chopped chives or sprigs of coriander.

Serves 6–8.

CHARD AND FENNEL PIE

In our house we call this Victory Pie, because the first time I made it we took it to an exciting election night party. It's a big, generous pie, delicious and undoubtedly good for you. And even though it's dark green, for some reason that I can't explain my kids usually eat it.

Note: You will need a 32 or 36 cm (13 or 14 inch) round gratin dish to make this pie. If you only have 23 or 25 cm (9 or 10 inch) pie dishes, divide both dough and filling in half, and make two pies.

for the dough
1½ teaspoon dried yeast
1 teaspoon sugar
60 ml (2 fl oz) warm water
425 g (15 oz) white flour
1 teaspoon salt
1 egg
150 ml (5 fl oz) low-fat milk
1 tablespoon olive oil

for the filling
1.4 kg (3 lb) Swiss chard
1½ large onions, chopped
12–15 spring onions, sliced
3 cloves garlic
1 medium fennel bulb
2 tablespoons olive oil
1 tablespoon cider vinegar
2 tablespoons chopped fennel greens
6 tablespoons chopped flat-leaf parsley
pinch of salt
freshly ground black pepper to taste
4 eggs
120 ml (4 fl oz) milk
300 g (10 oz) feta cheese, crumbled
3 tablespoons raw white rice

First make the dough: dissolve the yeast and sugar in the warm water and leave it a few minutes, until it starts to bubble and foam. Meanwhile, put all but 30 g (1¼ oz) of the flour into a large bowl and stir in the salt. Beat together the egg, milk, and olive oil, stir in the yeast mixture, and then mix the liquid into the flour. Stir it with a big wooden spoon until it forms a dough.

When the stirring gets tough, spread the remaining flour on an ample board and turn the dough out on it. Knead it gently, turning often at first to keep it coated with flour, until it is smooth and becoming elastic. Form the dough into a ball and put it into a lightly oiled bowl. Cover the bowl with a towel and set it aside to rise in a warm, sheltered place for 45 minutes to an hour; it should double in size.

To make the filling: first thoroughly clean the chard, cut off and discard the thick parts of the stems, and chop it coarsely. Peel and chop the onions, and trim and slice the green onions. Mince the garlic cloves, and trim and chop the white part of the fennel bulb.

Heat the olive oil in a large, non-stick sauté pan and cook the onions, spring onions, and garlic in it over a medium flame for a few minutes, then add the chopped fennel and keep cooking until the vegetables are soft and beginning to colour.

Add the chard by handfuls, tossing it with the hot vegetables to wilt it down, until it's all in the pan. Add the cider vinegar, the fennel greens and parsley, a dash of salt, and some pepper, and keep cooking until the chard is much reduced and all the excess liquid is gone.

Remove the pan from the heat and allow the mixture to cool slightly. Separate one of the eggs, reserving the yolk in a small bowl, then add the other 3 eggs to the remaining white and beat them with the milk. Stir the egg mixture into the cooled vegetables along with the crumbled feta cheese and the uncooked rice.

Mix everything together well, taste it, and adjust the salt and pepper if needed.

To assemble and bake: punch down the risen dough and divide it into two parts, one a bit larger. On a lightly floured board, roll the larger part out into a circle with a diameter 5 cm (2 inches) bigger than your gratin dish or casserole. Yeast dough is harder to roll out than pastry, because it keeps springing back together. I find it helps to lift it up and stretch it gently over the backs of my hands, just like pizza dough (it's the same thing, really), then lay it down and roll again, adjusting the shape.

Oil a 32 or 36 cm (13 or 14 inch) round gratin dish lightly and lay the circle of dough into it, bringing it evenly up the sides and letting the extra inch hang over the edges. Spread the prepared filling inside the dough.

Roll out the smaller piece of dough into a circle just large enough to cover the dish and lay it over the filling. Fold the overhanging edge of bottom crust over the edge of the top crust and pinch them together, making a design if you like.

Beat the reserved egg yolk lightly with a tablespoon of water and brush the glaze over the pie. Poke a few holes in the top crust with a fork and bake the pie at 180°C/350°F/Gas 4 for 45 minutes, or until the crust is golden brown. Cool the pie slightly before cutting it in wedges and serving.

Serves 8—10.

BROWNIES

I have this recipe from my friend and neighbour of many years, Martha Bates Jura, who had it from her mother in Boston. Martha told me that she never could do a thing in the kitchen except this – but she felt this was enough.

125 g (4 oz) unsweetened baking chocolate	450 g (1 lb) sugar
125 g (4 oz) butter	2 teaspoons vanilla extract
3 eggs	150 g (5 oz) flour
½ teaspoon salt	175 g (6 oz) chopped walnuts
	icing sugar for dusting

Melt the chocolate and butter together in a heavy-bottomed saucepan. As soon as it is almost all melted, remove it from the heat and allow it to cool slightly.

Beat the eggs with a pinch of salt until they are foamy. Gradually add the sugar and keep beating until the mixture is thick and pale. Beat in the vanilla and the cooled chocolate mixture, then the flour. Stir in the walnuts.

Butter a 32 × 20 cm (13 × 8 inch) baking tin, and pour the

mixture into it, spreading it evenly. Bake at 180°C/350°F/Gas 4 for 25–30 minutes, or until a toothpick inserted in the centre comes out nearly clean. The brownies should still be moist and slightly sticky when they come out of the oven; they achieve the right texture as they cool.

Allow the brownies to cool to room temperature, cut into squares, and dust with icing sugar.

Makes 24 brownies.

A SPAGHETTI DINNER
FOR AUTUMN

❧

White Bean Salad with Sautéd Radicchio

Spaghetti with Garlic and Oil

Green Apple Sorbet

The classic pairing of beans and pasta has been perfected in a hundred variations of *pasta e fagioli* – usually as a soup or a stew.

In this simple meal, the same elements are brought together in another way. The beans are tossed with sautéd radicchio and a few other delicious things and served as a substantial antipasto salad.

The pasta that follows is one of the plainest and best – each strand of spaghetti touched with garlic, oil, and parsley.

To clear the palate after that marvellous dose of garlic, serve a sorbet made from a new crop of tart green apples.

If you want to dress this dinner up for company, expand the antipasto by adding another little salad of chopped tomatoes and basil and perhaps a Simple Focaccia (see page 218) or one of the other focaccias. Then, with the sorbet, serve some thin butter cookies or biscotti (see page 467).

WHITE BEAN SALAD WITH SAUTÉD RADICCHIO

The flavours of cannellini and radicchio make a very satisfying combination. In this salad, the radicchio is quickly sautéd first, then combined with the beans, and some raw ingredients for a contrast in texture. It's an excellent antipasto salad, or a light main course when served with some good bread. Also sensational on bruschetta.

700 g (1½ lb) cooked
   cannellini beans or
   equivalent in canned
   beans
1 small head radicchio
2 tablespoons olive oil
1 large clove garlic, minced
dash of salt
4 tablespoons aged red wine
   vinegar

1 stalk celery, chopped
¼ medium red onion, sliced
   very thin
25 g (1 oz) slivered cured
   black olives
25 g (1 oz) coarsely chopped
   flat-leaf parsley
freshly ground black pepper

If using canned beans, drain them and rinse them well, and be very careful when mixing because they tend to be mushy. Beans you have cooked yourself need only be well drained.

Wash the radicchio, cut it in half, then slice into 0.5 cm (¼ inch) ribbons. Heat a tablespoon of olive oil in a non-stick pan and throw in half the minced garlic. Stir for a minute, then add the shredded radicchio and a dash of salt. Toss the radicchio in the oil and garlic over a high heat for 4 minutes. Remove from the heat and sprinkle on a tablespoon of the wine vinegar. Toss again, then leave to cool slightly.

In a large, shallow bowl, combine the beans with the radicchio, celery, red onion, olives, parsley, and the remaining minced garlic. Drizzle on the rest of the olive oil and vinegar, grind on some fresh black pepper, and mix together gently but thoroughly. The salad improves if left to marinate for an hour or two. Serve cool or at room temperature.

Serves 6 as an appetizer, or 4 as a light main course.

SPAGHETTI WITH GARLIC AND OIL

This is one of those amazingly simple dishes that Italians do so well. Just a few assertive flavours – nothing shy about it, and nothing extra to confuse the issue. Of course, with this kind of food, the all-important rule of good cooking cannot be overstated: use good ingredients! The garlic must be fresh, the parsley must be Italian flat-leaf parsley, the olive oil must be virgin and fruity, full of real olive flavour. And don't even think about using pre-grated, packaged Parmesan cheese or you could get your culinary licence revoked.

450 g (1 lb) spaghetti
9–10 cloves garlic
3–4 tablespoons fruity green
    olive oil
salt to taste
¼ teaspoon red pepper
    flakes

9–10 tablespoons coarsely
    chopped flat-leaf parsley
lots of freshly grated
    Parmesan cheese

Put the spaghetti into a big pot of boiling salted water to cook until it is just *al dente.*

While it is cooking, peel and chop the garlic. Heat about 2½ tablespoons of the olive oil in a very large non-stick pan and cook the garlic in it over a low flame, stirring constantly, just until it begins to turn golden. Don't let it brown. Add a dash of salt if you like. Remove the pan from the heat, sprinkle in the red pepper flakes, add the chopped parsley, and set aside.

When the spaghetti is just tender-firm, drain it and add it to the garlic and oil mixture in the pan. Return the pan to a medium flame while you toss the spaghetti with the oil, garlic, pepper flakes, and parsley until everything is well mixed.

Add the remaining oil, toss again, and serve immediately on warm plates, with some grated Parmesan cheese spooned over each serving.

This should serve 6, but 4 of us have been known to eat up the whole thing. It's that kind of dish.

GREEN APPLE SORBET

575 g (1¼ lb) crisp green
  apples
2½ tablespoons freshly
  squeezed lemon juice

300 ml (10 fl oz) water
300 g (10 oz) sugar
dash of ground cinnamon

Wash the apples well, quarter and core them, then slice the quarters
thinly crosswise. Toss the apple slices in a bowl with the lemon
juice, until all are evenly coated. Cover the bowl tightly with a lid
or with plastic wrap and freeze the apple slices for several hours,
or overnight.

Combine the water and sugar in a saucepan and stir gently over
medium heat until all the sugar is dissolved. Bring the syrup to a
boil and let it boil for a few minutes. Transfer the syrup to a bowl
and let it cool completely.

Put the frozen apple slices and cooled syrup into the food processor and purée as smoothly as possible. This purée will always
have a little texture from the flecks of green apple peel. Add a little
dash of cinnamon – not too much – and give it another spin.
Put the purée into an ice cream maker and freeze according to
manufacturer's instructions.

This makes about 1.2 litres (2 pints), or 8 servings.

TAMALE PIE

❧

tossed salad with avocado and coriander

Tamale Pie

sliced fruit platter

Hot Chipotle Salsa

Café de Olla Sorbet

In neighbourhoods where good, real tamales are plentiful, the idea of Tamale Pie is sometimes greeted with laughter, but never mind – it's a delicious casserole, and has its own place in the culinary scheme of things.

The basis of my pie is a comforting vegetable stew; familiar winter vegetables are simmered in an Ancho Chilli Salsa that delivers pure, deep chilli flavour yet is mild enough for anyone (you can spike it with a hotter chilli if you want to). Cooked in a big casserole or gratin dish, the vegetable stew is covered with a rich, thick crust that gives the dish its name. A masa for tamales is softened and lightened to a delicate texture with beaten egg whites. When it is served hot from the oven, bubbling underneath and crisp on top, with a really hot salsa and a cool fruit salad, it's hard to beat this for a supper dish.

A tossed salad of your favourite greens, with some avocado and coriander, can be served at the same time as the Tamale Pie, or separately as a first course.

For dessert, you will certainly want something cool and refreshing. I suggest a sorbet of *café de olla*, a perfectly light froth of iced coffee that happily combines the traditional Mexican flavours of *canela*, *piloncillo*, and *café negro* – cinnamon, brown cane sugar, and strong black coffee. If you want something rich, serve it garnished with mounds of whipped cream, and even chocolate curls if you like.

TAMALE PIE

In the Southwest during the mid-sixties, tamale pie was a dish much present in certain magazine recipe sections, and at community functions. I think it was one of those inventions intended to make a convenience food out of a traditional, labour-intensive dish. A friend of mine recalls with amused nostalgia the awful tamale pie of her Arizona childhood – a leaden casserole made mainly from canned foods.

But the idea of a deep-dish pie, full of fresh vegetables in a chilli-laced broth, with a thick top crust made from masa lightened by beaten egg whites, is very appealing to me, so here's my version of the tamale pie.

A note about substitutions: If you cannot get ancho chillies, one full recipe of Red Chilli Salsa (see page 98) can be used in place of the Ancho Chilli Salsa. Green tomatoes can be used in place of tomatillos. And if masa harina is unavailable, it can be replaced in this recipe by maize meal, although the amount may have to be increased a little.

for the vegetable stew
3 medium carrots
450 g (1 lb) new potatoes
1 medium onion
2 leeks
500 ml (16 fl oz) vegetable
   stock (see page 459)
500 ml (16 fl oz) water
½ teaspoon salt
800 g (1¾ lb) Kabocha or
   acorn squash

6–8 spring onions
125 g (4 oz) tomatillos or
   green tomatoes
600 ml (1 pint) Ancho Chilli
   Salsa (see page 97)
350 g (12 oz) courgettes
6 tablespoons coriander
   leaves

optional: hot chilli salsa to taste

for the crust
450 g (1 lb) fresh corn kernels
400 ml (14 fl oz) milk
300 g (10 oz) + 2 tablespoons
   dry masa harina (see page
   38) (or approx. 350 g (12 oz)
   maize meal)

2½ teaspoons baking powder
1¼ teaspoons salt
225 g (8 oz) + 2 tablespoons
   butter, softened
7 egg whites
175 g (6 oz) Cheddar cheese

Scrape the carrots and cut them in thick slices. Wash and trim the potatoes and cut them in quarters, or into 2.5 cm (1 inch) pieces. Cut the onion in 2.5 cm (1 inch) pieces. Trim and thoroughly wash the leeks, cut them in half lengthwise, and slice them thickly. Combine these vegetables in a large sauté pan with the stock, water, and salt, and simmer for about 15 minutes.

Peel the squash and cut it in 2.5 cm (1 inch) cubes. Trim the spring onions and cut them in 2.5 cm (1 inch) lengths. Peel the dry husks off the tomatillos and cut them in quarters. Add these vegetables to the pan, along with the Ancho Chilli Salsa, and simmer, uncovered, for at least another 30 minutes, or until all the vegetables are completely tender and the liquid is reduced by about half. You should have a stew, not a soup.

Trim the courgettes and cut in thick slices. Add to the stew and simmer 5 minutes, then stir in the coriander leaves. Taste and correct the seasoning if necessary. For a spicier dish, you can add some hot salsa at this point, tasting until you achieve the heat you like. Ladle the stew into a large gratin dish, or into two 20 × 27 cm (8 × 11 inch) glass baking dishes.

To prepare the masa: simmer the corn in the milk for about 6 minutes, or until it's quite soft. Sometimes at this point I reserve a few spoonfuls of the corn kernels, and then stir them into the finished masa for more texture. Purée the mixture in a blender.

Sift together the 300 g (10 oz) dry masa, the baking powder, and the salt. If you are using maize meal, start with about 350 g (12 oz), and have a little more on hand to mix in later, if needed.

In a large bowl, whip the softened butter with an electric mixer until it is fluffy. Alternately add scoops of the corn purée and the dry mixture, beating each time, until everything is well combined.

The masa should be light, fluffy, just firm enough to hold a soft shape. If it seems too dry, beat in a little more milk. If it seems too wet, add a touch more dry masa harina (or maize meal). Fold in the whole corn kernels if you have reserved them.

Beat the egg whites until they are stiff. Stir a third of the beaten whites into the masa to lighten it, then gently fold in the remainder.

Coarsely grate the Cheddar cheese and toss it in a bowl with 2 tablespoons of masa harina. Sprinkle the cheese over the vegetables in the gratin dish, then spoon the prepared masa over it evenly.

Bake the pie in a 190°C/375°F/Gas 5 oven for about 40 minutes. The crust should be a bit puffed up and golden brown, and the juices of the vegetable stew bubbling.

Serve at once, with the hot salsa of your choice, and a fruit salad.

Serves 8–10.

Variations: This is a basic pie, and many things could be used for the filling. Black Bean Chili (see page 9) would be good, or leftover chilli combined with roasted or stewed vegetables. This recipe is based mainly on root vegetables, making it a good winter dish, but other combinations of vegetables could be used in other seasons. Add kidney beans or black beans to the stew, or green chillies to the crust; use crumbled white cheese instead of Cheddar, etc., etc . . .

HOT CHIPOTLE SALSA

This is a concentrated and intense version of chipotle flavour: a tiny bit will leave a nice hot afterglow in your mouth. Use it to spike a dish that needs some excitement, to turn up the volume on a milder salsa, or as a dip for tortilla chips.

175 g (6 oz) tomatillos (6–8)
40 g (1½ oz) dried chipotle
**   chillies (about 12 chillies,**
**   depending on size)**
1 large onion, thickly sliced

5 cloves garlic, peeled
1½ teaspoons salt
4 teaspoons cumin seeds
6 tablespoons chopped
**   coriander leaves**

Peel the dry outer husks from the tomatillos, wash them, and put them on a hot iron pan or a grill. Move them around and turn them frequently as they blister, allowing them to char in big black spots all over, about 10–15 minutes. Then drop them into a bowl of cold water, and take off the charred bits of skin wherever it wants to come off easily. Don't worry about the skin that still clings.

At the same time, put the dried chipotles, onion, garlic, and salt in a non-reactive pan with just enough water to cover. Bring the water to a boil, then simmer for about 15 minutes. Turn off the heat and let the chillies soak for about another 30 minutes, or until they are soft and plumped.

Remove the stems from the chillies, tear the pods open under running water, and discard the seeds.

Combine the tomatillos, chillies, onions, and garlic in the container of a blender, together with as much of the liquid as is needed to purée everything into a thick sauce.

Toast the cumin seeds in a small pan, stirring constantly over medium heat for a minute or two, until the seeds release their fragrance. Grind them roughly in a mortar and add them to the sauce in the blender, processing again briefly.

Add the chopped coriander leaves, process only if you want the leaves minced into the sauce, and taste. Add salt if needed.

This makes about 750 ml (1¼ pints) of salsa. It can be kept in the refrigerator, tightly covered, for about a week.

CAFÉ DE OLLA SORBET

Mexican *café de olla* (see page 101), a sweet, strong coffee brewed with cinnamon and brown cane sugar, is usually something we enjoy in cooler weather. Traditionally, it's not brewed during heat waves, and yet it's just the flavour I want after a chilli-laced Mexican lunch or dinner, so here's the frozen dessert version.

600 ml (1 pint) spring water
15 cm (6 inch) stick cinnamon,
   broken up
125 g (4 oz) piloncillo (solid
    brown cane sugar)

125 g (4 oz) granulated sugar
about 350 ml (12 fl oz)
   double-strength coffee

garnishes: whipped cream
  additional cinnamon sticks

Combine the water and broken-up cinnamon sticks in an enamelled or stainless steel pot, bring to a boil, then turn off the heat, add the *piloncillo* and leave it to steep for at least an hour, longer if possible. Add the granulated sugar to the cinnamon water and bring it slowly to a simmer again, stirring occasionally until all the sugar is completely dissolved. Let the syrup boil gently for 5 minutes, then remove it from the heat.

Meanwhile, brew some double-strength coffee, using excellent beans; you want this to be flavourful, not bitter or acidic. As soon as the coffee is ready, pour it into a measuring cup. Add a cup of the coffee to the cinnamon syrup, stir it, and taste it. Add a little more coffee, a spoonful at a time, until the sweetness of the cinnamon syrup is balanced with the coffee flavour to your taste.

Allow the liquid to cool, then chill it in the refrigerator. Freeze it in an ice cream freezer, according to the manufacturer's instructions. Let it harden in your freezer, packed into a container and tightly covered, for a couple of hours before serving. Serve it in chilled, stemmed glasses, garnished with whipped cream and a cinnamon stick.

This makes about 1.2 litres (2 pints) of sorbet.

A WINTER PILAF DINNER

❦

Bulgur Pilaf with Fennel, Sultanas, and Pine-nuts

Oven-roasted Kabocha Squash

Red Cabbage Stewed with Apples and Wine

baby broad beans
ripe pears and blue cheese

This meal is built upon an earthy, satisfying pilaf of quick-cooking bulgur. Around it are arranged several vegetables, each with a distinct flavour and character. The bright red cabbage is tart and fruity; the golden squash is effortless to prepare and tastes rich, dense, and sweet; baby broad beans are a simple finishing touch. It's a comforting dinner for an autumn or winter night. Easy to serve, it all looks nice together, arranged on your biggest dinner plates.

A more elaborate meal can be made of this by adding a nice soup and a superb winter dessert, such as crème caramel or pumpkin cheesecake.

Substitutions: If you can't find Kabocha squash, acorn or butternut squash could be used. If you can get Chinese broccoli (chop suey greens) you could use it instead of the broad beans. The important thing is to keep the flavour and texture simple.

BULGUR PILAF WITH FENNEL, SULTANAS, AND PINE-NUTS

2 medium onions
2 small fennel bulbs
2–3 cloves garlic, minced
2 tablespoons olive oil
salt and pepper to taste
450 g (1 lb) bulgur

900 ml (1½ pints) hot vegetable stock (see page 459)
75 g (3 oz) sultanas
75 g (3 oz) pine-nuts

optional: 2 tablespoons chopped fresh parsley, or
2 tablespoons chopped fresh fennel greens

Peel and chop the onions. Trim the fennel bulbs, wash them carefully, and cut them into 1 cm (½ inch) dice. Sauté the onions, fennel, and minced garlic in the olive oil, stirring often, until the vegetables take on a nice golden-brown colour. Add some salt and pepper – more or less, depending on the saltiness of the stock you will use.

Add the dry bulgur and stir it in the hot pan with the vegetables for a few minutes. Then add the hot vegetable stock and the sultanas.

Pour the whole mixture into a large casserole or gratin dish, cover tightly, and bake it in a 180°C/350°F/Gas 4 oven for 40 minutes.

Meanwhile, toast the pine-nuts: heat them in a small pan, stirring constantly, until they begin to brown. Do not turn away to answer the phone! This only takes a few moments, and they'll burn in an instant if you take your eyes off them. When they are toast-coloured and give off a divine fragrance, just set them aside in a bowl.

After 40 minutes, when the pilaf is ready, remove the cover from the pilaf and check to make sure all the liquid has been absorbed. If not, leave it in the oven for a few more minutes. Then fluff the pilaf with a fork and stir in the toasted pine-nuts. Sprinkle with the chopped fresh herbs if you like and serve hot.

Serves 10–12.

OVEN-ROASTED KABOCHA SQUASH

The main job is done at the market. Get the right squash and you don't have to do much more. Kabocha squashes are pumpkin-shaped, and vary in size from about 900 g to 3.5 kg (2 to 7 or 8 lb). They are usually a dark greenish-grey colour, although I have seen some with an amber cast, and they often have rough patches or warts on the skin. Inside this homely shell, the exquisitely tasty flesh is dense and bright orange.

An uncut squash will keep for months in a cool, dry place, so you can buy several at once.

**2.2–2.8 kg (5–6 lb) Kabocha   2–3 tablespoons olive oil
   squash   salt to taste**

Cut the squash in half, scrape out and discard the seeds, then cut the halves into thick wedges. If you are using several smaller squashes, you can simply quarter them.

Brush the wedges with olive oil, sprinkle them lightly with salt, and arrange them on a baking sheet.

Roast the squash for 45 minutes to an hour at 190°C/375°F/Gas 5. The squash is ready when it is completely tender, and spotted golden-brown in places. If you want it browner and crustier, you can put the wedges under the grill for a moment at the end, just until they colour.

Serve hot with pilaf, rice, or with a mixed vegetable platter and polenta.

Serves 10–12.

RED CABBAGE STEWED WITH APPLES AND WINE

1 medium head red cabbage
(about 900 g/2 lb)
1 large onion
2 stalks celery
1½ tablespoons olive oil
2–3 cloves garlic, minced
1 small bay leaf
¼ teaspoon dried thyme
salt and pepper to taste

2 tart green apples, peeled,
cored, and grated
3 tablespoons chopped
flat-leaf parsley
300 ml (10 fl oz) dry red wine
1½ tablespoons red wine
vinegar, or 3 tablespoons
balsamic vinegar
2–3 teaspoons brown sugar

Wash the cabbage, cut it into large sections, trim away the core, and shred it either by hand or in a food processor with a slicing disc. Blanch the cabbage in boiling, salted water for 2 minutes, drain it, and set it aside.

Peel and chop the onion. Trim the celery, de-rib it, and dice it finely. Sauté the onion and celery in the olive oil, along with the garlic, until all the vegetables have softened. Add the bay leaf, thyme, and salt and pepper to taste, and continue cooking over medium heat until the onion begins to colour.

Stir in the blanched cabbage, grated apple, parsley, and wine. Cover the pan and simmer the mixture over low heat for about 20 minutes. Remove the lid, stir in the wine vinegar and sugar, correct the salt and pepper if needed, and continue cooking, stirring occasionally, for about 30 minutes. The liquid will reduce to a light glaze.

Serves 10–12.

BUCKWHEAT CRÊPES WITH ONIONS AND APPLES

※

Wild Mushroom and Charred Tomato Soup

Buckwheat Crêpes with Onions, Apples, and Cheese

Cranberry-Chilli Sauce

Watercress and Frisée Salad

Pear Sorbet and chocolate cookies
or fresh fruit and Biscotti

This is a delicious dinner to have with company, or for a special occasion with your family.

Buckwheat crêpes are the basis of many meals in Brittany. There are restaurants that serve only these crêpes, with a great range of savoury and sweet fillings.

These buckwheat crêpes are especially evocative of Brittany to me, because they are filled with a mixture of onions and apples, moistened with Calvados, and enriched with a little cheese. The apples add a mysterious quality, a light touch that is not at first identifiable, but alters the whole character of the dish.

A deeply flavoured soup of mushrooms and charred tomatoes begins the meal, preparing the way for the rich-tasting blend of melted onions and cheese. A spicy cranberry sauce and a peppery green salad provide the right contrast with the hot crêpes.

Pear Sorbet with chocolate cookies is a dessert of true elegance, and light enough to be welcome after any meal. If you have an ice cream freezer, take the time to make this sorbet. It's very easy, and the result is ambrosial.

WILD MUSHROOM AND CHARRED TOMATO SOUP

50 g (2 oz) dried porcini
1 tablespoon + 1 teaspoon
 olive oil
2 tablespoons butter
3 large onions, quartered and
 sliced
4 cloves garlic, chopped
1 bay leaf
salt and pepper to taste

½ teaspoon dried whole
 thyme, or 1–2 teaspoons
 fresh
1.4 kg (3 lb) ripe tomatoes
125 g (4 oz) fresh shiitake, or
 other wild mushrooms
250 ml (8 fl oz) dry red wine
750 ml (1¼ pints) vegetable
 stock (see page 459)
120 ml (4 fl oz) cream

Cover the dried porcini with boiling water and set them aside to soak for at least 30 minutes or longer, until soft.

Heat half the olive oil and half the butter in a large non-stick sauté pan, and add the sliced onions, three-quarters of the garlic, the bay leaf, some salt, and the thyme. Regulate the heat and cook slowly, stirring occasionally, until the onions are golden brown – as long as an hour if needed.

Meanwhile, scald and peel the tomatoes, cut them in halves or quarters, and mix them in a large bowl with the remaining olive oil, a sprinkle of salt, and the remaining chopped garlic. Spread them on a baking sheet with edges, and roast in a very hot oven (220°C/425°F/Gas 7), turning once or twice, until charred spots are appearing around their edges.

Check the tomatoes every 10 minutes or so, and then more frequently when they begin to colour – remember, you want them subtly charred, not burnt. When they're ready, allow them to cool a little on the baking sheet, then scrape them into a blender and process for a few seconds only; they should be roughly chopped.

When the porcini feel soft and flexible, drain them, reserving the liquid. Rinse them very carefully to get rid of all the sand, and chop any large pieces. Strain the liquid through a paper filter, adding water if needed to make 750 ml (1¼ pints). Wash the shiitakes, cut off the stems, and slice them.

Melt the remaining butter in a non-stick pan and sauté all the mushrooms in it until the shiitakes begin to colour. Deglaze the pan with the wine, then combine the mushrooms and wine with the caramelized onions in a soup pot.

Add the soaking liquid from the porcini, the vegetable stock, and the tomatoes, and simmer everything together for about 10 minutes to marry the flavours. Taste, and correct the seasoning with salt or pepper if desired. Stir in the cream.

Makes 8 — 10 servings.

BUCKWHEAT CRÊPES WITH ONIONS, APPLES, AND CHEESE

18–20 Buckwheat Crêpes (recipe follows)
2.8 kg (6 lb) onions
2 tablespoons olive oil
2 tablespoons butter
1 teaspoon salt, more to taste
black pepper

700 g (1½ lb) tart green apples, such as pippins or Granny Smiths
3 tablespoons Calvados
225 g (8 oz) mature Cheddar cheese, grated

Prepare the Buckwheat Crêpes and set aside.

Peel the onions, cut them in half lengthwise, and then slice them thickly. Heat a tablespoon of olive oil and half the butter in each of two large non-stick pans, and divide the onions between them. Sprinkle about ½ teaspoon of salt over each batch and cook the onions on medium heat, stirring occasionally, until they are golden brown. This will take about 45 minutes. Add black pepper to taste.

Meanwhile, peel the apples, cut into wedges, and slice the wedges crosswise. When the onions are lightly browned and much reduced in volume, consolidate them into one pan. Add the Calvados to the onions and stir quickly to deglaze the pan. Add the sliced apples, and a touch more salt if needed. Continue cooking, stirring often, until the liquid is entirely gone, the onions are a deep caramel colour, and the apples are tender.

Spoon 2–3 rounded tablespoons of the onion mixture across the centre of a crêpe, then sprinkle about 15 g (½ oz) of grated cheese over it. Roll the crêpe loosely over the filling and place it seam side down on a buttered baking sheet. Continue filling and rolling crêpes until all the onions and cheese are used up. You should have at least 16–18 filled crêpes. Reserve any leftover crêpes for another use.

Cover the crêpes loosely with a piece of aluminium foil, and bake them in a 180°C/350°F/Gas 4 oven for 10–15 minutes, or until they are hot through and the cheese is completely melted. If you have filled the crêpes earlier and kept them in the refrigerator for a while, adjust the oven time upward by at least 5 minutes.

Serve the crêpes at once, with a green salad or a tart relish.

Serves 8.

BUCKWHEAT CRÊPES

These buckwheat crêpes have a distinctive, nutty flavour, as well as a tenderness that makes them delightful to eat but a bit tricky to handle. If you let them brown before trying to flip them, and work gently when filling them, you'll be fine.

Note: This batter needs to rest at least 2 hours before you make the crêpes, so make it in the morning, or the night before – it only takes a few minutes.

325 ml (11 fl oz) low-fat milk
2 eggs
2 egg whites
120 ml (4 fl oz) beer
325 ml (11 fl oz) water
2 tablespoons vegetable oil,
    more for the pan

2 tablespoons sugar (slightly
    more for dessert crêpes)
½ teaspoon salt
250 g (9 oz) buckwheat flour

Combine the milk, eggs, egg whites, beer, water, and oil in a blender and process for a few seconds. Add the sugar, salt, and buckwheat flour, and process again until smooth, working in two batches if you need to. Stop and scrape down the sides, and process again.

Put the batter in a bowl, cover it, and refrigerate for at least 2 hours, or as long as overnight. Stir the batter up and check its consistency. It should be like double cream; you can thin it with a spoonful or two of water if you need to.

To cook the crêpes, heat a 23 cm (9 inch) non-stick pan (a well-seasoned crêpe pan can also be used if you have practice). Brush the pan with oil or rub it with a paper towel dipped in oil. Pour a ladleful of batter (equivalent to 3–4 tablespoons) into the hot pan and immediately tilt the pan around to spread the batter evenly over the bottom. Cook the crêpe on a medium flame for about 45 seconds, or until the edges are just beginning to brown. Loosen the edges gently with a thin spatula or a butter knife, then turn the crêpe over and cook on the other side for 20–30 seconds.

If a crêpe sticks, oil the pan a bit more next time, and let the crêpe cook slightly longer before turning. You may have a torn crêpe or two before your pan temperature and timing are worked out, as these are rather fragile – you'll just have to eat those as you work.

Stack the crêpes on a plate as they are finished, and keep them covered with a slightly damp kitchen towel.

Makes about 24 crêpes.

Variation: For sweeter crêpes, increase the sugar to 3 tablespoons. These are perfect for dessert, filled with jam or fruit compote.

CRANBERRY-CHILLI SAUCE

350 g (12 oz) fresh or frozen
   cranberries
1 orange
2 tablespoons tequila

125 g (4 oz) sugar
1 medium jalapeño chilli or
   2 small fresh green chillies

Rinse the berries and discard any that are brown and soft. Finely grate the zest only of the orange peel, then cut the orange in half and squeeze out the juice. Add enough water to the orange juice to make one cup of liquid.

Combine the berries, grated orange zest, juice and water, tequila, and sugar in a large non-reactive pan, and bring it to a slow boil, stirring occasionally as the sugar dissolves. Trim the chilli, discarding the seeds, and chop finely.

When the berries begin to pop, add the chopped chilli and boil everything together for about 5 more minutes, stirring with a long wooden spoon. If the sauce seems too thick, add a little more water.

Remove the sauce from the heat and allow it to cool, stirring now and again to prevent a skin from forming. Spoon it into a pretty dish, and chill if you like.

This delicious, slightly spicy sauce is perfect alongside stuffed crêpes, or any similarly rich-flavoured dish.

Makes about 500 ml (16 fl oz).

WATERCRESS AND FRISÉE SALAD

This is another of those excellent salads that can be served with wine. The peppery tastes of good watercress and radishes provide bite without acid, and contrast with the sweetness of fennel and raisins. Only a few drops of a fruity vinegar are used, letting the olive oil and walnuts dominate.

Make this salad only when you can get really fresh, dark green watercress. Watercress is great when just picked, but loses its flavour and character after a few days in the refrigerator.

2 bunches fresh watercress
1–2 heads young frisée
small handful of fresh basil
   leaves
small handful of fresh
   coriander
1 fennel bulb
5–6 red radishes

75 g (3 oz) raisins
fruity green olive oil, to taste
2–3 teaspoons raspberry
   vinegar
salt
black pepper
75 g (3 oz) chopped walnuts

Wash the watercress well to remove any mud, and break off and discard heavy stems. Wash the frisée and tear it into bite-sized pieces. Spin the leaves in a salad spinner to remove excess water.

Cut the larger basil leaves in wide strips and leave smaller ones whole. Snip the coriander leaves off their stems. Clean and trim the fennel bulb, quarter it lengthwise, and cut it in paper-thin slices. Trim and thinly slice the radishes.

Toss together the leaves, herbs, fennel, radishes, and raisins. Drizzle on a very small amount of fruity green olive oil and the raspberry vinegar, then add a dash of salt and pepper and toss again until the leaves are all lightly touched with dressing. I use only a couple of tablespoons of oil for this salad, as the walnuts add richness.

Sprinkle the chopped walnuts over the salad in the serving bowl, or over each serving.

Serves 8 as a side salad, or small dinner salad.

PEAR SORBET

600 ml (1 pint) water
400 g (14 oz) sugar
several strips lemon peel
1.2 kg (2½ lb) pears, ripe and
   juicy but not mushy

3–4 tablespoons freshly
   squeezed lemon juice
3 tablespoons pear brandy or
   liqueur

Make a simple sugar syrup by heating the water gently with the sugar, stirring with a wooden spoon, until all the sugar dissolves. Add the lemon peel and simmer the syrup for about 5 minutes.

Peel, core, and slice the pears, removing any blemished areas, and add them immediately to the sugar syrup. Poach them in the syrup, keeping it at a gentle simmer, until they are just tender. Remove the pears and set them aside. Discard the lemon peel.

Measure out 750 ml (1¼ pints) of the syrup, combine it with the pear slices and 3 tablespoons of lemon juice, and purée in a blender in batches until perfectly smooth.

Taste the purée, and add a little more lemon juice if it seems too sweet. The exact amount of lemon juice will depend on the sweetness of the pears. Stir in the pear brandy or liqueur.

Chill the mixture first, then freeze according to manufacturer's instructions in an ice cream freezer.

For a divine treat, serve the sorbet with Chocolate-dipped Biscotti (page 469).

Makes a little more than 1.2 litres (2 pints) of sorbet.

Biscotti (see page 468)

AFTER THE HOLIDAYS

❧

A Big Tossed Salad

Winter Vegetable Stew

Simple Couscous

Cranberry Chutney or Cranberry Sauce

ripe pears

After the winter holidays, we all want to retreat a little from food. We probably ate a little more, and a little fancier, than we normally do. We celebrated! It was fun, but we're carrying the memory of it on our hips. A certain sluggishness creeps over us. We feel the need to lighten the load.

It's time for simple food, with true and satisfying flavours but no heaviness on the palate or elsewhere.

Here it is, both raw and cooked: a bright-flavoured tossed salad, followed by a delicious vegetable stew served with plain couscous and a dab of cranberry sauce, and then fresh, ripe fruit for dessert.

The salad is big, full of crunchy things, contrasting sweet fennel, hot radishes, dark greens and herbs. It can be adapted to what is available in the shops and needs only a touch of the lightest dressing.

Winter Vegetable Stew is just a great combination of vegetables simmered together in a reduction of clear broth and white wine; a little vinegar, honey, and soy sauce are added at the last moment to form a savoury glaze. This stew could be served with almost any rice or grain, and I chose the easiest one I know – plain couscous, which I love not only for its ease. Cranberry sauce or chutney is the little condiment that spikes this combination. If you're tired of cranberries, almost any tart little relish will do.

A perfectly ripe pear for dessert finishes a meal that is in every way just what the moment requires.

A BIG TOSSED SALAD

This is not a salad for which a precise formula can be given. The idea is to have a balance of dark and light leaves, some pungent and some sweet, with a few very crunchy things for contrast, and perhaps a little taste of fruit as an extra flourish. All the ingredients listed are suggestions.

This salad is made from the good things that are available in colder weather, when tomatoes and basil and sweet peppers are still far away. It has clear, strong flavours and doesn't need much dressing.

leaves	*crunchy vegetables*
radicchio	celery
curly endive	fennel
watercress	radishes
rocket	kohlrabi
oak leaf or lollo rosso lettuce	red onion
small spinach leaves	

herbs
Italian flat-leaf parsley
coriander leaves
chives

garnishes: toasted walnuts, almonds, or pistachios
  raisins or dried cranberries
dressing: olive oil and wine vinegar, or Ginger-Sesame Dressing
  (page 449)

I use mixed, torn leaves and more solid ingredients – thinly sliced vegetables, toasted nuts, etc. – in a ratio of roughly 3 parts leaves to 1 part other ingredients. These proportions give nice body and texture to the salad.

Select your leaves, mixing peppery ones with sweet ones. Wash and trim them as needed, tear into bite-sized pieces, and spin them dry in a salad spinner. Clean the herbs the same way, and add them to the leaves – I add a big handful of herbs for a medium-sized bowl of salad, but follow your own taste in this.

Clean and trim the celery, fennel, radishes, kohlrabi, or whatever you like from the crunchy category, cutting it into very thin slices. If you are adding onion, taste it to see how sharp it is, and add it sparingly.

Add the raisins or dried cranberries, and toss everything in a large salad bowl. Dress the salad lightly with your best oil and vinegar, or a touch of Ginger-Sesame Dressing, and toss again. Scatter some toasted nuts on top and serve.

WINTER VEGETABLE STEW

1 medium to large Kabocha squash (1.4–1.6 kg/ 3–3½ lb) (or acorn squash if you can't get Kabocha)
2 large onions
2 fennel bulbs
2½ tablespoons olive oil
salt and pepper to taste
2 medium red-skinned potatoes
500 ml (16 fl oz) light vegetable stock (see page 460) or chicken stock

250 ml (8 fl oz) white wine
2 cloves garlic, finely chopped
450 g (1 lb) mushrooms, preferably wild, thickly sliced
¼ teaspoon cayenne
3 medium tomatoes, peeled and cut in chunks
1 bunch kale
3 tablespoons cider vinegar
1–2 tablespoons honey
1 teaspoon soy sauce

Cut the squash in half, scrape out all the seeds, and, using your biggest, sharpest knife, cut it into slices 2.5 cm (1 inch) thick. Pointing your knife always away from you, cut away the thick green peel, and cut the orange flesh into 2.5 × 5 cm (1 × 2 inch) chunks.

Peel the onions and cut them into thin wedges. Wash and trim the fennel, halve the bulbs lengthwise, and cut them in thick slices.

Heat 1½ tablespoons of olive oil in a large non-stick sauté pan and add the squash, onions, fennel, about ½ teaspoon of salt, and black pepper to taste. Cook the vegetables over medium heat, stirring and turning them often, until the onions and fennel are limp and all the vegetables are beginning to colour in spots – about 20 minutes.

Meanwhile, peel and cut the potatoes into 2.5 cm (1 inch) chunks. Put them in a small pot with the stock and white wine, bring the liquid to an easy boil, and cook them for about 10 minutes.

In another non-stick pan, heat ½ tablespoon of olive oil, add 1 chopped garlic clove, and stir it in the hot oil for a minute. Add the sliced mushrooms, a dash of salt, and the cayenne pepper, and sauté the mushrooms, stirring often, until they release their juice, it cooks away, and the mushrooms are beginning to brown.

Add the mushrooms, the tomatoes, and the potatoes in their stock to the squash mixture. Lower the heat, cover tightly, and let the stew simmer for about 30 minutes. The vegetables should be tender, and the potatoes and squash will fall apart around the edges just enough to thicken the juices slightly. If the mixture seems dry, add a drop of water or white wine.

Wash the kale thoroughly, slice it off its stems, and cut the leaves into big pieces. Heat the remaining olive oil in the same pan you used for the mushrooms, and stir the rest of the garlic in it for a minute. Add the kale and toss it with the garlic and oil and a little salt just until it wilts, then stir it into the stew.

Add the cider vinegar, honey, and soy sauce to the stew and turn up the flame. Stir everything together for a few minutes as the juices cook down a little and form a glaze. Taste, correct the seasoning with more salt or pepper if needed, and serve on big, deep plates, with couscous or any rice pilaf.

Serves 6–8.

SIMPLE COUSCOUS

825 ml (28 fl oz) liquid: a light
  vegetable stock (see page
  460), or a combination of
  stock and water

½ teaspoon salt, if needed
1 tablespoon butter
400 g (14 oz) couscous

optional garnish: chopped fresh parsley or coriander

Bring the liquid to a boil in a medium-sized pan. You can use a
delicate vegetable stock, or a combination of half water and half
stock. Do not use a stock that is too salty or strongly flavoured.
Add the salt, if needed, and the butter.

Reduce the heat to a simmer, stir in the couscous, cover the pot
tightly, and leave it on the lowest possible heat for 3 minutes. Then
turn off the heat and leave the pot covered for another 5 minutes.
Uncover and fluff the couscous with a fork before serving.

Serves 8−10.

CRANBERRY CHUTNEY

350 g (12 oz) cranberries
175 g (6 oz) brown sugar
75 g (3 oz) dried pears,
  chopped
1 large crisp apple, peeled,
  cored, and chopped
1 large onion, chopped
90 ml (3 fl oz) cider vinegar
2 tablespoons finely chopped
  fresh ginger root

grated zest of 1 lemon
pinch of salt
350 ml (12 fl oz) water, more
  if needed
1½ teaspoons whole mustard
  seeds
1−2 small hot red chillies,
  dried or fresh

Rinse the berries and pick them over, discarding any that are soft
and brown. In a large, non-reactive pan, combine the berries with

all but the last two ingredients, and bring everything to a slow boil, stirring to dissolve the sugar.

Toast the mustard seeds in a small pan, shaking them over medium heat until they begin to pop and jump. Toast the chillies in a very hot pan or directly over a flame until they blister and turn black in spots, then mince them. Stir the mustard seeds and minced chilli into the cranberry mixture.

Lower the heat and simmer the chutney for about an hour, stirring occasionally, adding a little more water if the chutney becomes too thick and threatens to scorch.

The chutney can be kept refrigerated and covered for several weeks, or put into sterilized jars and processed in a hot-water bath for longer storage. Flavour improves after a day or two.

This makes about 900 g (2 lb).

Cranberry Sauce (see page 195)

ABOUT ROASTING VEGETABLES

My favourite way to cook vegetables at the moment is to roast them. I love grilling things, but this is much easier, and you don't have to have charcoal and get soot all over yourself. Nothing touches water, so nothing can get soggy or lose taste. I get very satisfying results using very little fat; flavours are subtly enriched as juices caramelize, and edges crisp up.

Almost any vegetable that has a solid, as opposed to leafy, texture can be successfully roasted. Of course, everyone's been roasting potatoes for ever, but roasted green beans have become a staple in my house now, and have you ever tasted roasted asparagus? Or a pasta sauce made from slowly oven-roasted tomatoes? Or a combination of roasted onions, peppers, squashes, and aubergine? It's like a ratatouille done entirely in the oven, with just a little oil and a great depth to the flavour. Wonderful.

I like to find sympathetic combinations of vegetables, depending on what's in season, roast them all together, and serve them alongside a ladleful of polenta with a dab of tomato sauce or a few slivers of cheese. If the vegetables include some softer, juicier ones, I like to toss them with great big noodles like rigatoni. The denser vegetables, roasted to an almost crispy finish, make a great finger food with drinks. And almost any combination can make the taco of your life, wrapped up in a warm corn tortilla with a spoonful of beans and some salsa.

Preparation time is minimal, and you only have to stir the vegetables once or twice while they're in the oven, so life can go on. The whole house smells great, and when you take them out of the oven and serve them, there's so much reward for so little effort.

What's more, they're good cold the next day. Of course, I love them in salad – I toss them with some crisp greens, a splash of oil and vinegar, some chopped herbs, maybe some big gratings of Parmesan or slices of fresh mozzarella, and there's lunch.

The three dinner menus that follow are good examples of different approaches to roasted vegetables. In the first, a combination of vegetables are cut up, mixed up, and all roasted together. The second concentrates on a couple of assertive flavours. The third, Polenta and Roasted Vegetables, presents a whole array of vegetables, roasted simply but separately, for a rustic feast.

Roasted vegetables also turn up in many other menus. See A Celebration for Everyone (page 426), or Tomato Risotto for the Family (page 64).

A RUSTIC AUTUMN DINNER

❧

Fresh Herb Salad

Roasted Autumn Vegetables

Brown and Wild Rice Pilaf

Plum and Walnut Galette

This is a nice menu for the turning of the season, when you want to taste the winter squashes that are turning up in the markets, and to have a glass of red wine. Yet it takes advantage of the late summer produce that is still abundant in September and October.

A salad that tap-dances with flavours starts the meal. It's full of fresh herbs tossed with tender lettuces, bitter greens, hot radishes – and a touch of honey in the dressing.

After that, one of the simplest and nicest ways to enjoy the time of the harvest – a great platter of assorted vegetables, roasted in the oven until they develop a sweet intensity of flavour, and served with a Brown and Wild Rice Pilaf.

In keeping with the rustic, straightforward style of this dinner, the Plum and Walnut Galette is a generous, juicy tart, casually shaped but bursting with the flavour of autumn plums.

This is not a fussy meal, and can be adapted infinitely as autumn deepens into winter. Almost all the winter vegetables are very suitable for roasting, and the plums in the galette can be replaced with apples or pears later in the season.

FRESH HERB SALAD

This salad has exciting flavours. Handfuls of herbs are mixed with lettuces, green onions, and radishes, and a touch of fruit for contrasting sweetness.

300–350 g (10–12 oz) mixed mild-flavoured lettuce leaves

1 bunch dark green watercress or rocket

6 tablespoons fresh mint leaves

6 tablespoons coriander leaves

6 tablespoons flat-leaf parsley leaves

6 tablespoons fresh basil leaves

4–5 spring onions, sliced paper thin

6 red radishes, thinly sliced

1 large, juicy apple

75 g (3 oz) raisins

2½ tablespoons fruity green olive oil, or walnut oil

2 tablespoons balsamic vinegar, or sherry vinegar

2 tablespoons honey

2 teaspoons Dijon mustard

salt and freshly ground pepper to taste

Rinse all the leaves, tear them into bite-sized pieces if needed, and spin in a salad spinner or blot with towels. Combine the leaves, herbs, onions, and radishes in a large salad bowl.

Cut the apple into wedges, core it, and slice the wedges thinly crosswise. If the raisins are very dry, plump them briefly in hot water, then drain. Add the sliced apples and the raisins to the leaves. Whisk together the oil, vinegar, honey, and mustard. Pour the dressing over the salad and toss it gently until every leaf glistens. Sprinkle on a little salt and grind on some pepper, toss again, and serve.

Serves 8.

ROASTED AUTUMN VEGETABLES

If Kabocha squash is not available, use another dense orange or dark yellow squash, such as acorn, or pumpkin.

2–3 large aubergines
salt as needed
1 medium Kabocha squash
  (900 g–1.4 kg/2–3 lb)
2 large onions
3–4 medium red, green or
  yellow peppers
700 g (1½ lb) small potatoes,
  preferably red-skinned, or
  about 15–20 new potatoes

8–10 whole cloves garlic
3 tablespoons fruity green
  olive oil
2–3 tablespoons fresh
  rosemary leaves, coarsely
  chopped
1 teaspoon dried crushed
  whole oregano leaves
freshly ground pepper to taste

The whole idea here is to scrub and trim the vegetables and cut them in fairly large pieces of a more or less uniform size so that they will roast evenly.

Trim the aubergines, quarter them lengthwise, then slice about 1 cm (½ inch) thick. Toss the pieces in a bowl with a couple of teaspoons of salt and transfer to a colander to drain while you prepare the remaining vegetables.

Cut the squash in half, scoop out and discard the seeds, and cut each half into 2.5 cm (1 inch) wedges. Trim off the skin with a very sharp knife, leaving only the firm, dark yellow flesh, and cut it in 2.5 cm (1 inch) pieces.

Peel the onions, halve them lengthwise, then cut each half into 6 or 8 chunks. Trim the peppers and cut them in pieces about 2.5 cm (1 inch) square.

Scrub the potatoes, trim away any rough spots, and cut them in 1.5 cm (¾ inch) dice. Peel the garlic cloves.

Put all the vegetables except the aubergines into your largest bowl, add the olive oil, rosemary, oregano, 1½ teaspoons of salt, and as much fresh pepper as you think you might like. Mix everything together thoroughly. All the vegetables should be lightly coated with oil and herbs. Now rinse and drain the aubergine pieces, and mix them into the other vegetables.

Spread the vegetables out on 2 medium-sized baking sheets, and roast them in a 200°C/400°F/Gas 6 oven for about 1½ hours. After the first 30 minutes, turn them with a spatula, stir them around a bit, and reverse their positions in the oven so the one that was underneath can have a turn on top. Move them around again after 30 minutes, and after that check them every 15 minutes.

They're done when the biggest chunk of squash is tender, when golden brown patches appear here and there, when the peppers look soft and the potatoes have crisp edges – when they just look *done*.

Serves 8 – 10 generously.

Variation: Substitute 7 – 8 medium courgettes for the aubergine.

BROWN AND WILD RICE PILAF

The chewy texture and sweet, almost nutty flavour of this pilaf make it a very satisfying dish. It is an ideal companion to autumn or winter vegetables, either roasted or stewed.

1½ tablespoons olive oil
1 onion, finely chopped
pinch of salt
175 g (6 oz) wild rice
225 g (8 oz) long-grain brown
   rice

750 ml (1¼ pints) vegetable
   stock (see page 459)
550 ml (18 fl oz) water

Warm the olive oil in a medium-sized sauté pan and cook the onion in it with a pinch of salt, stirring often, until the onion is soft and translucent. Add the wild and the brown rice and stir them with the onions for a couple of minutes, then add the stock and water.

Bring the liquid to a simmer, lower the heat, and cover the pan tightly. Leave the rice to simmer for 55 minutes, then turn off the heat and let it stand, without lifting the lid, for another 5 minutes. Fluff the rice up with a fork before serving.

Serves 8.

Leftovers: I made such a tasty little frittata once with some of this leftover pilaf that I thought I'd include the recipe here.

RICE PILAF FRITTATA

1 ½ tablespoons olive oil
350 g (12 oz) chopped white
  of leek
salt and pepper to taste
225 g (8 oz) Brown and Wild
  Rice Pilaf (see previous
  recipe)

8 eggs
75 g (3 oz) freshly grated
  Parmesan cheese

Heat the olive oil in a medium-sized non-stick pan and cook the leeks in it, with a dash of salt and pepper, until they are beginning to colour. Add the rice pilaf and stir it over a medium heat until it is thoroughly heated.

Meanwhile, beat the eggs with salt to taste and the Parmesan cheese. Add the hot rice and leek mixture, and immediately stir everything together well.

Wipe the pan clean or start fresh with another one, lightly brushed with olive oil, and pour the egg and rice mixture into it. Turn the heat down low, and cover the pan. Check the frittata after about 10 minutes. If the eggs on top are no longer runny, loosen the frittata gently with a spatula, then invert it on to a plate or lid and slide it back into the pan to brown for a moment on the other side. Serve the frittata warm, cut into wedges.

Serves 6.

PLUM AND WALNUT GALETTE

This is a flat, open-faced tart. It is shaped casually, with the pastry edge pulled over the filling around the sides in loose pleats or folds, leaving the fruit in the centre exposed. Under the juicy plums, a layer of sweetened ground nuts and flour absorbs the excess moisture, and adds a nice flavour.

for the pastry
225 g (8 oz) plain flour
1½ teaspoons sugar
¾ teaspoon salt
150 g (5 oz) cold unsalted
    butter
4–5 tablespoons ice water

for the filling
1.2 kg (2½ lb) sweet plums
75 g (3 oz) toasted walnuts
    (see below)
3 tablespoons flour
175 g (6 oz) sugar

optional: 75–125 g (3–4 oz) plum or raspberry preserve, strained

To make the pastry, put the flour, sugar, and salt into the container of a food processor, and add the cold butter, cut into bits. Process very briefly, until the mixture resembles coarse meal. Sprinkle in the ice water, running the processor, just until the pastry starts to hold together – only a few seconds.

Remove the pastry from the processor, form it into a ball, then roll it out on a floured board to a circle or oval about 40–45 cm (16–18 inches) across. Drape the pastry over the rolling pin and transfer it to a large baking sheet. Cover the pastry with a towel or with plastic wrap and chill it for at least 30 minutes.

Slice the plums off their stones into 1 cm (½ inch) wedges. Preheat the oven to 200°C/400°F/Gas 6. Put the toasted walnuts, 3 tablespoons of flour, and 25 g (1 oz) of sugar into the food processor and process into a fine meal.

Remove the pastry from the refrigerator and spread the walnut mixture evenly over it, leaving a 5 cm (2 inch) border all around. Arrange the plums over the walnut mixture, and sprinkle them evenly with all but 1 teaspoon of the remaining 50 g (2 oz) of sugar.

If the pastry is still stiff, wait a few minutes for it to reach room temperature and become pliable, in order to avoid cracking. Then fold the 5 cm (2 inch) border of the pastry up over the filling, gathering it into loose folds. The fruit in the centre of the pie remains uncovered. Sprinkle the last teaspoon of sugar over the pastry border.

Bake the galette in the bottom half of the hot oven for about an hour. I cover it loosely with foil for the first 30 minutes to keep the crust from browning too much, but that's a matter of taste.

When it is done, remove it from the oven and, while it is still hot, brush the strained preserve over the exposed fruit to make a beautiful, shiny finish (not essential but very pretty). Allow the tart to cool somewhat, then loosen it from the baking sheet with a spatula or knife and slide it on to a cooling rack.

Serve at room temperature from a large, flat platter or board, cut into wedges.

Serves 8 – 10.

To toast walnuts: Spread the nuts on a baking sheet and toast them in a 120°C/250°F/Gas ½ oven for about 25 minutes, then allow them to cool.

GREEN TOMATOES AND COUSCOUS

❧

Black Bean Soup

Roasted Yams with Green Tomatoes

Cranberry Couscous

Cinnamon Custard Ice Cream

Yams and cranberries are wonderfully evocative of autumn, and this is an unusual but very straightforward way to enjoy them. Because the cranberries are dried, you can use them in any season. However, you must have fresh green tomatoes, which pair up with roasted yams like Fred Astaire and Ginger Rogers.

Savoury Black Bean Soup begins the meal, garnished with a hot and smoky sauce made from chipotle chillies. The ice cream that finishes it is a simple custard infused with a subtle touch of cinnamon, and frozen.

This meal can be served with no last-minute fuss. The soup can be prepared ahead, and the ice cream must be. Once the vegetables are cut up, it only takes putting them in the oven 1½ hours before dinner, and turning them over a couple of times. Even the couscous could be partly prepared ahead of time, and in any case, it only takes a few minutes.

BLACK BEAN SOUP

450 g (1 lb) black beans
pinch of bicarbonate of soda
2 large onions
6 cloves garlic
2 bay leaves
6–8 branches coriander
2 teaspoons salt, more to taste
1 tablespoon olive oil

1 tablespoon butter
6 medium carrots, sliced
3 stalks celery, sliced
2 tablespoons cumin seeds
white pepper to taste
2 teaspoons paprika
pinch of cayenne
1 tablespoon cider vinegar

garnishes: fresh limes
  coriander sprigs
  Simple Chipotle Sauce (see page 281)

Soak the beans overnight in about 3.4 litres (6 pints) of water with a pinch of bicarbonate of soda. In the morning, drain the beans and rinse them, then put them in a large pan with enough fresh water to cover them by at least 5 cm (2 inches). Add ½ an onion, 3 peeled cloves of garlic, 2 bay leaves, and a few branches of coriander. Simmer the beans very gently until they are tender, probably about 2 hours. Discard the onion, garlic, bay leaves, and coriander. Add 2 teaspoons of salt.

Meanwhile, chop the remaining 1½ onions and finely chop the remaining garlic. Heat the oil and butter together in a large non-stick pan and sauté the chopped onion, sliced carrots, sliced celery, and chopped garlic in it, stirring often, until the vegetables are tender and beginning to brown. Add the vegetables to the cooked beans, deglazing the pan with some of the bean liquid.

Toast the cumin seeds lightly in a frying pan, then grind them in a mortar and add them to the soup with the remaining ingredients. Simmer everything together for about another 30 minutes. Taste and correct the seasoning with a bit more salt, pepper, or cayenne, as needed. Purée the soup in batches in a blender and return to the pot.

Serve the soup hot, passing lime wedges, fresh coriander sprigs, and Simple Chipotle Sauce as garnishes.

Serves 8–10 generously.

ROASTED YAMS WITH GREEN TOMATOES

The essential thing in this dish is the balance between the dense, sweet yams and the tart, juicy green tomatoes. You could get away with using all green tomatoes if you can't find decent red ones in the autumn or winter, and of course the amount of olive oil is very discretionary.

900 g (2 lb) yams
900 g (2 lb) green tomatoes
3 medium red tomatoes
3 medium red onions

6 large cloves garlic
1–2 tablespoons olive oil
salt and pepper to taste

Peel the yams and cut them in 1–2.5 cm (½–1 inch) dice. Trim the green and red tomatoes and cut them in large chunks. Peel the onions and cut them in 2.5 cm (1 inch) chunks. Peel the garlic and, if the cloves are very large, cut them in half lengthwise.

Combine all the vegetables in a large bowl, drizzle on the olive oil, add some salt and pepper, and mix well. Spread the vegetables out on two baking sheets, preferably non-stick.

Roast the vegetables at 190°C/375°F/Gas 5 for about 1½ hours, moving them around and turning them twice during the cooking time. They should be very tender, and browning here and there.

Serve with couscous, or with a rice pilaf.

Serves 6–8.

CRANBERRY COUSCOUS

1 large onion
2 teaspoons olive oil
2 teaspoons butter
salt as needed

2.2 litres (3¾ pints) vegetable
    stock (see page 459)
75 g (3 oz) dried cranberries
400 g (14 oz) couscous

Peel the onion, cut it lengthwise into 8 wedges, then slice the wedges very thinly crosswise. Heat the olive oil and butter in a large non-stick sauté pan and sauté the onion, with a little salt, until it is lightly browned.

Add the vegetable stock and the dried cranberries and bring the stock to a boil. Lower the heat to a mere simmer, add the couscous, cover the pan, and leave it to simmer for 5 minutes. Remove from the heat and leave covered for another 2 – 3 minutes, then fluff up the couscous with a fork and serve.

Serves 8 – 10.

CINNAMON CUSTARD ICE CREAM

500 ml (16 fl oz) milk	**2 large sticks cinnamon**
500 ml (16 fl oz) double cream	**4 egg yolks, beaten**
175 g (6 oz) sugar	

In a medium-sized, heavy-bottomed saucepan, combine the milk, cream, sugar, and cinnamon sticks. Heat the mixture until it simmers, stirring to dissolve the sugar. Remove from the heat and leave to steep, covered, for 2 – 3 hours. You can leave the cinnamon to soak in the cream mixture even longer if you want a more defined cinnamon flavour.

Heat the liquid again to just below a simmer. Stir a ladle of the hot liquid into the egg yolks, then whisk the yolks into the cream mixture. Continue stirring over very low heat, never allowing the mixture to boil, until the custard thickens, about 8 – 10 minutes.

Pour the custard into another container and allow it to cool, then chill it. Remove the cinnamon sticks, strain the custard if needed, and freeze it in an ice cream freezer according to manufacturer's instructions.

This makes slightly more than 1.2 litres (2 pints) of ice cream.

POLENTA AND ROASTED VEGETABLES

❦

polenta, plain or grilled

Roasted Whole Garlic

Roasted Radicchio and Endive

Roasted Carrots

Roasted Green Beans with Garlic

Roasted Fennel and Red Onions

Sautéd Winter Greens

Roasted Winter Squash and Apples

fresh fruit plate

Biscotti

Here is polenta as an anchor for ten wonderful tastes – nine vegetables and a little surprise fruit. Polenta (see page 260) served with an assortment of roasted vegetables is a popular meal for good reason.

The right selection of contrasting vegetables, each roasted to its peak texture and flavour, is the crowning glory of vegetable roasting. It is spectacular to look at and spectacular to eat, yet it is simplicity itself.

The entire technique of roasting consists of putting something in the oven at the correct temperature, leaving it there the right amount of time, and letting nature take its course.

With this meal, the trick is to divide the vegetables into categories based on cooking time. Carrots and winter squash go into the oven first. Then the garlic, the fennel, and the red onions. A little later, you add the green beans and the apple slices. You finish with the radicchio and endive, which, being lettuces, wilt quickly at 200°C/400°F/Gas 6.

Meanwhile, you have stirred the polenta and sautéd the greens on top of the stove.

Roasting times always vary a little, depending on the size of things and how well calibrated the oven is, but this kind of food is very forgiving. If you need to take something out and put it aside while other things finish roasting, it's no big deal.

You can serve all these vegetables on huge platters, put an earthenware pot full of polenta on the table, and let all your guests serve themselves.

The combination of vegetables I propose here can be changed, reduced, or expanded. I would always want to include garlic and sautéd greens, and at least one root vegetable or squash, but after that just be guided by your taste and what's available.

Other good things that could be part of this plate are:

new potatoes	**spring onions**
green or red peppers	**turnip wedges**
tomato halves	**Chinese leaves**
sweet potato slices	**leeks**
courgettes	**mushrooms**

ROASTED WHOLE GARLIC

8–10 heads garlic   **2 tablespoons olive oil,**
salt to taste   **approx.**

There are two ideas about roasting garlic: one is to separate the cloves, and the other to leave the head whole. To roast whole head garlic, first slice off about 1 cm (½ inch) from the sprouting end with a very sharp knife. This will help you to separate the cloves later, when the garlic is soft.

If you're keeping up with kitchen fashion, you can put the trimmed garlic heads into clay garlic roasters, or into the larger onion roaster, or you can arrange them snugly in any casserole or baking dish that is the right size for them. Drizzle a few drops of olive oil over the cut top of each head, and sprinkle them lightly with salt. Put 2 or 3 tablespoons of water in the bottom of the dish.

This is the important part: cover the dish tightly, or the garlic will dry out and become hard. Ideally, the dish should be sealed up. The best method is to use a casserole with a close-fitting cover, or to cover a dish with aluminum foil first and then fit a lid over that to hold it down.

Roast the garlic at 200°C/400° F/Gas 6 for 45–60 minutes. You should be able to squeeze the soft garlic easily out of a clove.

Serve one head of garlic per person, with plenty of good country bread to spread it on, and be ready for the fact that everyone within a mile of your house will know what you're having for dinner.

Serves 8–10.

ROASTED RADICCHIO AND ENDIVE

These two vegetables can easily be roasted together, because they have a similar density.

2 large or 4 small heads   **2 tablespoons olive oil**
    radicchio   **salt to taste**
4 Belgian endives

Peel away any badly bruised or torn outer leaves, and wash the vegetables. Cut the radicchio into quarters, or, if the heads are very small, into halves. Cut each endive in half lengthwise.

Arrange the radicchio and endive on a baking sheet, cut side up. Brush the olive oil evenly over all the cut parts. Sprinkle them with salt.

Roast the radicchio and endive in a 200°C/400°F/Gas 6 oven for about 15 minutes, or until they feel soft and the tops are beginning to colour. They can be finished under a hot grill for a few moments if you like them a little more charred.

Serves 8.

ROASTED CARROTS

900 g (2 lb) carrots
1½ tablespoons olive oil
salt to taste

4–5 tablespoons vegetable stock (see page 459), more if needed
1 tablespoon lemon juice

Scrape and trim the carrots. If you have thin or very small carrots, you can roast them whole. Otherwise, you will need to cut them into carrot sticks no more than 1 cm (½ inch) thick at their thickest point.

Put the carrots in a bowl and drizzle the olive oil over them. Toss them around until the oil is evenly distributed over all the carrots. Spread them on a shallow baking pan and sprinkle them lightly with salt. Mix together the vegetable stock and lemon juice and sprinkle it over the carrots.

Roast the carrots in a 200°C/400°F/Gas 6 for 45–60 minutes, turning them and moving them around every 20 minutes or so. After a while, the vegetable stock will cook away, and the carrots will begin to colour. If they are turning too dark before they are tender, you can add a tiny bit more stock, but you certainly don't want any left by the time they are done.

Serves 8–10.

Roasted Green Beans with Garlic (see page 250)
Roasted Fennel and Red Onions (see page 432)

SAUTÉD WINTER GREENS

You can cook a wide variety of winter greens this way. I've done Swiss chard, ruby chard, kale, Chinese leaves, and, of course, spinach. Cooking times will vary with the density of the greens.

about 900 g (2 lb) greens
2 tablespoons fruity green olive oil
2–3 cloves garlic, peeled and chopped

salt to taste
dash of vinegar or lemon juice
black pepper to taste

Wash the greens thoroughly. Discard any leaves that are yellowed or wilted. Trim off heavy stems, particularly with kale or chard. If your greens are large, cut them into smaller pieces.

Heat the olive oil in your largest non-stick sauté pan and add the chopped garlic. Stir the garlic around in the hot oil for 1 minute, then add as much of the prepared greens as the pan will hold and start turning them gently as they wilt. Continue adding greens and turning them over until you've added them all. It will look like a lot to start with, but it's amazing how greens shrink.

Salt the greens lightly and keep cooking until there is no excess liquid in the pan. By this time, most greens are completely cooked. With something a little sturdier, like kale, you might have to add a few drops of water and keep cooking for a few minutes more.

Just before serving, toss the greens with a little dash of vinegar, or some lemon juice if you prefer, and grind on a little pepper.

Serves 8–10.

ROASTED WINTER SQUASH AND APPLES

Use Kabocha squash, or ask your greengrocer about the best variety available in your area. Use firm, tart apples.

900 g (2 lb) winter squash   **1½ tablespoons olive oil**
900 g (2 lb) apples   **½ teaspoon salt**
2 teaspoons lemon juice

Peel and seed your squash and cut it in large cubes or in slices, whatever works for you. Cut the apples in quarters, and core them, then toss them with the lemon juice.

Put the squash pieces in a big bowl, drizzle them with the olive oil, sprinkle on a little salt, and turn them over and over with your hands until all are lightly and evenly coated with oil.

Combine the squash with the apples and spread them on a baking sheet. Roast them at 200°C/400°F/Gas 6 for about an hour, turning and moving them every 20 minutes or so.

Serves 8 – 10.

Biscotti (see page 468)

ABOUT WILD MUSHROOMS

A mycologist once said that the world is divided into two types of people – mycophiles and mycophobes. As nations and cultures, we seem to be either fanatics for wild fungus, or else have a dread of it, and there's not much middle ground.

I'm definitely with the mycophiles, by heritage and by personal inclination. I just love wild mushrooms of all sorts, love to find them, love to eat them, and love to cook with them.

I remember on a visit to Poland going mushroom hunting in the cool, deep forest with my relatives. That was when my husband became enamoured of wild mushrooms; he later studied them diligently so that he could hunt on his own at home.

I should say here that I do not encourage anyone to find and eat mushrooms on casual information. Do not experiment. There are poisonous mushrooms, and a few of them can kill you, or make you so sick you wish they had. But if you have studied mushrooms or are with someone who has, and you know how to make a positive identification, then collecting mushrooms in the damp and quiet wilderness can be a rewarding experience.

In Poland, as in much of Europe, the forests and meadows are well known to the local inhabitants, and traffic in the woods can be heavy on an autumn morning. The dedicated foragers are there at dawn, baskets on their arms, eyes cast down and scanning. They are there in the cold mist or drizzle, as well as on a bright morning. The first ones in the forest find the prizes. Those who follow in the warmth of the day have to search hard and walk farther to fill their baskets. These are the woods where mushrooms have been harvested for generations, or centuries.

But I have seen a virgin forest. We were in Utah, on our way to a summer workshop in a beautiful, sparsely populated region known for its spectacular mountain landscapes but not for its cuisine. As we were driving into the mountains, my husband suddenly hit the brakes and pulled off the road, his eyes fixed on the forest floor that sloped away from us. 'Mushrooms! I see some, right there!'

We got out and tramped into the trees, to a nice, rich stand of what appeared to be boletus, and quite large ones. He was already cutting and gathering when he looked up and exclaimed again. We moved a little farther into the woods, barely away from the road, and stared in speechless wonder. Neither of us had ever seen a forest floor so carpeted with big, glorious, perfectly undisturbed mushrooms. There were thousands. They spread in every direction, as far as we could see.

We rushed back to the car and dumped books and papers out of carry-alls so we could fill them up with fungus. We must have gathered forty or fifty pounds in half an hour, stunned with the knowledge that no one had ever gathered mushrooms there before us. We were in a land of mycophobes.

Later, during the workshop, we went about our business with writers and film-makers, secretly on fire with the knowledge that in our cabin there were sacks of mushrooms waiting to be made into soup, or pickled the way I had seen my Polish aunt pickle hers. And a funny thing happened. We walked into another cabin for a meeting, and there, on the kitchen counters, all over the tables, on every available surface, mushrooms were laid out on paper towels to dry. The scripts and notebooks were on the floor. It turned out that this film-maker was Czech.

It was a rare experience, not to be repeated, and probably now there are chic restaurants in that region with chefs who send foragers into the woods. It is becoming easier to buy fresh wild mushrooms in this country than it was even a decade ago. They turn up in delicatessens and even in supermarkets.

Oyster mushrooms and shiitake mushrooms are cultivated now, so we cannot really call them wild, but they are very tasty indeed, and their ready availability in many markets shows a great improvement over the days when champignons, the little white buttons, were the only thing you could find.

I get cultivated Portobello mushrooms at my local farmshop; they resemble very large field mushrooms. Sometimes I also see chanterelles there, which grow locally in foggy areas near the sea. If you want something that the good restaurants are getting and don't know where to find it, just ask them who *their* supplier is. Most of the time they'll be happy to tell you, and many wholesalers are perfectly willing to deal with a home chef – though you might have to drive to the warehouse at odd hours of the morning.

Still the most difficult to get in this country, at least in my area, are *Boletus edulus*, the greatest of the edible fungi – with the possible exception of truffles. *Boletus* are called cèpes in France, and porcini – little pigs – in Italy. Their Italian nickname is becoming more and more frequently used here, and it may one day sound as American as pizza. Better that than what my father called them in Poland: *prawdjiwki*. It means 'the real ones', in an affectionate form.

They are the real ones to me, and though they may be expensive and hard to find, it is worth searching them out. Fortunately, dried porcini are more easily available, and while they may seem very costly, their flavour is so intense that even an ounce can add a depth and woodsy perfume to a dish of other fungi.

The simplest way to cook most fresh mushrooms is this. Clean them well, and use minimal water if they aren't especially muddy or sandy. If you need to use water, do, but pat them dry on towels. Slice them. Sauté a little garlic into some olive oil or butter, or a combination of the two, and then add the mushrooms. Sauté them until they release their juice and it cooks away. When they are tender, salt and pepper them to your taste and eat them.

This method can be elaborated with the addition of a little chopped parsley, or a dash of wine. Some people like to add a bit of cream at the end. Fresh mushrooms, quickly sautéd in this manner, are great with eggs for breakfast, with a piece of toast or a roll any time, with rice or pasta for dinner. But there are many wonderful ways to cook mushrooms, and I mean to try them all before I die.

The following four dinners are little celebrations of the great culinary gift of fungus. The ragout and the risotto are classic, incomparably good ways to feast on mushrooms in lavish amounts. Wild Mushroom Cobbler is an easy casserole, and in the fourth menu, buckwheat crêpes are wrapped around a filling of mushrooms and potatoes.

So, when you have gathered mushrooms, whether you foraged in the woods or at the market, then gather a few fellow mycophiles, open a wonderful bottle of Burgundy, and enjoy a treat that is all the more delightful because it is rare.

Note: For other mushroom dishes, see Oyster Mushroom Chowder (page 285), Roulade of Fresh Wild Mushrooms (page 366), and my own favourite, pure essence of mushrooms, Wild Mushroom Soup (page 451).

A WILD MUSHROOM DINNER

✤

Gingered Squash and Apple Soup

Ragout of Wild Mushrooms

Rice Pilaf

Cranberry Sauce

Basque Cake

This dinner is elegant in its simplicity. Great seasonal ingredients are cooked and presented in an uncomplicated and satisfying way. The ragout calls for a great bottle of Burgundy, making this a meal for a special occasion; we had a Grands Échézeaux once, and it was memorable. The delicate, buttery pastry at the end also adds a celebratory touch. On the other hand, any time you come into a windfall of fresh wild mushrooms, this can be a wonderful family dinner.

The Gingered Squash and Apple Soup is a golden purée with a lovely flavour kick from fresh ginger and coriander. It offers a nice introduction to the Ragout of Wild Mushrooms, with its deep woodsy flavours, fully developed by a combination of sautéing and then simmering in red wine. Serve with it a very plain Rice Pilaf and a bright little relish – Cranberry Sauce spiked with orange and cinnamon.

The Basque Cake is nothing more than a sweet shortcrust pastry filled with vanilla crème pâtissière and dusted with icing sugar. It follows the style of the rest of this meal: no frills, just pure, voluptuous flavour and texture.

Except for the Rice Pilaf, everything in this menu can be made in advance. The soup, ragout, and Cranberry Sauce can be made the day before, and at a pinch so could the cake, though the cake is better made the same day.

GINGERED SQUASH AND APPLE SOUP

You can use almost any of the dark yellow or orange winter squashes for this, such as Kabocha or acorn, though you may find yourself needing more seasoning with some than others.

1.2 kg (2½ lb) Kabocha or
  acorn squash
2½ tablespoons butter
2 medium red onions,
  coarsely chopped
450 g (1 lb) sweet apples,
  peeled, cored, and
  sliced
salt to taste

1 litre (1¾ pints) vegetable
  stock (see page 459)
175 ml (6 fl oz) dry white
  wine
1½ tablespoons minced fresh
  ginger
2 tablespoons chopped fresh
  coriander
pepper to taste

garnish: additional coriander leaves

Cut the squash in half, or in thick slices, and place cut side down on a lightly oiled baking sheet. Roast in the oven at 190°C/375°F/ Gas 5 for 50–60 minutes, or until soft. Cover with foil during roasting if the squash is cut in slices. Let it cool until you can handle it, then scoop out the soft flesh, discarding any seeds, and measure out enough to fill a measure to the 750 ml (1¼ pint) level.

In a very large non-stick sauté pan, melt the butter and cook the onions in it over medium heat, stirring often, until they are very soft. Add the apple slices and a little salt, and keep cooking for 15 minutes more, stirring frequently.

Add the cooked squash, vegetable stock, wine, ginger, and chopped coriander, and simmer for another 15 minutes. Everything should be very soft.

Purée the soup in the blender in batches until perfectly smooth, then add salt and pepper to taste. Serve hot, sprinkled with coriander leaves.

Of course, a splash of cream could be added for a richer soup, or a spoonful of crème fraîche plopped in the centre of each bowl, but the pure flavours of the vegetables and fruit are so lively and concentrated in this purée that I prefer it this way.

Serves 6–8.

RAGOUT OF WILD MUSHROOMS

The success of this dish will depend mainly on the flavour and quality of the mushrooms used. It pays to go out of your way to find good wild mushrooms, or the more interesting cultivated varieties, and a combination is more satisfying than all of a kind. You can use porcini, morels, field mushrooms, oyster mushrooms, shiitakes, or other varieties if you live in a good area for mushrooms. Add champignons, the ubiquitous white buttons, if you need to, but try not to use more than half champignons in your mix, as they have the blandest flavour.

800 g (1¾ lb) fresh wild
   mushrooms, or a
   combination of wild and
   cultivated
1 large onion
1 large red onion
1 tablespoon olive oil
2 tablespoons + 1 teaspoon
   butter
3 cloves garlic, chopped
salt and pepper to taste

250 ml (8 fl oz) dry red wine
1 bay leaf
½ teaspoon thyme leaves
2 stalks celery, sliced thinly
pinch of cayenne
1 tablespoon flour
500 ml (16 fl oz) heated
   vegetable stock (see
   page 459)
3 tablespoons chopped
   flat-leaf parsley

Clean the mushrooms thoroughly, trim off tough or woody stems, and slice the mushrooms or cut them in generous pieces.

Cut the onions in very thin wedges or wide slices. Heat 1 teaspoon of olive oil and 2 teaspoons of butter in a non-stick sauté pan and sauté the onions in it, stirring often, until they begin to soften. Add the chopped garlic and some salt and pepper and continue cooking until the onions and garlic begin to brown. Add half the red wine, the bay leaf and thyme, and the sliced celery. Turn down the heat and simmer gently until the wine cooks away.

Meanwhile, in another non-stick pan, heat 2 teaspoons of olive oil with 2 teaspoons of butter. Sauté the mushrooms in it with a sprinkle of salt and a pinch of cayenne until their excess liquid cooks away and they begin to colour. Add the remaining wine, lower the heat, and allow the wine to simmer down. Add the onions to the mushrooms.

Add the remaining butter to the pan in which you've sautéd the onions and let it melt. Stir in a tablespoon of flour and keep stirring over medium heat for a few minutes as it turns golden. Whisk in the hot stock and continue whisking as it thickens. Add this sauce to the mushrooms and onions, along with the parsley.

Simmer everything together very gently for about 10 more minutes. Serve with steamed rice or Rice Pilaf.

Serves 6.

Variation: If you can't find any fresh wild mushrooms at all, you could use 700 g (1½ lb) of fresh cultivated mushrooms, and about 50 g (2 oz) of dried porcini. Cover the porcini with hot water and let them soak until they are soft and pliable, at least 30 minutes, then drain, reserving the water. Clean the mushrooms well and slice them. Proceed as above, combining the soaked porcini with the sliced fresh mushrooms. Filter the soaking liquid and add it to the broth.

RICE PILAF

6 spring onions, thinly sliced
1 tablespoon butter
250 g (9 oz) long-grain white rice

825 ml (28 fl oz) vegetable stock (see page 459), heated
salt to taste

optional: chopped flat-leaf parsley, basil, or tarragon
freshly grated Parmesan cheese

In a medium sauté pan, sauté the sliced spring onions in the butter until they are soft. Add the rice and stir it into the onions and butter for a minute or two. Add the heated stock, and a little salt only if needed.

Cover the pan, lower the heat, and simmer very gently for 25 minutes. Turn off the heat and leave the rice covered for another 5 minutes. Uncover, fluff with a fork, and serve, with or without the optional garnishes.

Serves 6.

CRANBERRY SAUCE

350 g (12 oz) fresh cranberries   1 teaspoon ground cinnamon
1 large orange   dash of ground cloves
175 g (6 oz) sugar

Wash the cranberries and discard any that are soft or spoiled.

Finely grate the zest of the orange. Cut away and discard all the white pith, and cut the orange into a few pieces. Put the orange pieces and the grated zest into the container of a blender with enough water to make 250 ml (8 fl oz), and process until the orange is roughly chopped.

Combine the liquid in a heavy-bottomed saucepan with the sugar, cinnamon, and cloves, and bring to a boil, stirring to dissolve the sugar. Add the cranberries, return to a boil, and stir over medium heat for 8–10 minutes. Use a long-handled wooden spoon – this stuff can really spit.

When most of the cranberries have popped and the liquid is somewhat thickened, the sauce is done. Pour it into a serving dish and allow it to cool, then chill.

Serves 6–8 as a garnish.

BASQUE CAKE

This is a lovely cake, made from a delicate, biscuit-like pastry filled with crème patissière.

for the crème pâtissière
3 large egg yolks
125 g (4 oz) sugar
45 g (1¾ oz) flour
pinch of salt
500 ml (16 fl oz) milk
2 tablespoons cream
1 teaspoon vanilla extract

for the pastry
300 g (10 oz) + 2 tablespoons
  white flour
125 g (4 oz) sugar
pinch of salt
1 teaspoon baking powder
150 g (5 oz) cold butter
grated zest of 1 orange
grated zest of ½ lemon
1 egg
2 tablespoons melted butter
icing sugar

Make the crème pâtissière first, so that it has time to cool completely. Beat the egg yolks with the sugar until they are pale and creamy. Beat in the flour and salt. Combine the milk, cream, and vanilla in a heavy-bottomed saucepan and heat to a simmer. Beating constantly with a whisk, gradually add the hot milk to the egg yolk mixture. When all the milk has been whisked in, return the mixture to the saucepan and whisk over a medium flame as it returns to a simmer. Continue whisking steadily as the sauce thickens to the consistency of custard. This will take about 5 minutes.

Transfer the crème pâtissière to a bowl and allow it to cool completely, giving it a stir with the whisk every now and then to keep the top from drying out.

The pastry can be made in moments with a food processor. Put 300 g (10 oz) of flour, the sugar, salt, and baking powder into the container of a food processor fitted with the steel blade. Add the cold butter, cut in 6 or 7 pieces, and the grated orange and lemon zest. Process until the mixture resembles fine breadcrumbs. Add the egg and process again until a dough forms and begins to hold together.

To make the pastry by hand, sift together 300 g (10 oz) of flour with the sugar, salt, and baking powder. Add the cold butter, cut in small pieces, and the zest, and cut in the butter with 2 knives or with a pastry cutter until the mixture resembles fine breadcrumbs. Lightly beat the egg, add it to the flour mixture, and stir it in with a fork until a dough forms and begins to hold together. Work the dough lightly with your hands for a few moments, just until it can be formed into a ball.

Cover the pastry dough and chill it for about 20 minutes. Divide the dough into 2 equal parts. Roll out the first half of the dough between 2 sheets of waxed paper into a circle 30 cm (12 inches) in diameter. Put the rolled pastry away to chill again, still covered with waxed paper. Roll the second piece out the same way into a circle about 27 cm (11 inches) in diameter, and allow it to chill again.

Butter a 25 cm (10 inch) springform tin. Gently peel away the waxed paper from the larger circle of pastry and fit it into the cake tin, forming a 2.5 cm (1 inch) high edge all around. Brush the bottom of the pastry with the melted butter, and dust it lightly with the 2 tablespoons of flour. Fill the pastry with the crème patissière.

Remove the waxed paper from the smaller circle of pastry and lay it over the filling. Press the edges of pastry together carefully to seal them, and form a smooth, even rim around the perimeter of the cake. This pastry is very tender, and easy to mould with your fingers.

Bake the cake at 150°C/300°F/Gas 2 about 45–50 minutes. It should be a light golden brown, and tremble only slightly when moved.

Allow the cake to cool on a rack in its tin for about 10 minutes, then remove the outside of the tin and let the cake finish cooling to room temperature. Dust the top of the cake with sieved icing sugar.

Makes one 25 cm (10 inch) cake, 10–12 servings.

WILD MUSHROOM RISOTTO DINNER

❧

Toasts with Grilled Chèvre

Roasted Beetroot, Asparagus and Garlic Salad

Wild Mushroom Risotto

Apple Crisp

Here's a terrific dinner that can be served to company or to family. It can be simplified if need be, or can be as elegant as you want.

It is a good winter dinner, and one of the best things about it is how beautifully it goes with your best red wines. 'Buy on bread and sell on cheese' is the wine merchant's motto, and you know why when you bite into creamy, warm goat's cheese on a slice of baguette, then sip your wine.

Wild mushrooms are also known for their affinity to red wines. Burgundies and generous Italian Chiantis are our favourites with this risotto.

The salad of roasted beetroot and asparagus can be served as a course of its own, between the chèvre and the risotto, if you've got someone willing to stand at the stove and stir risotto. If that risotto-stirrer is you, then sip wine and nibble cheese toasts while you stir, and just serve the salad on a smaller plate alongside the bowls of risotto.

Dessert is a refreshing, old-fashioned Apple Crisp.

For a simpler meal, eliminate the Toasts with Grilled Chèvre, and replace the Apple Crisp with a good store-bought ice cream or sorbet.

TOASTS WITH GRILLED CHÈVRE

This is a very tasty little nibble before dinner, and just the idea of layering butter and cheese this way adds a quality of thrilling recklessness to any event.

1 baguette
butter to taste

225–300 g (8–10 oz) fresh
white chèvre (goat's cheese)

Cut the baguette into 18–20 slices, and spread them thinly with softened butter. Arrange the buttered slices on a baking sheet and toast them in a hot oven (200°C/400°F/Gas 6) until they are crisp and evenly golden on top, about 7 or 8 minutes.

Allow the toasts to cool slightly, then spread them thickly with a semi-soft fresh goat's cheese, using about 2 tablespoons per slice. Put the cheese toasts under a preheated grill for a few minutes, until the cheese is soft and hot through, about 3 or 4 minutes. Watch them carefully to be sure they don't burn, and serve at once when they are done.

Serves 6–8.

ROASTED BEETROOT, ASPARAGUS AND
GARLIC SALAD

This is a beautiful salad – red and bright green, arranged together at the last minute. The flavour is superb as the sweetness of the garlic-infused beetroot plays against the freshness of asparagus, all of it lightly marinated.

900 g (2 lb) beetroots (small if
**   possible)**
1 head garlic
450 g (1 lb) slender green
**   asparagus**
60 ml (2 fl oz) + 1 tablespoon
**   olive oil**

salt to taste
2 tablespoons balsamic
**   vinegar**
60 ml (2 fl oz) fresh orange
**   juice**
1 tablespoon minced onion
pepper to taste

Trim the beetroots, leaving 2.5 cm (1 inch) of stem, and scrub them well. Break the garlic up into individual cloves, but don't peel them. Put the beetroots in a glass baking dish, and scatter the garlic cloves evenly over them. Add about 120 ml (4 fl oz) of water to the dish, cover tightly with a lid or with foil, and cook in a 200°C/400°F/Gas 6 oven for about 1 hour, until perfectly tender. The time will vary a bit depending on the size of the beetroot.

Meanwhile, wash the asparagus stalks and trim off any tough ends. Drizzle them with a tablespoon of olive oil, roll them around on a baking sheet until they are evenly coated, spread them out, and sprinkle them with salt. Set aside until the beetroots are cooked.

When the beetroots are tender, allow them to cool slightly so you can handle them, then peel and cut them into wedges or slices.

At the same time, raise the oven temperature to 230°C/450°F/Gas 8 and roast the prepared asparagus stalks for 15–20 minutes, depending on their thickness, until tender but not browned.

Squeeze about 10 cloves of the soft, cooked garlic into a bowl and mash it well with a fork. Add the remaining 60 ml (2 fl oz) of olive oil, the balsamic vinegar, orange juice, minced onion, salt, and pepper, and whisk together thoroughly.

In separate bowls, add 4 tablespoons of the dressing to the beetroots and 2 tablespoons to the asparagus. Toss gently to coat, and leave the vegetables to marinate for a few hours.

Just before serving, arrange the beetroot and asparagus on individual plates in an alternating pattern. Don't toss them together, or the beetroot will stain everything! Serve this salad at room temperature.

Serves 6–8.

WILD MUSHROOM RISOTTO

A delicious risotto can be made with almost any of the commonly available edible wild mushrooms, but the ones with the most intense, woodsy flavours are my favourites. I like porcini the best, and if I can get fresh ones I'm thrilled. Because they are not often available where I live, I usually combine 450 g (1 lb) of other fresh mushrooms with a small amount of dried porcini to intensify the flavour of the dish, which works very well.

700 g (1½ lb) fresh wild mushrooms (porcini, morels, shiitake, or other flavourful varieties), or 450 g (1 lb) fresh wild mushrooms and 40 g (1½ oz) dried porcini
1.5–1.7 litres (2½–3 pints) vegetable stock (see page 459) or chicken stock
2 tablespoons olive oil

1 teaspoon butter
1 clove garlic, minced
dash of salt
1 medium onion, chopped
350 g (12 oz) Arborio rice
90 ml (3 fl oz) Marsala
175 ml (6 fl oz) dry white wine
75 g (3 oz) grated Parmesan cheese, more for the table
6 tablespoons chopped flat-leaf parsley

Prepare the mushrooms. Clean them carefully under running water to get rid of all the grit, and trim them as needed. Cut them into thin strips or small chunks, depending on the size and variety. If you are using dried porcini, soak them in enough boiling water to cover for about 30 minutes, or until they are pliable, then rinse them carefully under running water. Chop them coarsely, and strain the soaking water through a coffee filter. Add the strained water to the stock and set aside.

Heat 1 tablespoon of olive oil and the butter in a non-stick pan, and stir the garlic in it for a minute. Add the prepared fresh mushrooms and a dash of salt, and sauté them, stirring frequently, until they release their moisture. Add the soaked and chopped porcini and keep stirring over medium heat until all the mushrooms are tender and colouring around the edges.

Heat the remaining tablespoon of oil in a large non-stick sauté pan and stir the chopped onion in it over medium heat until it is soft and barely golden. At the same time, heat the stock to a simmer, cover it, and keep it warm.

Add the rice to the sautéd onion and stir together for a few moments. Add the Marsala and keep stirring as it cooks away – this will take a few seconds. Add the white wine, and when it has cooked away, stir in the sautéd mushrooms and about 250 ml (8 fl oz) of the hot stock. Adjust the flame so that the stock simmers gently with the rice, and stir it slowly with a wooden spoon.

When the stock has almost all been absorbed, add another 250 ml (8 fl oz) or so, and continue in the same manner, stirring as often as possible, until most of the stock is used and the rice is *al dente* – tender but firm. It will take about 20–25 minutes.

When the rice has reached the right texture, stir in a last 120 ml (4 fl oz) of broth, 75 g (3 oz) of Parmesan cheese, and the chopped parsley. Serve the risotto at once, in warmed shallow bowls, and pass additional Parmesan cheese at the table.

Serves 6–8.

APPLE CRISP

for the filling	*for the topping*
1.6 kg (3½ lb) crisp, juicy apples	75 g (3 oz) coarsely chopped walnuts
2 tablespoons freshly squeezed lemon juice	65 g (2½ oz) flour
125 g (4 oz) sugar	175 g (6 oz) dark brown sugar
1 teaspoon ground cinnamon	½ teaspoon ground cinnamon
2 tablespoons plain flour	3 tablespoons cold butter
	75 g (3 oz) rolled oats
	1 egg white

Quarter the apples, peel and core them, and slice them crosswise. Toss the apple slices with the lemon juice, sugar, cinnamon, and flour. Spread the prepared apple mixture evenly in a large, shallow gratin dish.

Spread the chopped walnuts on a baking sheet and toast them in a 120°C/250°F/Gas ½ oven for about 25 minutes, then remove them and set them aside.

For the topping, combine the flour, brown sugar, and cinnamon in a food processor and process briefly. Add the cold butter, cut in pieces, and process again until the mixture has an evenly grainy texture, with no large chunks of butter. Add the rolled oats and process for a few seconds only. Add the egg white, and process for a few seconds again, until the mixture starts to form clumps.

Using your hands, sprinkle the topping evenly over the apples, breaking apart the largest clumps if necessary. Bake the crisp in a 190°C/375°F/Gas 5 oven for about 35 minutes. The apples should be simmering and the topping crisp and brown.

Allow the crisp to cool slightly, then sprinkle the toasted walnuts over the top and serve. This is best served warm, with a little scoop of vanilla ice cream.

Serves 8.

WILD MUSHROOM COBBLER DINNER

❦

Revised Caesar Salad

Wild Mushroom Cobbler

Cranberry-Chilli Sauce

Pumpkin Cream

Deep-dish pies are among the homey, familiar foods that children and adults alike adore, especially when the days close in with darkness, damp, and chill. I was fooling around with the idea of a hearty pie for supper and started with an assortment of flavourful mushrooms and lots of onions. Then, because I wanted to keep it simple and not too heavy, I made a buttermilk scone topping. My children took one look and said, 'That's not a pie, Mom. It's a cobbler.' And so it is.

A big plate of cobbler with a spoonful of cranberry sauce is the centre of this meal. A crunchy green salad completes it. While you can serve any tossed salad you like, I decided on an old favourite, the Caesar, slightly revised to eliminate the raw egg and reduce the amount of olive oil a bit.

In keeping with the mood, dessert is a lovely Pumpkin Cream – everything a cream should be yet reminiscent of pumpkin pie. This is a perfect 'nursery sweet' but completely elegant as well. It's even more beautiful than a classic cream when unmoulded on to a platter in its glaze of liquid caramel.

REVISED CAESAR SALAD

The original Caesar salad is an abiding favourite, having survived time, changing fashion, numerous weird and perverse variations, and the certain knowledge that too much oil just isn't good for us. It's a delicious salad, and that's a fact.

But nothing's sacred, that's another fact, so here's a delicious variation. It calls for a lighter hand with the olive oil, and replaces the nearly raw egg with a spoonful of mayonnaise. These are minor changes – the essential flavours of olive oil, lemon juice, Worcestershire, and Parmesan cheese remain clear and true, and the crunchy, home-made garlic croûtons are there. It's just a little less of a production to make and a little easier on your health, so now, if you like, *you can have it every day*!

2 cloves garlic
5 tablespoons fruity green
   olive oil
12–16 slices from a baguette
   (sourdough if possible)
salt to taste
3–4 heads romaine lettuce,
   hearts only
3 tablespoons freshly
   squeezed lemon juice

1 tablespoon Worcestershire
   sauce
1–2 tablespoons reduced-fat
   mayonnaise
50–75 g (2–3 oz) freshly
   grated Parmesan cheese
freshly ground black pepper

Crush the garlic cloves a little with the flat of a knife, then peel and chop them coarsely. Combine the garlic in a dish with 2 tablespoons of olive oil and let steep for about 15 minutes.

Cut 12–16 thick slices from a baguette. (You can use ordinary French bread, but I prefer sourdough.) Using a pastry brush, very lightly brush a little garlic oil on both sides of each slice, then sprinkle with salt. Cut the slices into thirds or quarters, spread them on a baking sheet, and toast them in a 200°C/400°F/Gas 6 oven for 15–20 minutes, or until they are crisp and golden brown around the edges.

Wash the lettuce, set aside the large, dark green outer leaves for another use, and tear up the crisp, lighter green inner leaves. Spin them dry in a salad spinner and put them in a big, wide salad bowl.

In the container of a blender, combine the remaining 3 tablespoons of olive oil, the lemon juice, Worcestershire sauce, a pinch of salt, and 1–2 tablespoons of mayonnaise, depending on how 'creamy' you like your dressing. For a more assertive garlic taste, add a bit of the chopped garlic you used for the croûton oil. Give all this a brief spin, drizzle it over the lettuce, and toss. Add the grated Parmesan cheese and a few turns of the pepper mill, and toss again. Scatter the croûtons over the top, or toss them in with the lettuce, and serve.

Serves 6–8.

WILD MUSHROOM COBBLER

for the filling
900 g (2 lb) red onions
2½ tablespoons olive oil
2½ tablespoons butter
salt to taste
25 g (1 oz) dried porcini
450 g (1 lb) fresh wild
  mushrooms, such as porcini,
  field mushrooms, oyster
  mushrooms, or a
  combination
2 cloves garlic, chopped
pinch of dried thyme
pinch of cayenne
freshly ground black pepper
  to taste
120 ml (4 fl oz) dry red wine
1½ tablespoons flour
350 ml (12 fl oz) low-fat milk,
  heated

for the topping
350 g (10 oz) plain flour
1 teaspoon bicarbonate of
  soda
2 teaspoons baking powder
1 teaspoon salt
4 tablespoons chilled butter
75 g (3 oz) freshly grated
  Parmesan cheese
300–325 ml (10–11 fl oz)
  buttermilk

Prepare the filling: peel, quarter, and slice the red onions. In a large non-stick pan, heat a tablespoon of olive oil and a tablespoon of butter, add the onions and a good sprinkle of salt, and cook over low heat, stirring often, for about an hour. The onions will gradually soften and eventually caramelize to a golden-brown colour and incredible sweetness.

Pour boiling water over the dried porcini and leave them to soak for at least 30 minutes. Clean, trim, and slice the fresh mushrooms. When the dried porcini are soft, rinse them carefully and chop them finely. Strain the soaking water through a coffee filter and reserve it.

In another large non-stick pan, heat 1½ tablespoons of olive oil and ½ tablespoon of butter. Add the chopped garlic to it and stir for 1 minute, then add the sliced fresh mushrooms and a little salt. Sauté the mushrooms, stirring often, until they start to release their liquid. Add the chopped porcini, a pinch of thyme, a pinch of cayenne, and freshly ground black pepper to taste, and keep cooking over medium heat until the excess liquid has cooked away, and the mushrooms are sizzling and beginning to colour.

Add the red wine, stirring as it cooks away, then add the soaking liquid from the dried mushrooms. Combine the mushrooms with the caramelized onions and simmer them all together for a few minutes.

In a small, heavy-bottomed saucepan, melt the remaining tablespoon of butter and stir in 1½ tablespoons flour. Stir the roux over a medium heat for 3−4 minutes, until it is golden. Add the heated milk, whisking steadily. Keep stirring with a whisk for several minutes, as the sauce thickens. Stir the white sauce into the onions and mushrooms. Taste, and correct the seasoning with more salt or pepper as needed.

Pour the mushroom mixture into a lightly buttered medium-sized gratin dish, spreading it evenly.

Prepare the scone dough: combine the flour, bicarbonate of soda, baking powder, and salt in the container of a food processor. Add the chilled butter, cut in chunks, and process briefly, until the mixture has the texture of coarse meal. Add the Parmesan cheese and process for a few seconds.

Transfer the mixture to a bowl and stir in the buttermilk, just until a dough forms. It will be thick and sticky; don't overmix it.

Spoon the scone dough on to the mushrooms, distributing it more or less evenly over the top. Bake the cobbler in a preheated 200°C/400°F/Gas 6 oven for about 25 minutes. The scone topping should be lightly golden brown.

Serve hot, with a green salad, with cranberry sauce or a chutney, or with your favourite relish.

Serves 8.

Cranberry-Chilli Sauce (see page 157)

PUMPKIN CREAM

This excellent dessert combines some of the best qualities of those two universal favourites, pumpkin pie and crème caramel. It makes a nice change from classic crème caramel, and the flavour of the pumpkin is beautiful with the caramel sauce.

400 g (14 oz) sugar
300 ml (10 fl oz) whole milk
300 ml (10 fl oz) evaporated milk
5 large eggs
¼ teaspoon salt

400 ml (14 fl oz) puréed pumpkin
2 teaspoons ground cinnamon
1 teaspoon ground ginger
¼ teaspoon ground allspice

Select a 2.4 litre (4 pint) baking dish, perhaps a soufflé dish or a casserole. Heat the dish in a 200°C/400°F/Gas 6 oven as you melt 225 g (8 oz) of the sugar in a heavy-bottomed pan over a medium flame. When the sugar is entirely melted and a rich golden caramel colour, put on your thickest pot-holder gloves, take out the heated baking dish, pour the caramel into it, then immediately tilt the dish around so that the caramel coats both the bottom and the sides. Set the prepared dish aside.

Scald all the milk, stopping short of boiling. In a mixing bowl, beat the eggs with the remaining sugar until they are smooth and getting thick. Add the salt, the pumpkin, and the spices, and beat again. Pour the scalded milk through a strainer and add it to the pumpkin mixture, still beating.

Pour the pumpkin mixture into the prepared baking dish, and place that dish in a larger baking pan which has at least 2.5 cm (1 inch) of water in it. Put the dish carefully into the oven, lower the heat to 180°C/350°F/Gas 4, and bake for an hour, or slightly longer. The cream should be golden brown on top, it should tremble only slightly when shaken, and a thin knife inserted in the centre should come out clean.

Set the dish on a rack and allow it to cool to room temperature, then cover it tightly and chill it in the refrigerator. To unmould, first loosen the sides by slipping a very thin, sharp knife around the edges. When the cream moves freely in its dish, invert a large serving plate over the baking dish and, holding the two securely together, quickly turn them over. The cream will drop out on to the serving platter, and the gleaming brown caramel sauce will pour out around it – a thing of beauty. Cut it into thick wedges to serve, and spoon a little of the sauce over each wedge.

Serves 8.

BUCKWHEAT CRÊPES WITH WILD MUSHROOMS

✤

Tomatillo and Squash Soup or Green Tomato and Squash Soup

Buckwheat Crêpes with Potato and Mushroom Filling

small green salad

Winter Fruit Compote

Gingerbread Biscotti

I don't think I ever had such an instant hit with a new recipe as I did with this soup. Everyone who ate it at my dinner party immediately asked for the recipe, and then they all went home and actually *made* it. By week's end, there wasn't a Kabocha squash to be found in our small-town markets.

Buckwheat crêpes filled with a hearty mixture of mushrooms, onions, and potatoes are a quintessential winter dish – substantial food, yet not overwhelmingly rich. The distinct flavour and texture of buckwheat is a pleasure. With the wild mushrooms and the little bit of cheese, this is a dish that calls out for a wonderful big red wine. Plates can be garnished with a small side salad, but avoid sharp, piquant dressings, as they fight with the wine.

If you are preparing this meal for company, it is nice to know that most of it can be prepared well ahead of time. The soup, crêpes, and compote can all be made the day before with no loss of quality at all. You should, however, rewarm both the crêpes and filling before rolling the crêpes, and that part should be done just before dinner.

TOMATILLO AND SQUASH SOUP

700 g (1½ lb) tomatillos
450 g (1 lb) ripe red tomatoes
10–12 cloves garlic, unpeeled
salt to taste
800–900 g (1¾–2 lb) Kabocha
squash, peeled and diced
(or acorn squash if you
absolutely can't get
Kabocha)
900 ml (1½ pints) vegetable
stock (see page 459)

600 ml (1 pint) water, more if
needed
1 tablespoon olive oil
2 large onions, quartered and
sliced
1 small bunch coriander,
de-stemmed and coarsely
chopped
2 dried red chillies

Take the husks off the tomatillos, wash them, and cut in half. Trim the tomatoes and quarter them. Arrange the tomatillos, tomatoes, and all but one clove of the unpeeled garlic on a baking sheet. Sprinkle lightly with salt and roast in a 230°C/450°F/Gas 8 oven for 35–45 minutes, until the vegetables are soft and beginning to char in spots. Remove and let them cool for a few minutes.

While the vegetables are roasting, combine the diced squash, the vegetable stock, and 500 ml (16 fl oz) of water in an ample pan and simmer, covered, for at least 45 minutes, or until the squash is very tender.

At the same time, heat the olive oil in a large non-stick pan and add the onions and the remaining clove of garlic, peeled and minced, and a dash of salt. Cook over medium heat, stirring often, until the onions are caramelized to a dark golden brown.

When the roasted vegetables are ready and cool enough to handle, scrape the red tomatoes off their skins with a spoon. Squeeze the soft garlic out of the cloves and discard the husks. Combine the red tomato pulp, the tomatillos, and the soft garlic in a blender or food processor with a little water, and purée them.

Add the purée to the stock and squash, along with the caramelized onions and the chopped coriander. If the stock has been greatly reduced during cooking, add back some water.

Toast the dried red chillies in a hot pan or over a flame until

they blister or show black spots. Chop them, removing some of the
seeds for a milder flavour, and stir them into the soup. Simmer
everything together for 5–10 minutes. Serve hot, with warm corn
tortillas or any good bread.

Variation: If tomatillos can't be found, a very tasty version of this
soup can be made using green tomatoes and fresh lemon juice in
their place.

Quarter and roast 700 g (1½ lb) of green tomatoes along with
the red tomatoes, and when they are soft, peel off and discard their
skins. Then proceed as above until you purée the soup and combine
all the ingredients. At that point, stir in 1½–2 tablespoons of fresh
lemon juice and taste. Add more lemon juice to taste, or a touch
more salt if needed.

BUCKWHEAT CRÊPES WITH POTATO AND MUSHROOM FILLING

12–14 large Buckwheat Crêpes (see page 155)

for the filling
450 g (1 lb) shiitake or wild
  mushrooms
1 tablespoon + 1 teaspoon
  olive oil
1 tablespoon butter
2 cloves garlic, minced
salt to taste

3 large onions, chopped
2 large potatoes
120 ml (4 fl oz) dry white wine
coarsely chopped flat-leaf
  parsley
freshly ground black pepper
125 g (4 oz) grated Swiss or
  Fontina cheese

Clean the mushrooms and cut them in 1 cm (½ inch) dice. Heat a
tablespoon of olive oil and a teaspoon of butter in a large non-stick
pan and stir the minced garlic in it for a minute. Add the mushrooms
and a little salt, and sauté for 10–12 minutes, until they are tender
and starting to sizzle.

In another pan, cook the chopped onions in the remaining olive oil
and butter, with a dash of salt, until they are soft and turning golden.

Peel the potatoes and cut them in 1 cm (½ inch) dice. Combine them in a saucepan with the white wine and enough water just barely to cover them, as well as ½ teaspoon of salt. Bring the water to a boil, lower the heat to a simmer, cover the pan tightly, and cook for 10–15 minutes, until the potatoes are just tender. Remove the lid and continue cooking gently, stirring once or twice, until the liquid is reduced and thickened to a sauce. Stir in the sautéd onions and mushrooms, as well as chopped parsley and freshly ground black pepper to taste.

Allow the potato and mushroom mixture to cool slightly, then fill the crêpes. Spoon 2–3 rounded tablespoons of filling across the centre of each crêpe, then sprinkle a little grated cheese over the filling before rolling or folding the crêpe loosely over it. You should have about a dozen filled crêpes.

Cover the crêpes loosely with aluminium foil and bake in a 180°C/ 350°F/Gas 4 oven for 10–15 minutes, or until they are hot through and the cheese is completely melted.

Serves 6.

WINTER FRUIT COMPOTE

225 g (8 oz) dried nectarines or peaches (or a combination)
125 g (4 oz) dried plums
225 g (8 oz) dried figs
600 ml (1 pint) spring water

500 ml (16 fl oz) dry red wine
peel of 1 lemon
7.5 cm (3 inch) stick cinnamon
75 g (3 oz) cup sugar
1 teaspoon Pernod

garnish: ice cream

Cut the nectarines or peaches and the plums into wide strips. Leave the figs whole. Combine the fruit in a medium-sized non-reactive pan with the water and the wine. Remember – when cooking with wine, the rule is, if you don't want to drink it, don't cook with it. You don't have to use a rare or expensive wine, but it must be good; its flavour will tell.

Cut the lemon peel off in wide strips, and with a thin, sharp knife slice away the thick white pith and discard. Add the peel to the fruit, along with the cinnamon stick, sugar, and Pernod. Bring everything to a boil, lower the heat, and gently simmer for about 30 minutes. Add a bit more water if needed to keep everything just covered.

The fruit should be soft, but not falling apart. The liquid will have the consistency of a thin syrup, not too sweet and just slightly spicy from the cinnamon and lemon peel. The peel can be left in the syrup while the compote is refrigerated, but should be removed before serving.

Serve warm or cool, in wide, shallow bowls, with a scoop of ice cream added at the last moment. Cinnamon or anise ice cream would be great; so would a good, plain vanilla.

Serves 8–10.

Gingerbread Biscotti (see page 469)

LITTLE DINNER PARTIES FOR AUTUMN AND WINTER

A SIMPLE AUTUMN DINNER PARTY

❧

Simple Focaccia

cured olives, fennel wedges, celery, radishes
goat's cheese

Butter Bean Soup with Herbed Croûtons

Torta di Polenta with Three Cheeses

Roasted Tomato Sauce

Parfaits of Fruit and Mascarpone

This straightforward meal consists of a few easy foods that I really like. It's a warming, relaxing meal, good for appetites sharpened by chill air, and a very nice menu for a good bottle of red wine.

A focaccia hot from the oven turns a platter of raw vegetables and some cheese into a great first course. An old-fashioned bowl of steaming Butter Bean Soup with croûtons is a universal favourite, and the baked polenta is richly flavoured with cheese, then accented with the smoky taste of roasted tomatoes. The flavours are big and hearty, and familiar. A touch of elegance is added by the pretty dessert of sweet, ripe fruit, discreetly layered with mascarpone.

A practical note: Nothing is complicated to serve, and almost all the work can be done in advance, so you can enjoy the meal in the easygoing atmosphere it creates. The polenta just needs to be put in the oven at the right time. The parfaits should be assembled not long before you serve them, but the fruit and the mascarpone can be prepared ahead. Only the vegetables should be cut up at the last minute – fennel wedges really need to be fresh – but that's no problem.

SIMPLE FOCACCIA

A fresh, warm focaccia is a wonderful addition to almost any meal, and it's not much more trouble to make than stirring up a batch of cornbread. You need to start about 2½ hours before you want to eat, but there's only about 20 minutes of actual work involved.

It's a great thing to serve with an aperitif wine and some olives or chopped tomatoes if you have a gang of people hanging around in the kitchen while you finish cooking dinner. This is a very basic recipe, which can be varied endlessly with herbs and flavourings. Remember, don't make more than you need, because it's only good when it's fresh – but people love it, so you'll need more than you think.

7 g (¼ oz) dried yeast
300 ml (10 fl oz) warm water
pinch of sugar
1 teaspoon salt
3 tablespoons olive oil

350–400 g (12–14 oz) flour –
white, wholemeal, or a
combination
coarse sea salt to taste

In a large mixing bowl, dissolve the yeast in the warm water with the sugar, and leave it for about 15 minutes, until it starts to foam. Add the salt and half the olive oil, then start stirring in the flour, a scoop at a time.

When the dough is too stiff to stir with a spoon, turn it out on a well-floured board, sprinkle more flour on top of it, and begin kneading. Knead it gently, working in as much more of the flour as you must to keep it from sticking. When the dough is smooth and elastic, form it into a ball and put it in an oiled bowl, turning it once to coat it. Cover the bowl with a tea towel or with plastic wrap, and leave the dough in a warm place to rise for about 45 minutes, or until almost double in size.

Punch the dough down, lift it out of the bowl on to an oiled baking sheet, and pat or roll it out into a large, thick oval, about 30 × 40 cm (12 × 16 inches). Cover it with a tea towel and leave it to rise again for at least 30 minutes, or until almost doubled in size.

Brush the focaccia delicately with the remaining olive oil, and sprinkle it with some coarse sea salt. If you like, you can cut shallow diagonal slashes in the top with a sharp knife, in a crisscross pattern. Or dimple the top of the focaccia with your fingertips, but don't be too aggressive − you don't want to punch it down again.

Bake the focaccia in a preheated 230°C/450°F/Gas 8 oven for 20−30 minutes, or until it is golden on top and sounds hollow when the bottom crust is tapped. Cut it in squares and serve it hot or warm.

This makes 1 loaf, and the recipe may be doubled.

BUTTER BEAN SOUP

**450 g (1 lb) dried butter beans
   or lima beans
pinch of bicarbonate of soda
1 head garlic
1 large red onion
1 teaspoon salt
2−3 sprigs rosemary**

**1 bay leaf
2 tablespoons green olive oil
750 ml (1¼ pints) vegetable
   stock (see page 459) or
   chicken stock
freshly ground black pepper
   to taste**

garnishes: Herbed Croûtons (recipe follows)
   grated Parmesan cheese

Soak the beans overnight in plenty of water with a pinch of bicarbonate soda in it. Drain and rinse the beans.

Peel the garlic, and peel and coarsely chop the red onion. In a large, heavy-bottomed pan, combine the beans, 2.4 litres (4 pints) water, the salt, rosemary, garlic, onion, bay leaf, and a tablespoon of olive oil. Bring the water to a boil, reduce the heat, and simmer gently for about 2 hours, until the beans are very soft and much of the water is absorbed.

Remove the bay leaf and the stems from the rosemary, then purée the soup in batches in a blender until it is creamy. Add the stock and heat to simmering, then taste and correct the seasoning with additional salt and some pepper if needed.

Serve hot, drizzled with the remaining olive oil and garnished with Herbed Croûtons and Parmesan cheese.

Serves 8.

HERBED CROÛTONS

This is one of the best things to do with leftover bread, but you have to get around to it before the bread becomes completely dry. The type of bread is not too important, as long as it's a type you like, and the herbs can be varied.

225 g (8 oz) bread cubes (white, sourdough, whole wheat, or rye, or a mix; fresh or a few days old, but not dry)

2 tablespoons olive oil

1 teaspoon fresh rosemary leaves, chopped

1 teaspoon fresh thyme leaves

1 teaspoon minced garlic (optional)

salt and pepper

Cut your bread into cubes of the size you like.

Heat the olive oil, herbs, and garlic in a large, non-stick sauté pan for a minute, then add the bread cubes and immediately start tossing them in the oil until all of them are as evenly coated with oil and herbs as possible; this will never be perfect, but don't worry.

Spread the croûtons on a baking sheet, sprinkle them liberally with salt and, if you like, pepper, and bake them in the oven at 160°C/325°F/Gas 3 for 20–30 minutes, or as long as it takes to make them crispy and golden brown. You might want to move and turn them once during the baking time.

Allow the croûtons to cool and use them as you like, in salads and soups.

TORTA DI POLENTA WITH THREE CHEESES

Polenta can be made plain or fancy. In this version, simple polenta is mixed with a number of savoury ingredients, moulded into a nice round shape, then baked in the oven and served with a sauce. It's extremely tasty, and does not suffer at all from being prepared hours ahead of time, so is an ideal party dish.

1 large clove garlic, minced
1 leek, white part only, chopped
1 red onion, chopped
2 tablespoons olive oil
900 ml (1½ pints) light vegetable stock (see page 459)
1 teaspoon butter

175 g (6 oz) yellow cornmeal (polenta) (see page 260)
40 g (1½ oz) fresh white goat's cheese
25 g (1 oz) smoked Gouda cheese, cut in 0.5 cm (¼ inch) dice
25 g (1 oz) Parmesan cheese, grated
salt, if needed

Sauté the garlic, leek, and onion in the olive oil, in a non-stick pan, until they are golden. Heat the stock with the butter, whisk in the cornmeal, and simmer it, stirring constantly with a wooden spoon, for about 10–15 minutes, or until it is thick. Remove the polenta from the heat and stir in the cooked onions and the goat's cheese, then the diced Gouda cheese and the grated Parmesan. Taste, and add salt only if needed. Pour the hot polenta into a buttered deep pie dish or round casserole, and smooth the top. Cover and chill for 45 minutes or longer.

Slide a butter knife around the edges of the polenta to loosen it, then invert it on to a buttered baking sheet. Bake the torta at 200°C/ 400°F/Gas 6 for 12–15 minutes. It should be hot through and just barely crisping on the outside.

Cut the torta into wedges and serve with Roasted Tomato Sauce.

Serves 6–8.

ROASTED TOMATO SAUCE

For years I thought the simple tomato sauce I made in a pan, sautéing garlic and tomatoes in a bit of olive oil, was as easy as it could get, but this may be even easier. It takes time in the oven, but hardly any work. More important, roasting tomatoes concentrates their flavour to a dark, rich essence that is a mystical experience for tomato addicts.

1.8 kg (4 lb) very ripe
  tomatoes
450 g (1 lb) mild onions
5 large cloves garlic
2 tablespoons fruity green
  olive oil

1 teaspoon salt, more to taste
3 tablespoons coarsely
  chopped fresh basil

Peel the tomatoes in the usual way: cut a cross in the bottom of each one with a sharp knife and put them into boiling water for 1 minute. Remove them from the hot water directly into cold water, then slip off their skins and trim them over a bowl, catching all the juice.

Cut the tomatoes into large chunks or wedges. Peel and chop the onions. Peel and slice the garlic cloves.

Toss together all the ingredients, including the juice of the tomatoes, and spread it all evenly over a large baking sheet with edges.

Put the tomatoes in a 190°C/375° F/Gas 5 oven and roast them for about 2–2½ hours, stirring once after the first hour, then every 30 minutes or so. Most of the liquid will cook away, and the tomatoes will melt into a soft, thick, slightly caramelized marmalade. It's wonderful.

Serve this on pasta, with rice, on pizza, with polenta, in soups, in an omelette – alongside anything that goes well with tomatoes.

Makes about 600 ml (1 pint).

PARFAITS OF FRUIT AND MASCARPONE

I'm suggesting pears and berries for this dessert, but you could use many combinations of soft, ripe fruits. Sliced strawberries, kiwis, seedless grapes, pitted cherries, and cut-up peaches or apricots are all good ideas. You need 1 – 1.2 kg (2¼–2½ lb) of fruit in all.

4 ripe pears
juice and grated zest of 1 large
  lemon
350 g (12 oz) raspberries
350 g (12 oz) blackberries

3–4 tablespoons sugar
225 g (8 oz) mascarpone
175 ml (6 fl oz) cream
75 g (3 oz) icing sugar

garnish: grated sweet chocolate

Peel and core the pears and cut them into pieces. Sprinkle them with the lemon juice and toss. Add the berries and the sugar; a drop of cognac or some sympathetically flavoured liqueur could be added as well – entirely optional. Mix gently and leave for about 20 minutes.

Stir the mascarpone slowly with a whisk to soften it. Add the cream, icing sugar, and grated lemon zest. Continue whisking gently only until the mixture is smooth and holds soft shapes. Do not beat this with any vigour, as it can become stiff quickly.

Select 6 – 8 large goblets or parfait glasses. Put a rounded teaspoon of the mascarpone in the bottom of each glass, then spoon in the macerated fruit. Top with a rounded tablespoon of mascarpone. Dust the top with some grated sweet chocolate.

Mascarpone is heavenly, but a little goes a long way. Think of it as a garnish to the fruit compote, which is the body of this dessert.

Serves 6–8.

A MOROCCAN COUSCOUS DINNER

❧

A Relish Plate

Yogurt-cucumber Dip

pitta bread

Roasted Kabocha Squash and Green Tomatoes

Couscous with Moroccan Spices

*Chilled Orange Slices
in Grand Marnier and Cognac*

You will be surprised at how little effort it takes to prepare this interesting dinner. It looks like a dinner party, but can just as well be a comfortable family meal.

Each dish is quite simple. A relish plate that includes mint sprigs and green onions is the traditional start of many Middle Eastern meals. You could include other fresh herbs, such as basil, and add multi-coloured peppers or other vegetables to make it more elaborate. A fresh Yogurt-cucumber Dip, flavoured with more mint, and warmed pitta bread are served at the same time.

The roasted vegetables and couscous are an easy and plain dish, until they are enlightened by a sauce of gently fried spices in a reduction of stock. Then they take on a subtly exotic quality.

Orange slices chilled in a light, sweet syrup are the most refreshing dessert I know, and pure pleasure after anything rich or spicy. And because this meal, while delivering both rich and spicy flavours, is in fact not at all a heavy meal, you might even be tempted to add vanilla ice cream to those orange slices.

A RELISH PLATE

This can be simple or elaborate, as you wish. For me, the important thing is that there be some balance between the biting, peppery tastes and the cool, cleansing ones. Choose vegetables that are beautiful, fresh, and unblemished, and vary quantities according to the taste of your family or friends.

peppery tastes	*somewhere in between*
radishes	red or green peppers
green onions	fennel wedges
pickled peppers	mint sprigs

cool tastes
cucumbers
cherry tomatoes
sugar peas (eat the whole pod)

Wash and trim all the vegetables and cut them in spears, wedges, or strips, as desired. Arrange them to look pretty on a big platter, and try to do it as close as possible to the time you will serve it, so the vegetables do not lose their freshness. You can certainly prepare the plate an hour or two ahead of time, but if you do, sprinkle the vegetables with water, cover tightly with clingfilm, and refrigerate until it's time to serve.

YOGURT-CUCUMBER DIP

750 ml (1¼ pints) plain yogurt, or 250 ml (8 fl oz) yogurt + 225 g (8 oz) Yogurt Cheese (see page 85)	½ teaspoon salt, more if needed
	1 tablespoon chopped fresh dill
1 large cucumber, peeled, seeded, and chopped	1 tablespoon chopped fresh mint

Line a colander with 3 layers of cheesecloth and spoon the yogurt into it. Leave it to drain for several hours so that it is reduced in volume by at least a third. Discard the liquid that drains away. Or, for a quick way to get the same result, combine equal parts of plain yogurt and Yogurt Cheese.

Toss the chopped cucumbers in a bowl with the salt, then leave them in a colander to drain for at least 30 minutes. Rinse them quickly and squeeze out excess moisture.

Combine the drained yogurt, cucumbers, and chopped herbs, mix well, and taste. Add a touch of salt if you feel it is needed. Chill the mixture and stir it up again before serving. Serve with pitta bread, cut into wedges and lightly toasted.

Makes about 750 ml (1¼ pints).

ROASTED KABOCHA SQUASH AND GREEN TOMATOES

Tart green tomatoes, if you can find them, are the perfect foil for sweet Kabocha squash. If you can't find Kabocha, use acorn squash. Or try another great recipe, Roasted Yams with Green Tomatoes (see page 178), which is similar to this – and yams are easy to find.

1.4 kg (3 lb) Kabocha or acorn squash
900 g (2 lb) green tomatoes
700 g (1½ lb) red onions
575 g (1¼ lb) small red-skinned potatoes

6–8 cloves garlic
2 tablespoons olive oil
1–1½ teaspoons salt

Peel the squash, seed it, and cut it in 2 cm (¾ inch) cubes. The best method I've found to do this is to cut the squash in half with your biggest, sharpest knife, and scoop out the seeds. Then lay the halves cut side down and slice them in wide strips. Lay the strips on their sides and cut off the thick, hard rind in pieces, then cube the orange flesh. This method allows you to keep the cutting edge of your knife always safely aimed down towards the board, very important when applying pressure to a tough hide.

Cut the green tomatoes in 2.5 cm (1 inch) chunks. Peel the red onions and cut them in thin wedges. Scrub the potatoes and cut them in pieces no larger than the squash pieces. Peel the garlic cloves and slice the larger ones in half lengthwise.

Toss all the vegetables together with the olive oil and salt until they are evenly coated, spread them on two baking sheets, and roast them at 200°C/400° F/Gas 6 for about 1¼–1½ hours. Stir and turn the vegetables a couple of times in the course of the cooking time. They should be perfectly tender, with crisped, browned edges here and there.

Serve the vegetables with Couscous with Moroccan Spices.

Serves 8–10.

COUSCOUS WITH MOROCCAN SPICES

for the sauce
1 tablespoon olive oil
½ large onion, chopped
6 cloves garlic, finely chopped
1 teaspoon cumin seeds,
   lightly toasted and
   ground
1 teaspoon ground turmeric
½ teaspoon ground cinnamon
½ teaspoon ground coriander
¼ teaspoon cayenne or red
   pepper flakes
½ teaspoon sweet paprika
500 ml (16 fl oz) light
   vegetable stock (see
   page 460)

3 small red tomatoes, peeled
   and puréed
75 g (3 oz) dried currants
1–2 tablespoons fresh lime or
   lemon juice

for the couscous
500 ml (16 fl oz) vegetable
   stock (see page 459)
350 ml (12 fl oz) water
1 tablespoon butter
½ teaspoon salt
400 g (14 oz) couscous

Heat the olive oil in a non-stick pan and cook the chopped onion and garlic in it until the onion is soft and translucent. Stir in the ground, toasted cumin, turmeric, cinnamon, coriander, cayenne, and paprika. Continue stirring over medium heat for 2–3 minutes, then add the vegetable stock, puréed tomatoes, and currants. Simmer the sauce for 10 minutes.

Remove the sauce from the heat and stir in freshly squeezed lemon or lime juice to your taste. If you are not planning to use the sauce immediately and want to reheat it before serving, wait to add the citrus juice at the last minute.

To cook the couscous, heat the stock, water, butter, and salt together in a medium frying pan until the liquid boils. Reduce to a simmer, add the couscous, cover the pan tightly, and leave it on lowest heat for 5 minutes. Then remove the pan from the heat and leave it covered for another couple of minutes before fluffing the couscous with a fork.

Serve the couscous with roasted vegetables and pass the spicy sauce separately to spoon over it.

Serves 8—10.

CHILLED ORANGE SLICES IN GRAND MARNIER AND COGNAC

This is a very refreshing dessert, perfect after rich or spicy food. It happens to be a non-fat dessert, but that could be solved by adding a scoop of vanilla ice cream.

peel of 1 large orange, cut in julienne strips	8 medium navel oranges
450 g (1 lb) sugar	2 tablespoons Grand Marnier
600 ml (1 pint) water	2 tablespoons cognac

Prepare the peel first. Choose a large, firm orange with thick skin and cut away wide strips of the peel, 5—7.5 cm (2—3 inches) long. Using a very thin, sharp knife, slice away every bit of the white pith, until you have only the pure orange zest. Cut this lengthwise into matchsticks, discarding the trimmings.

In a medium-sized saucepan, dissolve the sugar in 500 ml (16 fl oz) of water. Add the orange peel strips and bring the liquid to a boil.

Adjust the flame and keep the syrup at a gentle boil for 10–15 minutes.

Meanwhile, peel all the oranges, cutting away all the white pith and outer membrane with a very sharp knife. Cut them crosswise into thick slices, about 1 cm (½ inch), and arrange them in close-fitting layers in a glass dish.

With a slotted spoon or a fork, lift out the strips of orange peel, allowing the syrup to drip off them back into the pan, and lay them out on a sheet of waxed paper. Cover them with another sheet, and set them aside. Add the Grand Marnier and the cognac to the syrup in the saucepan, as well as the additional 120 ml (4 fl oz) of water.

Pour the syrup over the orange slices in the dish; there should be just enough to cover them. If not, try using a dish in which they fit more compactly, or thin the syrup with a tiny bit more water. Cover the dish tightly with clingfilm and chill the orange slices for several hours or overnight.

Serve the oranges in individual shallow glass bowls, with a little of the syrup poured over several slices, and garnish each serving with a few strips of the candied peel.

Serves 8–10.

STUFFED CORN CRÊPES
IN MOLE

❧

*Salad of Frisée, Avocado, Grapefruit, and
Fennel*

*Corn Crêpes with Goat's Cheese Stuffing
in Mole Poblano*

Baked Pears in Caramel Syrup

Once, in Santa Fe, where there is so much good food that it makes
me dizzy to think about it, I had an amazing stuffed poblano pepper.
It was filled with goat's cheese, which in turn was studded with a
phantasmagoria of spicy, sweet, and tart flavours. I adapted the idea
of that cheese filling for these corn crêpes.

The *mole* sauce is a Mexican classic, combining chillies, hot and
sweet spices, savoury onions and garlic, and the richness of nuts and
chocolate, in an exotic and sensational amalgam. Making *mole* is
easier today than it was in the sixteenth century, when the nuns in
Puebla ground their spices and pounded almonds by hand in great
stone mortars, following formulas that were closely guarded secrets.
Where once religious dedication was required, now you just need
a food processor, and making *mole* is fun.

What's more, when your family and friends say, 'Wow, what's
in this sauce?' you can answer, 'Chocolate and chillies.'

Because the *mole* and the crêpes do take some time, the other
elements of the menu have been kept very simple. Start with a
tossed salad, combining frisée with avocado, grapefruit, and fennel.

Finish with a delicately spiced fruit dessert: pears, baked in a light
syrup infused with ginger and cinnamon. But don't hesitate to serve

fresh fruit if you'd like to; a perfectly ripe pear, served whole with a little paring knife, is both an elegant and a delicious ending to a meal. Sliced mangoes and papayas, or any sweet melon, would also be an excellent choice.

Leftovers: When you make *mole*, and go to the trouble of assembling all those ingredients, you may as well make a lot. Fortunately, it keeps terrifically well. Refrigerated, tightly covered, it will keep for at least 2 weeks. Frozen in a good container, it will keep for several months.

And what a useful sauce it is. Spoon it on tacos, stir it into soups and beans, spread it on quesadillas, and serve it with scrambled eggs. In Mexico, it is most frequently used as a basis for a turkey or chicken stew – large pieces of fowl are simmered in *mole* and then served with rice. And finally, it's a nice thing for dipping into with a tortilla chip.

SALAD OF FRISÉE, AVOCADO, GRAPEFRUIT, AND FENNEL

350 g (12 oz) frisée (1 large
  head or 2 small)
2 fennel bulbs, sliced
4 spring onions, thinly sliced
6 tablespoons coriander
  leaves

1 large avocado
1½–2 tablespoons lemon juice
3 tablespoons fruity green
  olive oil
salt and pepper to taste
2 large pink or red grapefruit

Wash the frisée well, tear it into bite-sized pieces, and spin it in a salad spinner or use kitchen towels to remove excess moisture. Wash and trim the fennel bulbs, cut them in half lengthwise, and slice very thinly. In a large salad bowl, toss together the endive, fennel, green onions, and coriander leaves.

Halve and peel the avocado, slice it, put the slices in a glass dish or bowl, and immediately pour the lemon juice over them. Drizzle the olive oil over the salad greens, add the avocado and lemon juice and a little salt and pepper, and toss the salad very gently with your hands until everything is well combined and lightly coated with dressing.

With a very sharp knife, slice the peel off the grapefruit, cutting away all the white pith, and then pull them apart into sections, peeling away the membranes. Scatter the grapefruit sections over the salad and serve.

Serves 8.

CORN CRÊPES WITH GOAT'S CHEESE STUFFING IN MOLE POBLANO

½ recipe Mole Poblano (recipe follows)

for the corn crêpes
3 large eggs
350 ml (12 fl oz) milk
175 ml (6 fl oz) water
½ teaspoon salt
150 g (5 oz) flour
65 g (2½ oz) masa harina (see page 38)
3 tablespoons melted butter + more for the pan

for the stuffing
450 g (1 lb) fresh white goat's cheese
3 eggs
2 fresh ears of corn
2 courgettes, diced
75 g (3 oz) sultanas
75 g (3 oz) lightly toasted pine-nuts
2–3 tablespoons diced green chillies
salt if needed
melted butter

garnishes: sour cream
coriander sprigs

Prepare the Mole Poblano (see next recipe).

To make the crêpes: beat the eggs, milk, water, and salt together, then beat in the white flour, the masa harina, and the melted butter. Or combine all the ingredients in a blender and blend until perfectly smooth, stopping to scrape down the sides as needed. Let the batter rest for at least an hour.

Heat a crêpe pan and brush it with butter, then pour in just enough batter to cover the bottom of the pan by quickly tilting it around – about 3–4 tablespoons. Cook for a minute or two on medium heat, until the crêpe is golden brown on the bottom, then gently peel it up and flip it over. Cook the other side until golden and spotted with brown, usually less than a minute. Continue this way until all the batter is used.

Stack the crêpes and keep them covered with a slightly damp tea towel as you work. The crêpes can be made several hours or a day ahead and kept in the refrigerator, tightly covered with clingfilm. If you refrigerate crêpes, allow them to return to room temperature before filling or rolling them. If handling crêpes that are still cold, heat a non-stick pan and place each crêpe in it for a few seconds to warm it up before filling it; this softens the crêpe and keeps it from cracking.
Makes about 18–20 crêpes.

To make the filling: first sauté the diced courgettes in a little butter with a drop of lemon juice and set aside. Soften the goat's cheese with a fork. Lightly beat the eggs and stir them thoroughly into the cheese.

Strip the corn kernels from the cobs and blanch them for about a minute, then drain them completely.

Stir together the cheese mixture, the courgettes, the corn kernels, and all the remaining ingredients except the melted butter. Taste, and add salt only if it is really needed.

To assemble and serve the crêpes: lightly butter a large baking sheet. Take one pliable crêpe at a time and mound 2 rounded tablespoons of filling down the centre of it, leaving plenty of room all around. Roll the crêpe over the filling, folding in the sides envelope-style as you finish rolling it up. Fill and fold all the crêpes this way. Arrange the crêpes, seam side down, close together on the prepared baking sheet. Brush their tops lightly with softened or melted butter. Bake the crêpes for about 25 minutes at 180°C/350°F/Gas 4 – they will be slightly puffed and golden brown.

Meanwhile, heat the *mole* to a simmer. Spoon about 6 tablespoons of *mole* on to each plate, place one or two of the hot stuffed crêpes on top of the *mole*, and garnish with a little dollop of sour cream and a few coriander sprigs. Serve at once.
Serves 8–10 as a main course, 18–20 as a little dish in a series of courses.

MOLE POBLANO

Mole is to Mexican cuisine what pesto is to Italian – any sauce in which a number of different ingredients are ground or pounded together into a paste. However, the rich, dark *mole* from Puebla, in which chillies and chocolate combine with a great many other ingredients, is probably the most famous. This recipe is very faithful to the classic version, the main exception being that I eliminate the lard. In my view it's an improvement, as this is already a very rich sauce.

75 g (3 oz) dried ancho
  chillies*

75 g (3 oz) dried pasilla
  chillies*

50 g (2 oz) dried mulato
  chillies*

750–900 ml (1¼–1½ pints)
  water

450 g (1 lb) tomatoes, peeled,
  with their juice, or
  equivalent weight of
  canned tomatoes

2 large onions, peeled and
  quartered

4 cloves garlic, peeled

1 teaspoon salt, more to taste

1½ teaspoons coriander seeds

1½ teaspoons anise seeds

4 tablespoons sesame seeds,
  lightly toasted

175 g (6 oz) blanched almonds

75 g (3 oz) pine-nuts

75 g (3 oz) raisins

½ teaspoon ground cloves

1½ teaspoons ground
  cinnamon

500 ml (16 fl oz) vegetable
  stock, more if needed (see
  page 459)

250 ml (8 fl oz) white grape
  juice or apple juice

40 g (1½ oz) unsweetened
  chocolate

optional: dash of red wine

---

* If you cannot get mulato chillies, add more ancho and pasilla chillies in their place, or replace them with guajillo chillies. Likewise, if you don't have pasilla chillies, you can increase the amounts of the other two. Ancho chillies are the ones you *must* have – they are also called poblano chillies, and it isn't Mole Poblano without them.

All of these chillies can be ordered by mail; see p. 470 for details.

Remove the stems and seeds from the chillies, wash them, and put them in a non-reactive pan with the water, tomatoes, onions, garlic, and salt. Bring the liquid to a boil, then lower the heat and simmer gently for about 30 minutes. Add a little more water if needed to keep all the chillies covered. When the vegetables are soft, purée everything in batches in a blender, and return it to the pan.

Grind the coriander and anise seeds in a stone mortar. Put the sesame seeds, almonds, and pine-nuts in a food processor with the steel blade and process until the nuts are ground. Add the ground coriander and anise, the raisins, cloves, and cinnamon, and process again until a thick and sticky paste is formed. Scrape the paste out with a spatula and stir it into the chilli purée.

Add the vegetable stock and the fruit juice to the chilli sauce and stir as you bring it back to a simmer. Add the chocolate, broken up into pieces. Keep simmering and stirring as the chocolate melts. The *mole* should have the consistency of thick cream. If it seems too thick, you can add a little more stock.

Once when I was making this *mole*, at the very end I added a dash of the Châteauneuf-du-Pape that we planned to serve with it. It was wonderful. So, though it's not traditional and certainly not required, know that you can add a bit of wine to finish it off.

This makes about 3 litres (5 pints) of mole.

BAKED PEARS IN CARAMEL SYRUP

6–8 medium-sized ripe pears
3 tablespoons fresh lemon
  juice

ground cinnamon
ground ginger
225 g (8 oz) sugar

optional garnish: vanilla ice cream, or mascarpone

Cut the pears in half, scoop out their cores, and peel them. Combine the pear halves in a bowl with the lemon juice, moving them around gently until they are coated. Be careful not to bruise the pears.

Choose a baking dish just large enough to hold all the pears in one layer and arrange them cut side down, close together. Drizzle the pears with the lemon juice remaining in the bowl, then sprinkle them with a light dusting of cinnamon and a tiny pinch of ginger.

In a medium-sized, heavy-bottomed saucepan, heat the sugar over medium heat until it melts and begins to turn golden brown. Stir it gently as it completely liquefies, then pour it evenly over all the pear halves. It will bubble and spit a little as it comes in contact with the liquid in the baking dish.

Bake the pears in a 190°C/375°F/Gas 5 oven for 30 minutes, or until the pears are completely tender. A sharp, thin knife inserted near the centre of a pear should slide through effortlessly.

The pears will be dotted with brown on top, and the fruit juices will have combined with the caramelized sugar to make an exquisite pool of glistening brown syrup around them.

Baste the pears with a little of this syrup just before serving. Serve them hot or warm, with some syrup spooned around them, and garnish them with a little scoop of vanilla ice cream or a spoonful of mascarpone if you like.

Serves 6–8.

AN INDIAN DINNER

❧

Stewed Chickpeas and Potatoes
in Indian Spices

Fragrant Rice Pilaf with Currants and Almonds

Yogurt with Cucumber, Mint, Raisins, and Nuts

Green Chilli and Mint Chutney

Major Grey's chutney

Naan

or any other Indian bread

fresh sliced fruit with Cardamom Ice Cream

Although it looks very exotic and complex, this is really a pretty straightforward meal. It is built around a vegetable stew and a rice dish, with an assortment of condiments and side dishes.

A nice, lightly spiced dish of stewed chickpeas and potatoes is the centrepiece. It has a long list of ingredients, but most of them are spices which combine to produce a flavour that has a little kick to it but isn't too hot. The stew is served with a rice pilaf of great delicacy, perfumed with ground coriander and cinnamon, and studded with sweet currants and toasted almonds.

For a little drama and contrast, we add a cool, cool yogurt dish, a hot, *hot* fresh chutney, and a sweet-sour mango chutney – my old favourite, Major Grey's, straight off the shelf of your grocery store.

A bread completes the array of savoury foods, which are all served at once and eaten together on one big plate. The perfect beverage with this is an ice-cold lager. I've also served an iced tea blended with berry juice and fresh lemon juice, and a peppermint tea with honey would be fine as well.

Besides being a delicious meal, this makes a very enjoyable afternoon of cooking, filling the house with gently exotic fragrances I'd like to bottle and keep.

On the other hand, if you want to enjoy this meal at a busier time, preparation can be streamlined: pitta breads, available in markets almost everywhere, are delicious and close enough to naan, especially when brushed with a little butter, wrapped in foil, and heated in the oven. Whole wheat tortillas, available in packets at good supermarkets and specialist shops, can also be used; they only need to be heated. And the Cardamom Ice Cream is a treat, but a good commercial pistachio ice cream would also be an excellent dessert for this meal.

STEWED CHICKPEAS AND POTATOES IN INDIAN SPICES

450 g (1 lb) dried chickpeas
pinch of bicarbonate of soda
1½ teaspoons salt, more to
    taste
3 large onions
8–10 cloves garlic
2 tablespoons peanut oil, or
    vegetable oil
½ tablespoon butter
900 g (2 lb) potatoes
2 tablespoons whole cumin
    seeds
2 teaspoons ground coriander
¼ teaspoon cayenne pepper
2 teaspoons turmeric

2 teaspoons whole mustard
    seeds
2 small, hot green chillies,
    trimmed and finely
    chopped
2.5 cm (1 inch) piece of fresh
    ginger root, peeled and
    chopped (about 2
    tablespoons)
900 g (2 lb) ripe tomatoes
8–9 tablespoons chopped
    coriander leaves
3–4 tablespoons freshly
    squeezed lemon juice
1 tablespoon Major Grey's or
    other mango chutney

Soak the dried chickpeas overnight in cold water with a little bicarbonate of soda and drain. (The soaking process can be omitted, but in that case the chickpeas will take longer to cook.)

In either case, simmer them in a large pot with enough fresh water to cover them by at least 2.5 cm (1 inch); if you have hard water, add a pinch more soda to the water. When the chickpeas are starting to be tender, add about a teaspoon of salt to the water. The cooking time will vary with the age of the beans – it might take an hour or two, or maybe even longer. They're ready when they're tender.

Peel the onions, halve them lengthwise, and cut them in thick slices. Peel and coarsely chop the garlic. Heat the peanut oil and butter in a large, non-stick sauté pan and sauté the onion in it, stirring frequently, until it begins to colour. Add the chopped garlic and a dash of salt and keep stirring over medium heat until both onions and garlic are golden brown.

Meanwhile, peel the potatoes and cut them in 2.5 cm (1 inch) chunks. Toast the cumin seeds lightly in a little pan, stirring and watching until they release their fragrance, then grind them briefly in a stone mortar or a spice grinder.

When the onions and garlic are ready, add the cumin, coriander, cayenne, turmeric, and mustard seeds. Stir over medium heat for about 3 minutes. Add the potatoes, the cooked chickpeas, and enough of the cooking liquid from the chickpeas to just barely cover everything in the pan. Bring the liquid to a simmer.

Add ½ teaspoon of salt, the chopped chillies, and the chopped ginger, stir everything, cover the pan, and leave it to simmer for about 15 minutes.

Scald and peel the tomatoes, trim out their cores, and cut them into wedges or big chunks.

Uncover the pan, add the tomatoes, coriander leaves, fresh lemon juice, and chutney. Simmer the mixture, uncovered, for about another 10–15 minutes. The liquid will be thickened, and all the vegetables will be tender yet still maintaining their separate identities. Taste, and correct the seasoning with a bit more salt or lemon juice if needed.

Serve the stew hot, with a rice pilaf, a chutney or two, and a cool yogurt dish.

Serves 8–10.

FRAGRANT RICE PILAF WITH CURRANTS
AND ALMONDS

1 small onion
1 clove garlic
2.5 cm (1 inch) piece of fresh
   ginger root
1 tablespoon sesame oil
1 teaspoon butter
450 g (1 lb) long-grain rice
5 cm (2 inch) stick cinnamon,
   broken in little pieces

1 teaspoon ground coriander
1 litre (1¾ pints) hot water
1 teaspoon salt
75 g (3 oz) currants
75 g (3 oz) almonds
2–3 tablespoons sesame seeds

Peel the onion, halve it lengthwise, and cut it in thin slices. Peel and chop the garlic and the ginger root. Heat the sesame oil and the butter in a medium-sized sauté pan and sauté the onion, garlic, and ginger in it, stirring almost constantly, until the onion begins to turn golden brown in spots.

Add the rice, cinnamon stick, and coriander, and continue stirring over heat for a couple of minutes. Stir in the hot water, salt and currants, cover, lower the heat, and leave the rice to simmer very gently for 25 minutes. Turn off the heat and leave the pan covered for another 5 minutes, then uncover and fluff up the rice with a fork.

While the rice is cooking, spread the almonds on a baking sheet and toast them in a 180°C/350°F/Gas 4 oven for about 15 minutes; they should be releasing a delightful fragrance and have a very light golden-brown colour when broken. Let them cool, then chop them coarsely. Toast the sesame seeds for a few minutes in a little pan on the stove top, stirring them vigilantly, just until they start to turn golden.

To serve, pile the rice pilaf on to a big, beautiful platter, then

sprinkle the chopped almonds and the sesame seeds all over it. For a party, garnish the plate with lacy coriander sprigs or edible flowers.
Serves 8–10.

YOGURT WITH CUCUMBER, MINT, RAISINS, AND NUTS

This is a *raita*, one of the many variations on yogurt that are always present in an Indian meal. It's a lovely side dish to spicy or hot food – soothing, refreshing, and a little bit surprising.

1.2 litres (2 pints) plain low-fat yogurt
125 g (4 oz) raisins
75 g (3 oz) walnut pieces
1 large cucumber

3 tablespoons chopped fresh mint leaves
plenty of freshly ground black pepper

Drain the yogurt in a colander, lined with 3 layers of cheesecloth, for about an hour. It will lose about 250 ml (8 fl oz) of liquid and gain a nice, thick texture.

Put the raisins in a small pot with enough water to cover them, bring the water to the boil, then turn off the heat and let the raisins soak for an hour.

Toast the walnut pieces in a 180°C/350°F/Gas 4 oven for 10–15 minutes, just until they release their fragrance. Take them out and allow them to cool, then chop them a little if the pieces are very large.

Peel the cucumber, trim off the ends, quarter it lengthwise, and slice out the seeds. Cut into pea-sized bits.

Drain the soaked raisins, pressing them gently in a strainer to squeeze out excess water. Combine the yogurt in a bowl with the chopped mint leaves, raisins, walnuts, cucumber, and a generous amount of freshly ground black pepper. Stir and taste. Add more black pepper if you like. Some people would add salt to this – you can try it if you want to, but I prefer it without.

This makes about 1.2 litres (2 pints) of cooling yogurt raita, enough for 8–10 servings.

GREEN CHILLI AND MINT CHUTNEY

This is so refreshing and exciting in your mouth that it's well worth the short time it takes to make. The green chillies give it heat, but when fresh coriander and fresh mint join forces, it's terrific.

**6 fresh hot green chillies
(about 50 g/2 oz)
1 large clove garlic
10–12 tablespoons chopped
coriander leaves
5 tablespoons chopped fresh
mint leaves**

**8 spring onions, chopped
¾ teaspoon salt
1 tablespoon whole mustard
seeds
3 tablespoons freshly
squeezed lemon juice**

Char the chillies and the unpeeled garlic clove in a hot frying pan or under a grill for about 10 minutes, turning them often, until their skins are blackened almost all over. Drop them into a bowl of cool water, then peel both chillies and garlic. Trim the stems off the chillies, and take out their seeds.

In the container of a food processor, combine the chillies, garlic, coriander, mint, spring onions, and salt. Process briefly a few times, scraping down the sides of the container in between.

Heat the mustard seeds in a pan until they jump and crackle, then remove them to a stone mortar and grind them roughly. Add the mustard to the chillies and herbs, along with the fresh lemon juice, and process again, scraping down as needed, until you have a thick, coarse-textured sauce. Taste, and add a pinch of salt or a drop of lemon juice as needed.

Serve this as a relish with Indian or Middle Eastern foods, or spread it on warm pitta toasts for a sensational little appetizer.

Makes about 175 g (6 oz).

NAAN

This is an Indian flatbread, but unlike most flatbreads it is slightly leavened with baking powder. The result is a somewhat thicker, moister bread than a chapati or tortilla. It resembles pitta bread, but the yogurt that is used to moisten the dough gives it a wonderfully tangy flavour. Naan are great eaten hot from the oven, but can also be made ahead of time and reheated in foil packets just before serving.

575 g (1¼ lb) plain flour,   1 teaspoon salt
   slightly more as needed   500 ml (16 fl oz) plain low-fat
1 teaspoon baking powder   yogurt

optional: melted butter

Sift together the flour, baking powder, and salt. Stir in the yogurt until the dough is too stiff for a spoon, then knead it in the bowl until it holds together well. Turn it out on a floured board and continue kneading for about 5 minutes, until the dough feels smooth and elastic.

Form the dough into a ball and put it in an oiled bowl, covered with a damp kitchen towel, to rest for an hour or longer.

Take the dough out and cut it into 10 equal pieces. Form each piece into a ball, and press the balls flat into round discs.

Heat a large cast-iron or non-stick frying pan. Take 1 piece of dough at a time, and roll it out on a floured board until it is about 20–25 cm (8–10 inches) across and less than 0.5 cm (¼ inch) thick. Lay it in the hot pan and cook it over a medium flame for 4–5 minutes. It will puff up in places, or all over, and there will be some blackish-brown spots on the bottom. Slide a spatula under the naan and place it under a hot grill for a minute or two, just until it finishes puffing up into a balloon and begins to colour lightly on top.

Remove the naan from the oven and brush it lightly with melted butter if you like.

Continue this way with all the dough, stacking the breads into a napkin-lined basket. Serve the breads hot, fresh from the oven, or let them cool and wrap them up. To reheat, wrap them in aluminium foil, in packets of 4 or 5 breads, and put them in a 200°C/400°F/ Gas 6 oven for 10–15 minutes.

Makes 10 flatbreads, approximately 25 cm (10 inches) across.

CARDAMOM ICE CREAM

A sweet cream, delicately flavoured with cinnamon and fragrant cardamom seeds, is cooked with a bit of rice, puréed to a silky texture, and frozen. The result is an ice cream that evokes both the rice pudding of childhood and an aromatic sweet from somewhere faraway and exotic.

7.5 cm (3 inch) stick cinnamon
500–750 ml (16–24 fl oz)
** spring water**
1½ teaspoons cardamom
** seeds**

600 ml (1 pint) milk
300 ml (10 fl oz) double cream
175 g (6 oz) sugar
50 g (2 oz) white rice

First make some cinnamon water by boiling the cinnamon stick with the water for a few minutes, then leaving it to steep for at least an hour. (You only need 175 ml (6 fl oz) of cinnamon water for this recipe, but it's a nice thing to have around for making tea or coffee. I sometimes throw a few pieces of cinnamon into a teapot so I can have cinnamon water on hand whenever I want it.)

Crush the cardamom seeds in a mortar or grind them in a small spice grinder. In a medium-sized saucepan, combine 175 ml (6 fl oz) of cinnamon water, the crushed cardamom seeds, the milk, cream, sugar, and rice. Bring the mixture gently to a simmer, stirring to dissolve the sugar completely. Lower the heat to the smallest possible flame, cover the saucepan, and let the mixture barely simmer for 40 minutes. You can lift the lid occasionally to give it a stir.

Allow the mixture to cool, then purée it in a blender, processing as long as necessary to get a truly smooth texture. It may take a couple of minutes.

Chill the mixture in the refrigerator, then freeze it in an ice cream freezer according to manufacturer's instructions.

Makes approximately 1.2 litres (2 pints) of ice cream.

AN INFORMAL WINTER BUFFET

❧

Baked Rigatoni with Grilled Vegetables

Tuscan White Beans with Chard

Tri-colour Salad

Roasted Green Beans with Garlic

assorted breads

DESSERT TABLE

Cranberry Tart

Chocolate Spongecake with Raspberry Coulis

Chocolate Caramel Nut Tart

strawberries with whipped cream

Apple Crisp

coffee, tea

Twenty or thirty people were going to drop by for dinner after a little book-signing party for my friend David Debin. I didn't know how many would turn up, and I was going to be at the bookstore beforehand, drinking champagne with everyone else, so I needed a plan that was festive but loose, with great 'do-ahead' factor.

I made several big gratins of Baked Rigatoni with Grilled Vegetables – a hearty, beautiful, and warming dish that could be prepared earlier, put in the oven when we all arrived home, baked while we had a glass of wine, and served bubbling hot half an hour later.

With the gratins I served three salads: some fresh rocket and radicchio for bite, and two bean salads that taste best at room temperature: Tuscan White Beans with Chard, and Roasted Green Beans with Garlic. I added a selection of breads and an extravagant dessert table which included a huge platter of fresh strawberries along with two beautiful tarts, one cake, and a crisp.

The atmosphere was celebratory but relaxed. There was nothing to do at the last minute except pour oil and vinegar on the salad and take the whipped cream out of the refrigerator. And the next day, we had some great leftovers.

Quantities: Expecting about thirty guests, I prepared three gratins, a double recipe of the white beans, and a triple recipe of the green beans. I refilled the Tri-colour Salad as needed, filling the bowl first with prepared salad leaves, then adding oil and vinegar. This is preferable to having a huge quantity ready and dressed all at once, as it may become limp. I made one of each dessert.

If you are preparing this menu for eight or ten guests, make just one of each recipe and select two or three desserts – unless you want lots of leftovers in that department.

BAKED RIGATONI WITH GRILLED VEGETABLES

2 large, firm aubergines
  (900 g/2 lb)
2 large red, green or yellow
  peppers
olive oil for grilling
2 large red onions
2–3 cloves garlic
2 tablespoons olive oil
900 g (2 lb) tomatoes, peeled
  and coarsely chopped

3 tablespoons chopped fresh
  basil
3 tablespoons chopped flat-
  leaf parsley
1–2 teaspoons chopped fresh
  oregano
salt and pepper to taste
120 ml (4 fl oz) dry red wine
450 g (1 lb) rigatoni
225 g (8 oz) grated mozzarella
  cheese

Slice the aubergines lengthwise, 1 cm (½ inch) thick. Salt the slices lightly on both sides and leave them to drain for at least 30 minutes. Pat them dry. Cut the peppers in quarters lengthwise and remove the seeds and stems. Brush the vegetables with a small amount of olive oil.

Grill the aubergines over charcoal or under a grill until they are tender. Grill the peppers, skin side down, until they are charred and blistered. Put the peppers in a paper bag for a few minutes to sweat, then slip off their skins. Cut the vegetables in wide strips and set aside.

Peel, halve, and slice the onions. Peel and chop the garlic. Sauté the onions and garlic in 2 tablespoons olive oil until they begin to colour. Add ¾ of the chopped tomatoes, the chopped herbs, some salt and pepper, and the wine. Simmer the sauce until it has a nice, semi-thick consistency – about 30 minutes.

Cook the rigatoni in a large pot of boiling salted water until it is just barely *al dente*. Drain the pasta and mix it gently but thoroughly with the tomato sauce and the grilled vegetables. Spoon the mixture evenly into a large oiled gratin dish. Scatter the remaining chopped tomatoes over the top, and then the grated mozzarella.

Bake the gratin at 180°C/350°F/Gas 4 for 30–40 minutes, until it is very hot right through and beginning to turn colour on top.

You can put it under the grill for about a minute at the end if you like the cheese to bubble and brown more. Serve at once, with a good Italian red wine.

Serves 8—10.

TUSCAN WHITE BEANS WITH CHARD

This is a variation of the slow-cooked Tuscan White Beans with Garlic and Sage (see page 377) that I frequently prepare for an antipasto or a buffet. The beans make a great marriage with chard.

450 g (1 lb) small white beans
pinch of bicarbonate of soda
handful of fresh sage leaves, or 2 tablespoons dried whole-leaf sage
1 head garlic, separated into cloves and peeled

3–4 tablespoons fruity green olive oil
salt
450 (1 lb) fresh Swiss chard
freshly ground black pepper
juice of 1 or 2 lemons
additional green olive oil for garnish

Soak the beans in cool water for a few hours, or overnight. A pinch of bicarbonate of soda can be added if you have hard water. Drain the beans and put them in a large, shallow pan with enough fresh water to cover them by at least 2.5 cm (1 inch). Add the sage leaves, the garlic cloves, and about half the olive oil. Bring the water to a boil, then lower the heat and simmer the beans gently until they are tender – this may take anywhere from an hour to all afternoon.

Do not stir the beans more than 2 or 3 times, and then very gently with a wooden spoon. Add water if needed to keep the beans covered at all times. When the beans are beginning to feel tender, add about 2 teaspoons of salt.

Meanwhile, clean the chard, slice away the stems, and cut the firm green leaves into strips about 2.5 cm (1 inch) wide.

Add the prepared chard to the beans when the beans are just becoming soft, and continue simmering until the beans are done.

Stir in the other half of the olive oil and additional salt if it's needed, and grind in some black pepper.

Allow the vegetables to cool slightly, then squeeze in some lemon juice, taste, and add more in discreet amounts until you have the balance you like. Chard comes alive with a touch of citrus.

Serve the beans and chard at room temperature in a wide, deep platter, drizzled with a bit more green olive oil.

Serves 10–15.

TRI-COLOUR SALAD

This is the simplest of dinner salads, just green leaves with oil and vinegar, only in this case the 'greens' are also red and white. The flavours are great together, and this can be used as a basis for many more elaborate salads.

1 medium bunch rocket
1 medium head radicchio
2–3 heads Belgian endive
2–3 tablespoons fruity green
  olive oil

balsamic vinegar, or any good
  wine vinegar
salt and pepper to taste

Wash all the leaves. Trim the rocket, discarding the thicker stems. Tear the rocket and radicchio into bite-sized pieces. Slice the endive crosswise, discarding any tough inner core. Spin the leaves in a salad spinner to get rid of any excess water, and toss them together in a large bowl.

Drizzle on the olive oil and toss again until every leaf glistens. Sprinkle on a few drops of vinegar, and a little salt and pepper, and toss again before serving.

Serves 8–10.

ROASTED GREEN BEANS WITH GARLIC

If you've never had green beans done this way in the oven, you will be amazed at the flavour. Use only thin, tender haricots verts or another stringless variety. Avoid larger, mature beans, as they will be tough.

1.4 kg (3 lb) tender young   **2 tablespoons fruity olive oil**
   green beans   **¾ teaspoon salt, more to taste**
1 head garlic

Wash and trim the green beans. Separate and peel the cloves of garlic. Combine the beans, garlic cloves, olive oil, and salt in a large bowl, and mix until all the beans are lightly coated with oil.

Spread the beans and garlic on two large baking sheets and roast them in a 200°C/400°F/Gas 6 oven for about 35–45 minutes. Roasting time will vary with the size of the beans. They are done when they have a somewhat blistered look and are beginning to brown in spots. Try one – if you like it, it's done.

Pile the roasted beans on a platter and serve them hot or at room temperature, as a finger food or on a plate with other foods.

Serves 8–10.

CRANBERRY TART

for the pastry
125 g (4 oz) + 2 tablespoons
  flour
125 g (4 oz) cold butter, cut
  in pieces
pinch of salt
2 tablespoons ice water

for the filling
900 g (2 lb) firm fresh
  cranberries

175 g (6 oz) sugar
zest of 1 large orange, finely
  grated
dash of ground cinnamon
⅛ teaspoon salt

for the topping
125 g (4 oz) flour
350 g (12 oz) sugar
150 g (5 oz) cold butter, cut
  in pieces

To make the pastry: combine the flour, cold butter pieces, and salt in the container of a food processor fitted with a steel blade, and process until the mixture resembles coarse meal. Sprinkle the ice water over it and process for a few more seconds, until it starts to hold together. Form the dough into a ball, flatten it somewhat, wrap it in plastic or waxed paper, and refrigerate for 30 minutes.

On a large, floured board, roll out the chilled dough into a circle about 30 cm (12 inches) across. It should be less than 0.5 cm (¼ inch) thick. Lay it carefully into a 25 cm (10 inch) tart pan with a removable bottom. Fit the pastry gently against the fluted sides of the pan and fold in the excess, reinforcing the edge of the shell and leaving it slightly higher than the rim of the pan. Cover the pastry shell and chill again for about 1 hour.

Line the pastry with foil, covering the edges, and fill it with dry beans or rice. Bake it in a 220°C/425°F/Gas 7 oven for 25 minutes. Remove the beans and foil and prick the bottom and sides of the pastry with a fork. Put it back in the oven and bake for another 5–7 minutes, or until it is golden brown.

To make the filling: wash the cranberries and pick them over carefully, discarding any soft ones. Drain them well, then toss the berries in a bowl with the sugar, orange zest, cinnamon, and salt.

To make the topping: put the flour and sugar into the food

processor fitted with a steel blade, along with the butter, and process until it starts to clump together in walnut-sized bits.

To assemble: pile the cranberries into the prebaked pastry crust, mounding them up somewhat in the centre. Using your hands, gently press together bits of the topping and then drop them over the berries, covering them pretty evenly. Some of the topping will stay in small clumps, some will fall apart.

Bake the tart at 190°C/375°F/Gas 5 for about 40–45 minutes, or until the topping is golden and the filling bubbles up around the edges. Cool the tart on a rack, and serve at room temperature.

Serves 10–12.

CHOCOLATE SPONGECAKE

This is a virtually fat-free cake, based on egg whites and cocoa. It tastes very chocolatey and stays moist – I love it. I serve it with a fresh berry sauce and whipped cream on the side. Those who want a rich dessert can have one, and those who don't still eat like kings.

2 tablespoons minced dried apricots
40 g (1½ oz) raisins, chopped
2 tablespoons cognac
2 tablespoons water
½ teaspoon almond extract
125 g (4 oz) flour
3 tablespoons Dutch cocoa powder, e.g. Drostes
2 teaspoons espresso or other dark-roast instant coffee powder

1 teaspoon baking powder
1 teaspoon bicarbonate of soda
½ teaspoon ground cinnamon
pinch of cream of tartar
250 ml (8 fl oz) plain non-fat yogurt
325 g (11 oz) light brown sugar
6 large egg whites, at room temperature
icing sugar

garnishes: Raspberry Coulis (page 374)
  whipped cream

Prepare a 23 cm (9 inch) springform cake tin: oil or butter it lightly and dust it with flour. Preheat the oven to 180°C/350°F/Gas 4.

Combine the minced dried apricots, chopped raisins, cognac, water, and almond extract in a small pan and warm over low heat until the liquid begins to steam. Stir it a bit and leave the fruits to macerate while you prepare the batter.

Sift together the dry ingredients, except the brown sugar. In an ample mixing bowl, beat together the yogurt and brown sugar until smooth. In another bowl, whisk or beat the egg whites until they hold firm, glossy peaks.

Stir the macerated fruits and their liquid into the yogurt-sugar mixture. Then stir in the dry ingredients. You will have a stiff batter. Mix in about a third of the egg whites very thoroughly to loosen it, then fold in the remaining whites.

Pile the batter carefully into the prepared tin and bake at 180°C/350°F/Gas 4 for about 35 minutes. Test by inserting a toothpick or a very thin knife near the centre; the cake is done when the toothpick comes out clean.

Cool the cake in its tin for about 10–15 minutes, then carefully remove it and cool it completely on a rack. Dust it with sifted icing sugar and serve with a fresh berry coulis and with whipped cream on the side.

Serves 8–10.

CHOCOLATE CARAMEL NUT TART

for the pastry
185 g (6½ oz) plain flour
2½ tablespoons sugar
½ teaspoon salt
125 g (4 oz) cold unsalted
 butter
1 large egg
1 teaspoon vanilla extract

for the filling
175 g (6 oz) whole almonds
175 g (6 oz) whole hazelnuts
200 g (7 oz) best quality
 bittersweet chocolate
250 ml (8 fl oz) sweetened
 condensed milk
½ teaspoon vanilla extract
125 g (4 oz) sugar
175 ml (6 fl oz) single or
 double cream

Make the pastry first. Combine the flour, sugar, and salt in the container of a food processor. Add the cold butter, cut in pieces, and process until the mixture has the texture of coarse meal. Beat the egg lightly with the vanilla, add it to the flour mixture, and process until the pastry starts to hold together and form a ball.

On a lightly floured board, roll the pastry into a circle about 36 cm (14 inches) across. Lay it into a 30 cm (12 inch) loose-bottomed flan tin, and fold the excess in to shape a thick fluted edge. Chill the pastry for at least an hour, or overnight.

Prick the chilled pastry here and there with a fork, and then line it with foil and fill with dry beans or rice. Bake the pastry in a preheated 200°C/400°F/Gas 6 oven for 15 minutes. Remove the dry beans and the foil and bake for another 20 minutes. The pastry should be lightly golden. If it is browning too quickly, cover it very loosely with the foil. When it is ready, allow it to cool, then carefully remove it from the pan on to a serving platter.

Meanwhile, spread the almonds and hazelnuts on a baking sheet and toast them in a 150°C/300°F/Gas 2 oven for about 20 minutes. Allow them to cool until you can handle them, then rub the hazelnuts between your hands to remove as much skin as possible.

Combine the chocolate, cut up in pieces, with the condensed milk and vanilla in a heavy-bottomed saucepan. Heat gently, stirring often, until the chocolate is completely melted and the mixture forms a thick, glossy fudge. Allow the fudge to cool slightly, until it just begins to thicken, then pour it into the prepared tart shell and spread it evenly over the bottom.

To make the caramel sauce, heat the sugar over a medium flame in a heavy bottomed, enamelled saucepan until it begins to melt. Stir it with a fork as it melts completely and just begins to caramelize. Heat the cream to a simmer. Remove the caramelizing sugar from the heat and very carefully stir in the heated cream. It will boil up dramatically, and the caramelized sugar will harden at first, but never fear, it will dissolve back into the cream. Whisk the sugar and cream together over low heat until they form a smooth sauce.

Put the toasted nuts in a bowl, pour the caramel sauce over them, and stir together. Allow this mixture to cool slightly, stirring it up now and then. As the sauce cools it will thicken. After 5–10 minutes, when the caramel forms an even, shiny coat on all the nuts, but before it hardens, spread the nuts over the chocolate layer in the tart shell. Allow the tart to cool to room temperature; if the weather is hot, you can chill it briefly. To serve, cut the tart in thin slices with a very sharp knife.

Serves 10–12.

Apple Crisp (see page 202)

SOUP SUPPERS, PASTA DINNERS, AND OTHER EASY FAMILY MEALS

FAMILY DINNER FROM TUSCANY

❧

Tuscan Salad

*Simple Polenta with goat's cheese and
Chunky Tomato Sauce*

seasonal fresh fruit

I could eat this meal at least once a week, and there are times when I do. My children have always loved polenta, the simpler the better, so it's a mainstay in our house. It's one of those easy foods that needs no planning, and it can be combined with any leftover pasta sauce. This version is drizzled with green olive oil, scattered with chunks of feta or fresh white goat's cheese, and served with a ladleful of Chunky Tomato Sauce. In the winter I use tomatoes from my garden that I put up in jars when they were plentiful.

The salad is one of the best – just fresh rocket bathed in the same green olive oil, with big shavings of Parmesan cheese and a spoonful of those good Tuscan White Beans on top. Of course my kids won't eat rocket yet – it's too peppery for them – so sometimes I make two salads, one with sweet butter lettuce or romaine for them and one with rocket for the grown-ups. I suppose the day will come when they'll start eating rocket – and next they'll be drinking our Chianti.

For dessert, we have what we usually have, the best fresh fruit of the season. All in all, if you have a pot of those Tuscan beans on hand, this meal can be prepared in not much more than 30 minutes. If you add a focaccia or other special bread, a bottle of wine, and some biscotti with the fruit, it could be a great casual company meal.

TUSCAN SALAD

This is the salad we always have when we've had Tuscan White
Beans with Garlic and Sage the day before.

2–3 bunches fresh rocket   **350–500 ml (12–16 fl oz)**
4–5 tablespoons fruity green   **Tuscan White Beans with**
  olive oil   **Garlic and Sage (see page**
salt   **377)**
freshly ground black pepper   **50–75 g (2–3 oz) Parmesan**
                                        cheese

optional: 1 – 2 tablespoons balsamic vinegar

Wash the rocket, spin it dry in a salad spinner, trim off the tough
stems, and tear it into manageable pieces. Toss it in a bowl with
just enough fruity green olive oil to make the leaves glisten. Then
add a dash of balsamic vinegar if you like, and a little salt and pepper,
and toss again.

Divide the salad between 6 plates and ladle 3–4 tablespoons of
the Tuscan White Beans over each one. Then grate some Parmesan
cheese on the coarse side of the grater, making nice big shavings,
and scatter them over the salads.

Serves 6–8.

SIMPLE POLENTA

I use a coarse-ground polenta, which I buy in a local Italian deli or
in a health food store. It needs longer cooking than the fine grind,
but I prefer the texture. I've also had excellent results with cornmeal
from the supermarket.

The simplest polenta can be made with water and salt, or a stock
can be used for the liquid. Some people like to use a home-made
chicken stock. I use a light vegetable stock, and I've been known
to use a vegetable stock powder that I keep in the freezer for those

times when you just need it. The thing to remember is not to use any stock with a very assertive flavour, as it could take over the delicate taste of the polenta.

2 litres (3½ pints) water or vegetable stock (see page 459)
350 g (12 oz) coarse-ground yellow cornmeal (polenta)

salt to taste
butter or olive oil
75 g (3 oz) grated Parmesan cheese

garnishes: 175–225 g (6–8 oz) goat's cheese, broken into pieces
Chunky Tomato Sauce (recipe follows)

In a deep saucepan, combine the cold water or stock with the polenta and additional salt if needed. Use about 2 teaspoons of salt if you are using water, otherwise adjust to the saltiness of the stock. You can use slightly less liquid if you want a very firm polenta, which will set up nicely in a pan and can later be sliced and grilled.

Whisk the polenta into the liquid to break up any lumps. Gradually bring the liquid to a boil, stirring often with a long-handled wooden spoon, then lower the heat to a simmer. Continue stirring the polenta over low heat for about 40 minutes, a bit less if you are using the fine-ground cornmeal. Constant stirring is best, but frequent stirring will do if reality so dictates. The polenta will thicken quickly, and has a tendency to splatter, which is why I recommend a deep pot and long-handled spoon.

Before serving, stir in about a tablespoon of butter and about 75 g (3 oz) of grated Parmesan cheese. Ladle the steaming polenta into shallow bowls, and serve at once, with additional Parmesan cheese, or with a few chunks of goat's cheese and a tomato sauce.
Serves 6–8.

Variations: A superb way to enjoy polenta, if you are ever lucky enough to get your hands on a fresh truffle or two, is this – put a rounded tablespoon of mascarpone in the plate, ladle a serving of polenta over it, then scatter shavings of fresh truffle over the polenta. Polenta also goes beautifully with sautéd porcini, or any other mushroom (see also page 390).

CHUNKY TOMATO SAUCE

This type of sauce takes only about 15 minutes to make and has a wonderfully fresh, bright flavour.

1.4 kg (3 lb) ripe red tomatoes	**salt to taste**
2–3 cloves garlic	**chopped fresh basil**
1 large onion	**chopped flat-leaf parsley**
2 tablespoons green olive oil	**pepper to taste**

optional: splash of balsamic vinegar

Plunge the tomatoes into boiling water for no more than a minute, then into a bowl of cold water. Remove their skins, trim them, and cut them into wedges or large chunks, saving all the juice.

Finely chop the garlic and coarsely chop the onion. Heat the olive oil in a large pan and sauté the garlic and onion in it over high heat, adding a little salt and stirring often, until the onions begin to colour.

Add the tomatoes and all their juice to the pan, and as much chopped basil and parsley as you like. Salt and pepper to taste and stir frequently, still over high heat, until most of the juices have evaporated. If the tomatoes seem to need a little bite, add just a little balsamic vinegar – some tomatoes have less acid than others.

Makes 600–750 ml (1–1¼ pints).

Soup is often the basis of a family supper, especially in the cold and rainy months, when nothing can warm and sustain the way a steaming bowl of soup can.

In this easy supper, a Broccoli Soup thickened with potatoes and touched with mustard is paired with Cheese Popovers, hot out of the oven. The combination makes a nourishing and delicious meal, with the additional advantage that children are always enchanted with popovers and the interesting caverns they find when they tear them open.

A simple green salad before and a juicy Apple Pudding to finish complete the menu. If you can't find the time to make a pudding, a bowl of home-made Chunky Applesauce (see page 128) with a little cream poured over it will do very well.

BROCCOLI SOUP

800 g (1¾ lb) broccoli
3 large onions
salt to taste
1 tablespoon olive oil
2½ tablespoons butter
450 g (1 lb) potatoes
1 stalk celery
750 ml (1¼ pints) water

900 ml (1½ pints) vegetable
    stock (see page 459)
juice of ½ lemon
1½ tablespoons flour
500 ml (16 fl oz) hot milk
2 tablespoons Dijon mustard
generous pinch of cayenne

optional garnish: sour cream

Trim the broccoli, peel the stems and chop them coarsely, and break the heads into small florets.

Coarsely chop the onions and sauté them with a sprinkle of salt, in a large non-stick sauté pan, in the olive oil and 1 tablespoon of butter, until they are just becoming golden.

Peel and dice the potatoes and chop the celery, and combine them in a soup pot with the water and vegetable stock, and about ½ teaspoon of salt if needed. Bring to a boil, lower the heat, and simmer for 10 minutes. Add the broccoli pieces and the sautéd onions and simmer another 8–10 minutes, until everything is tender. If you like, you can reserve some of the broccoli florets to steam separately and use as a garnish, or to stir into the soup at the end for greater texture.

When the vegetables are tender, stir in the lemon juice, and then purée the soup in batches in a blender. Don't overprocess: the texture should remain somewhat rough.

Melt the remaining 1½ tablespoons of butter in a heavy-bottomed pan and stir in the flour. Cook this roux for a few minutes, stirring, until it has a pale gold colour. Whisk in the hot milk, bring the mixture to a boil, then reduce the heat and simmer, stirring or whisking, until it thickens. Whisk in the mustard and the cayenne, and mix the white sauce into the soup.

Bring the soup back to a simmer, taste, and correct the seasoning with more salt, mustard, or cayenne if needed. If you have reserved some steamed broccoli florets, you can stir them in now, or put a few on top of each serving as a garnish.

Serves 10—12.

CHEESE POPOVERS

5 large eggs
385 ml (13½ fl oz) milk
225 g (8 oz) flour
2 tablespoons melted butter, and extra for muffin cups
½ teaspoon salt

⅛ teaspoon cayenne
3 tablespoons grated Parmesan cheese
75 g (3 oz) grated Cheddar or Gruyère cheese

Preheat the oven to 200°C/400°F/Gas 6.

Beat the eggs with the milk, then beat in the flour, melted butter, salt, cayenne, and grated Parmesan cheese. The mixture should be completely smooth. You can do all this in a few seconds in a blender.

Brush 12—15 non-stick muffin cups lightly with butter. Distribute the grated Cheddar or Gruyère cheese among the prepared muffin cups, then pour the popover batter over the cheese, filling each cup about two-thirds full.

Put the popovers in the oven, immediately reduce the temperature to 190°C/375°F/Gas 5, and bake the popovers for about 50 minutes. They will balloon up over the rims of the muffin cups, and should be a deep golden brown.

Popovers are best when served hot out of the oven. Just ease them out of the muffin cups. However, if you need to keep them for a little while, loosen them gently, tilt them sideways in their cups to allow some air flow, and cut a small slit in each one with a sharp knife so that steam can escape. Let them cool this way for 10—15 minutes, then serve within the next hour.

Makes 12—15 popovers.

APPLE PUDDING

1.8 kg (4 lb) pulpy apples,
such as Rome or Golden
Delicious
600 ml (1 pint) water
175 g (6 oz) sugar
2 teaspoons ground cinnamon
dash of ground nutmeg
225 g (8 oz) French bread, cut
in 1 cm (½ inch) cubes

6 tablespoons melted butter
75 g (3 oz) raisins
4 eggs
500 ml (16 fl oz) milk
½ teaspoon vanilla extract
125 g (4 oz) chopped walnuts
2 tablespoons brown sugar

garnish: softly whipped double cream

Peel and core the apples, quarter them, and cut the quarters cross-wise in thick slices. Combine the prepared apples in a large non-reactive pan with the water, sugar, cinnamon, and nutmeg. Bring the water to a boil, then lower the heat to medium and let the apples simmer, stirring often, until they are perfectly soft and most of the liquid has cooked away. This may take 30–45 minutes, and some of the apple slices will fall apart into a sauce.

Put the bread cubes in a large mixing bowl. Drizzle the melted butter over the bread and immediately toss the cubes, distributing the butter as evenly as possible. Spread the buttered bread cubes on a baking sheet and toast them in a 200°C/400°F/Gas 6 oven for about 10 minutes, or until they are golden brown.

Return the toasted bread to the big mixing bowl, and stir in the cooked apples and the raisins.

Beat together the eggs, milk, and vanilla, and mix this custard into the apples and bread. Let the pudding mixture stand for a few minutes as the bread absorbs liquid, then give it another stir and spoon it into a large buttered gratin dish. Sprinkle the chopped walnuts and brown sugar over the top.

Bake the pudding at 180°C/350°F/Gas 4 for 40 minutes. Serve it warm, with softly whipped double cream on the side.

Serves 10–15.

TACOS FOR DINNER

※

Corn and Squash Soup

Black Bean Tacos with Salsa Cruda

sliced mangoes, papayas, and pineapple

Living in California, which historically is part of Mexico, we eat a lot of tacos — and that's a good thing. The corn tortilla is the principal bread of Mexico, and the taco is like a sandwich: whatever you want to make it.

In this version, tacos are made with black beans, white cheese, and a raw salsa, providing what is probably a complete balanced meal that you can hold in your hand. But the real beauty of it is the balance of flavours, the sweet corn and savoury beans, and the hot chillies jumping around in your mouth.

The golden soup has a gorgeous flavour and delicacy, but you must have genuinely fresh sweet corn and a good squash to do it. Fortunately, Kabocha and other flavourful varieties are becoming more commonly available.

The combination of this soup and the tacos is so good, and when I wrote down this menu and looked at it, I realized an interesting thing. Without thinking about it, I had concocted a meal almost entirely of pre-Columbian ingredients. Corn, squash, black beans, chillies, tomatoes, and the tropical fruits are all New World foods.

CORN AND SQUASH SOUP

This is a delicious autumn soup, and virtually fat-free. You must use a very good squash and fresh sweetcorn for this, for those are the ingredients that most define the flavour. If you can't get Kabocha squash, try acorn. (You will not get the same results with butternut squash.)

4–5 branches young kale
1 large potato, cut in 1 cm (½ inch) dice
700–900 g (1½–2 lb) Kabocha or acorn squash, peeled and cubed
225 g (8 oz) fresh tomatoes, peeled and coarsely chopped
8 spring onions, chopped
1 teaspoon salt, more to taste

1½ large onions
1 tablespoon olive oil
1 medium green pepper
1 medium red pepper
4 large ears sweetcorn
750 ml (1¼ pints) vegetable stock (see page 459)
1½ tablespoons cumin seeds, lightly toasted and ground
6 tablespoons coarsely chopped fresh coriander

garnishes: fresh lime or lemon wedges
 any chilli salsa, or chilli flakes to taste

Trim the stems from the kale, cut the leaves in half lengthwise, then thickly slice them. Combine the kale, potato, squash, tomatoes, and spring onions in a large pot and add enough water to cover and a teaspoon of salt. Simmer these vegetables until the potatoes and squash are tender, about 20 minutes.

Meanwhile, chop the onions and begin sautéing them in the olive oil in a medium non-stick pan. Trim the peppers, cut them in 1 cm (½ inch) dice, and add them to the onions. Sauté the vegetables, stirring often, until the onions begin to brown. At the same time, slice the kernels off the sweetcorn – you should have enough to fill a 900 ml (1½ pint) measure.

When the potatoes are tender, add the sautéd vegetables and the corn kernels to the soup, along with the vegetable stock. Continue simmering for about 10 minutes.

Lightly toast the cumin seeds in a little pan, then crush them in a mortar and stir them into the soup. Stir in the chopped coriander leaves. Taste the soup, and correct the seasoning if needed.

Serve the soup with a squeeze of fresh lime or lemon juice, and pass a chilli salsa or chilli flakes.

Serves 10.

BLACK BEAN TACOS

Tacos are anything you like folded into a warm corn tortilla. Deep-fried, prefolded taco shells are an invention of American fast food operations, and until recently they were unheard of in Mexico. The soft taco, on the other hand, is to Mexico as the sandwich is to northern parts – indispensable, and a thing of infinite variety. Packets of corn tortillas can be found in specialist shops and some supermarkets.

1 recipe Everyday Black Beans (recipe follows)	10–12 tablespoons chopped coriander leaves
225 g (8 oz) crumbled feta cheese	225 g (8 oz) shredded cabbage or lettuce
500 ml (16 fl oz) Salsa Cruda (page 272)	18 corn tortillas (see page 38)

Since tacos should be made the instant before they are eaten, it is best to let folks make their own. Simmer the beans in an open pan until they are thick enough to spoon into a tortilla. Then line up the beans, feta cheese, salsa, coriander, and shredded cabbage or lettuce on the table.

Last, heat the corn tortillas. Put them in a couple of large non-stick pans, doing as many at a time as you can fit. Heat them for about a minute on one side, then about ½ minute on the other. They should be hot, pliable, and releasing a toasty corn fragrance – don't let them get crisp or browned.

As the tortillas are ready, put them immediately into a basket lined and covered with a folded kitchen towel to keep them warm for the few moments between stove top and table. Alternatively, wrap a bundle of warm tortillas tightly in foil and keep them warm in a low oven.

To assemble the tacos, spoon about 2 heaped tablespoons of black beans into a warm tortilla, sprinkle on some cheese, add salsa to taste, garnish with chopped coriander and shredded cabbage or lettuce, fold the tortilla over everything, and eat. Yes, it's a finger food, and might be a touch messy, so be ready to lick your fingers.

Allowing 2–3 tacos per person, this will serve 6–8.

EVERYDAY BLACK BEANS

This is a very easy recipe that's become a staple in my kitchen because it's so accommodating. The beans are savoury but not spicy. They make a perfect taco when spooned into a warm corn tortilla with a little cheese and salsa. They taste great with rice. I love them cold or lukewarm on salads. Puréed with a little stock, they instantly become a delicious soup.

450 g (1 lb) dried black beans
pinch of bicarbonate of soda
3 large onions
6–8 cloves garlic
small bunch coriander
salt

1½ tablespoons olive oil
1 large green pepper, cored
   and chopped
2 tablespoons cumin seeds
1 tablespoon sweet paprika

Soak the beans overnight in plenty of water with a pinch of bicarbonate of soda in it. In the morning, drain them, rinse them, and put them in a pot with enough water to cover them by 5 cm (2 inches), 1 peeled onion, 2 or 3 peeled garlic cloves, and a small handful of the coriander. Simmer the beans gently until they are tender, an hour or two, or however long it takes – beans vary tremendously in cooking time, depending on age. Add a little water if needed to keep them covered, and stir in about a teaspoon of salt towards the end of the cooking time. Remove and discard the onion, garlic cloves, and coriander.

Chop the remaining onions and garlic, and sauté them in the olive oil in a large non-stick pan until they are limp. Add the chopped pepper and continue cooking, stirring often, until all the vegetables are beginning to colour.

Meanwhile, lightly toast the cumin in a small pan, then quickly crush it in a mortar. Chop about 2 tablespoons of coriander leaves. Add the cumin and paprika to the vegetables, then stir in the beans with their remaining liquid, the chopped coriander, and a little more salt to your taste. Simmer the beans with the vegetables and spices until the liquid has thickened a bit and you like the consistency.

Makes 1.2 – 1.4 litres (2 – 2¼ pints), or 6 – 8 servings.

SALSA CRUDA

This is also called *pico de gallo*, or *salsa fresca*. It is the staple item of the south-western table, the garnish that accompanies almost anything. A simple combination of freshly chopped tomatoes, onions, chillies, and coriander, it depends on the excellence and freshness of its few ingredients.

900 g (2 lb) vine-ripe tomatoes
½ medium onion (sweet
varieties are best)
4 – 5 small green chillies (5 – 6
tablespoons chopped)

6 tablespoons chopped
coriander
salt to taste

optional: 1 – 2 teaspoons lemon juice
cumin seeds, toasted and crushed

Cut the tomatoes into small dice, using a sharp, serrated knife. Don't use the food processor for this, as it will turn the tomatoes into soup. If the tomatoes are very, very juicy, you could drain them a few minutes in a colander.

Finely chop the onion. Cut the chillies in half lengthwise, remove the ribs and seeds, and chop them finely. Remove the coriander leaves from their stems and chop them roughly.

Toss all these things in a bowl, add salt to your taste, and lemon juice if you like. Sometimes I add a little toasted, crushed cumin, and sometimes not, depending on my mood and the time.

Makes about 900 ml (1½ pints), which is less than you think.

STEWED WHITE BEANS WITH BABY POTATOES

tossed green salad

White Beans with Baby Potatoes and Herbs

Parmesan and Rosemary focaccia

fruit sorbets

Dinner in a bowl is not only an attractive idea during our busier times, sometimes it's a downright necessity. But plain food can be wonderful – sometimes more delicious and satisfying than any elaborate meal. This bowlful of beans with potatoes and tomatoes, all swimming in a savoury broth, fills that bill for me.

It's an easy thing to make, although the beans take their unhurried hours of simmering. If you can't be around the house, that part could be done in a crockpot, following manufacturer's instructions.

Also in keeping with the down-home style, this is a generous recipe – you'll have more than you need for one dinner, but with a dish like this, you want leftovers. Combine some with pasta for an instant *pasta e fagioli*.

I paired these beans and potatoes with a focaccia, one of the easiest yeast breads and the perfect flavour to accompany cannellini, but any good chewy, crusty bread is fine. Your favourite green salad can be added as starter.

For dessert, refreshing fruit sorbets are perfect. This kind of comforting peasant food is filling, and a heavy dessert could be too much. An old-fashioned baked apple would be just as nice, or a bowl of fresh seasonal fruit with some walnuts and a wedge of cheese.

WHITE BEANS WITH BABY POTATOES AND HERBS

450 g (1 lb) dried white
    cannellini beans
pinch of bicarbonate of soda
½ head garlic, parted into
    cloves and peeled
1 teaspoon dried sage
3 tablespoons olive oil
salt to taste
900 g (2 lb) very small
    red-skinned potatoes
6 cloves garlic, minced
6 tablespoons chopped
    flat-leaf parsley

2 teaspoons chopped fresh
    rosemary leaves
1 bay leaf
pinch of oregano
¼ teaspoon crushed red
    pepper
900 g (2 lb) ripe tomatoes,
    peeled and cut in chunks
250 ml (8 fl oz) water
250 ml (8 fl oz) vegetable stock
    (see page 459)
pepper to taste

optional garnish: grated Parmesan cheese

Wash the beans and put them in a large, shallow saucepan with
water to cover and a pinch of bicarbonate of soda. Bring the water
to a boil, let it boil for 5 minutes, then remove the beans from the
heat and let them soak for an hour. Drain and rinse the beans and
return them to the saucepan with fresh water to cover by 5 cm
(2 inches). Add the garlic cloves, crumbled sage leaves, and about
a tablespoon of olive oil.

Simmer the beans gently until they are tender, anywhere from 1
to 3 hours. Add more water as needed to keep the beans covered,
and towards the end of the cooking time add about ½ teaspoon of
salt, or more to taste.

Put the potatoes into a pot of cold, salted water, bring it to the
boil, and cook them until they are just tender, 10–15 minutes,
depending on their size.

Meanwhile, heat the remaining 2 tablespoons of olive oil in a
large non-stick sauté pan, and stir the minced garlic in it for a minute
or two over medium heat. Add the parsley, rosemary, bay leaf,
oregano, and crushed red pepper. Continue stirring for 3 or 4

minutes, then add the tomatoes, water, and vegetable stock. Add some salt and pepper to taste and simmer the mixture for 10 minutes.

Add the cooked beans with their remaining liquid and the cooked potatoes to the herb mixture. Let everything heat through together, then spoon it into generous bowls, pouring a little of the herb-scented broth over each serving.

Pass grated Parmesan cheese to sprinkle on top, and have big hunks of chewy country bread with this for a perfect supper. *Serves 8–10.*

PARMESAN AND ROSEMARY FOCACCIA

Parmesan cheese marries well with many herbs. It's good with basil in pesto, delicious with parsley in spaghetti *aglio e olio*, and here it sings with rosemary in a fragrant bread. Start this bread about 3 hours before dinner and serve it warm – it will vanish.

7 g (¼ oz) dried yeast
300 ml (10 fl oz) warm
   water
½ teaspoon sugar or honey
1 teaspoon salt
2 tablespoons fruity green
   olive oil
1½ tablespoons chopped fresh
   rosemary leaves
450 g (1 lb) unbleached white
   flour, approx.
125 g (4 oz) freshly grated
   Parmesan cheese
½ teaspoon coarse salt

In a large mixing bowl, dissolve the yeast in the warm water with the sugar or honey. When it starts to foam, stir in the salt, 1 tablespoon of the olive oil, the chopped rosemary, as much of the flour as it takes to make a thick batter, and half the Parmesan cheese.

Continue adding flour and stirring until the dough is too stiff for a spoon, then turn it out on a floured board. Knead it gently, sprinkling it liberally with more flour to keep it from sticking, until it is smooth and elastic, about 10 minutes.

Form the dough into a ball, and put it in a large, oiled bowl, turning it to coat it with oil. Cover the bowl with a tea towel and leave the dough to rise in a warm place for about an hour, or until more or less doubled in size.

Punch the dough down, lift it out of the bowl, and lay it on an oiled baking sheet. Pat it out into a large oval of uniform thickness, about 40 × 30 cm (16 × 12 inches). Cover it loosely with a tea towel again and leave it to rise for about 30 minutes, until almost doubled.

Brush the focaccia very gently with the remaining olive oil, and sprinkle it with the remaining Parmesan cheese and the coarse salt. If you like, you can cut a few diagonal slashes in it with a sharp knife, or dimple it here and there with your fingers. Bake it in a preheated 200°C/400°F/Gas 6 oven for about 35 minutes, or until it is golden brown on top and sounds hollow when the bottom crust is tapped. Let it cool on a rack for just a few minutes, then cut it in squares and serve.

Serves 6–8.

A CASSEROLE SUPPER

❧

Rice and Corn Salad

Squash Custard

Simple Chipotle Sauce

warm tortillas or sourdough bread

fresh fruit in season

A salad and a casserole are a good, homely combination that has been done a thousand times, and this is yet another.

In this case, the salad is rice and corn, crunchy and a little bit spicy. The casserole is Squash Custard, a generous, savoury pudding of sweet winter squash, semolina, and eggs, punctuated with flecks of blue cheese and walnuts. A sauce made of my favourite chilli, the smoky chipotle, is served on the side. In the tradition of casseroles, this is make-ahead food, but there is no compromise of flavour.

The same Squash Custard could also be served with a very simple green salad, and the chipotle salsa could be replaced by any salsa or relish you like – try cranberry sauce, or piccalilli.

RICE AND CORN SALAD

This is a refreshing salad of bright colours and flavours — citrus, cumin, and fresh coriander with the sweetness of corn. It's good as a tostada topping, in tacos, with black beans, and just fine on its own.

2 tablespoons olive oil
350 g (12 oz) courgettes, cut
   in 1 cm (½ inch) dice
salt to taste
juice of 2 large lemons
4 medium ears fresh
   sweetcorn
1 tablespoon cumin seeds
225 g (8 oz) long-grain white
   rice, cooked

9–10 tablespoons coarsely
   chopped coriander leaves
1 large red pepper, trimmed
   and cut in 0.5 cm (¼ inch)
   dice
2 fresh green chillies, diced
6 spring onions, thinly sliced

Heat a tablespoon of the olive oil in a non-stick pan. Add the courgettes, lightly salted, and sauté over very high heat, tossing and stirring constantly, until they are flecked with brown spots — about 7–8 minutes. Remove from the heat, sprinkle with about 2 table-spoons of the lemon juice and toss again.

Plunge the shucked corn into boiling salted water for 5 minutes, then remove and let it cool slightly before slicing the kernels off with a sharp knife.

Heat the cumin seeds in a little pan, stirring constantly, until they release a toasty aroma, then crush them in a mortar. Strip the coriander leaves from their stalks and chop.

In a large bowl, combine the courgettes, sweetcorn, cumin seeds, rice, coriander, diced red pepper, diced chillies, and spring onions. Toss everything together with the remaining olive oil, and as much more lemon juice and salt as you like. Let the salad chill in the refrigerator, in a covered bowl, for about an hour.

Serves 6–8.

SQUASH CUSTARD

There are so many kinds of squash available now that it can get confusing. On the other hand, there's a lot of good eating to be had. Make this custard with Kabocha or acorn squash, or ask your greengrocer what varieties are best, but be sure to use a sweet, flavourful one.

450 g (1 lb) thick purée of cooked Kabocha or acorn squash
1 teaspoon salt
600 ml (1 pint) milk
50 g (2 oz) semolina
50 g (2 oz) cornmeal
1 tablespoon + 2 teaspoons butter
5 eggs, beaten

2 tablespoons molasses
½ teaspoon grated nutmeg
½ teaspoon ground cinnamon
1 medium onion
½ teaspoon ground ginger
40 g (1½ oz) small walnut pieces
40 g (1½ oz) Roquefort cheese, crumbled

To cook any winter squash into a purée, seed and peel it and cut the flesh into pieces. Simmer the squash in a heavy-bottomed pot with about 2.5 cm (1 inch) of water and a little salt, tightly covered, until it is falling apart. Lift the lid and give it a stir now and then, adding a little water if necessary. When the squash is completely tender, remove the lid, raise the heat, and stir constantly as you cook away all the excess moisture. Then mash the pulp with a potato masher or purée it in a food processor. The finished purée should have the consistency of a thick applesauce. Another method is to roast squash in the oven (see page 150).

Heat the milk in a medium-sized saucepan and whisk in the semolina, cornmeal, and 2 teaspoons of butter. Continue stirring with a whisk or a wooden spoon until the mixture thickens, then remove it from the heat, let it cool for about 5 minutes, and whisk in the beaten eggs a little at a time.

Stir in the squash purée, the molasses, ½ teaspoon of salt, nutmeg, and cinnamon. Whisk all this together or process it in a blender for a few seconds – the mixture should be silky smooth, with no lumps. Taste, and add more salt if needed.

Peel and quarter the onion and slice it rather thickly. Sauté the onion in a tablespoon of butter with the ginger and a dash of salt until it begins to colour. Lower the heat and keep cooking the onion until it is an even caramel colour.

Stir the walnut pieces and the crumbled cheese gently into the squash mixture; the cheese should not get too mushy and blend into the custard, but rather should stay in distinct lumps. Pour the mixture into a large, shallow, buttered baking dish, and scatter the sautéd onions over the top. Put the dish into a preheated 200°C/400°F/Gas 6 oven; after 10 minutes, lower the heat to 180°C/350° F/Gas 4 and bake for 40–45 minutes more.

Serve the custard hot or warm, with some Simple Chipotle Sauce on the side.

Serves 6–8.

SIMPLE CHIPOTLE SAUCE

Chipotle chillies have become quite fashionable now, and it's high time. These searingly hot and smoky nuggets, in reality nothing more mysterious than smoked green jalapeño chillies, have been a favourite of mine for years. I buy them in their simple, dried form, pounds at a time, and keep a huge jar of them on my kitchen counter. Chipotle chillies can sometimes be found in cans, but that is not the pure chipotle. If possible, seek out a specialist shop and get the dried ones or order them by mail (see page 470).

This sauce is so fast, easy, and good that it is a staple in my kitchen. It keeps for about a week refrigerated.

3–4 dried chipotle chillies
  (see page 88)
2 medium tomatoes, peeled
½ large sweet onion
4 cloves garlic

½ teaspoon salt
5 tablespoons coriander
  leaves, coarsely chopped
1 tablespoon cumin seeds

In a small non-reactive pan, pour enough hot water over the chipotle chillies to cover them and let them soften for a few minutes. Take them out, pull out their stems and remove the main cluster of seeds, and return them to the pan.

Cut the peeled tomatoes in wedges, and the onion into large chunks. Peel the garlic. Add the tomatoes, garlic, salt, and coriander leaves to the chillies. Add a little more water if needed, just barely to cover the vegetables, and simmer it all for about 30 minutes.

Toast the cumin seeds lightly in a small pan, then grind them in a mortar and add them to the chilli mixture. When everything is soft, purée the mixture in a blender. Taste, add a bit of salt if needed, and you're done. Serve the sauce warm or cold, with quesadillas, with soup, with beans, with any kind of taco or enchilada, as a dip for tortilla chips, or with your morning eggs for a real wake-up call.

This makes 250–350 ml (8–12 fl oz) of sauce.

A SALAD AND
CHOWDER DINNER

❧

Salad of Bitter Leaves
with Gorgonzola Cheese and Walnuts

Figs Marinated in Spiced Wine

Oyster Mushroom Chowder

Fast Buttermilk Yeast Rolls

Apple and Pear Crumble

The salad is substantial, interesting, and on the fancy side. With a garnish of spiced figs, it could qualify for what used to be called a 'company meal'. The rest of the food is very straightforward and homey, though – you could substitute a salad of whatever you have on hand and eat this dinner any night of the week, with the children, at the kitchen table. On the other hand, share it with friends and they'll appreciate you.

After the pungent, complex flavours of the salad, the Oyster Mushroom Chowder makes a pleasing change, with delicate tastes and a rich texture. The Fast Buttermilk Yeast Rolls use a speeded-up version of yeast dough, simple to make but allowing you to enjoy that freshly baked quality that you can't get any other way. Serve them with both the salad and the chowder. Finish with Apple and Pear Crumble, a seasonal favourite.

Both the chowder and the crumble can be prepared ahead of time, if need be, but don't put the crumble in the oven until shortly before dinner, so that you can enjoy it hot.

SALAD OF BITTER LEAVES WITH GORGONZOLA CHEESE AND WALNUTS

350 g (12 oz) rocket
1 medium head radicchio
½ head curly endive
12 large fresh basil leaves
¼ red onion, cut in slivers
175 g (6 oz) Gorgonzola
   cheese

125–150 g (4–5 oz) walnut
   pieces, lightly toasted
2 tablespoons fruity green
   olive oil
1 tablespoon walnut oil
sprinkle of balsamic vinegar
salt and pepper to taste

garnish: 16 Figs Marinated in Spiced Wine (recipe follows)

Wash and trim all the salad leaves, spin them dry in a salad spinner, and tear them into manageable pieces. Combine the leaves in a large bowl with the slivered red onion.

Break the cheese into pea-sized nuggets and scatter it over the greens. If the walnut pieces are very large, chop them just a little, then add them to the salad. Drizzle on the olive oil and walnut oil, and toss everything together gently. Add a few drops of balsamic vinegar and some salt and freshly ground black pepper, and toss again.

Divide the salad among 8 large salad plates and garnish each plate with 2 of the marinated figs.

Serves 8.

FIGS MARINATED IN SPICED WINE

450 g (1 lb) dried figs
600–750 ml (1–1¼ pints) dry
   red wine
60 ml (2 fl oz) balsamic
   vinegar

125 g (4 oz) sugar
1 stick cinnamon
6–7 whole cloves

Pierce the figs in several places with the tip of a sharp, narrow knife or with the tines of a fork.

Combine the wine, vinegar, sugar, and spices in an enamelled saucepan and heat, stirring, until the sugar is completely dissolved. Add the figs and simmer gently for about 30 minutes. Remove from the heat and allow the figs to steep in the wine for several hours at room temperature, or overnight in the refrigerator. The figs can be kept for several days, in their marinade, refrigerated in a covered container. Or they can be drained and used at once.

Makes 450 g (1 lb) of spiced figs.

OYSTER MUSHROOM CHOWDER

2 large onions
1 tablespoon olive oil
1 tablespoon butter
salt to taste
450 g (1 lb) fresh oyster mushrooms, well cleaned
175 ml (6 fl oz) dry white wine
800 g (1¾ lb) potatoes
750 ml (1¼ pints) cold water
1 leek, white part only, chopped
1 stalk celery, trimmed and chopped
1 bay leaf

½ teaspoon dried thyme leaves
500 ml (16 fl oz) vegetable stock (see page 459)
2 tablespoons Marsala
1 small red pepper, finely diced
pinch of cayenne
pinch of freshly ground black pepper
500 ml (16 fl oz) milk (low-fat if desired)
60 ml (2 fl oz) double cream
chopped coriander

Peel the onions, cut them in half lengthwise, and slice them in very thin wedges. In a large non-stick sauté pan, cook the onions slowly in the oil and butter and a little salt until they begin to colour.

Add the sliced oyster mushrooms and keep cooking on medium-low heat, stirring often, until the mushrooms are turning golden brown. This may take about 30 minutes. Add half the white wine and continue stirring as it cooks away. When the mushrooms are dry and crackling in the pan and turning an even deeper brown, add the remainder of the wine, and let it cook away again. This long, slow cooking of the onions and mushrooms develops a flavour that is worth waiting for.

Meanwhile, peel the potatoes, quarter them lengthwise, and slice them thinly. Put them in a pot with the water, ½ teaspoon of salt, the chopped leek, chopped celery, bay leaf, and thyme. Bring the water to a boil, then lower the heat and let it simmer for about 20 minutes. The potatoes should be very soft.

Add the potato mixture to the mushrooms, along with the vegetable stock, Marsala, diced red pepper, cayenne pepper, and black pepper. Simmer everything together for about another 10 minutes, then stir in the milk and cream, and about a tablespoon of chopped coriander. Correct the seasoning with salt and more pepper if needed.

Serve the chowder hot, with additional chopped coriander to sprinkle on top.

Serves 6–8.

FAST BUTTERMILK YEAST ROLLS

Yeast-leavened bread has a quality of its own that cannot be duplicated with any amount of soda or baking powder, but it usually takes hours to make. These rolls are a hybrid: a combination of leavenings is used, as well as a greater amount of yeast and higher temperatures, to speed the process. The result is a delightful, soft dinner roll, with the inimitable character of a yeast roll but in about a third of the time.

300 ml (10 fl oz) buttermilk
60 ml (2 fl oz) water
1 tablespoon butter
425 g (15 oz) plain flour
15 g (½ oz) dried yeast

1 tablespoon sugar
1 teaspoon salt
½ teaspoon bicarbonate of
  soda
40 g (1½ oz) rolled oats

Heat the buttermilk, water, and butter together, stirring over a low flame just until the butter begins to melt. Remove from the heat and pour the liquid into another container. Stir as the butter finishes melting. The liquid should feel hot to the touch, but not scalding.

Sift together 365 g (12½ oz) of flour with the yeast, sugar, salt, and bicarbonate of soda. Stir in the oats. Mix the warm liquid into the dry mixture, and stir until a sticky dough forms.

Sprinkle the remaining flour on a board and turn the dough out on it, coating the dough with the flour. Knead it gently for about 5 minutes, working in more flour as you go. The dough should remain fairly soft, but become much smoother and more elastic.

Form the dough into a rope about 50 cm (20 inches) long, then cut it into 12 equal pieces. Shape each piece into a ball, pulling the sides down and pinching together the bottom.

Arrange the balls on a buttered baking sheet, seam side down, and cover them with a tea towel. Or put the balls of dough close together in a buttered 25 cm (10 inch) cake tin; they will grow together as they rise, forming a 'loaf' of rolls that will easily pull apart. Either way, leave the rolls to rise in a warm, sheltered place for about an hour.

Bake the rolls in a preheated 180°C/350°F/Gas 4 oven for 20–22 minutes, or until they are lightly browned and sound hollow when the bottom is tapped.

Cool the rolls on a rack for a few minutes before serving.

Makes a dozen rolls.

APPLE AND PEAR CRUMBLE

Here's a simple, homely dessert to make when autumn fruits are plentiful and freshly picked. This should be eaten warm, so prepare it ahead if you need to, but put it in the oven about an hour before you want to serve it. For a divine experience, have a scoop of vanilla ice cream alongside.

for the filling
900 g (2 lb) apples, mixed
    sweet and tart
900 g (2 lb) pears
3 tablespoons lemon juice
125 g (4 oz) sugar
75 g (3 oz) raisins
dash of grated nutmeg
dash of ground cinnamon

for the crumble
85 g (3½ oz) white flour
175 g (6 oz) brown sugar
pinch of salt
1 teaspoon ground cinnamon
¼ teaspoon grated nutmeg
5 tablespoons butter
2 tablespoons ice water
75 g (3 oz) rolled oats, or
    slightly more to taste

Peel and core the apples and pears, quarter them, and slice them crosswise about 0.5 cm (¼ inch) thick. Toss them in a bowl with the lemon juice, sugar, raisins, and just a whiff of nutmeg and cinnamon.

Combine the flour, sugar, salt, and spices in the container of a food processor fitted with the steel blade. Process for a few seconds. Then cut the butter into chunks, add it to the dry mixture, and process again until the mixture resembles coarse meal. There should be no large bits of butter left.

Sprinkle in the ice water and process again, about 5 or 6 seconds, until the crumble mixture is holding together and forming little clumps. Add the rolled oats and pulse for a few seconds only, just enough to mix everything together but not so much that you grind up the oats. If the mixture seems too sticky, add a bit more oats.

If you are not using a food processor, mix together all the dry ingredients thoroughly, then rub softened butter in with your fingers until the mixture feels like very coarse cornmeal. Sprinkle the ice water over it and toss together with forks until it is all well combined and starting to clump together.

Spread the apples evenly in a large glass or ceramic gratin dish – I use a 32 cm (13 inch) round, or a 23 × 36 cm (9 × 14 inch) oval – and scatter the topping evenly over them, leaving some of it in larger chunks and letting some crumble finely.

Bake the crumble at 190°C/375°F/Gas 5 for about 40–45

minutes, or until the top is crisp and brown and the juice of the apples is bubbling up around the edges. Serve it hot or warm, with vanilla ice cream, with crème fraîche, with whipped cream, or all by itself.

Serves 8–10.

Variation: I have also made this with summer fruits. I used a combination of peaches, nectarines, apricots, and plums – a total of 1.8 kg (4 lb). The result was slightly more tart and much juicier, but a great success. If you want to thicken the juices a little, dissolve 2 teaspoons of cornflour in the lemon juice before stirring it into the fruit.

FIVE EASY PASTA DINNERS

❧

A Bowl of Noodles

Pasta with Cream Cheese and Pistachio Nuts

*Penne with Oyster Mushrooms and
Chinese Broccoli*

Greek Pasta Casserole

*Rigatoni with Garlic, Olives, and
Raw Tomatoes*

There is nothing like a good plate of pasta. First of all, I just love it. Furthermore, everyone else loves it, too. Of all the foods I know, pasta is the one most likely to be met with universal enthusiasm at any given moment. It presents itself in infinite variety, and on top of all that, it's healthy.

That would be reason enough to have pasta every day, but it also is *fast and easy*. It's the most satisfying hot meal to prepare when you have little time to think about it and less to do it, but want real food.

So here, as a friend to the working mother, the impromptu host, or anyone who needs a friend, are five pasta dinners. Each is a little different, each answers a particular need. With perhaps one exception, each could stand alone as a meal; a loaf of bread and something good to drink, and you're in business. A fresh green salad could be added to the plan, and would be nice, but is not required. A plate of fresh fruit, whatever is in season, makes an ideal ending, as does a scoop of sorbet and a biscuit from the biscuit jar.

In other parts of this book you'll find more pasta dishes that should also be in everyone's repertoire – pasta with simple tomato sauce, with garlic and oil, with fresh herbs, with goat's cheese and chard. They are all suggested in specific menu combinations, but any of them can also be treated in exactly the same way as the recipes given here.

A BOWL OF NOODLES

We've all had times when we've walked into the kitchen at dinnertime, tired and distracted, and just grabbed whatever was at hand and thrown it together in some fashion to make a meal. Sometimes it works. This time it came together into a brothy bowl of noodles with lightly cooked, fragrant, fresh-tasting vegetables, just hitting the spot. I wrote it down at once, and have enjoyed it many times since.

Only the simplest of salads is needed, because there are so many vegetables in the bowl.

5 cloves garlic, chopped
6–8 spring onions, sliced
1½ tablespoons olive oil
450 g (1 lb) fresh mushrooms, sliced (shiitake, oyster, or whatever you have)
splash of white wine
450 g (1 lb) fresh spinach leaves, whole or sliced

1.5 litres (2½ pints) light vegetable stock (see page 460) (chicken stock would be OK)
salt and pepper to taste
450 g (1 lb) fettucine or linguine
700 g (1½ lb) tomatoes, peeled and chopped

garnishes: grated Parmesan cheese
red pepper flakes

Put a pot of water on to boil for the pasta.

In a large non-stick sauté pan, toss the garlic and sliced spring onions in the heated olive oil for a couple of minutes. Add the sliced mushrooms and sauté everything together, stirring often, until the onions and mushrooms begin to colour and everything smells great.

Pour in a little white wine, then add the spinach leaves, the stock, and salt and pepper to taste. Bring it to the boil, lower the heat, and let the soup simmer for a few minutes.

Meanwhile, cook the fettucine or linguine in plenty of boiling salted water until it is *al dente*, then drain.

About 2 minutes before serving, add the chopped tomatoes to the broth. Taste, and correct the seasoning with more salt or pepper if needed.

Using generous soup bowls, put a serving of cooked pasta into each bowl, then ladle a cup or so of broth and vegetables over it. Serve at once, passing Parmesan cheese and red pepper flakes at the table.

Serves 6–8.

PASTA WITH CREAM CHEESE AND PISTACHIO NUTS

I made this in a few minutes for my children when they didn't want to eat the 'grown-up' pasta I was preparing. But the grown-ups had no qualms about eating this right along with theirs. It was a forbidden pleasure, with all that cream cheese! It's delicious, and very pretty too, with the light green pistachios against the white sauce.

I would serve a plate of crudités while the pasta is cooking, the kind that children will eat – carrot sticks, cucumber spears, celery, and sugar snap peas. Some children love cherry tomatoes, and mine will eat lightly steamed broccoli on occasion.

450 g (1 lb) rigatoni (or the pasta of your choice)
2½ tablespoons butter
175 g (6 oz) cream cheese

300 ml (10 fl oz) milk
75 g (3 oz) shelled, roasted pistachio nuts

Put the pasta on to cook in a big pan of boiling salted water.

Melt the butter in a large sauté pan, and add the cream cheese, broken into chunks. Stir it over medium heat with a wooden spoon as it softens. Add the milk and keep stirring, and in a little while you'll have a smooth, creamy sauce.

When the pasta is *al dente*, drain it and add it to the cream cheese sauce. Stir until all the pasta is coated with sauce, then serve on warmed plates. Sprinkle each serving with some pistachio nuts. Now, wasn't that easy?

Serves 6−8.

PENNE WITH OYSTER MUSHROOMS AND CHINESE BROCCOLI

I started buying Chinese broccoli at the local market, and for a while I practically abandoned the ordinary heads of broccoli I used to get. I love the flavour of this, and I like using the stems, the leaves, and the little flower buds for a real variety of texture. If you can't get Chinese broccoli (sometimes known as chop suey greens), use ordinary sprouting broccoli, though the result will be different. Oyster mushrooms are pretty widely available now in supermarkets.

These ingredients combine well and add a whisper of Asian influence to what is essentially an Italian dish. We drink Chianti with it and this seems to work just fine. A salad of mild-flavoured lettuces would go well with this, and fresh sweet oranges for dessert.

350 g (12 oz) fresh oyster mushrooms
1 medium onion
2 cloves garlic
2−3 tablespoons olive oil
salt and pepper to taste
450−575 g (1−1¼ lb) Chinese broccoli or sprouting broccoli

1 teaspoon rice vinegar
about 1 teaspoon soy sauce
450 g (1 lb) penne pasta
2−3 fresh red tomatoes
125 g (4 oz) pine-nuts, lightly toasted
freshly grated Parmesan cheese as needed

Clean the mushrooms gently but thoroughly, and cut them in wide strips. Chop the onion and garlic.

Heat half the olive oil in an ample non-stick pan and sauté the onions and garlic in it for a few minutes. Add the oyster mushrooms and continue cooking over high heat, stirring occasionally, until the mushrooms release their water, it cooks away, and they begin to colour. Lower the heat to medium, add salt and pepper to taste, and stir more frequently until both mushrooms and onions are flecked with golden-brown spots. This may take up to 30 minutes. Remove the mushrooms from the heat.

Meanwhile, wash the broccoli, trim off the tough ends, and peel the thick bottoms of the stalks as you would asparagus. Slice the stalks diagonally about 1 cm (½ inch) thick and put them aside. Cut off the florets and cut the largest leaves and thin stems into big pieces.

Heat the remaining olive oil in another non-stick pan or wok, and stir-fry the broccoli stems in it for a few minutes. Add the leaves and flowers and continue stirring over high heat until the stems are beginning to colour and everything is just tender. Sprinkle on the rice vinegar and soy sauce and toss together for a moment. Remove from the heat.

Cook the penne pasta in several quarts of boiling salted water until it is just *al dente*. While the pasta is cooking, cut the tomatoes in 1 cm (½ inch) cubes. A couple of minutes before the pasta is ready (you're tasting it, right?), toss the mushrooms over high heat again for a moment, then add the cut-up tomatoes and stir just until the tomatoes are heated through. Add the broccoli to the mushrooms.

When the pasta is *al dente*, drain it and add it immediately to the vegetables. Toss everything together in the hot pan and serve at once on warm plates, passing toasted pine-nuts and Parmesan cheese to scatter over each serving.

Serves 6.

GREEK PASTA CASSEROLE

This is a big, oven-baked dish that takes a little more preparation than some other pastas, but the great thing is that it can all be done completely ahead of time, and just put in the oven about 40 minutes before you serve it. It makes it a great party dish, and it's much easier to put together than lasagne. Have fresh baguettes or a big

Greek loaf with sesame seeds, some red wine, and, for dessert, ripe melons cut into wedges.

This recipe can, of course, be halved.

1 **large aubergine (at least 450 g/1 lb)**	150 **ml (5 fl oz) dry red wine**
2 **large green or red peppers**	1 **tablespoon chopped fresh Greek oregano or 1 teaspoon dried (more to taste)**
1.4 **kg (3 lb) ripe tomatoes**	
2 **large onions**	
2 **large cloves garlic**	900 **g (2 lb) shell pasta**
3 **tablespoons fruity green olive oil**	75 **g (3 oz) sliced Kalamata olives**
75 **g (3 oz) sun-dried tomatoes, halved or sliced**	350 **g (12 oz) mild feta cheese, coarsely crumbled**
salt and pepper	

Trim the aubergine and slice it 1 cm (½ inch) thick, crosswise. Salt the slices lightly on both sides and leave them in a non-reactive tray to drain for about 30 minutes. Rinse the aubergine quickly and blot it dry on paper towels, pressing gently. Cut the aubergine slices into cubes.

Trim and seed the peppers, cut them to a similar size, and set aside.

While the aubergine is draining, scald the ripe tomatoes, slip off their skins, and cut them into medium-sized wedges. Coarsely chop the onions and finely chop the garlic. Sauté the onions and garlic in 2 tablespoons of the olive oil over a high flame, stirring often, until they begin to colour. Add both the ripe and dried tomatoes, and a little salt and pepper, and simmer for a few minutes. Add the wine and about a tablespoon of chopped fresh oregano, and simmer for about 5–6 more minutes, until the liquid is slightly reduced.

Heat the remaining tablespoon of olive oil in a heavy-bottomed, non-stick pan and sauté the aubergine and peppers with a sprinkle of salt and pepper, until the vegetables are tender and the aubergine is beginning to colour.

Cook the pasta in vigorously boiling salted water just until it is *al dente*, then drain.

In your largest bowl, combine the cooked pasta, the tomato sauce, the sautéd aubergine and peppers, the sliced olives, and half the feta cheese. Using big wooden spoons or your hands, mix everything together well.

Spoon the mixture into two large, oiled gratin dishes, or one enormous one. Scatter the remaining feta cheese over the top. At this point, you can cover the dishes tightly and refrigerate them for a day with no harm done.

Cover the dishes with foil, and bake at 180°C/350°F/Gas 4 for about 20 minutes if the mixture is still warm, or about 35–40 minutes if it has been refrigerated. Remove the foil for the last 5 minutes, and raise the heat to brown the cheese slightly.

Serve hot, with a green salad, a wonderful bread, and a full-bodied red wine.

Serves 16.

RIGATONI WITH GARLIC, OLIVES, AND RAW TOMATOES

This is a summer dish; everything in the sauce is barely cooked or not cooked at all. Pungent, salty olives, garlic, hot peppers, and the freshness of herbs combine with juicy raw tomatoes. Salad is almost redundant. I'd like a chewy, dense country bread and some creamy goat's cheese with this, and then lots of peaches, apricots, and cherries.

450 g (1 lb) rigatoni
3 tablespoons olive oil
5 cloves garlic, chopped
75 g (3 oz) sliced Kalamata
    olives
5 tablespoons coarsely
    chopped fresh basil
8–9 tablespoons coarsely
    chopped flat-leaf parsley

½ teaspoon red pepper flakes,
    more to taste
900 g (2 lb) ripe tomatoes,
    peeled and cut in 1 cm
    (½ inch) dice
salt to taste
coarsely grated Parmesan
    cheese
freshly ground black pepper

Cook the rigatoni in a large pot of boiling salted water until it is *al dente*.

While the pasta is cooking, heat 2 tablespoons of olive oil in a large non-stick sauté pan. Sauté the chopped garlic in it for just a minute or two — you want to take the raw edge away, but don't let it brown. Add the sliced olives, chopped herbs, and red pepper flakes to the garlic and remove the pan from the heat.

Just before draining the pasta, add the diced tomatoes to the pan and toss them with the other ingredients over high heat for about a minute, just to warm them and start releasing their juices. Add a sprinkle of salt if the olives are not too salty.

Drain the pasta, add it to the tomato mixture in the pan with the remaining tablespoon of olive oil, and fold everything together thoroughly. Serve at once on warmed plates, and pass a generous bowl of coarsely grated Parmesan cheese and a pepper grinder.

Serves 6.

DINNER IN A BOWL

Sometimes basic is best, and that's what the following four menus are. Each one is a hearty, nourishing bowl of soup, paired with the right bread. A dessert can be added to fancy up a meal like this, but a piece of good, ripe fruit and a sliver of cheese are always welcome.

These are the easiest meals in winter, and satisfy in many ways, even before you eat them. Cook a big soup on a dark, cold day and comforting aromas fill each part of the house. The heart of the home is beating, and everyone is reassured. If you bake bread or muffins – even the easiest popovers – this effect is multiplied.

And there is no more restorative food when you sit down to eat on a raw and blustery day than that steaming bowl of home-made soup and the fragrant loaf, warm from the oven. It replenishes the body and cheers the spirit. Add a glass of wine and the cares of the day melt. By the time you're having the pear and the cheese, all's well.

So it is not surprising that we sit down to a big bowl of soup often on a winter day, as do so many other families I know. Here is a series of family meals based on that welcoming bowl.

All the soups here are of a type – the rib-sticking, appetite-quenching main course soup, full of vegetables and full of taste. The breads are all quick breads – only one is yeast-leavened and even that is a batter bread. For those times when it's just about getting dinner on the table before you drop dead, these menus can be really stripped down: a good country bread from a bakery to replace home-baked bread, fresh fruit for dessert, a glass of wine, and you're fine.

FOUR EASY SOUP DINNERS

❧

Guillermina's Lentil Soup

Fresh Green Chilli and Cheese Cornbread
or pumpernickel bread and a slice of smoked cheese

Greens and Garlic Soup

Toasted Polenta Slices
or sourdough bread and hummous

Leek and Potato Soup

Irish Soda Bread
*and Cheddar cheese or
olive bread and fresh goat's cheese*

Sweet Potato and Corn Soup

Tomato and Onion Batter Bread
or baguettes with any pesto or tapenade

GUILLERMINA'S LENTIL SOUP

As Laurie Colwin once pointed out, lentils never let you down. They're good plain or complicated, marrying easily with almost anything. This big, nourishing lentil and vegetable soup has been the *soupe du jour* in my house on many blustery days. I first watched my friend and fellow cook Guillermina make it. She never measured anything, never even thought about it. One day I asked her to tell me the recipe so I could write it down.

'Do you put chard in? Or spinach?'

'Yes.'

'Which one?'

'Which one do you have?'

'How about potatoes?'

'OK.'

'But how many?'

'How many do you want?'

'Do you use spring onions or ordinary onions?'

'Which ones do you like?'

'Just make the soup, and I'll watch.'

450 g (1 lb) lentils	1 large red or green pepper
2 teaspoons salt, more to taste	3–4 leeks, white part only,
3 medium carrots	chopped
2 stalks celery	2 tablespoons olive oil
small bunch fresh coriander	4 cloves garlic, minced
6 spring onions	2 tablespoons cumin seeds
8–10 Swiss chard leaves,	freshly ground black pepper
chopped (or 450 g (1 lb)	to taste
chopped spinach)	pinch of cayenne
575 g (1¼ lb) potatoes	juice of 1 lemon
2–3 ripe tomatoes	

Boil the lentils in about 3.4 litres (6 pints) of water, with a teaspoon of salt, for about 30 minutes.

Meanwhile peel and slice the carrots; trim and slice the celery;

wash the coriander well and remove the leaves, discarding the stems; trim and slice the spring onions; wash the chard leaves, remove the tough part of the stems, and coarsely chop the leaves; scrub the potatoes and cut in 1.5 cm (¾ inch) dice; peel and coarsely chop the tomatoes; trim and seed the pepper and coarsely dice it; clean and chop the leeks.

Heat the olive oil in a medium-sized pan and sauté the leeks, spring onions, and garlic in it, stirring often, until softened and beginning to colour. Add the chard and cook a few minutes more. Then add the sautéd mixture, as well as all the other vegetables and another teaspoon of salt, to the lentils. Continue simmering the soup for another 30 minutes.

Toast the cumin seeds in a small pan, stirring constantly, until they release their fragrance. Grind them in a mortar and add them to the soup, along with freshly ground black pepper to taste, a good pinch of cayenne, and the juice of a lemon.

Simmer the soup a few minutes more, or until all the vegetables are tender. Taste and correct the seasoning if needed.

This is a big soup — it will yield 12—15 servings, but you'll want to have that much, because people will have seconds, and you'll want it around the next day, and you'll be putting it in thermoses for kids' lunches . . ..

FRESH GREEN CHILLI AND CHEESE CORNBREAD

Cornmeal and flour, green chilli peppers, Cheddar cheese, onions, fresh corn, milk and eggs — this bread is the entire food pyramid in one dish. When you mix it up and bake it, it comes out crunchy, chewy, a little bit spicy, and a little bit sweet — in short, just a great cornbread. The chillies, searingly hot when raw, lose a lot of their fire when baked in a batter, so don't be afraid to use them. If you cannot find jalapeños, use the small fresh green chillies (about 5 cm / 2 inches long) that are easily found in many shops, and increase the quantity to 5 or 6.

185 g (6½ oz) white flour
450 g (1 lb) yellow cornmeal
2 teaspoons salt
5 teaspoons baking powder
2 tablespoons sugar
500 ml (16 fl oz) low-fat milk
300 g (10 oz) fresh or frozen
  sweetcorn kernels
3 tablespoons butter
3 eggs
4 fresh jalapeños or 5–6 fresh
  green chillies
1 small onion, chopped
125 g (4 oz) coarsely grated
  Cheddar cheese

Sift together into a mixing bowl the flour, cornmeal, salt, baking powder, and sugar.

Heat together the milk, sweetcorn kernels, and butter, until the butter melts. Scoop out some of the sweetcorn kernels and set them aside, then process the mixture briefly in a blender, just enough to chop up the sweetcorn roughly. Add back the whole sweetcorn.

Beat the eggs in a bowl, and beat in the warm milk and corn mixture. Stir the liquid into the dry ingredients. Seed and chop the chillies, and stir them into the batter, along with the chopped onion and grated cheese.

Spoon the mixture evenly into a large (23 x 32 cm/9 x 13 inch) buttered baking dish. Bake at 220°C/425°F/Gas 7 for about 35 minutes, or until the bread is puffed up, the top is golden brown, and a thin knife inserted near the middle comes out clean. Serve hot or warm, cut in squares.

Serves 8–10.

GREENS AND GARLIC SOUP

This soup packs a punch. It starts with a whole head of garlic and moves on to stronger flavours from there, making the kind of robust, assertive bowlful you want on a cold winter day. With a good bread and maybe some Hummous (see page 115), it's a meal.

I've made it with a combination of Chinese leaves, Swiss chard, and spinach, and another time with a mix of chard and kale. For best results, use 2–3 kinds of greens, mixing stronger flavours with milder ones.

1 head garlic, separated into
  cloves, peeled and chopped
1 onion, chopped
2 tablespoons fruity green
  olive oil
350 g (12 oz) *each* young kale
  and chard, or 700 g (1½ lb)
  mixed other leafy greens,
  such as escarole, spinach,
  Chinese leaves, etc.

700 g (1½ lb) potatoes, peeled
  and diced
500 ml (16 fl oz) water
salt and pepper to taste
2 litres (3½ pints) vegetable
  stock (see page 459) (or low-
  salt chicken stock)
175 ml (6 fl oz) white wine
3 tablespoons rice vinegar

garnishes: additional olive oil
  hot red chilli pepper flakes
  175 g (6 oz) feta cheese, crumbled

Sauté the garlic and onion in the olive oil in a large non-stick pan, until they begin to colour. Wash the greens, trim away any tough stems and ribs, and shred the leaves with a sharp knife. If you're using one of the sturdier greens, such as kale or escarole, add it to the pan when the garlic starts to turn golden, and sauté them together for a few minutes, stirring often.

Meanwhile, combine the diced potatoes, water, salt and pepper to taste, and stock in a soup pot and bring to a boil. When the potatoes are tender, add the garlic and onion mixture, all the shredded greens, the white wine, and the rice vinegar. Simmer everything together for about 30 minutes, then taste and correct the seasoning if needed.

Put on the table a carafe of good green olive oil, some dried red chilli flakes, and a bowl of crumbled feta cheese, then serve steaming bowls of soup. The best way is with a little of everything: a tiny drizzle of the oil, a sprinkle of chilli, and a spoonful of crumbled feta in the middle.

Serves 10.

TOASTED POLENTA SLICES

This is essentially a dish made from leftover polenta. Cold polenta is cut into slices and used instead of bread for making Parmesan cheese toasts. Any kind of polenta can be used, as long as it's thick enough to cool to a solid consistency. If you're starting from scratch, prepare the polenta earlier in the day so that it has time to become firm.

leftover polenta, chilled in a loaf tin, or 1 recipe Simple Polenta (page 260), made with 400 g (14 oz) dry polenta

olive oil
Parmesan cheese

Make the polenta as always, using the slightly larger quantity of dry polenta to make it thicker. When it's ready, pour it into loaf tins and allow it to cool completely, then chill it in the refrigerator.

When the polenta is completely firm, turn it out of the tins and cut it into 1.5 cm (¾ inch) slices, as you would a loaf of bread. Cut the slices in half or into triangles if they are very large.

Lay the slices on lightly oiled baking sheets, and brush them with a very small amount of olive oil. Sprinkle them with a little Parmesan cheese.

Bake the polenta on the lower rack of a 190°C/375°F/Gas 5 oven for 3–5 minutes, until they are hot through, then put them under the grill for a moment, watching them carefully, until lightly browned on top.

Serve hot, with a soup or stew, or alongside grilled vegetables.
Serves 8–10, if using a whole recipe of polenta.
Variation: Brush the polenta slices with olive oil in which you have crushed some garlic, lightly salt them, and omit the cheese. For spicy flavour, sprinkle on some hot red chilli flakes.

LEEK AND POTATO SOUP

This is genuine comfort food – one of the simplest and best soups, in any of its variations. The recipe given here has a large yield and can be cut in half, but for me it's a big-pot kind of soup, the kind I like to have around for a couple of days because no one gets tired of it.

700 g (1½ lb) (trimmed weight) leeks, white and light green parts only, sliced
1½ tablespoons butter
1.8 kg (4 lb) potatoes
900 ml (1½ pints) water
1 teaspoon salt

900 ml (1½ pints) vegetable stock (see page 459)
2–3 tablespoons chopped fresh dill
2–3 tablespoons chopped fresh parsley
juice of ½ lemon
freshly ground black pepper

optional: milk or cream to taste

Thoroughly wash the leeks, quarter them lengthwise, and slice them thinly. Melt the butter in a large non-stick pan and cook the leeks in it over medium heat, stirring often, until they are limp and just hinting at the idea of colouring.

Meanwhile, peel the potatoes and cut them in 1 cm (½ inch) dice. Combine them in a saucepan with the water and the salt, adding a little more water only if needed to cover them. Bring the water to a boil, lower the heat, and simmer the potatoes until they are completely tender.

For a more intense potato flavour, cook the peels in a separate pot, in just enough water to cover (be sure you scrubbed the potatoes first). When the potatoes are tender, strain the water off the peels and add it to the soup.

Add the cooked leeks to the potatoes, along with the vegetable stock, chopped herbs, lemon juice, and pepper. Cook everything together for about 10 more minutes, then taste and correct the seasoning with more salt or pepper if desired.

If you like a chunky soup, it's ready. If you want it less chunky, use a potato masher. If you want it smooth, purée it in the blender in batches, but be sure to blend very briefly, as potatoes suffer from overprocessing. For a creamier soup, stir in a little milk or cream now.

Makes 3.4–4 litres (6–7 pints), or about 12 servings.

IRISH SODA BREAD

I've revised this recipe a little over the years. This version has a little butter, some rolled oats, and raisins.

400 ml (14 fl oz) buttermilk	**1¼ teaspoons salt**
1 egg	**215 g (7½ oz) plain flour**
2 tablespoons melted butter	**215 g (7½ oz) wholemeal flour**
1 teaspoon bicarbonate of soda	**75 g (3 oz) rolled oats**
3 teaspoons baking powder	**75 g (3 oz) raisins**

Beat together the buttermilk, the egg, and the melted butter.

Sift together the bicarbonate of soda, baking powder, salt, white flour, and wholemeal flour. Stir in the rolled oats and the raisins, and then the buttermilk mixture.

Turn the dough out on to a well-floured board and knead it gently, dusting with a bit more flour to keep it from sticking, just until it all holds together. Divide the dough into 2 parts and form each part into a smooth ball.

Place the loaves on a buttered baking sheet, press down slightly, and cut a shallow cross in the top of each one.

Bake the loaves for 35–40 minutes at 190°C/375°F/Gas 5. Allow the loaves to cool slightly on a rack before cutting them, if you can stand to wait. They will smell so delicious that you may have to cut right into them, but they will tear a little until they've had time to cool off.

Makes 2 medium loaves.

SWEET POTATO AND CORN SOUP

1 large onion, chopped
1½ tablespoons butter
salt to taste
900 g (2 lb) sweet potatoes
500 ml (16 fl oz) water
900 ml (1½ pints) vegetable
   stock (see page 459)
450 g (1 lb) yellow or white
   sweetcorn kernels

1 medium red pepper, finely
   diced
1 small green chilli, finely
   chopped
250 ml (8 fl oz) milk
juice of ½ lemon
pinch of cayenne
2–3 tablespoons cream

garnish: chopped coriander leaves

Cook the onion slowly in the butter, with a little salt, stirring often, until it is golden brown. At the same time, peel and dice the sweet potatoes, combine them in a pan with the water and the stock, and simmer until the potatoes are tender, about 20–30 minutes. Add the caramelized onions to the soup, deglaze the onion pan with a little of the stock, and add it back, then purée this mixture in batches in a blender.

Return the purée to the pan and add the sweetcorn kernels, diced red pepper, chopped chilli, and milk. Simmer until the peppers and sweetcorn are tender. Stir in the lemon juice and cayenne, taste, and correct the seasoning if needed. Finish the soup with a little cream.

Serve hot, garnished with coarsely chopped coriander leaves.

Serves 8.

TOMATO AND ONION BATTER BREAD

50 g (2 oz) sun-dried
  tomatoes, chopped
250 ml (8 fl oz) hot water
2 large onions
3½ tablespoons olive oil,
  more for the pans
2 teaspoons salt

700 g (1½ lb) fresh tomatoes,
  scalded and peeled
150 g (5 oz) wholemeal flour
575 g (1¼ lb) plain white flour
2 envelopes dried yeast
2 tablespoons sugar

Put the sun-dried tomatoes in a bowl with the hot water and leave them to soak for at least 30 minutes.

Peel the onions, quarter them lengthwise, and slice them. Heat 1½ tablespoons of olive oil in a non-stick pan and add the onions and a teaspoon of salt. Cook the onions in the oil over medium heat, stirring very often, until they are golden brown all over, then set them aside until needed.

Cut the fresh tomatoes into chunks, working over a bowl so as not to lose their juice. Simmer them in their own juice for 5–10 minutes, just until they are tender and their juice is slightly thickened. You should have 500 ml (16 fl oz) of chunky sauce. Combine the cooked fresh tomatoes, the soaked sun-dried tomatoes with their water, 2 tablespoons of olive oil, and a teaspoon of salt in a bowl and allow the mixture to cool slightly.

In the bowl of a food processor, fitted with the short plastic blade, combine the wholemeal flour and 215 g (7½ oz) of the white flour with the yeast and sugar, and spin briefly to blend. Add the tomatoes and liquid, and process for several seconds at a time, scraping the sides down with a spatula in between, until you have a soft batter. Start adding the remaining flour, a little at a time, and process briefly after each addition. Continue adding flour only until the batter is thick and elastic but not yet stiff. Add the cooked onions and process for a few seconds only.

To prepare the batter by hand, combine the wholemeal flour and 215 g (7½ oz) of the white flour with the yeast and sugar in a large mixing bowl and stir with a whisk to blend. Add the tomatoes and liquid and beat vigorously with a wooden spoon for several minutes. Add as much of the remaining flour as is needed, a little at a time, beating it in thoroughly each time, until the batter is thick and elastic. You should use almost all the flour. Add the cooked onions and stir them into the batter.

Generously oil two deep pie dishes, or one large oblong baking dish, about 23 × 30 cm (9 × 12 inches). Using a large spoon or spatula, scoop the batter out into the prepared dishes. It should be thick enough to hold a shape, but softer and stickier than a dough that you would knead. Spread the batter evenly in the dishes, and push it into the corners. The surface will remain rough, which is fine.

Cover the dishes with clingfilm and leave the loaves to rise for about 45 minutes. The batter will nearly double in size.

Bake the bread in a preheated 190°C/375°F/Gas 5 oven for 35–40 minutes, or until it is lightly browned on top and the bottom sounds hollow when tapped. A thin knife inserted near the middle should come out dry.

Let the bread cool on a rack for a little while, then cut it into wedges or squares to serve.

Makes 2 normal loaves, or 1 very large loaf.

How do children actually stay alive and keep growing, since they refuse to eat almost everything? This is the question I keep asking myself, and every other mother I know asks the same.

You may think that, because I write about food, my children come in a docile manner to the table and eat everything that is put in front of them. Not so. My children, like yours, turn up their noses at almost everything I cook. Then, just when I've given up in despair, and cooked one thing for them and something entirely different for the adults, they come and snatch the adult food from our plates.

Why will a child who categorically refuses to touch anything green suddenly eat watercress sandwiches? Or Japanese seaweed? The same kid will painstakingly pick the raisins out of his coffee cake and leave them on the plate. He will demand to have his pasta completely plain, without even butter on it, but pizza can have everything. Probably they are programmed this way just to keep us paying attention.

One thing is clear – kids are so quirky that the marvellous solutions devised by one mother may be perfectly useless to another. Nevertheless, here is what I have observed in eleven years of fascinated observation.

My children will eat many kinds of Mediterranean foods. I think there are two reasons why. First, we live in a Mediterranean sort of climate, so we are surrounded by that kind of produce, that style of cooking. Second, it's just awfully good. They will eat pasta, polenta, and risotto as often as I make them.

They will eat Mexican food erratically. They love tortillas and tamales, but there are times when they will not eat food that has even one atom of chilli in it, and other times when they unaccountably lap up hot salsa.

They will always, always eat quesadillas. Quesadillas have saved them from starvation and me from a nervous breakdown many times.

They will eat crêpes if the fillings are not too weird. Jam is always all right. Cheese and mushrooms are fine, but nothing green will be accepted inside a crêpe; that is considered a betrayal of the whole idea of crêpes.

Rice and couscous are almost always accepted. Beans get the nod from one, vehement refusal from the other.

Fruit is either passionately devoured or completely ignored. Sometimes we go through intense fads for yogurt smoothies. Salads will turn to compost before they get a second look. And sometimes my children demand sausages, or hamburgers, or steak!

So what are we to do? My basic approach is to offer them a variety of healthy and tasty things, and then let them do pretty much what they want. (If after three years they have not touched a vegetable, I will go ahead and force them to eat one.) When they ask for sausage, I send them out to a restaurant with their father. Let them eat sausage. Eventually, they will work out for themselves how they want to eat, anyway, just as we all do. And I teach them to cook anything they are interested in learning.

Meanwhile, I let them eat the grain-based diet they seem to prefer. I bake bread when I can. I make a hundred quesadillas and plates of fruit. I give them carrot sticks and smoothies, and make pasta, risotto, and polenta as often as possible.

Here is the 'children's menu' of an ideal restaurant, as it would be written by *my* children:

1. **Quesadillas and a fruit plate.**
2. **Spaghetti with a little butter and cheese, or with nothing at all. Steamed broccoli on the side.**
3. **Baked potatoes with everything on the side – sour cream or cottage cheese, butter, spring onions, and so on.**
4. **Plain polenta, with grated Parmesan on the side. Carrot sticks and sugar snap peas.**
5. **Tomato and Rice Soup (see page 313). Muffins.**
6. **Pizza.**
7. **Fruit Smoothie (see page 314).**

Here are four recipes that you can stencil on the refrigerator door for the baby-sitter.

Quesadillas

Take a plain flour tortilla and heat it in an ungreased pan for a few seconds on each side. Sprinkle about 25 g (1 oz) of grated Cheddar cheese over one half of it, and fold the other half over the cheese. Keep toasting it in the pan for about a minute, turning once, until both sides are golden and the cheese is melted. Serve at once.

Cheese Toasts

I think in other parts of the world the quesadilla might be replaced by one of my childhood favourites (I grew up in Michigan), the toasted cheese sandwich. I used to make them the classic way, buttering the outside of a plain cheese sandwich and grilling it in a pan. Now I pile grated cheese on top of a thick slice of good bread and put it under the grill until the cheese bubbles.

Almost Instant Tomato and Rice Soup

You can start from scratch and make this soup in about 30 minutes. Or you can start with a tomato sauce you have made before, and some leftover cooked rice, and be done in a minute.

Combine 500–750 ml (16–24 fl oz) of good, home-made tomato sauce (but nothing fancy) with an equal amount of delicate vegetable stock (see page 460) or chicken stock. Add a slightly smaller amount of cooked rice, white or brown. Let everything simmer together for a couple of minutes. Serve with cheese toasts or any kind of bread.

You can add a little milk or cream. This makes a rather thick soup, becoming more porridge-like as the rice expands, and children love it that way.

Fruit Smoothie

Put into a blender 1 banana, a few strawberries, sliced peaches, or other soft fruit, about 120 ml (4–6 fl oz) of milk or yogurt, a little honey, and a drop of vanilla. Purée. Add 2 or 3 ice cubes and process until the ice cubes are completely ground up. Pour and serve.

Pizza

This is one for you to make when you're ready for détente. You make it. They eat it. There's peace in the house. It's plain cheese pizza, the abiding favourite of my two sons.

There are great techniques for making pizza. You can put a stone tile in your oven, and slide the pizza on to it with a peel, but not everyone has such things. These instructions are for anyone with an oven and a baking sheet. They will result in a very good pizza, and your children will adore you for it. It takes a little over an hour to do.

for the dough
120 ml (4 fl oz) milk
175 ml (6 fl oz) hot water
1 tablespoon dried yeast
  (1 envelope)
1 teaspoon sugar
1 teaspoon salt
1 tablespoon rye flour
about 450 g (1 lb) plain white
  flour
a little olive oil
a little cornmeal

for the sauce
700 g (1½ lb) red tomatoes
2 cloves garlic, minced
1 tablespoon olive oil
salt to taste
1 tablespoon chopped fresh
  basil
¼ teaspoon dried oregano
¼ teaspoon dried thyme
¼ teaspoon dried marjoram
2–3 tablespoons tomato paste,
  or sun-dried tomato paste

optional: dash of balsamic vinegar
garnish: 225 g (8 oz) mozzarella cheese, grated

In a large mixing bowl, combine the milk and the hot water. Add the yeast to this lukewarm liquid, along with the sugar and salt. Wait for a few minutes to see if it begins to froth, then stir in the rye flour and about 400 g (14 oz) of the plain flour. Stir until a thick dough forms.

Sprinkle the rest of the flour on a board and turn the dough out on to it. Knead the dough for about 10 minutes, working in as much more flour as it wants to become smooth and elastic. Form the dough into a ball and put it in a lightly oiled bowl, turning it over once, then cover the bowl with a kitchen towel and leave it in a warm place to rise for about 45–50 minutes.

While the dough rises, prepare the sauce. Scald the tomatoes, peel them and core them, then process them briefly in a blender to make a rough purée. Sauté the garlic in the olive oil for a minute or two, then add the tomatoes, some salt, and the herbs. Stir occasionally over fairly high heat until the tomatoes cook down to a thick, dark red. Stir in the tomato paste, and the vinegar if you want it. Taste, and correct the seasoning. You should have about 350 ml (12 fl oz) of sauce.

Lightly oil 2 pizza pans or large baking sheets, and sprinkle them with cornmeal. Preheat the oven to its hottest temperature, and be sure one of the racks is in the lowest position.

Punch down the dough and cut it into 2 equal parts. Form each part into a smooth ball. Take one of the balls and pat it, stretch it, roll it, and otherwise persuade it to be a circle about 32 cm (13 inches) across. It will want to spring back at first, but it will comply, don't worry. If it's very stubborn, leave it to relax for 5 or 10 minutes. Do the same to the other ball, and lay the finished circles of dough on the prepared baking sheets.

Spread half the sauce over each circle, and then sprinkle on the cheese. Bake at your oven's highest temperature, on the lowest rack, for about 12–14 minutes, or until the crust is lightly browned around the edges and the cheese is bubbling. For an extra-crispy crust, slide the pizza off the baking sheet directly on to the oven rack for the last few minutes of baking.

Slice each pizza into 8 wedges and eat while they are hot.

Serves 4–8, depending on how you feel about pizza.

SALAD LUNCHES,
A BRUNCH, AND TEA

A SALAD BOWL LUNCH ON THE PATIO

Salad with Sautéd Mushrooms

Semolina Focaccia with Onion and Garlic

Gorgonzola cheese

Clafouti with Apricots

This is a true salad-eater's lunch – wonderful leaves and lots of them. The salad starts with a mix of spinach, rocket, curly endive, watercress, and delicate young lettuces; on top there's a generous scattering of wild mushrooms, seared in hot oil with garlic and ginger.

The combination is refreshing, surprising, and delicious.

With a cool main-dish salad, it's nice to serve a focaccia warm from the oven, and a little wedge of Gorgonzola cheese. Add a glass of cold white wine and it's just what you'll want on a hot, sunny day.

Since the meal is light, you can have a dessert with a little more substance. I like the Clafouti with Apricots, but you can make a clafouti with whatever fruit is best at the time.

SALAD WITH SAUTÉD MUSHROOMS

for the sautéd mushrooms
450 g (1 lb) oyster mushrooms
225 g (8 oz) fresh shiitake
    mushrooms
2 tablespoons olive oil
1 teaspoon dark sesame oil
4 cloves garlic, minced
2 tablespoons minced fresh
    ginger
2–3 tablespoons rice vinegar
2 teaspoons soy sauce

for the salad
450 g (1 lb) assorted salad
    leaves, such as frisée, oak
    leaf, lollo rosso, curly or
    butterhead lettuce
1 large bunch watercress or
    rocket
6 spring onions, thinly sliced
10–12 tablespoons
    de-stemmed coriander
    leaves

for the dressing
olive oil
dark sesame oil
wine vinegar
salt and pepper

garnishes: coriander sprigs
    big gratings of Manchego or Parmesan cheese

Clean and trim all the mushrooms carefully, and cut the large ones into 1 cm (½ inch) strips.

Heat the olive oil and sesame oil in a large non-stick pan, add the minced garlic and ginger, and stir for a minute or so, until the garlic begins to soften. Add the mushrooms and toss over a medium-high flame until they start to give up their moisture. Continue cooking the mushrooms, stirring frequently, until they are tender and beginning to brown in spots.

Wash, spin, and tear all the salad leaves, and combine them in a large salad bowl. Use any combination of lettuces you like, but remember that you need a balance between sweet, delicately flavoured lettuces and peppery greens such as watercress or rocket. The coriander is essential.

Dress the salad sparingly with olive oil and a trace of dark sesame oil, a little splash of wine vinegar, and some salt and pepper. Toss it until each leaf glistens, taste, and correct the seasoning if needed. Divide the salad leaves among 8 plates.

When the mushrooms are starting to colour, drizzle on the rice vinegar and soy sauce and toss the mushrooms with the seasonings for a few moments. Divide the warm mushrooms evenly over the 8 salads, garnish with coriander sprigs, grated cheese, or both, and serve at once.

Serves 4–6 as a light main dish for lunch, or 8 as a first course.

SEMOLINA FOCACCIA WITH ONION AND GARLIC

7 g (¼ oz) dried yeast
300 ml (10 fl oz) warm water
½ teaspoon sugar or honey
3 tablespoons fruity green
  olive oil
1 large onion, finely chopped

2 cloves garlic, finely chopped
1 teaspoon salt
375 g (13 oz) semolina flour*
215 g (7½ oz) unbleached
  white flour, approx.

In a large mixing bowl, dissolve the yeast in the warm water with the sugar or honey, and put it aside for a few minutes. Meanwhile, heat 2 tablespoons of the olive oil in a non-stick pan and cook the chopped onion and garlic in it over a low heat, stirring constantly, just until they soften. Put this aside to cool.

When the yeast begins to foam, stir in the teaspoon of salt, the onions and garlic in their oil, and the semolina, about 100 g (3½ oz) at a time. Keep stirring with a wooden spoon as you add white flour, little by little, until the mixture is too stiff for a spoon.

Turn the dough out on to a floured board and knead it gently, working in as much of the white flour as it wants to absorb, until it feels quite smooth and elastic. Continue sprinkling it with flour as needed to keep it from sticking.

Form the dough into a ball and put it into an oiled bowl, turning

* Pasta flour – see page 59.

to coat it on all sides. Cover it with a tea towel and leave it in a warm place to rise for about 1½ hours, or until the dough has doubled in size.

Punch it down, lift it out of the bowl, and lay it in an oiled Swiss roll tin (40 × 27 cm/15½ × 10½ inches). Pat the dough evenly into the tin, out to the edges and corners. Cover it loosely and leave it to rise again, this time about 45 minutes, until almost doubled.

Brush the focaccia with the remaining olive oil, dimple the top with your fingertips if you like, and bake it in a preheated 200°C/400°F/Gas 6 oven for about 35 minutes, or until it is golden brown on top and the bottom crust sounds hollow when tapped. Let it cool for just a few minutes on a rack.

Cut the focaccia in squares and serve it hot or warm.

Focaccia, like cornbread or biscuits, really should be eaten shortly after it is out of the oven. This one, however, makes a delicious toast the next day. Cut it in 1 cm (½ inch) slices and grill or toast in the oven until golden.

Makes 1 large loaf.

CLAFOUTI WITH APRICOTS

A clafouti is a pudding-like dessert, made by pouring a pancake batter over fruit and baking it in a hot oven. It's quick and easy, and best eaten hot or warm, dusted with powdered sugar.

900 g (2 lb) ripe apricots	1 teaspoon baking powder
2 tablespoons melted butter, more for the baking dish	pinch of salt
	4 eggs
175 g (6 oz) + 2 tablespoons sugar	400 ml (14 fl oz) warmed milk
	1 teaspoon vanilla extract
175 g (6 oz) flour	grated zest of 1 lemon

garnishes: icing sugar
   cream

Wash and dry the apricots, then cut them in half and remove their stones. Preheat the oven to 220°C/425°F/Gas 7. Butter a large, shallow baking dish (I use a 36 cm (14 inch) round gratin dish), sprinkle it with 2 tablespoons of sugar, and arrange the apricots in one layer, close together, cut side down. Put them in the oven for 10 minutes; they should just begin to release their juice.

Sift together the flour, baking powder, and salt. Beat the eggs with the remaining sugar until fluffy, then beat in the flour mixture, the warmed milk, melted butter, vanilla, and lemon zest to make a smooth batter.

Take the apricots out of the oven and pour the batter over them evenly. Push them down with a spatula if they float up, gently pressing out any trapped air. Put the dish back into the centre of the oven and reduce the heat to 200°C/400°F/Gas 6.

Bake the clafouti for about 35 minutes, but check it after 15. This clafouti has a little baking powder in the batter, so don't be surprised to see it rising in high, billowy shapes. If the edges are browning quickly, lay a sheet of foil loosely over the top for the remaining time.

The clafouti will sink gradually when you take it out of the oven. Serve it warm, sprinkled generously with sifted icing sugar. A little cream poured around it on the plate also goes very well.

Serves 8.

SALAD LUNCH FOR A HOT DAY

❧

*Cold Peach and Nectarine Soup with
Honey-sweetened Yogurt*

Salad with Wheat Pilaf and Red Grapes

*Roquefort cheese
French bread or crackers*

Coffee Granita

Make this salad the day after you've had pilaf for dinner. With leftovers on hand, this meal is almost effortless. I designed it for a very hot day, when no one wants to cook and no one cares to eat anything hot, but perhaps there's company coming or there's another reason why something nicer than a carton of yogurt is called for. Well, here it is.

Everything can be prepared ahead and, assuming the existence of the leftover pilaf, it takes no heat and very little time. The soup takes 15 minutes to prepare, then goes into the refrigerator. All the elements of the salad can be prepared ahead, to be dressed and assembled at the last moment. The granita is waiting in the freezer.

Now have a break and relax, then spend about five more minutes by your refrigerator, and you're ready to serve a beautiful lunch. Set a table outside, in a shady spot if you have one, and open a bottle of chilled wine. The whole meal is refreshing, and none of it overly filling.

COLD PEACH AND NECTARINE SOUP WITH HONEY-SWEETENED YOGURT

This soup is almost instant. It's whipped together in the blender and chilled, and is divinely refreshing in the dog days of August or here where I live in September, when the Santa Ana winds blow from the desert.

900 g (2 lb) peaches, peeled and sliced
900 g (2 lb) nectarines, peeled and sliced
750 ml (1¼ pints) plain low-fat yogurt

8 tablespoons honey
2 tablespoons freshly squeezed lemon juice
2 tablespoons Marsala
½ teaspoon ground cinnamon

optional garnish: mint sprigs

Use fully ripe, juicy peaches and nectarines. Working in batches, purée the fruit in a blender with 500 ml (16 fl oz) of the yogurt, 3 tablespoons of honey, the lemon juice, Marsala, and cinnamon. Chill the mixture well. (When I'm in a hurry, I put it in the freezer in a stainless steel bowl and give it a stir with a whisk every 15 minutes or so. It will be very cold in about an hour.)

Whisk together the remaining yogurt with the remaining honey, and chill.

Ladle the soup into shallow bowls and put a spoonful of the honey-sweetened yogurt in the centre of each serving. Garnish with mint sprigs if you happen to have some mint around.

Serves 6.

SALAD WITH WHEAT PILAF AND RED GRAPES

This is really a delicious salad, combining the pungency of fresh leaves with the rich chewiness of wheat and browned onions, and the sweetness of grapes. It makes a nice first course, and because the pilaf is quite substantial, it can also be the centrepiece of a summer lunch with no change except portion size.

450 g (1 lb) mixed tender salad
  leaves
1 large cucumber
2 small red peppers
50 g (2 oz) sunflower seed
  sprouts, or any
  mild-flavoured sprouts
50 g (2 oz) radish sprouts, or
  50 g (2 oz) very thinly sliced
  radishes

3 tablespoons virgin olive oil
1½ tablespoons balsamic
  vinegar
salt to taste
350 g (12 oz) Wheat and Lentil
  Pilaf, cooled (page 83)
125 g (4 oz) toasted almonds,
  coarsely chopped
350 g (12 oz) seedless red
  grapes

The mix of salad leaves is important – use tender young lettuces and herbs, and be sure you have a balance of peppery flavours with the delicate, sweet ones. Mesclun, which is a mix of many salad leaves, is quite widely available now, but if you don't have it you can start with red and green oak-leaf lettuce or tender butterhead lettuce or Little Gem, add some young frisée and some rocket or watercress, and a bit of radicchio if you can get it. Wash all the leaves, remove heavy stems, if any, and spin the leaves dry in a salad spinner. Tear everything into bite-sized pieces.

Peel the cucumber, quarter it lengthwise, and slice thinly. Trim the peppers, quarter them lengthwise, and then cut crosswise in matchsticks.

In a large bowl, toss the leaves with the cucumber, peppers, sprouts, olive oil, vinegar, and a touch of salt.

Using ample salad plates, divide the various ingredients equally among them: first a mound of leaves, and on top of that a large spoonful of pilaf, then a tablespoon or more of chopped almonds scattered over everything. Finally, arrange some red grapes casually around the perimeter of the leaves, and serve.

Serves 6 as a light entrée, or 8 – 10 as a first course.

COFFEE GRANITA

900 ml (1½ pints) hot espresso, or triple-strength filter coffee	**3 thin strips lemon peel, or orange peel**
125 g (4 oz) sugar	**2 tablespoons Triple Sec or Grand Marnier**

optional garnish: whipped cream, or vanilla ice cream

Be sure to use very strong coffee. Stir the sugar and the citrus peel into the coffee. Allow it to cool, then chill it. Stir in the Triple Sec or Grand Marnier.

Put the coffee in a big, shallow bowl, or into old-fashioned ice-cube trays with the dividers removed. Put it in the freezer, and every 30 minutes or so take it out and stir it up well with a fork, scraping the ice down from the sides and breaking it up. Do this until the coffee has turned into a mass of coarse ice crystals, something like a rough-textured sorbet.

The granita can be kept in the freezer, tightly covered, for several days.

Serve the granita piled into sorbet goblets, alone or with whipped cream on top. Or place a small scoop of vanilla ice cream in the glass and then spoon the granita around it.

Serves 6 – 8.

A FRENCH SOUP AND SALAD LUNCH

⸙

Cream of Carrot Soup

*Haricot Vert, Red Potato,
and Cucumber Salad*

Goat's Cheese Toasts

Rustic Plum Pie or white peaches

Here's a lunch that takes me straight back to France, to an ancient stone table under a tree at the edge of the big lawn behind our little rented house at Beaureport.

Each nearby village had a market day, and so nearly every day you could drive a few kilometres and find seasonal vegetables, fresh farmhouse cheeses, beautiful fruits, and flowers for the table. In the hot Provençal afternoons we sat at the stone table, eating meals of easy summer food, drinking ice-cold rosé from Tavel.

The Cream of Carrot Soup is a classic purée. Sprinkle it with chopped chives or mint from the garden. After the soup, a big plate of salad that can only be had in summer, when *haricots verts* are plentiful and cucumbers sweet. They're mixed with new red potatoes cut in big chunks, and everything is scattered with fresh dill.

Along with the salad, serve toasted country bread with hot goat's cheese melting on top of it. Of course, one of the delicious Tavel rosés, well chilled, would be perfect with this.

For dessert, have either an easy fruit pie or a bowl of ripe, perfumed white peaches. These peaches have a short season, and are very delicate, so they don't travel well, but when you find them at the peak of their ripeness, juicy and fragrant, buy as many as you can – they'll make your day.

CREAM OF CARROT SOUP

1 leek, white part only, chopped	pinch of sugar
2 large onions, chopped	1 teaspoon salt
4 tablespoons butter	½ teaspoon crushed dried thyme
1 kg (2–2¼ lb) young carrots	1 small bay leaf
750 ml (1¼ pints) water	pinch of cayenne
750 ml (1¼ pints) vegetable stock (see page 459)	350 ml (12 fl oz) milk
5 tablespoons raw white rice	90 ml (3 fl oz) cream
	dash of grated nutmeg

garnish: chopped fresh chives

In a large, heavy saucepan, sauté the leek and onions in the butter, stirring often, until they are golden. Meanwhile, peel and thinly slice the carrots. Add the carrots, water, stock, rice, sugar, salt, herbs, and cayenne to the leek and onion mixture. Cover and simmer for about 40 minutes, or until the carrots and rice are completely mushy soft.

Remove the bay leaf and purée the soup in batches in a blender or food processor until it is velvety smooth. Return the soup to the rinsed saucepan and stir in the milk, cream, and a sprinkle of nutmeg. Heat the soup through, stirring gently, then taste and correct the seasoning with another pinch of salt or nutmeg. Sprinkle each serving with chopped fresh chives.

Serves 8–10 generously. This may be more than you need for one meal, but a soup like this one is a nice thing to have left over for lunch the next day.

HARICOT VERT, RED POTATO, AND CUCUMBER
SALAD

This salad came into my head at the market one day as I bought first a huge bunch of fresh dill, and then all the things I like best with dill. It's an excellent salad for picnics, and keeps well for a day or so in the refrigerator. But the thin, tender French green beans are important to this – don't try to cheat with any larger, tougher beans.

700 g (1½ lb) small
  red-skinned potatoes
  (about the size of walnuts)
450 g (1 lb) haricots verts
  (French green beans)
1 cucumber
6 tablespoons coarsely
  chopped fresh dill weed

½ red onion, finely chopped
2 tablespoons fruity olive oil
2 tablespoons fresh lemon
  juice
½ teaspoon salt
½ teaspoon sugar
1 teaspoon Dijon mustard
freshly ground pepper to taste

Scrub the potatoes clean and trim away any rough spots. Cut in half potatoes that are larger in size than a walnut. Salt the potatoes lightly and steam them for about 15 minutes, or until tender. Let them cool.

Wash and trim the haricots verts and steam them for 5–7 minutes, or until tender-crisp. Let them cool.

Peel, halve lengthwise and deseed the cucumber, then slice thinly.

Combine the potatoes, green beans, sliced cucumbers, coarsely chopped dill, and chopped red onion in a large bowl. Whisk together the olive oil, lemon juice, salt, sugar, Dijon mustard, and a dash of pepper. Pour the dressing over the vegetables and toss together gently but thoroughly. Try not to break up the potatoes.

Allow the salad to rest in the refrigerator for an hour or so, then taste, and correct the seasoning with more salt, pepper, or lemon juice if needed.

This serves 6–8 generously, or up to 10 in smaller servings.

GOAT'S CHEESE TOASTS

16–20 slices from a baguette
butter to taste
225 g (8 oz) soft white goat's cheese

Cut the French bread into slices about 1 cm (½ inch) thick, and butter them lightly. Toast the buttered slices under the grill or in the oven until they are just golden and slightly crisp – do not let them get brown.

Spread a thick slice of the goat's cheese evenly over each toast. Arrange the toasts on a baking sheet and bake them in a hot oven for about 2 minutes to soften the cheese, then put them under the grill until the cheese begins to turn golden brown in spots. Serve at once.

Serves 8.

RUSTIC PLUM PIE

for the pastry
185 g (6½ oz) flour
1 teaspoon salt
1 teaspoon sugar
125 g (4 oz) cold butter
3–4 tablespoons ice water

for the filling
1.6 kg (3½ lb) plums, sliced
165 g (5½ oz) sugar
3 tablespoons cornflour
dash of ground cinnamon
¼ teaspoon almond extract
1 egg

Combine the flour, salt, and sugar in the bowl of a food processor, and cut in the cold butter in chunks. Process briefly, until the mixture resembles coarse meal. Process again while trickling in the ice water, just until the pastry pulls together and starts forming a ball. Do not add more water than necessary to reach this stage.

On a lightly floured board, roll the dough out into a circle about 36 cm (14 inches) in diameter. Transfer it to a baking sheet, cover it with clingfilm, and put it away to chill for an hour or longer.

Wash the plums and slice them off their stones into thin wedges. In a dry bowl, whisk together the sugar and cornflour until there are no lumps left. Add the prepared plums, the cinnamon, and the almond extract, and mix well. Let the fruit sit for about 20 minutes.

Preheat the oven to 230°C/450°F/Gas 8. Remove the pastry from the refrigerator and give it a few minutes to soften. It should be cool but pliable, to prevent cracking. Centre the pastry over a 25 cm (10 inch) deep pie dish and fit it gently into the curve of the dish, pushing out all air bubbles and letting the excess pastry hang over the sides.

Whisk the egg in a bowl and brush the inside of the pie shell with it. Stir up the plums, then pour them into the prepared pie crust, distributing them evenly. You can make a pattern in the centre with plum wedges, or just leave it random.

You should have about a 5 cm (2 inch) border of pastry overhanging the edge of the pan. You can trim it a little to make it more even, or just leave it ragged around the edges as I do. Fold this edge in over the fruit, pleating it loosely as you go round. You will have a rustic-looking pie, something like a deep-dish galette. Only about a 12 cm (5 inch) circle of fruit will show in the middle.

Brush the pastry edge with the remaining egg, and put the pie into the lower half of the oven. Lay a sheet of foil loosely over the top of it, and bake for 20 minutes. Lower the heat to 190°C/375°F/Gas 5 and bake for another 40 minutes, removing the foil for the last 10 or 15 minutes to brown the crust. The fruit will be bubbling vigorously when you remove the pie.

Let the pie cool on a rack for a while, then serve it while it's still warm if you can. Enjoy it alone or with a scoop of vanilla ice cream. This is a juicy pie, so have a spoon ready as well as a pie server.

Serves 8.

A NOODLE SALAD LUNCH

❈

papaya halves with fresh lime wedges

Asian Noodle Salad

Lemon Cheesecake Ice Cream with blueberries

A salad made of nutty-flavoured Japanese buckwheat noodles, tossed with a combination of vegetables and mushrooms in a sesame and ginger dressing, makes the centrepiece of this cold lunch. The noodle salad is not overly spicy, but flecks of hot red pepper, ginger, and garlic keep it lively. A Gewürztraminer or a fruity white Riesling would be just right with this.

The salad is a subtle complex of tastes and textures, so the other parts of the meal should be kept as simple as possible – ripe papaya halves with lime wedges for a starter, and one of my favourites, Lemon Cheesecake Ice Cream, for dessert.

ASIAN NOODLE SALAD

225 g (8 oz) *haricots verts* (French green beans), or thin asparagus
2 tablespoons peanut oil
salt to taste
175 g (6 oz) baby courgettes, or small ones quartered lengthwise
225 g (8 oz) oyster mushrooms
½ large onion
1–2 cloves garlic
1 teaspoon dark sesame oil
60 ml (2 fl oz) rice wine
½ head Chinese leaves, shredded
2 tablespoons minced fresh ginger
2–3 tablespoons rice vinegar
soy sauce

450 g (1 lb) Japanese
   buckwheat noodles
6 spring onions, thinly sliced
2 small hot red chillies,
   minced
8–10 tablespoons coriander
   leaves, coarsely chopped

for the dressing
1 tablespoon sesame oil, more
   to taste
2½ tablespoons rice vinegar,
   more to taste
2 tablespoons soy sauce, more
   to taste

garnishes: coriander sprigs
   thin strips of red chilli
   sesame seeds

Trim the ends off the *haricots verts*; if using asparagus, trim off the tough parts of the stalks and cut each stalk in half. Toss the vegetables with a teaspoon of peanut oil and a little salt, and spread them out on a baking sheet. Quarter the courgettes lengthwise if necessary, toss them with another teaspoon of the oil and some salt, and spread on another baking sheet.

Roast the prepared vegetables in a 200°C/400°F/Gas 6 oven for 15–20 minutes, just until tender and barely beginning to colour. Remove and allow to cool.

Meanwhile, cut the oyster mushrooms in 1 cm (½ inch) strips, and thinly slice the onion and mince the garlic. Heat the remaining peanut oil and a teaspoon of sesame oil in a non-stick sauté pan, and sauté the mushrooms, onion, and garlic in it until they are lightly browned. Add 2 tablespoons of rice wine to the pan and continue to stir the vegetables for another minute. Remove the mushroom mixture from the pan and set it aside.

Add the shredded Chinese leaves to the pan, along with the minced ginger, and sauté it over medium heat until it is limp and starting to colour. Add the remaining rice wine, the rice vinegar, and a dash of soy sauce, and keep tossing the leaves over medium heat until the excess liquid is gone.

Cook the noodles in an ample amount of boiling, salted water until they are *al dente*. Drain them, then plunge them into ice water for a moment and drain again.

In a large bowl, combine the drained noodles, the roasted vegetables, the mushroom mixture, Chinese leaves, sliced spring onions, minced chillies, and coriander. Add sesame oil, rice vinegar, and soy sauce to taste and toss gently until everything is lightly coated with the dressing. Serve at room temperature, garnished with coriander sprigs, strips of chillies and sesame seeds.

Serves 6−8.

LEMON CHEESECAKE ICE CREAM

Because this is made with more buttermilk than cream, it is not as fatty as conventional ice cream, and it has the delicious, tangy taste of cheesecake. It's sensational with ripe summer blueberries.

60 ml (2 fl oz) freshly squeezed lemon juice
grated zest of 2 lemons
175 g (6 oz) + 1 tablespoon sugar

90 ml (3 fl oz) water
120 ml (4 fl oz) double cream
120 ml (4 fl oz) milk
250 ml (8 fl oz) low-fat buttermilk

In a small enamelled saucepan, combine the lemon juice, zest, sugar, and water. Heat to a simmer and stir until the sugar is completely dissolved. Cool the syrup, then chill it.

Combine the chilled lemon syrup with the cream, milk, and buttermilk, and freeze according to manufacturer's instructions in an ice cream freezer.

This makes about 1.2 litres (2 pints) of ice cream.

A TOSTADA LUNCH

❧

*Black Bean Tostadas with courgettes, feta
cheese, radishes and Guacamole*

fruit platter

Strawberry Ice Cream with Triple Sec

This lunch has the casual and relaxed quality of a picnic, whether it is eaten inside or out. Everyone makes their own tostadas, the way they like them. Bowls of tasty things are passed back and forth, you pick up tostadas in your hands to eat them, and things drip a little so fingers have to be licked.

Savoury black beans and crumbly white cheese, on a crisply toasted corn tortilla, are the foundation. After that, all sorts of toppings are added. Purists like a dab of salsa, or a few sliced radishes. Others pile sliced courgettes on top of guacamole, adding sliced spring onions, dousing it all with salsa, and decorating the top with coriander leaves. Having guests assemble their own tostadas is important not only because it's fun, but because freshness is essential when combining juicy toppings with crispy tortillas.

These are not so big, so you can have two or three, made different ways.

With spicy food, I always serve fruit. After Black Bean Tostadas I like more fruit for dessert, in the form of a terrific home-made ice cream with strawberries and Triple Sec.

BLACK BEAN TOSTADAS

These are not to be confused with restaurant tostadas – mounds of salad piled inside a deep-fried flour tortilla 'bowl'. The tostadas I make are much smaller, crisp-toasted corn tortillas spread with delicious things, and they can be picked up and eaten in the hand.

Packets of corn tortillas can be found in some supermarkets.

20–24 corn tortillas (see page 38)
olive oil
salt
900 g (2 lb) courgettes
butter
juice of 1 lemon
1 recipe Everyday Black Beans (see page 271)
350 g (12 oz) feta cheese, crumbled

1 bunch radishes, thinly sliced
6 spring onions, thinly sliced
10–12 tablespoons chopped coriander leaves
Hot Chipotle Salsa (see page 145), or Red Chilli Salsa (see page 98) or bought chilli salsa
Guacamole (recipe follows)

Everything you need for tostadas can be prepared ahead of time if you like, but it is important to assemble them a second before you eat them.

Lay the corn tortillas out on baking sheets. Brush them very lightly with olive oil and sprinkle with a little salt. Shortly before you're going to eat, toast the tortillas for a few minutes under a hot grill. Watch them carefully and remove them as soon as they start to turn golden brown in spots. Pile them in a basket, where they will become very crisp as they cool.

Slice the courgettes and sauté them lightly in a tiny bit of butter and a little lemon juice.

Have your black beans warm and ready in a bowl. Put everything on the table, and assemble the tostadas like this:

Spread about 2 rounded tablespoons of black beans on a crisp tortilla. Sprinkle crumbled feta cheese over the beans. Now add whatever toppings appeal to you, just as you would on a pizza. The combinations are endless, but what always works for me is the basic layer of black beans and cheese followed by something green or crunchy, and then something spicy. Some of my favourites:

Black beans, feta cheese, lots of courgettes or green beans, a little Guacamole, a dab of Chipotle Salsa.

Black beans, feta cheese, thin-sliced radishes.

Black beans, feta cheese, spring onions, radishes, and coriander.

Black beans, Guacamole, Chipotle Salsa, feta cheese.

The amounts given here are enough for 6–8 people, depending on what other food is served.

GUACAMOLE

Here is the most basic Guacamole, and it should be freshly made. You can elaborate this with the addition of chillies, hot salsas, or tomatoes. I cannot give exact proportions, as the acidity of lemons and the size and ripeness of avocados will vary.

2 large ripe avocados
2–3 tablespoons freshly squeezed lemon juice
salt to taste

2–3 spring onions, thinly sliced
chopped coriander leaves

Cut the avocados in half lengthwise, take out the stones, and scoop the soft flesh out into a bowl. Immediately add some lemon juice and mash the avocado with it. Add salt to taste, some thinly sliced spring onions, and as much chopped coriander as you like. Taste, and add more lemon if needed. Serve the Guacamole as soon as possible, with corn tortillas or chips, and as a topping for tostadas.

Makes about 500 ml (16 fl oz).

STRAWBERRY ICE CREAM WITH TRIPLE SEC

120 ml (4 fl oz) double cream
120 ml (4 fl oz) milk
300 g (10 oz) sugar
½ teaspoon vanilla extract
900 g (2 lb) ripe strawberries,
 sliced

2 tablespoons freshly
 squeezed lemon juice
1–2 tablespoons Triple Sec
250 ml (8 fl oz) buttermilk

Scald the cream and milk with 175 g (6 oz) of sugar and the vanilla, stirring until the sugar is completely dissolved. Allow the mixture to cool, then chill it. Crush the strawberries with the remaining 125 g (4 oz) of sugar, the lemon juice, and the Triple Sec. Pulse this mixture in a food processor until it is a rough purée. You want a little texture, but no great big chunks of strawberry. Chill the processed strawberries.

Combine the cream mixture, the strawberries, and the buttermilk, and freeze according to manufacturer's instructions in an ice cream freezer.

This makes about 1.7 litres (3 pints) of intensely flavoured ice cream, with a texture somewhere between true ice cream and sorbet.

NOTHING FANCY BRUNCH

❦

Mimosas

freshly squeezed orange juice

Green Chilli Potatoes

Huevos Mexicanos

fresh corn tortillas

Salsa Cruda

Molletes

Teddy's Fruit Salad

Buttermilk Coffee Cake

coffee

I've heard brunch praised as the most interesting and relaxed of meals, and dismissed as an aberration.

Well, let's lighten up, folks.

What I like about brunch is that anything goes. Breakfast foods, lunch foods (and, truthfully, some of those might be dinner foods), fruit juices, wine, coffee – they're all part of brunch. Of course, that's exactly the spirit of anarchy that drives some people crazy, but I remember what Duke Ellington said about serious music versus popular music: 'If it sounds good, it *is* good.' The same is true if it tastes good, and I've eaten all these foods in the middle of a nice Sunday, and it *was* good.

Brunches ultimately fall to the side of either the great, hearty breakfast, or the big, fancy buffet lunch, and this one is solidly in the breakfast camp.

There's nothing fancy here, nothing held warm in a chafing dish, only simple foods prepared just before they're eaten. If that sounds tricky for a company meal, let me hasten to add that all the component parts can be prepared well ahead of time, and you only need a few minutes at the stove before serving.

It starts with the classic brunch drink, a Mimosa. Ice-cold champagne mixed with freshly squeezed orange juice is equally welcome after hiking in the mountains all morning or sleeping till noon. Next, two great pan-cooked dishes, Green Chilli Potatoes and Huevos Mexicanos. The potatoes are savoury with onions, green chillies and cheese, and the eggs snappy with chillies too. Both can be served straight from the pans in which they're made.

To accompany the hearty hot foods serve warm corn tortillas (see page 38), your favourite salsa, fresh fruit, a sweet and easy coffee cake, and my personal favourite, Molletes – crusty rolls toasted and topped with warm refried beans and melted cheese.

MIMOSAS

This refreshing beverage is the traditional drink of many a brunch. There are only 2 ingredients, so they must both be excellent. You don't need to buy the most expensive vintage champagne, but you should be willing to drink it even without the orange juice (and someone is sure to do just that).

fresly squeezed orange juice   ice-cold champagne

Strain the orange juice to remove the heavy pulp, chill it thoroughly, and keep it cold without adding ice. Have the champagne completely chilled as well, and keep the bottle in an ice bucket.

Mix the Mimosas a moment before they are to be consumed. Half fill a champagne flute with juice, then fill to the top with champagne.

GREEN CHILLI POTATOES

This is roadside diner food the way you wish it would taste in the roadside diner. My father-in-law, Rudy, described it to me one day, and I made a panful right away, which the whole family ate for lunch. It's an old-fashioned pan-fried dish of potatoes, cheese and chillies. The original version was made with canned chillies, but any medium hot green chillies will do very well.

Use the smaller red-skinned potatoes if you can, for their taste and their texture. If they're unavailable, use the white-skinned variety.

1.6 kg (3½ lb) small red-skinned potatoes	salt and pepper to taste
2 tablespoons olive oil	2 canned chillis or fresh green chillies, chopped
2 large onions, chopped	125–150 g (4–5 oz) grated Cheddar cheese, to taste
1 clove garlic, finely chopped	

Boil the unpeeled potatoes in salted water until they are just tender – the time will depend on their size. Drain them and allow them to cool. Cut them up in 2.5 cm(1 inch) chunks.

Heat the olive oil in a large non-stick sauté pan, and sauté the chopped onion in it until it softens. Add the garlic, and stir for a minute. Add the potatoes and some salt and pepper.

Sauté the potatoes with the onions and garlic, stirring and turning gently but often, until they are becoming browned and crisp in spots. Stir in the chopped chillies and continue turning over medium-high heat for another 2 minutes.

Spread the potato mixture evenly in the pan, sprinkle the grated cheese over the top, cover tightly, and turn off the heat. Wait 2 minutes; the steam will melt the cheese over the potatoes in a delectable way. Then lift the lid and serve.

Serves 8.

HUEVOS MEXICANOS

For a traditional Mexican breakfast, serve these eggs with refried beans, warm corn tortillas, fresh fruit, hot chilli salsa, and café con leche or hot chocolate.

This recipe gives the amounts for 4 servings. For 8 servings, double the quantities, but do the cooking in 2 pans. It's easier, and the texture of the eggs will be good.

8 eggs
salt to taste
freshly ground black pepper
   to taste
5–6 tablespoons chopped
   coriander leaves
1 teaspoon olive oil

1 tablespoon butter
2 fresh green chillies, trimmed
   and finely chopped
1 medium onion, chopped
225 g (8 oz) fresh tomatoes,
   chopped and drained

Beat the eggs with salt, pepper, and coriander. Heat the oil and butter in a non-stick sauté pan, add the chillies and chopped onion, and stir and cook for about 5 minutes, just until the onion is trans-lucent and soft.

Add the drained tomatoes, stir them just until they are hot through, then add the eggs. Scramble the eggs over a medium-low flame until set, then serve at once with warm corn tortillas.

Serves 4.

Salsa Cruda (see page 272)

MOLLETES

These provide a great way for using leftover refried beans the next morning, and they are just delicious.

8 small, crusty French rolls (I   **125 g (4 oz) grated Cheddar**
   like sourdough rolls)   **cheese**
2½ tablespoons butter
600 ml (1 pint) Refried Pinto
   Beans (see page 36)

optional: roasted, chopped green chillies, hot or mild

Split the rolls in half lengthwise and butter them lightly. Toast them under the grill just until they start to turn golden.

Spread a generous, heaped tablespoon of warm refried beans on each toasted roll, covering it as completely as you can to prevent the edges from scorching when you toast it again. Sprinkle a little grated cheese over the beans. Put the rolls back in the oven or under the grill for about 2 minutes, or until the beans are hot through and the cheese is melted and bubbling. Serve at once with hot coffee or chocolate.

These can be made spicy to taste by stirring some chopped green chillies into the refried beans. I prefer them without the chillies, although I am a great fan of chillies in general, but don't be afraid to try.

Serves 8.

TEDDY'S FRUIT SALAD

No one needs a recipe for fruit salad. But just because it perfectly captures the spirit of fruit salad, here is one written by my son Teddy when he was six years old, for a little cookbook his school was putting together.

Just as he wrote it:

You need a medium sized bowl. Cut off the green part of at least 10 strawberries and put them in. Cut up some apricots. Any amount. And put them in. Put some mint leaves. One branch. And put some mango in. Cut up some peach. Drop it in. Cut up some honeydew. And drop it in. That's it. The end.

And in fact, if you do just that, you will have an excellent fruit salad.

BUTTERMILK COFFEE CAKE

This easy coffee cake is made with blueberries and walnuts, but I've made the same cake substituting chopped fresh apple and raisins, with excellent results.

225 g (8 oz) white flour
4 teaspoons baking powder
pinch of salt
125 g (4 oz) sugar
½ teaspoon ground cinnamon
40 g (1½ oz) rolled oats
40 g (1½ oz) finely chopped
   walnuts
1 large egg
120 ml (4 fl oz) buttermilk

3 tablespoons melted butter
1 teaspoon vanilla extract
175 g (6 oz) fresh or frozen
   blueberries

for the topping
20 g (¾ oz) rolled oats
3 tablespoons brown sugar
¼ teaspoon ground cinnamon
1 tablespoon softened butter

Sift together the flour, baking powder, salt, sugar, and ½ teaspoon of cinnamon. Stir in the 40 g (1½ oz) of rolled oats and the chopped walnuts.

In another bowl, beat the egg with the buttermilk, melted butter, and vanilla. Stir the wet mixture into the dry one, just until a batter is formed. If using fresh blueberries, rinse them and pat them dry. Stir the fresh or frozen blueberries gently into the batter.

Spoon the batter into a buttered 20 cm (8 inch) square baking pan. In a small bowl, combine all the topping ingredients and rub this together with your fingers until you have a crumbly mixture. Sprinkle this over the batter in the tin.

Bake the cake at 200°C/400°F/Gas 6 for about 40 minutes, or until a toothpick inserted near the centre comes out clean. Allow the cake to cool slightly, then cut it into squares to serve.

Serves 9–12.

THE CALIFORNIA TEA

Tea is not a meal where I live. Tea is something you drink if you don't drink coffee, or else it's an event.

Afternoon tea is an exotic idea here, associated with white gloves, cold weather, and polite conversation, all of which are things we believe in but some of us have never actually encountered.

In California, a pretty tea party can have the irresistible charm of something taking place in a storybook. Reality is left at the door, or at the garden gate, since gardens in bloom are the best venue for this sort of thing.

I once went to a very grand tea which was part of a fund-raising event for the local film society. I knew nearly everyone there, but didn't recognize a soul; the ladies were all in hats! And never have I seen such a stupendous array of lovely foods laid out on doilies.

A tea of that kind is sometimes mistakenly called a high tea in America. It sounds right, and many people have had no reason to find out that high tea does not translate to *haute cuisine*, and that the correct name for the white glove and doily event is 'afternoon tea'. Well, never mind – we love our tea events, and I think they are gradually evolving into a genre of their own. Maybe we'll call them California tea.

A FANCY TEA

❧

*Watercress Sandwiches on Oat Bread
with Maple Syrup*

*Chopped Egg and Dill Sandwiches
on pumpernickel bread*

Avocado Sandwiches on wholegrain bread

*Three-grain Cranberry Bread
with butter or Pumpkin Butter*

*Buttermilk Scones with
Sweetened Yogurt Cream and strawberries*

Russian Tea Cakes

Darjeeling or Earl Grey tea

This tea party stays pretty close to the traditional style of an English tea. There are savoury sandwiches – watercress, and egg with dill, and, because this is California, avocado. On the slightly sweet side are scones with strawberries and something reminiscent of clotted cream, as well as a very good cranberry bread with all-American Pumpkin Butter.

And for dessert, Russian Tea Cakes, the best biscuit ever made.

All this should be served with a fragrant tea, freshly brewed in an ample teapot, and very, very hot. And, as much as I love a good cup of tea, I think it's nice to have a little something more on hand for an occasion like this. For that little something, I suggest a medium-dry sherry. Finally, since this is a California tea, a bottle of champagne is never out of place.

AN EASY TEA

༜

For a simpler tea, something small for a couple of friends,
here is a pared-down version.

Watercress Sandwiches
on wholegrain bread

Buttermilk Scones with
Sweetened Yogurt Cream and strawberries

Russian Tea Cakes

Darjeeling or Earl Grey tea

This is a very nice yet sensible sort of tea that can be put together with a minimum of effort.

It provides the peppery bite of watercress, the pleasure of freshly baked scones (which are a snap to make) with ripe strawberries and cream, and those sensational biscuits, which could be replaced by something good from the bakery at a pinch. All the elements are there, in a restrained way that is actually very appealing.

WATERCRESS SANDWICHES

8 slices Oat Bread with Maple Syrup (recipe follows), or any good, fine-textured sandwich bread

50–75 g (2–3 oz) cream cheese
1 bunch or packet watercress sprigs, washed and dried

Spread each of the freshly cut slices of bread thinly with cream cheese. You can use reduced-fat cream cheese with perfect results; Yogurt Cheese (see page 85) would be fine also, though I wouldn't recommend non-fat Yogurt Cheese, which is a little too tart.

Take a quarter of the watercress sprigs, with all the heavy stems removed, and arrange them more or less evenly over a slice of bread. Cover with another slice, so that the watercress is held between cream cheese on both sides. This is a practical necessity as well as a tasty plan, since the sandwich would fall apart without the cementing properties of the cream cheese.

Construct all the sandwiches this way, then trim away the crusts if you must, and cut each of the 4 sandwiches in half diagonally, making 8 triangles. Keep them well covered with clingfilm until serving time.

Makes 8 small watercress sandwiches.

OAT BREAD WITH MAPLE SYRUP

My children love this bread, so I make it often. Once a whole loaf disappeared when I left it cooling on a rack in the kitchen. It's a crossover bread – loved by kids and grown-ups alike. A little bit of maple syrup enriches the flavour without making it noticeably sweet.

This is an excellent bread for sandwiches and for toast.

500 ml (16 fl oz) water
250 ml (8 fl oz) milk
135 g (4½ oz) rolled oats
1 packet dried yeast
120 ml (4 fl oz) pure maple
  syrup
2 teaspoons salt

2 tablespoons melted and
  cooled butter
425 g (15 oz) unbleached
  white flour
425 g (15 oz) wholemeal bread
  flour

Heat the water and milk together until scalding, and pour the liquid over the oats in a large bowl. Leave it to soak for about an hour.

Sprinkle the yeast over the oat mixture, which should be tepid, and stir it in. Then stir in the maple syrup, the salt, the melted butter, and the white flour. You will have a thick batter that can still be stirred with a big wooden spoon. Cover it with a tea towel or with clingfilm and leave it in a warm place to rise for about an hour.

Stir the batter down and start adding the wholemeal flour, about 65 g (2½ oz) at a time, stirring it in well. When the dough is too stiff for a spoon, turn it out on a well-floured board, sprinkle more flour on top, and begin kneading. Keep adding sprinkles of flour as long as the dough is sticky, but not past that point. Knead it until it is elastic and firm, and responds quickly to your push.

Divide the dough into 2 equal parts and shape them into loaves. Put the loaves into medium-sized, buttered loaf tins or on buttered baking sheets, and cover them loosely with a tea towel. Leave them in a warm place to rise for just under an hour, or until about doubled.

Bake the loaves in a preheated 180°C/350°F/Gas 4 oven for about 45–50 minutes. Check them along the way – if they're getting too dark, lay a piece of foil over them. They should be golden brown and sound hollow when tapped on the bottom crust.

Remove the loaves from the pans and cool them on racks before slicing.

Makes 2 loaves.

CHOPPED EGG AND DILL SANDWICHES

4 hard-boiled eggs
1 stalk celery, finely chopped
2 tablespoons minced sweet
  pickles
1½ tablespoons mayonnaise
1–2 teaspoons prepared
  mustard
pinch of cayenne
3 tablespoons chopped fresh
  dill

salt to taste
freshly ground black pepper
  to taste
8 thin slices pumpernickel
  bread
radish sprouts (dill or parsley
  sprigs can be used as an
  alternative)

Shell the eggs and chop them rather finely. Combine them in a bowl with the chopped celery and minced sweet pickles. Mix together the mayonnaise, mustard, cayenne, and dill, and add this to the eggs, mixing everything together thoroughly. Taste, and add salt and pepper as needed until the balance is right for you.

Spread this mixture evenly over 4 of the bread slices, and cover them with the other 4. Cut each of the sandwiches in half, crosswise or diagonally, depending on the shape of the bread.

Lift the top off each sandwich, place a few radish sprouts or dill or parsley sprigs so that they peek out over the edge of the bread in a decorative frill, then replace the top neatly.

Makes 8 small sandwiches.

AVOCADO SANDWICHES

2 ripe medium avocados
1 tablespoon mayonnaise
2 teaspoons freshly squeezed
  lemon juice

salt to taste
freshly ground pepper to taste
finely chopped chives
8 thin slices wholegrain bread

Cut the avocados in half lengthwise and take out the stones. Scoop out the soft flesh and immediately add the mayonnaise and lemon juice, and a little salt and pepper. Mash everything together, taste, and add more salt as needed. Stir in some chopped chives.

Spread 4 slices of bread evenly with the avocado mixture, and cover with the other 4 slices. Cut each sandwich in half.

Makes 8 small sandwiches.

THREE-GRAIN CRANBERRY BREAD

This bread is very easy and fast to make, not too sweet, and for a quick bread it is uncommonly low in fat. The dense, red-speckled slices look festive and taste great alone or with cream cheese.

150 g (5 oz) white flour	125 g (4 oz) rolled oats
150 g (5 oz) rye flour	325 ml (11 fl oz) buttermilk
1 teaspoon salt	50 g (2 oz) dark molasses
1 teaspoon bicarbonate of soda	125 g (4 oz) dried cranberries
1½ teaspoons baking powder	50 g (2 oz) chopped walnuts

Prepare 2 small loaf tins: butter them, line them with waxed paper, and butter the waxed paper. Preheat the oven to 180°C/350°F/Gas 4.

Sift the 2 flours together with the salt, bicarbonate of soda, and baking powder. Stir in the rolled oats. Mix together the buttermilk and molasses, and stir the wet mixture into the dry one, along with the cranberries and chopped walnuts.

Spoon the batter into the prepared tins, smooth it out, and bake at 180°C/350°F/Gas 4 for about 50 minutes, or until a toothpick inserted in the centre of a loaf comes out clean. Allow the loaves to cool in their pans for a few minutes, then remove them to racks and let them cool further before slicing.

Serve with butter or Pumpkin Butter (see page 465).

Makes 2 small loaves.

BUTTERMILK SCONES

This recipe calls for walnuts and raisins in a light-textured scone that is just sweet enough. The raisins could be replaced with currants, dried cranberries, dried cherries, or dried blueberries.

350–375 g (12–13 oz) white
   flour
3 tablespoons sugar
2 teaspoons baking powder
½ teaspoon salt
2½ tablespoons cold butter

2 tablespoons toasted
   wheatgerm
40 g (1½ oz) finely chopped
   walnuts
75 g (3 oz) raisins
250 ml (8 fl oz) buttermilk

Combine 300 g (10 oz) of flour, the sugar, baking powder, and salt in the container of a food processor and add the cold butter, cut into several pieces. Process briefly, until the mixture resembles a coarse meal.

Transfer it to a bowl, and stir in the wheatgerm, walnuts, and raisins. Add the buttermilk and stir just until a thick batter forms.

Turn the batter out on to a well-floured board, sprinkle a little more flour on top of it, flour your hands, and gently pull it together into a ball. Keeping it always well dredged in flour, fold the dough a couple of times to smooth it out. I don't even want to call this kneading. The secret to having light-textured scones is simply not to overhandle this moist, sticky dough.

Cut the dough in half, form each part into a ball, then pat each ball into an even circle a little less than 2.5 cm (1 inch) thick. With a sharp knife, cut each circle into 6 wedges. Lift the wedges with a spatula on to a buttered baking sheet.

Bake the scones in a preheated 220°C/425°F/Gas 7 oven for about 18–20 minutes, or until golden brown on top. Take them out of the oven and immediately transfer them to a rack to cool slightly, then serve. These are best eaten warm.

Makes 12 scones.

SWEETENED YOGURT CREAM

This combination of yogurt and cream is reminiscent of crème fraîche, and of English clotted cream, but is not quite as heavy as either, making it much more enjoyable to eat.

250 ml (8 fl oz) low-fat yogurt
250 ml (8 fl oz) non-fat yogurt
120 ml (4 fl oz) whipping cream
50 g (2 oz) icing sugar

Stir together the 2 yogurts and pour them into a colander lined with 3 or 4 layers of cheesecloth, set over a bowl. Leave it to drain for several hours. You should end up with about 300 ml (10 fl oz) of thickened yogurt, with the texture of sour cream.

Beat the whipping cream in a bowl until it starts to hold a soft shape. Add the icing sugar and continue beating until the cream just begins to hold a stiff shape. Beat in the drained yogurt.

Serve with any fresh, ripe berries.

Makes about 500 ml (16 fl oz).

RUSSIAN TEA CAKES

I have this recipe from my sister, Eve Lowry, but it's one of those fabulous recipes that have been around for a long time and are claimed by many nations. I've seen almost the identical thing called Mexican wedding cookies, and a crescent-shaped version of it called a Turkish something or other.

My sister is a registered dietitian, and spends most of her time developing low-fat food and providing educational tools about healthy diets to doctors and hospitals. I think it's very funny that among her family she is absolutely *famous* for these cookies, and everyone waits for the Christmas box that arrives each year. It proves that there is such a thing as a balanced life.

225 g (8 oz) unsalted butter, softened
50 g (2 oz) icing sugar
1½ teaspoons vanilla extract
½ teaspoon almond extract
¼ teaspoon salt
125 g (4 oz) chopped pecans or walnuts
325–350 g (11–12 oz) plain white flour
additional icing sugar as needed

Combine the butter, 50 g (2 oz) icing sugar, vanilla, almond extract, and salt in the container of a food processor, and cream everything until it is light and fluffy. Add the nuts and process in short pulses until the nuts are chopped finely. Add the flour and process in pulses until the dough is just combined.

Turn the dough out on to a large sheet of waxed paper. It will be quite soft. Use the paper to shape the dough into a cube, then wrap it and refrigerate for an hour or two, until the dough is firm enough to slice easily into small cubes without losing its shape. You can keep the dough in the refrigerator, well wrapped, for several days. However, when it gets completely chilled, you need to take it out and let it warm up a little before slicing, as it will be brittle.

Preheat the oven to 200°C/400°F/Gas 6. Using a thin-bladed knife, cut 1 cm (½ inch) slices off the cube, then cut each slice into 1 cm (½ inch) cubes. You can roll the cubes into balls if you want to take the time; we leave them square.

Put the biscuits on ungreased baking sheets, about 1 cm (½ inch) apart, or on parchment-lined sheets. Bake them, one sheet at a time, in the upper part of the oven, for about 10–12 minutes, or until they just barely start turning colour.

My sister points out that they should not brown, but they taste better if they develop a slightly golden colour on top. They do have a tendency to get dark brown on the bottom while the top still looks raw, so you just have to check every minute or so after the first 10 minutes, until you get the time right for your particular oven.

When done, remove them from the oven and allow them to cool on the baking sheet for 2 minutes. Then put about 225 g (8 oz) of icing sugar into a bowl, add about 20 warm biscuits at a time, and toss them around gently until they are well coated with sugar. Spread them out on waxed paper to cool, and when they have cooled completely, roll them in icing sugar one more time.

This makes about 4 dozen biscuits.

The Last Word

I must give one last variation on the tea theme. In summer, when tomatoes are dark red and sweet, the tomato sandwich is one of the great treats of life. It makes a superb replacement for the watercress sandwich, which is out of season in that weather.

TOMATO SANDWICHES FOR A SUMMERTIME TEA

Cut slices from a dense-textured loaf of French bread. Butter the slices thinly and sprinkle them with a little chopped parsley or basil. Cut large perfectly ripe tomatoes into thick slices, and use only the big middle slices, which match the size of the bread. Place one fat tomato slice on each piece of buttered and herbed bread, sprinkle on some salt and a few more herbs, and serve.

CELEBRATIONS AND FEASTS

A GALA DINNER FOR
LATE SPRING

❧

*Garlic Crostini with Sun-dried Tomato Pesto
and Fresh Cheese with Basil Pesto*

Cold Plum Soup

*Salad of Peppery Leaves
with Baked Goat's Cheese and Olives*

Roulade of Fresh Wild Mushrooms

Pink Grapefruit Sorbet

*Cornmeal Griddlecakes with Sweet Chipotle
Sauce, Peppers, Crème Fraîche, and Pine-nuts*

*White Peach Mousse in Chocolate Collars,
with Raspberry Coulis and Fresh Berries*

Towards the end of May, when the first summer fruits are appearing, this extravagant meal can be prepared to celebrate a milestone in someone's life – or just to have more fun at a dinner party than you've ever had before.

It's eclectic and interesting, cheerfully crossing cultural lines.

We start in Provence with Garlic Crostini, spread with two pungent versions of pesto. A champagne apéritif on the terrace would be perfect here – even if the terrace is only in your mind. Then skip to Eastern Europe for Cold Plum Soup, served with a delicate white Riesling – a refreshing pause between the garlicky appetizer and the peppery-salty salad that follows.

The first hot course is Roulade of Fresh Wild Mushrooms, a classic dish, subtle and rich with a woodsy flavour. That richness is gently erased by a dab of Pink Grapefruit Sorbet, and then the taste buds are really awakened by the sweet and fiery flavours from the Southwest. The chillies are slightly tempered, however, so you can enjoy a big, spicy, flavourful red wine for a great finale.

The dessert is a real concoction. It's the kind of thing that is often left in the 'don't try this at home' category, along with the spun sugar swans, but if you're an experienced cook, I say why not? It's absolutely wonderful.

Garlic Crostini (see page 75)

SUN-DRIED TOMATO PESTO

75 g (3 oz) sun-dried tomatoes
40 g (1½ oz) pine-nuts
50 g (2 oz) walnut pieces
60 ml (2 fl oz) fruity green olive oil
6 tablespoons chopped fresh basil
2 tablespoons balsamic vinegar

2 tablespoons reserved water from soaking tomatoes, or as needed
40 g (1½ oz) grated Parmesan cheese
pinch of tarragon
salt and freshly ground black pepper

optional: 1 – 2 garlic cloves

Put the dried tomatoes in a small pot with enough water to cover them, bring to a boil, reduce the heat, and simmer for a minute, then remove from heat and leave them to soak for about an hour. Drain the tomatoes, reserving the excess water.

If you want the taste of garlic in this pesto, peel a couple of garlic cloves, bruise them slightly, and leave them in the olive oil for about 30 minutes before using it.

Combine all the ingredients in a food processor and process for a few seconds at a time, scraping down the sides in between, until you have a thick, coarse-textured pulp. Taste, correct the seasoning with more salt and pepper if needed, and moisten the mixture with a little of the reserved tomato water if it seems too thick.

Serve at room temperature with Garlic Crostini (page 75), plain crackers, French bread, etc.

This makes about 350 ml (12 fl oz) of intensely flavoured, dark red paste.

Variations: This paste also combines well with goat's cheese or cream cheese, and when thinned a bit makes a nice sauce for pasta or a good addition to salad dressing.

FRESH CHEESE WITH BASIL PESTO

150–175 g (5–6 oz) fresh
    white goat's cheese
50 g (2 oz) cream cheese

125 g (4 oz) ricotta
4–8 tablespoons Fresh Basil
    Pesto (recipe follows)

Allow the goat's cheese and cream cheese to soften at room temperature, then combine all the ingredients in a bowl and beat with an electric mixer until smooth, or process briefly in a food processor. Mound the cheese on a serving plate and garnish with basil leaves. Serve cool but not cold, with crackers, crostini, or bread.

Makes about 350 g (12 oz) of cheese.

FRESH BASIL PESTO

150 g (5 oz) fresh basil leaves
    (enough to fill a 600 ml/
    1 pint jug)
75 g (3 oz) pine-nuts
75 g (3 oz) freshly grated
    Parmesan cheese

2 cloves garlic
5 tablespoons fruity green
    olive oil
salt and freshly ground
    pepper to taste

If you need to wash the basil leaves, spin them in a salad spinner or dry them in kitchen towels before proceeding. Remove any large or thick stems.

In the container of a food processor or blender, combine the basil leaves, pine-nuts, cheese, and garlic, and process until the nuts and garlic are finely chopped. Add the olive oil and process again, scraping down the sides of the container as necessary, until you have a paste of the consistency you like. Add salt and freshly ground black pepper to your taste.

Makes about 350 ml (12 fl oz).

COLD PLUM SOUP

1.4 kg (3 lb) mixed red and
    purple plums
500 ml (16 fl oz) water
500 ml (16 fl oz) dry red table
    wine
grated zest and juice of 1 large
    lemon

300 g (10 oz) sugar, more if
    needed
7.5 cm (3 inch) stick cinnamon
1 tablespoon cornflour
2 tablespoons icing sugar
250 ml (8 fl oz) sour cream

Wash the plums, cut them off their stones, and put them in a large non-reactive pan with the water, wine, lemon juice, lemon zest, sugar, and cinnamon. Bring to a boil, then lower the heat and simmer for 45 minutes.

Strain the cooked soup through a colander, stirring it down with a wooden spoon until the pulp remaining in the colander is mostly skins. Discard the skins, purée the soup in a blender in batches, and return it to the rinsed pan. Taste and correct the seasoning with a bit more sugar or lemon juice if needed. The soup should be both slightly sweet and slightly tart.

Dissolve the cornflour in 60 ml (2 fl oz) of cold water, and stir it into the soup. Bring the soup back to a boil and keep it boiling for 2 minutes, or until it clarifies. Allow it to cool, then chill it thoroughly.

Whisk the icing sugar into the sour cream, and serve the soup in shallow, chilled bowls with a spoonful of the sour cream in the centre of each one.

Serves 8.

SALAD OF PEPPERY LEAVES WITH BAKED GOAT'S CHEESE AND OLIVES

Do not scorn warm goat's cheese salad simply because it has enjoyed such popularity in recent times. Some things become popular for a good reason. This is marvellous.

2 bunches rocket
1 small head young curly
    endive
1 small head radicchio
3–4 heads Belgian endive
handful of fresh basil leaves
300 g (10 oz) log of fresh white
    goat's cheese
175 ml (6 fl oz) fruity green
    olive oil

50 g (2 oz) fine dry
    breadcrumbs
75 g (3 oz) coarsely ground
    walnuts
3–4 tablespoons balsamic
    vinegar
salt and freshly ground black
    pepper
25–30 cured black olives

optional garnish: marinated sun-dried tomatoes

Wash and trim the rocket, curly endive, and radicchio, spin dry in a salad spinner, and tear into manageable pieces. Wash the Belgian endive and slice it crosswise. Cut the basil leaves into slivers.

Cut the log of goat's cheese into 8 thick circles of equal size. Pour 90 ml (3 fl oz) of olive oil into a small bowl. In another bowl, combine the breadcrumbs and ground walnuts. Take one goat's cheese slice at a time, coat it lightly with the olive oil, then dip it on all sides into the breadcrumb mixture, pressing gently, until the goat's cheese is wearing a nice little coat of crumbs and walnuts. Arrange the coated goat's cheeses on a stainless steel baking sheet.

About 10 minutes before you are ready to serve the salad, preheat your oven to 200°C/400°F/Gas 6. Toss the salad leaves together in a big bowl with the remaining olive oil, some balsamic vinegar, and salt and pepper to taste. Divide the salad among 8 large plates.

Bake the goat's cheeses in the preheated oven for 5 minutes, then check them. Their crusts should just be turning golden brown. Leave them for another minute or two if necessary, but watch them carefully, because they can turn dark awfully fast once they warm up.

Remove the goat's cheeses from the oven and, working quickly but carefully, pick up one at a time with a spatula and slide it out on to the centre of a salad. Remember, they are very soft now. Garnish each salad with a few olives, and with marinated sun-dried tomatoes if desired. Serve at once.

Serves 8.

ROULADE OF FRESH WILD MUSHROOMS

In the spirit of celebration, I like to make this roulade with morels, a seasonal indulgence where I live, but it is also delicious with porcini, chanterelles, oyster or field mushrooms.

for the mushroom filling
450 g (1 lb) fresh wild
   mushrooms
4 tablespoons butter
1 medium onion, grated
2 tablespoons cognac
salt to taste
white pepper to taste
½ teaspoon paprika
3 medium tomatoes
60 ml (2 fl oz) double cream

for the roulade base
575 g (1¼ lb) courgettes
1 teaspoon salt, more to taste
125 g (4 oz) butter
1 small onion, chopped
85 g (3½ oz) flour
250 ml (8 fl oz) warm milk
4 eggs, separated
75 g (3 oz) grated Parmesan
   cheese
about 50 g (2 oz) fine, dry
   breadcrumbs

garnishes: melted butter
   additional grated Parmesan cheese

To make the filling: clean the mushrooms carefully. With morels in particular you must be very thorough, rinsing them under running water until you are certain there is no sand trapped in any of them. Trim away any soft or damaged parts and chop them coarsely.

Melt the butter in a large pan and sauté the onion in it for a few minutes, until it just begins to colour. Add the chopped mushrooms and cook over medium heat, stirring often, until they release their water and it cooks away. Add the cognac and stir for another minute or so. Then salt and pepper to taste and add the paprika.

Meanwhile, drop the tomatoes into boiling water for about 45 seconds, then remove them and slip off their skins. Purée the tomatoes in a blender and pass the purée through a sieve to eliminate the seeds. You should have about 250 ml (8 fl oz) of fresh tomato pulp.

Lower the heat under the mushrooms, pour in the tomato pulp, and simmer the mixture, continuing to stir it often, until it is reduced to a thick consistency, able to hold a soft shape. Stir in the cream, heat through, and set aside.

To make the roulade: wash and grate the courgettes and toss them with a teaspoon of salt. Leave them in a colander to drain for 20 minutes, then gently squeeze out the excess moisture.

Melt the butter in a medium saucepan and sauté the onions in it until they are just beginning to colour. Add the flour and stir constantly over low heat until the flour is golden, about 4–5 minutes. Add the warm milk and stir vigorously until the mixture is smooth and thick.

Remove the saucepan from the heat and let the mixture cool for 5 minutes. Beat in the 4 egg yolks, one at a time. Then stir in the grated, drained courgettes and the grated Parmesan cheese.

Beat the 4 egg whites until they hold peaks. Stir half the egg whites into the courgette mixture, then gently fold in the other half.

Butter a 25 × 35 cm (10 × 14 inch) Swiss roll tin and sprinkle it with fine, dry breadcrumbs. Be sure every bit of the tin is coated with butter and breadcrumbs or you could have trouble turning out the roulade. Carefully spoon the egg-courgette-cheeese mixture into the prepared tin and spread it gently over the entire surface, taking care not to smear the breadcrumb coating.

Bake in a preheated 190°C/375°F/Gas 5 oven for 15–18 minutes, or until it is puffed and coming away from the sides.

Lift the edges of the roulade gently with a spatula to be sure that it will come up. Then, using pot-holders or gloves to protect your hands, stretch a tea towel over the top of the tin, and swiftly turn the tin over on to a flat surface. The roulade should drop right out on to the tea towel.

While it is still warm, spread the roulade with the mushroom filling, leaving a 4 cm (1½ inch) border on one of the long sides. Starting at the edge with the border, and using the tea towel to help you lift the edge of the roulade evenly, roll it up just like a Swiss roll. Using long spatulas, lift the roulade carefully on to a baking sheet, and return it to the oven for about 5 minutes to heat through.

Slice the roulade with a thin, sharp knife and lay 2 slices on each plate, bottom to bottom. Drizzle each serving with melted butter and pass grated Parmesan separately.

Serves 8 generously, or 10–12 as an appetizer.

PINK GRAPEFRUIT SORBET

325 ml (11 fl oz) water
325 g (11 oz) sugar
600 ml (1 pint) strained fresh
   pink grapefruit juice

4–6 tablespoons strained
   fresh lemon juice
1–2 teaspoons grenadine
   syrup
2 teaspoons Pernod

Combine the water and sugar in a small saucepan and bring it to a simmer over a medium flame. Stir until all the sugar is dissolved. Allow the syrup to cool, then chill it for at least an hour.

Squeeze and strain the grapefruit juice and the lemon juice, and chill them in separate containers.

Combine the syrup with the grapefruit juice, 1 teaspoon of grenadine, 4 tablespoons of lemon juice, and the Pernod. Taste. Now add more lemon juice if needed – this will depend on the acidity of all the fruit. Remember, this sorbet should not be too sweet. Add more grenadine if you want it to be pinker.

Chill the mixture for 2 hours, then freeze it in an ice cream maker, according to manufacturer's instructions.

Makes a little more than 1.2 litres (2 pints) of sorbet.

CORNMEAL GRIDDLECAKES WITH SWEET CHIPOTLE SAUCE, PEPPERS, CRÈME FRAÎCHE, AND PINE-NUTS

When I make this dish in California, I use nopalitos instead of green peppers – they're ideal with corn and chillies. If you happen to find nopalitos, do snap them up. Use 450 g (1 lb) of nopalitos (cooked according to the directions on page 35) in place of the red and green peppers.

4–6 red and green peppers
olive oil
125 g (4 oz) pine-nuts
16 Cornmeal Griddlecakes
   (recipe follows)

750 ml (1¼ pints) Sweet
   Chipotle Sauce (see
   page 371)
500 ml (16 fl oz) crème fraîche

garnish: coriander sprigs

Remove the stalks and seeds from the peppers and cut the peppers into thin strips. Sauté briefly in a little olive oil.

Toast the pine-nuts by stirring them in a dry pan over a medium heat for 5–6 minutes, until they begin to turn golden brown and release a toasty fragrance.

If the griddlecakes were prepared earlier, put them under a hot grill now to reheat. Warm the Sweet Chipotle Sauce until it just simmers. Stir up the crème fraîche to soften it.

Put 2 hot griddlecakes on each of 8 large plates. Pour a ladleful of warm Sweet Chipotle Sauce alongside the griddlecakes on one side, and spoon some crème fraîche on the other side. Lay the sautéd peppers over the griddlecakes, and scatter toasted pine-nuts over the entire plate. Garnish the plates with big coriander sprigs and serve at once.

Serves 8.

CORNMEAL GRIDDLECAKES

My favourite way to serve these is with Sweet Chipotle Sauce (see page 371) and crème fraîche, garnished with nopalitos or peppers and pine-nuts, as in this menu. But they're also wonderful with sautéd mushrooms and tomato sauce, or topped with a little melted cheese and served alongside oven-roasted vegetables. My boys like them best snatched from the pan and eaten while running away.

2 large eggs, separated
50 g (2 oz) butter, melted and cooled
250 ml (8 fl oz) milk
120 ml (4 fl oz) single or double cream

150 g (5 oz) plain flour
175 g (6 oz) yellow cornmeal
4 teaspoons baking powder
1 teaspoon salt
vegetable oil for frying

Combine the egg yolks, melted butter, milk, and cream in a bowl and whisk together lightly. In another bowl, sift together all the dry ingredients. Add the egg yolk mixture to the cornmeal mixture and stir just until the wet and dry ingredients are combined; do not overmix.

Beat the egg whites, which should be at room temperature, until they hold stiff peaks, and then fold them gently into the batter. (Cold egg whites can be warmed quickly by putting them in a bowl, then setting that bowl into a larger bowl of hot water, and whisking the whites for about a minute.)

Heat a large frying pan until a drop of water sizzles on it, and brush it lightly with oil. Drop the batter on to the pan 2 – 3 tablespoons at a time, and cook for about 1½ minutes on one side, until the bottom is golden brown, then flip and cook briefly on the other side.

The griddlecakes can be served at once, or they can be cooled on racks, wrapped tightly in clingfilm, and kept for a day or so. To reheat them, lay them out on a baking sheet and allow them to come to room temperature. Then put them under a hot grill, about 12 – 15 cm (5 – 6 inches) away from the heat, for about 1½ minutes on each side, or until just heated through. Serve at once.

*Makes 16 medium-sized griddlecakes, enough for 8 servings in this menu,
or 4—6 servings if fewer other dishes are being served.*

SWEET CHIPOTLE SAUCE

In this recipe, the smoky spiciness of chipotle chillies is offset by
sweet red peppers and a touch of honey.

The sauce keeps well refrigerated. I often double the recipe, and
serve it with tortilla chips, on quesadillas, with eggs, with tamales
– with just about any Mexican food. A note about substitutions:
canned chipotle chillies can be used in place of dried in this recipe.
If New Mexican chillies cannot be found, the medium-sized dried
red chillies sold in most markets can be used, but be prepared to
taste and adjust quantity upwards a little for heat and flavour.

If you cannot get chipotle chillies at all, then increase the amount
of the other chillies you are using. It won't be chipotle sauce, but
it will be an interesting and delicious sauce nonetheless.

2 cloves garlic
1 medium onion
125 g (4 oz) dried New
  Mexican chillies (see page
  88)
2 dried chipotle chillies (see
  page 88)
250 ml (8 fl oz) water
120 ml (4 fl oz) white grape
  juice or apple juice

450 g (1 lb) cooked or canned
  tomatoes with their juice
1 teaspoon salt, more to taste
2—3 red peppers, roasted and
  peeled (see page 17) (you
  can use canned or bottled
  pimentos)
1 tablespoon lemon juice
1 tablespoon honey

Peel the garlic and peel and quarter the onion. Pull the stems and
seeds out of all the chillies and wash them. Put the garlic, onion,
chillies, water, fruit juice, tomatoes, and salt in a large non-reactive
pan and simmer gently for at least 30 minutes and up to an hour,
until the chillies are pulpy and soft.

Add the roasted and peeled red peppers – you can use the ones
sold in jars in Italian groceries, or roast and peel your own.

Purée the mixture in batches in a blender or a food processor until it is perfectly smooth. Stir in the lemon juice and honey, and taste. The sauce should be spicy but not searingly hot, with a slightly sweet taste under the chilli flavour.

Makes about 1.2 litres (2 pints).

WHITE PEACH MOUSSE IN CHOCOLATE COLLARS WITH RASPBERRY COULIS AND FRESH BERRIES

1 recipe White Peach Mousse (recipe follows)
1 recipe Raspberry Coulis (see page 374)
8 dark chocolate collars or cups

garnishes: fresh raspberries and blackberries
   chocolate curls and mint sprigs

This is one of those fantasy desserts, more likely to be found in a restaurant than at home, but now and again it's fun to do something wild.

I devised it for a fancy dinner I prepared as a fund-raising event for my boys' school. My crew and I slaved over it. We called it the peach mousse from hell, because it was so tricky to get the acid balance right without breaking down the texture of the mousse; because we had to send out for a good candy thermometer, as I hadn't used mine in so long that I couldn't find it; and because our arms were falling off from all the beating of egg whites. Of course, we were making enough for 120 people – it's easier for 8. Anyway, the dessert was such a spectacular success that I pass the recipe along here with warning for the inexperienced.

I had the bittersweet chocolate collars made to order by a wonderful chocolatier who has a small shop near where I live, and who makes everything by hand. You could use pre-formed dark chocolate cups, which are available at some specialist shops, or make your own by learning some of the chocolatier's art. In any case, what you need are thin chocolate containers into which you can mound the peach mousse.

To assemble the dessert: place the chocolate rings or cups in the centres of 8 large dessert plates. Spoon some chilled Raspberry Coulis around the chocolate and mound the peach mousse inside it. Scatter a few berries in the coulis, and tuck a mint sprig in each serving of mousse. Serve at once.

Serves 8.

WHITE PEACH MOUSSE

5–6 medium white peaches, to make 350 ml (12 fl oz) peach purée
3–4 teaspoons lemon juice
1½ teaspoons gelatine
175 ml (6 fl oz) whipping cream
3 egg whites, at room temperature

pinch of salt
pinch of cream of tartar
175 g (6 oz) sugar
½ teaspoon almond extract
grated zest of 1 orange (about 1 teaspoon)

garnishes: chocolate curls and mint sprigs

Peel and purée the peaches and add just enough lemon juice to bring out their best flavour. Cover and chill.

Sprinkle the gelatine into 60 ml (2 fl oz) of water and allow it to soften. Set it aside.

Whip the cream until it thickens so that it forms soft peaks when it falls back into the bowl. Set it aside in the refrigerator. Beat the egg whites with the salt and cream of tartar until they form soft peaks.

In a heavy saucepan, dissolve the sugar over medium heat in 60 ml (2 fl oz) of water. Bring the syrup to a boil, swirling the pan a little to wash down any crystals from the sides. Cook it over a medium flame until it reaches the soft ball stage (116°C/238°F).

Start beating the egg whites again with an electric mixer, on high speed, and pour the hot syrup into the egg whites in a thin, steady stream. As soon as the syrup is incorporated into the egg whites, and while the mixture is still hot, beat in the softened gelatine. Continue to beat at moderate speed until the mixture has cooled to room temperature, about 10–15 minutes.

Stir the almond extract and the orange zest into the peach purée, then pour the purée and the whipped cream over the meringue, and fold everything together gently but thoroughly with a spatula.

Chill the mousse for several hours. It is then ready to spoon into chocolate collars if you're doing the elaborate recipe on page 372, or it can be served in parfait glasses, garnished with chocolate curls and mint leaves.

Serves 8–10.

RASPBERRY COULIS

**700 g (1½ lb) fresh or frozen   50–125 g (2–4 oz) sugar
   raspberries**

Purée the berries and sugar together in a blender or food processor, then strain through a sieve. Taste and adjust the sugar if needed. Chill the coulis, covered, until needed. This can be prepared ahead and stored in the refrigerator for a day or two.

Makes a little more than 600 ml (1 pint).

A SUMMER BUFFET FOR
A CROWD

❧

Roasted Green Bean Salad

Tuscan White Beans with Garlic and Sage

Olives and Feta Cheese with Oregano

Pasta with Olive Oil and Fresh Herbs

Freshly Chopped Tomatoes with Basil

Chard and Parsley Frittata

Marinated Grilled Aubergine

Rosemary Focaccia

Sun-dried Tomato Pesto

salad of mixed leaves
assorted cheeses

summer fruits with
Honey-sweetened Mascarpone

assorted biscotti

An afternoon or evening party, in a garden, on a terrace, or anywhere, suitable for a crowd, casual or elegant – this is the kind of food everyone I know really likes the best. I cooked this exact menu once for about fifty people, doubling and tripling recipes, and then was able to enjoy the party myself. Everything is largely prepared ahead, and it's all delicious at room temperature, so there is a minimum of bother at serving time. The green beans, pasta, and frittata could be served hot or warm, but won't be harmed at all by cooling down.

This is a party that can be easily expanded or scaled down, depending on the numbers, and on your style. As given here, it will feed fifteen to twenty people. If you're having guests with mixed tastes, you can add a platter of prosciutto and melons, some spit-roasted chickens, or a big seafood salad – any of these would fit in perfectly. If it's a gala occasion, a spectacular cake could be added at the end. If it's a smaller group or a less ambitious time, the ten dishes could simply be pruned to six or seven and the home-made focaccia replaced by breads from a good bakery.

It's also a great menu for leftovers. Don't worry about making too much of anything. I just start recombining things, and eat this way for days. The herbed pasta can be put together with leftover chopped tomatoes and other vegetables for a lovely pasta salad. Or drop it into a broth with the white beans for an easy *pasta e fagioli*. Put slices of frittata into split and toasted focaccia with a dab of tomato pesto for a terrific sandwich. And so on.

ROASTED GREEN BEAN SALAD

900 g (2 lb) thin, tender green
   beans, such as haricots verts
1 head garlic
3 tablespoons green olive oil
salt and pepper to taste

2 large ripe tomatoes
a little balsamic vinegar
2 tablespoons chopped fresh
   basil leaves

Wash and trim the green beans, and separate and peel the cloves of garlic. Reserve one small clove of garlic and toss the remaining garlic and the beans in a bowl with half the olive oil, salt to taste, and a few grinds of black pepper. Spread them evenly over 2 baking sheets and roast them in a 200°C/400°F/Gas 6 oven for about 40 minutes. Stir and turn the beans at least once in the course of roasting them.

The roasting time will vary with the size of the beans. They are done when they have a somewhat wrinkled and blistered look, with light brown spots here and there. A marvellous toasty fragrance will alert you.

While the beans are roasting, peel the tomatoes and chop them, keeping all their juice. Mince the reserved clove of garlic. Combine the tomatoes, their juice, the garlic, the remaining olive oil, some balsamic vinegar, a little salt and pepper, and the chopped basil. Crush everything together a bit to blend the flavours.

When the beans are ready, transfer them to a big, shallow bowl and pour the tomato dressing over them. Serve hot, warm, or at room temperature.

This serves 6–8 as a first course, more in a buffet, but I always wish I had made more.

Variations: I have also served these roasted beans without the tomato dressing, just tossing them with a little additional oil and a few drops of balsamic vinegar. Sometimes I even omit the vinegar. Then they become a finger food, perfect for snacking in the kitchen with cheese crostini and a glass of wine while I finish cooking dinner. (See Roasted Green Beans with Garlic in the Informal Winter Buffet menu, page 251.)

TUSCAN WHITE BEANS WITH GARLIC AND SAGE

450 g (1 lb) small dried white beans

handful of fresh sage leaves, or 2 tablespoons dried whole-leaf sage

1 head garlic, separated and peeled

3–4 tablespoons fruity green olive oil

salt and freshly ground pepper

Soak the beans in cool water for a few hours, or overnight if you have the time. A pinch of bicarbonate of soda can be added to hard water.

Drain the beans and put them in a large, shallow pan, with enough fresh water to cover them by 2.5 cm (1 inch). Add the sage leaves, the garlic cloves, and a tablespoon of olive oil. Bring the water to a boil, then lower the heat to a gentle simmer.

Allow the beans to simmer this way until they are tender – this may take an hour, or 2, or 3. As always with dried beans, the cooking time varies quite a bit depending on the freshness of the beans.

Do not stir more than 2 or 3 times, and then gently, with a wooden spoon. If the water evaporates too much, carefully add more, always keeping the beans covered. The trick is just to leave the beans alone on that low flame for the right amount of time, so that they are soft to the bite but firm to the eye – you don't want them to fall apart into a mush.

Shortly before they're done, when they are just beginning to be tender, add about 2 teaspoons of salt. When they are soft, and the cooking water has become a savoury, sage-and-garlic-perfumed broth, pour beans and broth into a wide, shallow bowl, drizzle with 2–3 tablespoons of the best green olive oil, grind on some black pepper, and serve.

These are delicious as an antipasto, either warm or at room temperature, and also excellent cold in salads. Spoon them over bruschetta for a typical Tuscan dish, or add them to Pasta with Olive Oil and Fresh Herbs (see page 379) for an instant *pasta e fagioli*. And if you have lots of leftovers, these make a great soup; just purée them in a light vegetable stock (see page 460) (chicken stock will do if you don't have vegetable stock) with a bit of leftover rice or on their own. Then add a few slivers of any cooked greens and some croûtons – delicious.

Serves 6–8 in a small dinner, more in a buffet.

OLIVES AND FETA CHEESE WITH OREGANO

450 g (1 lb) cured olives,　　**olive oil**
　various kinds　　　　　　**fresh oregano**
700 g (1½ lb) feta cheese

optional garnishes: oregano branches or mint sprigs

Choose 2 or 3 types of cured olives. Kalamata olives are very good and quite easily available, so I use them often. I also like to get big green cured olives that you can find in good Mediterranean delis. Tiny black Niçoise olives are a nice addition, but very salty. About 450 g (1 lb) of olives altogether will be enough, unless your friends are all Greek.

I use fresh Bulgarian feta cheese, which I prefer to the Greek; the one I get seems a little creamier and less aggressively salty. Ask at your delicatessen which feta is the mildest, or taste some and see which you prefer.

Slice the feta cheese and then break it into large chunks. Arrange the various olives and the feta pieces on a platter, all mixed up, or any way you like. Drizzle a tiny bit of green olive oil on the feta, and scatter chopped fresh oregano over everything.

You can garnish this platter with oregano branches or mint sprigs.

Serves 15–20 in this menu.

Variation: Another nice presentation is to line the platter with rinsed vine leaves and arrange the olives and cheese on top.

PASTA WITH OLIVE OIL AND FRESH HERBS

This is a nice, easy pasta for warm weather. You can use a variety of different summer herbs, such as basil, Italian flat-leaf parsley, summer savory, thyme, oregano, as well as chives or rosemary in moderation. Use the more assertive herbs sparingly, and follow your nose. The formula here is a combination that I've used and particularly liked. The fragrance of the fresh herbs and olive oil is delightful, and this dish is good at room temperature as well as hot.

6 tablespoons chopped fresh basil

6 tablespoons chopped flat-leaf Italian parsley

1 tablespoon chopped fresh oregano

1 tablespoon chopped fresh thyme

60 ml (2 fl oz) fruity green olive oil

salt and pepper to taste

450 g (1 lb) spaghetti or linguine

garnishes: Parmesan cheese and toasted pine-nuts, or slivers of Kalamata olives, or red chilli flakes

optional: 1 small clove garlic, minced

Combine the chopped fresh herbs in a large ceramic bowl with the olive oil and a little salt and pepper. Add the optional minced garlic to the herbs if you want it. Cook the pasta in boiling salted water until it is *al dente*, then drain and immediately toss with the herbs and oil. Correct the seasoning if you need to, and serve.

This is delicious with some coarsely grated Parmesan cheese and a few toasted pine-nuts scattered over it. It's also nice with slivers of cured black olives, or some red chilli flakes.

Serves 6—8, more in a buffet.

FRESHLY CHOPPED TOMATOES WITH BASIL

During the late summer days, when I pick a big basket of ripe tomatoes almost every day, my favourite way to start dinner is with a bowl of these tomatoes, cut up just a few minutes before they're served, along with some focaccia, goat's cheese, and a glass of wine. Sometimes it turns out to be both the starter and the finisher, as we just have another helping and another glass . . . Make this only if you have great, vine-ripened tomatoes and fresh herbs.

1.4 kg (3 lb) ripe tomatoes

2–3 tablespoons chopped fresh basil

2 tablespoons chopped flat-leaf parsley

1 clove garlic, minced

2–3 tablespoons fruity green olive oil

1 tablespoon balsamic vinegar

salt and pepper to taste

Wash and trim the tomatoes and cut them into 1 cm (½ inch) dice. Chop the fresh herbs and mix them into the tomatoes along with the garlic, oil, and vinegar. Taste as you mix in some salt and pepper, as tomatoes can vary and some need less salt than others.

These tomatoes get quite soupy with their own juices, especially if you use a naturally juicy variety such as beefsteak, so serve them in little bowls with a good country bread to soak up the marinade. They're perfect spooned over bruschetta – grilled bread brushed with olive oil. They can be served at once, or kept covered at cool room temperature for 1–2 hours. They will keep longer in the refrigerator, but I really hate to put a great vine-ripened tomato into the refrigerator, and would only do it if I feared fermentation, as tomatoes lose both texture and flavour when refrigerated.

Serves 6–8 as an appetizer.

CHARD AND PARSLEY FRITTATA

All the dark, leafy greens, such as Swiss chard or spinach, go well with eggs. The taste of parsley does wonders for them, too, and so does Parmesan cheese. Be sure you use the flat-leafed Italian parsley, which has a much more pronounced flavour than the curly type.

1 medium onion, chopped

1 clove garlic

1 large potato

1½ tablespoons olive oil

1 teaspoon salt

8–9 eggs

4 tablespoons grated Parmesan cheese

10–12 tablespoons chopped flat-leaf parsley

freshly ground pepper

450 g (1 lb) Swiss chard, chopped

1 teaspoon cider vinegar

Chop the onion, mince the garlic, and scrub the potato and cut it in 0.5 cm (¼ inch) dice. Heat the olive oil in a 30 cm (12 inch) pan, preferably a good non-stick type. Sauté the onion and garlic for a few minutes, then add the diced potato and about ½ teaspoon of salt, and continue cooking over medium heat, stirring often, for about 10 minutes. The vegetables will be starting to brown.

Meanwhile, beat the eggs with the Parmesan cheese, the parsley, the remaining salt, and some pepper, and set aside. Add the chopped chard to the pan, sprinkle it with the cider vinegar, and toss it with the other vegetables until it is thoroughly wilted.

Pour the egg mixture into the vegetable mixture and give it a quick stir to make sure everything is more or less evenly distributed. Adjust the flame until it is very low, cover the pan, and let the frittata cook slowly for about 10–15 minutes, or until the eggs are completely set.

Loosen the frittata gently with a spatula until it slides freely in the pan, then invert it on to a flat lid or platter and slide it back into the pan to brown on the other side, just for a minute or two. Turn it out on to a platter and serve warm or cool, cut into wedges.

Serves 6–8, more if cut in thin wedges for a large antipasto buffet.

MARINATED GRILLED AUBERGINE

3 large purple aubergines
salt
2 cloves garlic
60 ml (2 fl oz) olive oil
60 ml (2 fl oz) balsamic
  vinegar

freshly ground pepper
½ large red onion, very thinly
  sliced
3 tablespoons slivered fresh
  basil

Wash the aubergines and cut them crosswise in 1 cm (½ inch) slices. Salt the slices lightly on both sides and leave them on a glass platter or tray for ½–1 hour to release their excess water. Pat the slices dry between paper towels, squeezing gently.

Mince or press the garlic cloves and stir them into the olive oil. Brush the aubergine slices lightly on both sides with the garlic oil, and grill them until they are charred in spots and tender throughout.

In a large glass or ceramic dish, arrange half the aubergine slices close together in one layer. Prick them here and there with a fork, sprinkle them with about half the balsamic vinegar, and salt and pepper them lightly. Scatter half the onion slices and half the slivered basil over them. Repeat with the remaining aubergines and other ingredients.

Cover the dish tightly with clingfilm and leave the aubergines at room temperature for a couple of hours, or in the refrigerator if longer.

Serve cool or at room temperature as a first course or as part of a buffet. This also makes a great sandwich, with a thick slice of ripe summer tomato and some fresh mozzarella, on coarse country bread.

Serves 6−8, more if served with other dishes.

ROSEMARY FOCACCIA

1 tablespoon dried yeast
250 ml (8 fl oz) warm water
pinch of sugar
300 g (10 oz) + 3 tablespoons
 unbleached white flour
85 g (3½ oz) wholemeal flour

1 teaspoon salt
3 tablespoons olive oil
2 tablespoons coarsely
 chopped fresh rosemary, or
 1 tablespoon dried
coarse sea salt

Dissolve the yeast and sugar in the warm water. Put the 300 g (10 oz) white flour and the wholemeal flour in a mixing bowl and begin stirring in the yeast mixture and salt, a little at a time, until you have a soft batter. Stir in 1 tablespoon of the olive oil and half of the chopped rosemary. Then continue adding flour until the dough is too stiff to stir.

Spread the remaining flour on a board, turn the dough out on it, and knead it gently for just a few minutes, working in only enough of the flour to keep it from sticking.

Form the dough into a ball, put it into an oiled bowl, and turn it once. Then cover the bowl with a towel and leave the dough to rise for 30–40 minutes, or until almost doubled. Meanwhile, oil a baking sheet and dust it with the 3 tablespoons of flour.

Punch down the dough and lay it on the board, then roll it into an oval about 1.5 cm (¾ inch) thick. Do not work the dough a lot at this point. Transfer the focaccia to the prepared baking sheet, cover it with a towel, and leave it to rise for about 30 minutes.

If you like, you can cut shallow crisscross patterns in the top of the focaccia with a sharp serrated knife and pull it apart a little to show the pattern. Or skip the cutting, and use your fingers to dimple it in a random pattern.

Brush the focaccia with the remaining 2 tablespoons of olive oil, sprinkle it with the remaining rosemary and about ½ teaspoon of coarse sea salt, and bake it in the middle of the oven at 230°C/450°F/Gas 8 for about 18 minutes. It should be turning golden brown on top. Serve the focaccia hot or warm, cut into squares.

This makes the equivalent of 1 small loaf of bread. It's easy to double this recipe, and I usually do, as my son Teddy can eat one of these by himself.

Sun-dried Tomato Pesto (see page 362)

HONEY-SWEETENED MASCARPONE

450 g (1 lb) mascarpone   **6–8 tablespoons honey**

Allow the mascarpone to come to room temperature, then stir it gently with a whisk until it is softened. Drizzle in the honey, and continue whisking slowly until smooth. Once the honey is incorporated, the mascarpone can be served at once, or cooled again.

Serve the sweetened mascarpone in small portions alongside summer fruits such as berries, sliced peaches, or figs.

Makes about 575 g (1¼ lb).

A CELEBRATION DINNER

❧

Bruschetta with Caramelized Fennel and Onion

*Salad of Rocket and Persimmons with Walnuts
and Roquefort Cheese*

Aubergine Pancakes in Sweet Red Pepper Purée

Rosemary Sorbet

*Grilled Polenta with Grilled Fresh Wild
Mushrooms*

*Warm Chocolate Cakes with Crème Anglaise
and Boysenberry Sauce*

Visiting dignitaries? Did someone finally get married? Publish a great book? Win the Nobel prize? Just get elected president? Finish a dissertation? Actually, if I can get good fresh wild mushrooms, that's reason enough to have a party. I remember travelling in northern Italy in the autumn, and seeing the big baskets full of giant fresh porcini proudly displayed in the entrances of restaurants. No need to look at the menu. We'd select our porcini and have them simply grilled, with a little garlic and parsley. Often they were accompanied by some polenta. I have never found a better way to have porcini. Get porcini if you can, or find some other meaty, woodsy wild mushrooms, and enjoy this simple but princely Tuscan dish.

In this meal, rustic country dishes alternate with more refined ones, but the flavours are all assertive, pungent, earthy, and interesting.

First the taste of caramelized fennel with onion – aromatic and a little mysterious. Then peppery rocket with one of my favourite fruits, the sweet but crisp Fuyu persimmon, in my favourite autumn salad. The Aubergine Pancakes have a smoky delicacy, punctuated by salty feta cheese and Greek olives. Rosemary Sorbet perfectly cools and cleanses the palate, and will amaze your guests with its subtle perfume and flavour. And it leaves you hungry again, ready for the marvellous, woodsy wild mushrooms. The dessert is extravagant, and you must wait a while for it, as it is baked at the last minute.

This is a great dinner for red wines, from beginning to end.

BRUSCHETTA WITH CARAMELIZED FENNEL AND ONION

4–5 large onions
4–5 large, trimmed white fennel bulbs
2 tablespoons olive oil
1 tablespoon butter
salt to taste
75 g (3 oz) slivered Kalamata olives

90–120 ml (3–4 fl oz) white wine, to taste
freshly ground black pepper to taste
1 loaf crusty, coarse-textured Italian bread

optional garnish: sprigs of watercress

Peel the onions, quarter them lengthwise, and slice them thickly. Trim and clean the fennel bulbs and slice them to a similar size.

In a heavy-bottomed non-stick pan, heat the olive oil and butter. Add the onion and fennel, salt them lightly, and cook over medium heat, stirring often, until the vegetables are a beautiful golden brown. This may take 45 minutes to 1 hour.

Stir in the slivers of Kalamata olives and the white wine. Continue stirring until the wine is completely absorbed. Taste and correct the seasoning with salt or freshly ground black pepper if needed.

Meanwhile, slice the bread about 1 cm (½ inch) thick. If it's a

large loaf, cut the slices down to about 7.5 × 5 cm (3 × 2 inches).
Toast the slices in a 200°C/400°F/Gas 6 oven or on a grill over
hot coals until they are crisp and golden brown on both sides. Brush
them lightly with olive oil.

Put 2 toasts on each plate and spoon the hot fennel and onion
mixture over them. Garnish the plates with sprigs of watercress if
desired, and serve at once.

I find the taste of caramelized fennel and onion intoxicating. It
can be varied with a shaving of Parmesan cheese, or you can up the
ante on the fennel by toasting some fennel seeds, crushing them,
and stirring them in. This dish is sensational with a glass of red
wine.

Serves 8—10.

SALAD OF ROCKET AND PERSIMMONS WITH WALNUTS AND ROQUEFORT CHEESE

Fuyu persimmons are eaten while hard and crisp, like apples (unlike
the Hachiya persimmons, which must be jelly-like before they are
ready). The sweetness of a Fuyu is delightful in a salad next to the
peppery snap of rocket and watercress. If they are not available to
you, you can use pears that are still just slightly firm, or one of the
varieties of crisp Asian (Nashi) pears that are now becoming much
more available.

3 good-sized bunches of
  rocket
1 small head radicchio
1 small bunch watercress
2 medium Fuyu persimmons
  or firm pears or Asian
  (Nashi) pears
1 medium onion, thinly sliced
½ medium red pepper

1 small yellow pepper
225 g (8 oz) Roquefort cheese
75 g (3 oz) walnut pieces
3–4 tablespoons green olive
  oil
2–3 tablespoons balsamic
  vinegar
salt and pepper to taste

optional: 50–75 g (2–3 oz) raisins

Wash the rocket, radicchio, and watercress, spin them dry in a salad spinner, and tear into manageable pieces. Peel and quarter the persimmons or pears, cut out the cores, and slice them thinly crosswise. Quarter and very thinly slice the onion and the red pepper. Cut the yellow pepper into thin rings, trimming out the ribs. Break the Roquefort cheese into little chunks.

Combine all the vegetables, fruits, cheese, and nuts in a large bowl. Drizzle on the olive oil and toss gently until every leaf glistens. Add a splash of balsamic vinegar and a little salt and pepper, toss again, and serve.

Makes 8 generous salads, or 10–12 small ones.

AUBERGINE PANCAKES IN SWEET RED PEPPER PURÉE

3 large aubergines
2 tablespoons olive oil
salt
1 large onion, finely chopped
3 large cloves garlic, minced
3 large eggs
40 g (1½ oz) flour
pinch of dried oregano

freshly ground pepper
additional olive oil for frying
Sweet Red Pepper Purée
  (recipe follows)
16 Kalamata olives, sliced off
  their stones
225 g (8 oz) feta cheese,
  crumbled

garnish: fresh mint sprigs

Pierce the aubergines in several places with a fork, brush them with a bit of olive oil, and roast them on baking sheets in a 200°C/400°F/Gas 6 oven for about an hour, or until they are completely soft and collapsing. Cut them open, let them cool a bit, then carefully remove and discard any pockets of dark seeds. Scoop out the pale flesh, toss it in a bowl with about a teaspoon of salt, and leave it in a colander to drain for an hour or more. Transfer the aubergine flesh to a board, chop it coarsely, then put it in a large mixing bowl.

In a small, heavy non-stick pan, sauté the onion and garlic in a tablespoon of olive oil until soft and translucent. Whisk together the eggs and the flour. Add the onion mixture, the egg mixture, and the oregano to the aubergine, and mix thoroughly. Add more salt and some freshly ground pepper to taste.

Brush a large, heavy-bottomed non-stick pan with olive oil and heat it over a medium flame. Place heaped tablespoonfuls of the aubergine batter evenly in the pan, shaping them into 7.5 cm (3 inch) pancakes. Cook the pancakes until they are lightly coloured on both sides, about 7–8 minutes total, and turn them very carefully.

Spoon a little warm Sweet Red Pepper Purée on each plate, and place 2–3 pancakes on top of it. Scatter some sliced olives and crumbled feta over the pancakes, and garnish with mint sprigs.

This serves 8 generously.

SWEET RED PEPPER PURÉE

2 large onions, chopped
1 tablespoon olive oil
salt
2–3 red peppers, roasted and
   peeled (see page 17)

3 tablespoons cider vinegar,
   more to taste
3 tablespoons brown sugar,
   more to taste

In a heavy-bottomed non-stick pan, cook the onions in the olive oil over low heat until they are a light-golden colour. Salt lightly. In a blender or food processor, combine the caramelized onions, the peppers, the vinegar, and the sugar, and process until you have a smooth purée. Add salt to taste, and correct the sweet-sour balance with a little more vinegar or sugar if needed.

Warm the sauce gently before serving.

Makes about 900 ml (1½ pints) of sauce.

ROSEMARY SORBET

for the rosemary syrup
225 g (8 oz) sugar
600 ml (1 pint) water
5 tablespoons chopped fresh
   rosemary leaves

to make the sorbet
600 ml (1 pint) rosemary syrup
500 ml (16 fl oz) good white
   Riesling
3–4 tablespoons fresh lemon
   juice, strained

Dissolve the sugar in the water, add the rosemary, and bring to a boil in a stainless steel or enamel pot. Lower the heat and simmer for 5 minutes. Cool and allow to steep for at least several hours, or overnight. Strain the syrup through a very fine sieve.

Combine 600 ml (1 pint) of cooled rosemary syrup with the wine and taste. Add the lemon juice a bit at a time, stirring and tasting as you go, until there's enough of an acidic little bite to make the mixture interesting. This sorbet is not meant to be overly sweet, and how much lemon juice you use will depend on how sour the lemons are, and how fruity or dry the wine.

Chill the mixture, and then freeze it in an ice cream maker, according to manufacturer's directions.

This should be served in small scoops. Chill the sorbet glasses first.

Makes about 1.2 litres (2 pints) of sorbet.

GRILLED POLENTA WITH GRILLED FRESH
WILD MUSHROOMS

For grilling, use large mushrooms with a firm, dense texture. Big porcini are ideal, as are large field mushrooms.

1 recipe Simple Polenta
   (page 260)
1–1.4 kg (2¼–3 lb) large,
   meaty wild mushrooms,
   such as porcini or large
   field mushrooms

120 ml (4 fl oz) fruity olive oil
2 cloves garlic, minced
6 tablespoons finely chopped
   flat-leaf Italian parsley
salt and freshly ground black
   pepper to taste

Prepare the polenta according to directions, using 400 g (14 oz) of cornmeal instead of 350 g (12 oz), and when it is cooked pour it into 2 shallow ceramic or glass tart dishes, quickly smoothing the top. It should be no more than 1.5 cm (¾ inch) thick. Allow the polenta to cool until it is completely firm. Then turn it out of its dishes on to a board and cut it into wedges.

Clean the mushrooms thoroughly, trimming away any soft spots and the hard bottoms of the stems. Separate the stems from the caps, and slice the stems lengthwise once or twice, depending on their thickness.

Whisk together the olive oil, minced garlic, and half the parsley, and brush this mixture over both sides of the porcini. Salt and pepper them lightly.

Brush the polenta wedges with olive oil and grill them over hot coals until they are golden brown and hot through – about 4–6 minutes on each side.

Grill the mushrooms over the coals alongside the polenta. They'll need 3–4 minutes a side, depending on how thick they are and on the type of mushroom. They're ready when they are golden brown on the outside, tender and juicy on the inside. If a charcoal grill is not available, the polenta and mushrooms can be placed under a very hot kitchen grill.

Serve the polenta wedges and mushrooms at once, sprinkled with the remaining chopped parsley.

Serves 8.

WARM CHOCOLATE CAKES WITH CRÈME ANGLAISE AND BOYSENBERRY SAUCE

This is a lovely dessert for a special occasion. The little cakes are served warm, and the insides remain soft, like puddings, spilling out when the cakes are cut with a fork. Use only the very best chocolate for these.

175 g (6 oz) best-quality semi-sweet chocolate
175 g (6 oz) unsalted butter
5 eggs, at room temperature

125 g (4 oz) sugar
pinch of salt
6 tablespoons flour

garnishes: icing sugar
    Boysenberry Sauce (recipe follows)
    fresh berries
    whipped cream or Crème Anglaise (see page 79)

Prepare 8 × 150 g (5 oz) baking dishes; I like to use the ordinary little Pyrex dishes with the slightly rounded bottoms, the kind you can buy in any supermarket, but I've also used individual soufflé dishes. Butter the dishes well, then dust them with flour.

In a heavy-bottomed saucepan, melt together the chocolate and the butter over low heat, stirring often, until you have a perfectly smooth sauce. In a mixing bowl, beat the eggs with the sugar and a little pinch of salt for about 6–8 minutes, or until they are thick and creamy. Beat in the flour, a tablespoon at a time, then slowly beat in the melted chocolate and butter.

Pour the batter into the 8 prepared baking dishes. Bake the cakes in a preheated 160°C/325°F/Gas 3 oven for 11–12 minutes. The edges of the cakes will be firm, and the centres will still look soft, and tremble slightly when you tap the edge of the dish.

While the cakes are baking, prepare the plates on which you will serve them, and any garnishes. As soon as the cakes are ready, invert them on to large dessert plates and lift off the baking dishes. Dust the cakes lightly with icing sugar, and spoon a little Boysenberry Sauce around each one. Garnish with fresh berries if you like.

Serve the cakes as soon as possible after removing them from the oven. Pass whipped cream or Crème Anglaise separately.

Serves 8.

BOYSENBERRY SAUCE

900 g (2 lb) fresh
  boysenberries, blackberries,
  raspberries or other soft
  berries

spring water
125 g (4 oz) sugar
freshly squeezed lemon juice
  if needed

Combine the clean berries in a non-reactive pan with about 120 ml
(4 fl oz) of spring water and about 125 g (4 oz) of sugar. Simmer
them, stirring, for about 5 minutes. Taste. If they are sour, add a
little more sugar. If they are too sweet, add a squirt of lemon juice,
then simmer again for a few minutes. If the liquid seems too thick,
add a bit more water; it all depends on the juiciness of the berries.

Makes about 900 ml (1½ pints) of sauce.

Crème Anglaise (see page 79)

A SMALL WINE TASTING

❧

WITH THE WHITE WINES

crostini with *Butter Bean Purée*

olives

Salad of Endive, Fennel, Roquefort, and Celery

Tomato and Onion Focaccia
goat's cheese

WITH THE RED WINES

Toasted Walnuts with Rosemary and Sage

Wild Mushroom Pâté with baguettes

Bocconcini di Parma

cheese tray: *Blue Castello, Camembert*
pastries
fresh fruit
nougats
coffee

A wine tasting can be a very interesting and pleasant way to have a little party. I'm not talking about a professional wine tasting, in which ratings are created which spell success or doom for particular vintages, but rather a tasting for fun-loving oenophiles, in which we learn a little something that we didn't know before, and a good time is had by all. In other words, we drink the wine, we don't spit it out.

This type of wine tasting can take several forms. A vertical tasting is a specific comparison of one wine through several vintages. Or you can compare the same kind of wine from one year but different vineyards.

On the other hand, we once had a tasting that simply introduced a few eager amateurs to some wines which they normally had little opportunity to taste, touching several of the great wine regions of the world.

After a couple of fine California Chardonnays to begin with, we went on to the serious reds: a Bordeaux, a Burgundy, a California Cabernet Sauvignon, and an Italian wine. These were the wines we drank that evening:

The white wines
1990 Stony Hill Napa Valley Chardonnay
1990 Kistler Dutton Ranch Chardonnay (Sonoma Valley)

The red wines
1982 Chateau Léoville-Lascases
1988 Chamertin-Clos-de-Bèze, Jadot
1986 Dunn Howell Mountain Cabernet Sauvignon
1985 Brunello di Montalcino, Poggio Antico

My mission was to provide some food that would accompany the wines in a satisfying way, but not overwhelm them. Bread and cheese instantly come to mind, but I wanted some variety, and when the tasting was all done, I wanted it to add up to a meal.

For the white wines, I arranged a little picnic of my favourite tastes from Italy and Provence – a wine-friendly salad, crostini, focaccia, and two kinds of cheese.

With the red wines, my choices were traditional. Toasted walnuts, wild mushrooms, and soft-ripened cheeses are flavours that will always be embraced by a red wine. The bocconcini, crêpes rolled around a delicate filling, are the only food served hot.

After the wines, we had a few sweet and refreshing nibbles served with coffee, and everyone went to bed happy in the wee small hours.

BUTTER BEAN PURÉE

This garlicky purée is nice to have on crostini, with a drizzle of green olive oil and a sprinkle of chopped parsley. It's very light, and makes a nice change from the somewhat richer tapenades, pestos, and cheeses that are often served on toast or crackers with an aperitif. A few cured olives alongside are perfect.

450 g (1 lb) dried butter or
   lima beans
pinch of bicarbonate of soda
salt
60 ml (2 fl oz) olive oil
5 cloves garlic, chopped
2 teaspoons chopped fresh
   rosemary leaves

pinch of red chilli flakes
1–2 tablespoons fresh lemon
   juice
freshly ground black pepper
   to taste

garnishes: additional olive oil
   chopped flat-leaf parsley

Soak the beans overnight in plenty of water with a pinch of bicarbonate of soda in it. Drain them, rinse them, and put them in a heavy-bottomed pot with fresh water to cover by at least 5 cm (2 inches). Bring the water to a boil, then lower the heat and simmer the beans for at least an hour, and perhaps longer, until they are perfectly tender.

Add more water, if necessary, to keep the beans just covered. Towards the end of the cooking time, add about a teaspoon of salt, or more to taste.

In a small pan, combine 1 tablespoon of the olive oil, about a third of the garlic, the chopped rosemary, and the red chilli flakes. Warm the oil and herbs on medium heat, stirring constantly, for about 2 minutes.

Drain the cooked beans, reserving the liquid. Combine them in a food processor or blender with 120 ml (4 fl oz) of their cooking liquid and the warm oil with herbs, and purée. Add the remaining minced garlic, the unheated olive oil, a tablespoon of lemon juice, and salt and pepper to your taste, and process again until everything is thoroughly blended. Taste, and correct the seasoning with a touch more salt or lemon juice if you like. If the purée seems too thick, add a little more of the cooking liquid. It should be light, but hold a shape.

Allow the purée to cool. Spread it in a pretty, shallow bowl, drizzle some fruity olive oil on top, and sprinkle with chopped parsley. Serve the purée with toasted or grilled bread.

Makes about 1.2 litres (2 pints).

Leftovers: Once I made this purée to serve among several other dishes, and had a lot of it left over the next day. Having no time to cook dinner, I combined the purée with a few cups of ready vegetable stock and some leftover cooked tomatoes. I put half a pound of radiatori (any chunky pasta would do) in a pot to boil, and when the pasta was barely cooked I added it to the soup. It was a delicious *pasta e fagioli.* With a little cheese on top and a slice of bread, it made a great 10-minute supper.

SALAD OF ENDIVE, FENNEL, ROQUEFORT, AND CELERY

This is the right salad to serve in a meal when you'd like to keep enjoying your wine with every bite. Salads usually fight with the wine, but this one, enriched with a bit of Roquefort cheese and some toasted almonds, and with virtually no acid in the dressing, is very agreeable.

2 medium fennel bulbs, thinly
  sliced
2 Belgian endives, sliced
2–3 stalks celery, thinly sliced
1 small head radicchio,
  shredded
75 g (3 oz) Roquefort cheese

fruity green olive oil
a few drops balsamic vinegar
salt to taste
125 g (4 oz) coarsely chopped
  toasted almonds (with
  skins)

Combine the fennel, endive, celery, and radicchio in a large bowl.
Break the Roquefort cheese into lumps and scatter them over the
salad.

Drizzle on a little green olive oil and toss everything together.
The vegetables should be barely glistening with oil, not dripping,
and the cheese must be dispersed through the salad. Add only a few
drops of balsamic vinegar, and a dash of salt if you feel it's needed,
and toss again.

Scatter the chopped toasted almonds over the salad and serve.

Serves 6–8.

TOMATO AND ONION FOCACCIA

Use a good, home-made tomato sauce for this, cooked down
until it's thick. This is delicious with tapenade and a glass of
wine.

3 tablespoons fruity green
  olive oil
2 large onions, coarsely
  chopped
1–1½ teaspoons salt
300 ml (10 fl oz) warm water

1 teaspoon dry yeast
1 teaspoon sugar
700 g (1½ lb) white flour
120 ml (4 fl oz) thick, puréed
  tomato sauce

Heat 2 tablespoons of the olive oil in a non-stick pan and cook the
chopped onions in it, with a sprinkle of salt. Stir them often over
a medium flame until they are limp and golden. Allow them to cool
slightly.

Meanwhile, put the warm water in a large mixing bowl and sprinkle the yeast over it. Stir in the sugar and leave the mixture in a warm place for a few minutes, until it begins to froth and foam. Stir in the salt and about 350 g (12 oz) of flour, making a soft sponge. Leave the sponge to rise, covered with a kitchen towel, for about 30 minutes.

Stir down the sponge and add the tomato sauce and the cooked onions. Stir in more flour, until the dough is too stiff to be stirred with a spoon.

Turn the dough out on to a heavily floured board and begin kneading in as much of the remaining flour as is necessary. Knead gently until the dough is smooth and beginning to pull back. It should still be soft.

Form the dough into a ball. Keeping the board well floured and turning the dough once or twice, roll it out to a large oval, about an inch thick. Lightly oil a baking sheet, preferably one with edges, and lay the loaf on it. Poke dimples in the bread with your fingers if you like. Cover the dough and let it rise about 40 minutes, or until it is almost doubled in bulk.

Brush the top of the bread very gently with the remaining olive oil, and bake the focaccia in a preheated 200°C/400°F/Gas 6 oven for about 35 minutes.

Remove it from the pan with the help of a large spatula and transfer it to a wire rack to cool slightly, then cut it in squares to serve.

Makes 1 large loaf.

TOASTED WALNUTS WITH ROSEMARY AND SAGE

1 tablespoon olive oil
1 tablespoon butter
2 tablespoons finely chopped
   fresh rosemary leaves
½ teaspoon rubbed sage

1 teaspoon sweet paprika
¾ teaspoon salt
350 g (12 oz) walnut halves, or
   large pieces

Heat the oil and butter together in a large pan. Stir in the herbs and salt. Add the walnuts and toss them in the herb mixture until they are evenly coated.

Spread the walnuts out on a baking sheet and toast them in a 150°C/300°F/Gas 2 oven for 20–30 minutes, stirring and turning them once or twice. They should be fragrant and somewhat darker in colour, but never blackened.

Allow them to cool to room temperature, then bite into one to make sure they are crisp. If not, they need a few more minutes in the oven.

These are delicious to nibble with an aperitif, or with cheese and a great glass of red wine at the end of a meal.

Makes about 350 g (12 oz).

WILD MUSHROOM PÂTÉ

25 g (1 oz) dried porcini
250 ml (8 fl oz) vegetable stock
(see page 459)
1 tablespoon olive oil
1½ tablespoons butter
4–6 shallots, chopped
2 large onions, chopped
salt and pepper to taste
575 g (1¼ lb) fresh wild
mushrooms – you can use
oyster mushrooms, field
mushrooms, or a mix of
shiitakes and cultivated
mushrooms if wild ones are
scarce

¼ teaspoon thyme
pinch of cayenne
120 ml (4 fl oz) port
120 ml (4 fl oz) dry red wine
125 g (4 oz) day-old bread,
torn into small pieces
3 tablespoons chopped
parsley

Pour boiling water over the dried porcini and let them soak for about 30 minutes. Drain them, reserving the water, and wash them well. Strain the water through a paper filter to eliminate all the grit and add it to the vegetable stock. You will have 350–500 ml (12–16 fl oz) of stock altogether. Chop the porcini.

Heat the oil and butter in a large non-stick sauté pan, and sauté the shallots and onions in it with a bit of salt until they are golden brown.

Wash and chop all the fresh mushrooms, and add them to the caramelized onions along with the chopped porcini, thyme, cayenne, and a little more salt and some pepper. Continue cooking, stirring occasionally, while the mushrooms release their water and the water cooks away. Stir more frequently as they begin to colour.

When the mushrooms are browning and beginning to stick to the pan, pour in the port to deglaze it. When that has cooked away, repeat with the dry red wine.

Add the torn bread, the chopped parsley, and about a cup of the vegetable stock. Lower the heat and keep stirring as the bread softens and absorbs the liquid. Add a little more stock if needed. The pâté mixture should be thick but moist.

Remove the mixture from the heat and allow it to cool somewhat, then put it all through the medium blade of the food mill. If you want a less chunky texture, you could put some of it through the fine blade.

Pack the pâté into a nice ceramic terrine, or mound it in a bowl. Garnish it with a few parsley sprigs and serve with toasted slices of baguette.

Makes about 700 g (1 ½ lb).

BOCCONCINI DI PARMA

Traditional bocconcini are made with no onion or parsley, just cheese, eggs, and butter. I like this variation, and another one I made once, in which I added chopped truffles to the cheese mixture instead of onions. All of them are fantastic.

1 recipe of basic crêpes
  (page 24)
1.2 kg (2½ lb) fresh ricotta
225 g (8 oz) finely chopped
  onion
7 tablespoons softened butter
4 whole eggs

225 g (8 oz) grated Parmesan
  cheese
salt and finely ground black
  pepper, if needed
3 tablespoons finely chopped
  flat-leaf parsley

Make the crêpes ahead of time and have them ready, at room temperature.

Drain the ricotta for about 30 minutes in a colander lined with a double thickness of cheesecloth. While it's draining, sauté the finely chopped onion in 2 tablespoons of the butter, stirring often, until it is golden. Beat the eggs lightly. Combine in a bowl the drained ricotta, eggs, Parmesan cheese, sautéd onion, and the remaining 5 tablespoons of softened butter. Mix everything together well, then taste and add salt and finely ground black pepper to taste. Stir in the chopped parsley.

Lay one crêpe at a time on a board and spread about 3 heaped tablespoons of filling down the middle of it. Roll the crêpe up around the filling, making a cylinder. Lay the rolled crêpes, seam side down, on a platter, cover with clingfilm, and chill in the refrigerator for at least 30 minutes.

Butter a large gratin dish, or a 23 × 32 cm (9 × 13 inch) baking dish. Take the chilled, rolled crêpes and lay them on a board. With a very sharp knife, cut each crêpe into 4 even pieces. Arrange the cut crêpes in the buttered gratin dish, standing up side by side and close together.

Bake the bocconcini for about 25 minutes at 190°C/375°F/Gas 5, and serve hot.

Serves 8–10.

A FORMAL DINNER PARTY FOR LATE SUMMER

❧

crostini with Mushroom Tapenade

Tomato and Provolone Tart

Cantaloupe and Nectarine Soup with Raspberry Purée

Salad with Wheat Pilaf and Red Grapes

Sweetcorn Soufflé with Tomato and Garlic Fondue

Chocolate and Chilli Torte

Orange and Mango Sorbet

coffee

This meal captures the voluptuous feeling of summer for me. It starts with a taste of salty Provençal olives, ripe tomatoes, strong cheese – and a glass of cold white wine. Already I want to be outside, in soft evening air.

Combining the formality of a five-course dinner with a relaxed outdoor setting has been refined to an art in the south of France, and you can do it too. Set a table somewhere on a balcony or in a garden, with white linen and your best china. Put wild flowers in a jug next to crystal glasses. Then let this dinner unfold in its leisurely pace through the evening and into the summer night.

The appetizers are finger food, and pungent tastes like tapenade are perfect with a slightly fruity champagne aperitif. The cooling fruit soup, which is the first sit-down course, is beautiful as well as delicious: you can paint a picture in each bowl, placing dots and spirals of raspberry purée on the pale orange of cantaloupes and nectarines. It's a delightful thing to come from aperitifs to the table and find these soup-paintings. The salad that follows, with a chewy, nutty pilaf mounded on salad leaves, is hearty without being heavy.

The only hot course in this meal is a puffy sweetcorn soufflé with tomato and garlic fondue, the essence of summer garden flavours. To have the hot soufflé coming out of the oven at exactly the right moment, put it in just as you're sitting down to eat soup. You can linger comfortably over two courses that have been prepared ahead, then serve the soufflé in its perfection.

A grand dessert ends this dinner. Some people accuse me of being unable to serve a meal without some chilli in it somewhere. This is not true – but I did find a way to bring some in here, in the Chocolate and Chilli Torte. Don't be afraid to try this. It's no spicier than a good gingerbread, and a scoop of Orange and Mango Sorbet is heavenly alongside it. End a summer celebration with little fireworks in your mouth.

MUSHROOM TAPENADE

A variety of mushrooms lends an earthy richness to the familiar pungency of tapenade. Serve this with thin slices of baguette, toasted crisp. It's delicious with a fruity wine or your favourite aperitif.

225 g (8 oz) cultivated
   mushrooms
125 g (4 oz) shiitake
   mushrooms
125 g (4 oz) oyster mushrooms
3 tablespoons olive oil

½ head garlic, peeled and
   chopped
1 teaspoon dried thyme
pinch of dried oregano
pinch of cayenne
¼ teaspoon salt

freshly ground black pepper
150 ml (5 fl oz) dry red wine
6 tablespoons chopped
   flat-leaf parsley

75 g (3 oz) sliced Kalamata
   olives
2 tablespoons fresh lemon
   juice

optional garnishes: additional olive oil
   parsley leaves
   additional olives

Clean and chop all the mushrooms. Heat 2 tablespoons of olive oil in a non-stick pan, add the garlic, and stir it for about a minute. Add the mushrooms, thyme, oregano, cayenne, salt, and pepper, and stir over high heat until the mushrooms release their liquid and it begins to reduce. Add the wine, and continue to stir frequently. Cook the mixture down until it sizzles in the pan and the mushrooms begin to colour.

Combine the mushroom mixture in the food processor with the parsley, olives, lemon juice, and the remaining olive oil. Pulse for 1 – 2 seconds at a time until it is chopped to your taste. I like it to be spreadable, but not mushy.

Serve the tapenade in a shallow bowl, with a basket of crostini – crisply toasted or grilled baguette slices. If you like, you can smooth the top, drizzle on some more green olive oil, and garnish with parsley leaves and whole olives.

Makes about 500 ml (16 fl oz).

TOMATO AND PROVOLONE TART

This tart is made with the same kind of cream cheese pastry I've used for years to make pierogi. It's delicious, and a slightly guilty pleasure. The mustard marries the tastes of the tomatoes and the provolone cheese in an unexpected and delightful way. Buy real Italian provolone cheese if possible, as it's quite different from the bland domestic version. If unavailable you can substitute Gruyère or another hard ripened cheese.

for the pastry dough
225 g (8 oz) butter
225 g (8 oz) cream cheese
¾ teaspoon salt
1 teaspoon crushed dried
   thyme or rosemary
300 g (10 oz) white flour, more
   for rolling out
3 tablespoons cold white wine

for the topping
1 tablespoon olive oil
3 tablespoons Dijon mustard
900 g (2 lb) ripe tomatoes,
   thinly sliced
salt as needed
125 g (4 oz) grated provolone
   or Gruyère cheese
3 tablespoons thinly sliced
   fresh basil leaves
freshly ground pepper

Cut the butter and cream cheese into chunks and combine them in the food processor with the salt, thyme or rosemary, and flour. Blend until the mixture has a dry and crumbly look. Sprinkle in the white wine and blend again until the pastry forms and holds together. Shape the pastry into a thick rectangle, wrap it well, and chill it in the refrigerator for an hour.

On a lightly floured board, roll the pastry out to a 36 × 45 cm (14 × 18 inch) rectangle, about 0.5 cm (¼ inch) thick. Brush the olive oil on a 30 × 40 cm (12 × 16 inch) baking sheet with edges. Fit the pastry into the sheet, folding it up against the sides and trimming away the excess.

Prick the pastry here and there with a fork, then bake it in a 190°C/375°F/Gas 5 oven for 25 minutes, or until light golden brown. Let it cool slightly. Brush the pastry evenly with the mustard. Arrange the tomato slices over the mustard. Sprinkle the tomatoes with a touch of salt and the grated provolone or Gruyère, and finally the sliced basil leaves. Grind on a little black pepper.

Bake the tart, again at 190°C/375°F/Gas 5, for about 20 minutes, or until the cheese is bubbling. Let the tart cool for a few minutes only, then cut it into 5 cm (2 inch) squares while it is still warm.

Serves 10–12 as a first course, 20 as part of a buffet.

Note: Leftovers are very popular, and especially tasty when popped into the oven for a moment first.

CANTALOUPE AND NECTARINE SOUP WITH RASPBERRY PURÉE

2 medium cantaloupe melons, about 900 g (2 lb) each
900 g (2 lb) nectarines
5–7 tablespoons lemon juice
3–4 tablespoons honey

350 ml (12 fl oz) plain yogurt
2 tablespoons chopped fresh mint leaves
300 g (10 oz) raspberries
2–3 tablespoons sugar

Choose the fruit with great care. Use only sweet, intensely flavourful cantaloupes, and ripe, juicy nectarines. There is nothing here to obscure the flavour of the fruit, only a few tweaks to heighten it.

Peel and seed the melons and cut the flesh in cubes. Peel and slice the nectarines. Purée all the fruit, with 5 tablespoons of fresh lemon juice, 3 tablespoons of honey, and the yogurt, until it is entirely smooth.

Taste the mixture and stir in a little more lemon juice or a little more honey – or both – until you have just the right sweet-tart balance. You must do this by taste; all fruit varies in sugar content, and lemons vary widely in acidity. When it tastes just fabulous, stir in the chopped mint and refrigerate the soup in a covered container for several hours.

Purée the raspberries and force the purée through a fine sieve to eliminate the seeds. Add a little sugar and stir until it's dissolved. Chill the sweetened purée.

Serve the soup in chilled bowls, and drizzle patterns of raspberry purée in each one.

Serves 8.

Salad with Wheat Pilaf and Red Grapes (see page 325)

SWEETCORN SOUFFLÉ

3 tablespoons + 2 teaspoons
    butter
1 large onion, chopped
salt
250 ml (8 fl oz) milk
5–6 ears fresh sweetcorn
30 g (1¼ oz) white flour
4 egg yolks
6 egg whites

6 spring onions, thinly sliced
125 g (4 oz) mature Cheddar
    cheese, cut in 0.5 cm
    (¼ inch) cubes
pinch of cayenne
freshly ground black pepper
    to taste
pinch of cream of tartar

garnish: Tomato and Garlic Fondue (recipe follows)

Melt 2 teaspoons of butter in a small non-stick pan and sauté the chopped onion in it, with a sprinkle of salt, until it begins to colour. Remove the onion and set it aside.

Heat the milk just to scalding point. In a blender, purée half the sweetcorn kernels with the hot milk.

Melt 3 tablespoons of butter in a heavy-bottomed saucepan, and stir the flour into it. Keep stirring with a wooden spoon over medium heat until the roux is golden and foaming, about 2 – 3 minutes. Then whisk in the hot milk and sweetcorn purée. Lower the heat and continue stirring with the whisk until the sauce thickens.

Remove the sauce from the heat and whisk in the egg yolks, one at a time. Return the saucepan to a very low flame and keep stirring steadily for about 2 more minutes. The egg whites, meanwhile, should be left in a bowl to warm to room temperature.

Allow the mixture to cool slightly, then stir in half the sautéd onions, the sliced spring onions, the cubed cheese, a pinch of cayenne, the remaining sweetcorn kernels, and some salt and pepper to taste. (At this point, the soufflé mixture could be covered and kept for several hours in the refrigerator. Allow it to return to room temperature before proceeding.)

Prepare a 2 litre (3½ pint) soufflé dish by forming a collar out of foil or heavy brown paper and tying it around the dish with strong twine. The collar should extend about 5 cm (2 inches) above the rim of the soufflé dish. Butter the dish and the inside of the collar. Preheat the oven to 220°C/425°F/Gas 7.

Beat the egg whites with a pinch of cream of tartar and a little salt until they hold stiff peaks. Stir about a third of the beaten whites into the sweetcorn mixture to lighten it, then gently fold in the remainder. Don't overmix.

Pile the soufflé mixture into the prepared dish, and sprinkle the remaining sautéd onions over the top. Bake the soufflé in the centre of the oven for 25 minutes. It should be crusty and brown on top, but wiggle slightly when moved. The inside will still be creamy and slightly runny. Serve it at once, and scoop out some of the crusty part and some of the saucy inside for each serving. Garnish each plate with a generous spoonful of Tomato and Garlic Fondue.

Serves 6–8.

TOMATO AND GARLIC FONDUE

This is so basic that you almost can't even call it a sauce. It's the perfect little condiment for a lot of things, redolent of garlic and intense tomato flavour.

4–5 large, very red tomatoes
6 cloves garlic, peeled and
  chopped

2 tablespoons fruity green
  olive oil ·
salt to taste

Scald the tomatoes, peel and core them, and trim them, and cut them in wedges or large chunks.

Sauté the minced garlic in the olive oil until it barely begins to turn colour. Add the tomato chunks with all their juice, and a little salt, and cook until the juices are reduced and the tomatoes are saucy rather than soupy. The texture will vary with the variety of tomatoes, but they should melt into a pleasant softness without completely losing their identity.

Makes about 500 ml (16 fl oz).

CHOCOLATE AND CHILLI TORTE

Mole Poblano, the famous chilli and chocolate sauce of Mexico, combines those two essentially American flavours, and numerous other spices, with a strong emphasis on the chilli. In this wonderful cake, the ratio is reversed, and Pasilla Chilli Paste adds a subtle kick to the rich chocolate flavour. The effect is something like that of a true gingerbread, sweet but genuinely spicy. If you don't tell people what it is, they never guess.

butter and flour for cake tin

175 g (6 oz) toasted almonds, with skins

75 g (3 oz) brown sugar

2 tablespoons ground cinnamon

¼ teaspoon ground cloves

2 teaspoons anise seeds, crushed in a mortar

½ teaspoon salt

250 g (9 oz) dark semi-sweet chocolate

3 tablespoons thick Pasilla Chilli Paste (recipe follows)

4 egg yolks

5 egg whites, at room temperature

125 g (4 oz) granulated white sugar

2 tablespoons unsalted butter

2 tablespoons cream

1 tablespoon golden syrup

Butter a 23 cm (9 inch) springform cake tin, and line the bottom with a circle of buttered waxed paper. Dust the tin with flour, tapping out the excess.

In the container of the food processor, fitted with the steel blade, blend together the almonds, brown sugar, spices, and salt until the texture resembles fine crumbs. Add 150 g (5 oz) of the chocolate, broken into bits, and blend again until the chocolate is finely ground. Add the chilli paste and the 4 egg yolks and pulse briefly, then scrape the mixture out into an ample bowl.

In a separate bowl, beat the egg whites with a pinch of salt until they hold soft peaks. Gradually beat in the granulated sugar and continue beating until the whites hold stiff peaks.

Stir about a third of this meringue thoroughly into the chocolate mixture to lighten it, then carefully fold in the remainder. Keep folding gently just until there are no large streaks of egg white left.

Pour the batter into the prepared tin, smooth the top with a spatula, and bake the torte in the centre of a preheated 160°C/ 325°F/Gas 3 oven for 50–55 minutes, or until it tests done. Let the torte cool a while in the tin, then remove it, invert it on to a wire rack, and let it finish cooling.

In a double boiler or a steel bowl set over a pot of simmering water, melt the remaining chocolate with the butter, cream, and golden syrup. Stir until completely smooth. Let this glaze cool until it is medium warm.

Set the torte, on its rack, over a large platter or a sheet of waxed paper, and pour the glaze over it. Smooth the glaze with a spatula and let it drizzle down the sides. It thickens as it cools, so you can adjust the look to your liking.

Transfer the torte carefully to a beautiful serving platter, and allow it to stand at cool room temperature for 2–3 hours. The glaze should set and remain glossy.

Serve each slice of torte accompanied by a scoop of Orange and Mango Sorbet, or some other refreshing fruit ice.

This is a moist cake, and keeps well for a couple of days if covered with clingfilm. You'll enjoy having some leftovers of this.

Serves 16.

PASILLA CHILLI PASTE

5–6 dried pasilla chilli pods (see page 88)

Rinse the pasilla chilli pods, break them open, pull out their stems and seeds, and put them in a small saucepan with water just to cover. Bring the water to a boil, lower the heat to a simmer for a few minutes, then remove from the heat and leave the pods to soak for 30 minutes.

Purée the softened chilli pods in a blender or food processor with enough of the remaining water to form a soft but thick paste. Put the purée through a strainer, measure out 3 tablespoons, and reserve the rest for another use, storing it in a tightly covered jar in the refrigerator.

ORANGE AND MANGO SORBET

125 g (4 oz) sugar
120 ml (4 fl oz) water
2 large ripe mangoes
350 ml (12 fl oz) freshly
   squeezed orange juice

5 tablespoons freshly
   squeezed lemon juice
finely grated zest of 1 large
   orange

In a small saucepan, dissolve the sugar in the water, bring it to a boil, and let it boil for 5 minutes. Allow the syrup to cool, then chill it.

Peel and slice the mangoes, and purée them with the orange juice, lemon juice, and orange zest. Stir the sugar syrup into the purée, a little at a time, until the sweet-tart balance is right.

Freeze the mixture according to manufacturer's instructions in an ice cream freezer.

Makes about 900 ml (1½ pints) of sorbet.

EASTER BRUNCH

✴

crostini with Aubergine and Olive Relish

Spinach, Green Garlic, and Mushroom Pie

painted eggs

Beetroot Salad in Raspberry Vinaigrette

Onion and Thyme Custard

*Roasted Asparagus with
Herb-roasted Baby Potatoes*

*Yogurt Cheese with honey
fresh strawberries
hot cross buns*

Easter Baba

Gypsy Mazurek

At our house, Easter means brunch on the terrace with several families, lots of kids, lots of beautiful food laid out on a buffet, and Easter egg wars.

The centrepiece of this brunch is a hearty spinach and mushroom pie, a big, wonderful-looking thing with a bread-like crust, something like an open calzone. Around it, I serve a bounty of spring vegetables – bright green asparagus, pink and gold beetroots with their leaves, little potatoes, and sweet onions in a custard.

There's flavourful Aubergine and Olive Relish to nibble with a cracker and a glass of champagne, and there are sweet strawberries and Polish pastries to linger over into the afternoon with a cup of coffee.

Most important, there are painted eggs. After the traditional egg hunt, everyone comes to the table and a big basket of painted hard-boiled eggs is passed around. We all choose our weapons for the egg war, and challenges are called out. The rules are simple: pointy end against pointy, blunt against blunt, the challenger usually does the hitting. The longest surviving egg wins. I don't need to say that the kids love this little event, and wait for it all year. Once only, one of my boys made a mistake and painted an egg that was still raw.

After the hilarity, there's a toast, and then food for as long as anyone likes. Most years we're lucky, the weather is beautiful, and we sit outside under the trees for hours.

On a practical note: most of the work for this brunch can be done the day before. The pie should be baked on Easter morning, but the filling can be done on Saturday. The asparagus and potatoes take about 10 minutes' preparation time before they go into the oven, and even the custard can be made the night before and then rewarmed slightly before being unmoulded on to a platter.

This is also a meal that adapts well to a potluck style. Almost anything seasonal that someone might bring along to a brunch will fit right in.

AUBERGINE AND OLIVE RELISH

3 medium aubergines (about
   1.4–1.8 kg/3–4 lb)
450 g (1 lb) tomatoes
125 g (4 oz) Kalamata olives,
   or a combination of black
   and green cured olives,
   coarsely chopped

lemon juice to taste
freshly ground black pepper
2–3 tablespoons chopped
   flat-leaf parsley

Prick the aubergines with a fork, put them on a baking sheet, and roast them in a 200°C/400°F/Gas 6 oven for at least an hour, or until they are soft enough to collapse when pushed. At the same time, quarter the tomatoes, arrange them skin side down on another baking sheet, and roast until they are blackened around the edges and most of the excess juice has cooked away, also about an hour.

When the aubergines have cooled enough so you can handle them, split them open and scoop the flesh out of the skins with a spoon. Scrape away and discard any clusters of very dark seeds. Allow the aubergine flesh to drain in a colander for about 30 minutes, then chop it coarsely.

When the tomatoes are ready, use a spoon to remove the tomato pulp gently from the skins. Discard the skins and stir the pulp into the aubergine flesh.

Add the chopped olives to the aubergine and tomatoes. Stir and taste. Add a few drops of lemon juice and some black pepper, and stir in the chopped parsley. You should not need any salt, as the olives will provide enough.

Serve the relish warm or at room temperature, with crostini, plain crackers, or pitta bread.

Makes about 500 ml (16 fl oz) of relish.

SPINACH, GREEN GARLIC, AND MUSHROOM PIE

Somewhere between calzone and quiche, and bigger than either one, is this substantial bread-like pastry filled with ricotta cheese, spinach, plenty of garlic, and sautéd oyster mushrooms. It's tasty when hot, and just as good at room temperature, and, because of its sturdy consistency, travels well to picnics.

Green garlic looks like slightly larger spring onions. It's garlic that hasn't bulbed yet, and it has a milder, fresher taste. If you can't find it, use a combination of spring onions and bulb garlic.

for the dough
1 tablespoon dried yeast
1 teaspoon sugar
175 ml (6 fl oz) lukewarm
   water

400–450 g (14–16 oz) plain
   flour
1 teaspoon salt
2 eggs
1½ tablespoons olive oil

for the filling

350 g (12 oz) fresh spinach

125 g (4 oz) sliced green
garlic, or 6–8 sliced spring
onions and 2 cloves garlic,
chopped

2 tablespoons olive oil

salt and pepper to taste

1–2 teaspoons lemon juice

1 egg

450 g (1 lb) ricotta

75 g (3 oz) grated Parmesan
cheese

3 leeks, white part only, thinly
sliced

225 g (8 oz) oyster mushrooms

2 tablespoons white vermouth

In a small bowl, dissolve the yeast and the sugar in the lukewarm water and leave it for 10–15 minutes, until it begins to foam. Mix 400 g (14 oz) of flour with the salt in a medium-sized mixing bowl.

Beat one egg lightly into the yeast mixture, and stir in the olive oil. Pour the liquid into the flour and mix with a wooden spoon until a ragged dough forms. Turn the dough out on a board lightly sprinkled with flour and knead it until it is smooth, about 5–6 minutes. If the dough feels very moist and sticks to the board, sprinkle on a little more flour, but don't let the dough get too dry.

Form the dough into a ball and put it into a lightly oiled bowl, turning it over once. Cover the bowl with a towel or with clingfilm and leave the dough in a warm place to rise for about 45 minutes, or until doubled in volume.

Meanwhile, prepare the filling. Wash the spinach very well, remove tough stems, and chop it coarsely. Clean and slice the green garlic, or slice the spring onion and finely chop the garlic.

Heat a tablespoon of olive oil in a large non-stick sauté pan and sauté the green garlic, or spring onions and garlic, in it until limp. Add the spinach and some salt and pepper. Continue cooking, stirring often, until the spinach is completely wilted, all the excess water has cooked away, and it begins to sizzle. Remove from the heat, and toss the spinach mixture with 1–2 teaspoons of lemon juice.

Beat the egg into the ricotta and stir in the Parmesan cheese, then the cooked spinach.

In another large non-stick pan, heat the remaining tablespoon of olive oil and sauté the leeks in it until they begin to be spotted with gold. Add the oyster mushrooms and continue sautéing, stirring often, until the mushrooms are also just beginning to colour. Add salt and pepper to taste, and the vermouth, and stir as the vermouth cooks away. Remove from heat.

When the dough is fully risen, punch it down and set it aside to rest for a few minutes. Then roll it out gently on a lightly floured board, to an oval about 21 by 15 inches. Very lightly oil a large baking sheet and sprinkle it with cornmeal. Lift the oval of dough and lay it down evenly on the baking sheet; the edges of the dough may overhang the baking sheet, which is fine.

Spread the ricotta cheese and spinach mixture over the dough, leaving a border of about 7.5 cm (3 inches) all the way around. Spread the cooked oyster mushrooms evenly over the spinach mixture.

Pull the edges of the dough up over the filling, pleating or folding them as you like. Beat the remaining egg with a spoonful of water and brush the dough lightly with it.

Bake at 200°C/400°F/Gas 6 for about 35 minutes. Check after 25 minutes, and if the crust is looking very dark, cover it lightly with a sheet of foil for the remaining time. It should be glossy and golden brown.

Allow the pie to cool slightly in its pan before removing it to a board and slicing it into wedges or squares.

Serves 8–10 as a main course, more as an appetizer.

BEETROOT SALAD IN RASPBERRY VINAIGRETTE

Raspberry vinegar and a little honey give this salad a surprising delicacy. This salad uses both the beetroots and their leaves, so choose young beetroots that have fresh, crisp leaves.

900 g (2 lb) young beetroots with their leaves	**2 tablespoons honey**
8 whole cloves garlic, unpeeled	**3 tablespoons raspberry vinegar**
1 tablespoon olive oil	**1 large stalk celery, diced**
2 cloves garlic, minced	**½ red onion, finely chopped**
	salt and pepper to taste

garnish: 75 g (3 oz) crumbled Roquefort or feta cheese

Cut the leaves off the beetroots, leaving about 1 cm (½ inch) of stem and reserving the leaves. Scrub the beetroots well. Arrange the damp beetroots close together on a sheet of heavy-duty foil and scatter 8 unpeeled garlic cloves over them. Wrap the beetroots in the foil, folding over and crimping the edges to make a tight seal. Bake the beetroots in the foil packet in a 200°C/400°F/Gas 6 oven for about 1 hour and 15 minutes.

Meanwhile, wash the beetroot leaves, discard those that are anything less than fresh and lovely, and cut off the stems. Slice the leaves in 1 cm (½ inch) strips; you should have enough to fill a measure to the 750 ml (1¼ pint) mark.

Heat the olive oil in a non-stick sauté pan, add the minced garlic, stir for ½ minute, then add the sliced beetroot leaves and a sprinkle of salt. Toss over a medium flame until the greens are completely wilted and sizzling in the pan, about 5–6 minutes. Remove the pan from the heat.

In a small bowl, whisk together the honey and the raspberry vinegar. Drizzle 2 tablespoons of this mixture over the beetroot leaves in the warm pan and toss to combine thoroughly.

When the beetroots are cool enough to handle, slip off their skins and cut them into slices or chunks. Squeeze out the soft garlic, mash it with a fork, and whisk it into the remaining vinegar-honey mixture. Pour this over the beetroots in a bowl, and add the diced celery, chopped red onion, salt and pepper to taste, and the sautéd leaves. Mix everything together well.

Serve the salad warm or at room temperature, alone or on a bed of tender young curly endive. Garnish each serving with a sprinkle of crumbled cheese.

Serves 6.

ONION AND THYME CUSTARD

This is a marvellous concentration of onions, married with a simple custard of eggs, milk, and cheese. The secret is in starting with good, sweet onions, and cooking them slowly for a long time.

1.6 kg (3½ lb) onions
1 teaspoon olive oil
1½ tablespoons butter
1½ teaspoons salt
1 teaspoon dried thyme
½ teaspoon white pepper
2 tablespoons sherry or
  Marsala

5 eggs
350 ml (12 fl oz) milk (low-fat
  is fine)
50 g (2 oz) Gruyère cheese,
  grated
50 g (2 oz) Parmesan cheese,
  grated

Peel and chop the onions. In a large non-stick sauté pan, heat the olive oil and butter, then add the onions and most of the salt, and begin stirring over medium heat. After a few minutes, lower the flame, and keep cooking the onions very slowly, stirring often, for about an hour.

It is essential to take your time in this process. The onions must not brown, but rather soften and melt slowly, and finally reduce to about a quarter of their original volume. Allow them to turn a pale shade of gold, then add the thyme and white pepper, and stir a few more minutes. Add the sherry or Marsala, and stir again until the liquid has completely cooked away. Remove the onions from the heat and let them cool slightly.

Whisk together the eggs and milk with a pinch of salt, then stir in the grated cheeses and the cooked onions.

Butter 1 large, straight-sided baking dish, or 10 individual ramekins. If you are using 1 baking dish, such as a medium gratin dish or large soufflé dish, and plan to unmould the custard to serve it, line the bottom of the dish with a buttered piece of waxed paper or parchment, cut to fit.

Pour the custard mixture into the prepared dish or ramekins. Place the baking dish or ramekins into a larger baking pan in which there is about an inch of water. Bake in a 180°C/350°F/Gas 4 oven for about 40–45 minutes for 1 large dish, about 25 minutes for individual ramekins. It is ready when the top is golden brown, the custard no longer trembles when the pan is jiggled, and a thin knife inserted near the middle comes out clean.

Remove the custard from its water bath, and allow to cool slightly before serving. The custard can be served hot, warm, or at room temperature. The large custard can be served in its baking dish, and spooned out casually, or it can be unmoulded, served on a platter and cut into wedges.

To unmould, slide a thin knife blade around the sides to loosen. Give the dish a little shake to check that the custard is moving freely. Place a large plate over the top of the baking dish, hold them together tightly, and flip. The custard will drop out on to the plate. Peel away the waxed paper. Now invert a serving platter over the custard and flip it again, revealing its nicely browned top.

Serves 10–12.

ROASTED ASPARAGUS

1.4 kg (3 lb) thin green   salt to taste
    asparagus   10 cloves garlic, peeled
2 tablespoons olive oil

optional: lemon juice or a fruity vinegar

Wash the asparagus and snap off the tough ends of the stalks. Drizzle the olive oil over the asparagus, sprinkle on some salt, and roll the asparagus around until all of it is evenly and lightly coated with oil. Spread the asparagus out on baking sheets, and tuck peeled garlic cloves in among it, here and there.

Roast at 200°C/400°F/Gas 6 for 20–30 minutes, depending on the thickness of the stalks. Check after 10 or 15 minutes, and when you see them getting a slightly blistered look, move the stalks around and turn them over.

The roasting time will vary. How long you leave the asparagus in the oven depends on how thick the stalks are, and even more on how you like them. Sometimes I like them just tender. Other times I like to let the thin tips get golden brown and crispy. When thin asparagus is roasted to this further stage, it makes an excellent finger food.

Serve the asparagus hot or at room temperature. You can sprinkle it with a few drops of lemon juice or a fruity vinegar if you like. I've used raspberry vinegar this way, and also a grapefruit vinegar once, which was very good.

Serves 10–12.

HERB-ROASTED BABY POTATOES

Here's one of those easy, practical things that are just delicious. These potatoes are best when they're hot, but also very good at room temperature. They are wonderful with eggs for a cooked breakfast or brunch, and make a delicious nibble with a glass of wine. I can make a meal of these with a green salad and a little slice of cheese.

1.4 kg (3 lb) baby red-skinned   salt to taste
  potatoes
2 teaspoons olive oil
1–2 tablespoons herbes de
  Provence (thyme, rosemary,
  basil, savory, marjoram)

Wash the potatoes thoroughly, scrubbing with a vegetable brush. Trim away any soft or damaged spots, and let the potatoes dry in a colander or on a tea towel. If some of the potatoes are much larger than others, cut them in half.

Put the potatoes in a bowl, drizzle them with the olive oil, and sprinkle on the crushed herbs and as much salt as you'd like, then tumble them around with your hands until all are evenly coated with oil and herbs – 2 teaspoons of oil really is enough! If you use more, the potatoes will be heavy, and taste greasy at room temperature.

Spread the prepared potatoes evenly on a non-stick baking sheet and roast them in the middle of a 200°C/400°F/Gas 6 oven for about 45 minutes to an hour. After the first 30 minutes, move them around and turn them over.

When the potatoes are tender, you can serve them at once or let them cool to room temperature.

Serves 6−8.

Yogurt Cheese (see page 85)

EASTER BABA

A sweet, rich yeast bread is an Easter tradition over most of Europe. This one is the Polish baba that I have eaten every Easter since I can remember. My mother made it by hand, slapping the glossy batter against the side of the bowl, and later worrying whether the butter-laden cake would rise properly.

The recipe to which she referred, in an old Polish cookbook with yellowed pages, called for 60 egg yolks and about 2 lb of butter. I have made a few modifications, in the amount of egg yolks as well as in some technique, but it is still a very traditional recipe, and the result is a true baba.

I serve it with Easter brunch or breakfast. It makes a fabulous coffee cake any time, and a slice of freshly baked baba with some crème fraîche and berries is a fine dessert.

2 eggs	1 teaspoon pure vanilla
2 egg yolks	extract
300 g (10 oz) sugar	½ teaspoon salt
500 ml (16 fl oz) warm milk	125 g (4 oz) butter, softened
2 tablespoons dried yeast	175 g (6 oz) plump raisins
700–800 g (1½–1¾ lb) white	150 g (5 oz) finely chopped
flour	blanched almonds
pinch of ground cardamom	icing sugar

Start by making a sponge. In a large mixing bowl, beat the eggs, egg yolks, and 2 tablespoons of sugar until creamy and light. Beat in the warm milk, the yeast, and about half the flour. Cover the bowl with a towel or with clingfilm and leave it in a warm place until the sponge rises to at least double its volume.

Stir down the sponge, and use an electric mixer to beat in the remaining sugar, the cardamom, vanilla, salt, and softened butter. Start beating in more flour, about 65 g (2½ oz) at a time, until the batter becomes too thick to use an electric mixer. Continue adding flour, beating it in now with a wooden spoon, until the batter starts to take on the consistency of a very soft dough. Do not let it get stiff.

Beat this dough vigorously with a wooden spoon, slapping it against the side of the bowl and giving the bowl an occasional turn, until the dough starts to pull away in a shiny, elastic mass. The consistency will be somewhere between a batter and a bread dough. It will fall *slowly* from the wooden spoon when lifted.

Work the raisins and chopped almonds into the dough, and let it rest while you prepare the tin.

Butter a large springform tin, and line the bottom with a round of buttered parchment or waxed paper, cut to fit. Spoon the soft dough into the prepared tin, spreading it evenly. It should come no more than half-way up the side of the tin. Cover the tin with a towel or with clingfilm, and put it away in a warm place to rise.

This rich dough will rise slowly, but after 1½ hours or so, it should reach the top of the pan. Find the warmest, stillest spot in your kitchen to help it along – an oven with a pilot light is great.

When the baba has doubled in size, preheat the oven to 170°C/ 325°F/Gas 3, and bake it for about 1 hour and 15 minutes. After the first 20 minutes, lay a sheet of foil or plain brown paper loosely over the top to keep it from browning too much. It should rise in a beautiful dome shape above the edge of the cake tin. When it is done, it should sound hollow when tapped, and a thin blade inserted near the middle should come out perfectly clean.

Remove the baba from the oven and let it cool slowly on a rack before removing the sides of the tin and lifting it off the bottom. Dust the top with sifted icing sugar. Do not slice the baba until it is completely cooled, then cut it in thin wedges to serve.

Serves 12–15.

GYPSY MAZUREK

We had several kinds of mazurek for Easter when I was little, and this was always my favourite. The flat, slightly crumbly pastry holds masses of raisins and almonds, and is cut into bars or squares to serve, making one of the nicest biscuits I know.

10 egg yolks	250 g (9 oz) plump dark raisins
2 whole eggs	250 g (9 oz) sultanas
450 g (1 lb) + 2 tablespoons sugar	175 g (6 oz) currants
pinch of salt	225 g (8 oz) blanched almonds, coarsely chopped
½ teaspoon grated nutmeg	3 tablespoons finely chopped candied orange peel
¼ teaspoon almond extract	
250 g (9 oz) flour	

In a large mixing bowl, beat the egg yolks and eggs until they are foamy. Gradually add the sugar, and keep beating until the mixture is thick and cream-coloured. Add the salt, nutmeg, and almond extract, and then stir in the flour, a little at a time, until you have a smooth batter. Stir in all the dried fruit, the chopped almonds, and the orange peel.

Prepare 2 medium-sized baking sheets with sides. Butter the sheets, and line them with buttered parchment. Spoon the batter on to the parchment and spread it evenly, about 1 cm (½ inch) thick. If your baking sheets are large and you don't have enough batter to fill two, simply fill one to the edges, and the other one as far as you can, maintaining an even thickness; the batter will hold its shape.

Bake the pastries at 170°C/325°F/Gas 3 for about 25–30 minutes. When done, the top will be a pale amber colour, and the pastry will sound hollow when tapped. Remove them from the oven carefully. Don't bend the baking sheets, as the pastry is fragile at this point. If the crusty top cracks a little, don't worry.

Allow the mazurek to cool, then slide it on to a board, trim away any dark or uneven edges, and cut into 2.5 × 5 cm (1 × 2 inch) bars, or into squares. The biscuits can be kept for a week in a tightly covered container, with waxed paper between the layers. If you want less brittle, chewier biscuits, put an apple slice in the container with them, and replace it every couple of days.

Makes about 5 dozen biscuits.

A CELEBRATION FOR EVERYONE

❦

crudité platter: radishes, carrot sticks, celery, sliced kohlrabi, cucumber spears, raw fennel, olives, peppers

Yogurt Cheese with Garlic and Herbs

crackers, sliced baguette

Cheddar Cheese Straws

Polenta Torta with Roasted Squash

Sautéd Spinach and Garlic

Roasted Fennel and Red Onions

Stewed Green Tomatoes with Chillies

Roasted Pearl Onions and Green Beans

Cranberry, Orange, and Red Wine Sauce

Gratin of Baked Yams with Pineapple

roast turkey

Bread Stuffing with Apples and Walnuts

Mashed Potatoes with Roasted Garlic

Apple Pie

Pumpkin Cheesecake with Caramelized Walnut and Ginger Sauce

or pumpkin pie with whipped cream

coffee

I don't know about you, but I don't live in an ideal world where everyone behaves the same way or wants the same thing. In my world – in my very own family, in fact – some are vegetarians and some want to eat meat. Some are even harder to define – the sortavegetarians, I call them.

So, when a special celebration like Thanksgiving comes around, I like to share a feast that is in the spirit of the celebration; it's a good time for us all to get together and accommodate each other.

With this harvest menu, a true vegetarian can have a memorable meal, yet tradition is satisfied and the turkey-eaters are content. I designed it around a great polenta dish, a torta made with caramelized onions and roasted squash. It's a beautiful golden thing, on a big platter, surrounded by dark-green sautéd spinach. Along with the polenta and spinach, I serve an array of vegetables, each one prepared its own way but always staying on the simple side, letting their individual characters and flavours shine.

Roasted Fennel and Red Onions develop a rich, deep flavour, and so do the green beans and pearl onions. The sautéd spinach with a whole lot of garlic just seems essential with the polenta. To counterpoint these flavours, I make an easy little stew of green tomatoes, tart and slightly spicy, and a cranberry sauce with oranges, cinnamon, and red wine.

Every one of these dishes crosses over beautifully into a turkey dinner, and the bread stuffing can be baked in casseroles so that everyone may enjoy it. The savoury menu is finished with the two tubers that are *de rigueur*: the yams are baked and baked again with pineapple, and the potatoes mashed with garlic. Everything goes with everything, and everyone is happy.

This all seems like a lot of food, but that's what great harvest festivals are all about. Still, it's nice to be able to try everything without feeling like a stuffed turkey yourself, so I've kept most of the dishes high in flavour but quite low in fat.

The appetizers are all 'walking around' food, the kind of thing that can be put out on a sideboard or a coffee table and nibbled through the course of the afternoon. They go well with champagne, with football, and with kids running in and out of a house. The desserts are a very traditional Apple Pie and Pumpkin Cheesecake or your favourite pumpkin pie.

Yields in the individual recipes are estimated at eight to ten servings, but in the context of a meal like this, with many more than the usual number of dishes, you can count on feeding at least a dozen comfortably.

YOGURT CHEESE WITH GARLIC AND HERBS

225 g (8 oz) thick Yogurt Cheese (see page 85)
2 tablespoons chopped fresh dill weed
2 tablespoons chopped fresh parsley

1 clove garlic, minced
freshly ground black pepper to taste
salt to taste

Mix everything together thoroughly and press into a small crock or mound on a plate. Chill for a few hours, allowing the flavours to marry. Serve with crostini, or with any good crackers.

This makes about 225 g (8 oz), and can be kept, tightly covered and refrigerated, for several days.

CHEDDAR CHEESE STRAWS

Long, thin, buttery pastries flavoured with lots of Cheddar cheese and a little snap of cayenne and mustard, these are a favourite with adults and kids alike. Their flavour can be dressed up with the addition of red pepper flakes, cracked black pepper, or a little Parmesan or blue cheese. But this recipe is the very tasty basic version.

300 g (10 oz) flour
¾ teaspoon salt
½ teaspoon cayenne pepper
125 g (4 oz) butter, cut in pieces
350 g (12 oz) mature Cheddar cheese, grated

4 tablespoons cold water, more if needed
1 teaspoon prepared mustard
1 teaspoon Worcestershire sauce

In the container of a food processor, combine the flour, salt, cayenne, butter, and grated cheese, and process until the mixture resembles coarse meal.

In a small bowl, whisk together the cold water, mustard, and Worcestershire sauce. Drizzle this over the mixture in the food processor and pulse for a few seconds at a time, until the pastry pulls together into a ball. Add a few drops more cold water if you need to, and do not overprocess.

Take the pastry out, divide it into 2 equal parts, and roll each part out between 2 sheets of waxed paper into rectangles about 20 × 40 cm (8 × 16 inches), and about 0.25 cm (⅛ inch) thick. Put the thin pastry sheets, still covered with waxed paper, into the refrigerator to chill for at least an hour.

Peel back the top sheet of paper and slice the pastry sheets crosswise into strips about a little less than 1 cm (⅓ inch) wide. Transfer the strips to baking sheets, either buttered or lined with parchment. Bake at 200°C/400°F/Gas 6 for about 10 minutes, or until the straws are golden and beginning to brown at the ends. Let the straws cool on a rack for a few minutes before serving.

This makes about 80–90 thin cheese straws, or enough for 10–15 people, but if children are involved, I suggest a double batch.

A Practical Note: You can make this pastry several days ahead of time and keep it in the refrigerator, well wrapped. Then slice and bake the straws not too long before you want to serve them. To recrisp leftover straws, put them in a hot oven for a minute or two.

POLENTA TORTA WITH ROASTED SQUASH

2 large Spanish onions,
  chopped
1 tablespoon olive oil, plus
  more to brush on top of
  torta
1 teaspoon butter
salt to taste
pinch of dried thyme
2 tablespoons Marsala
750 ml (1¼ pints) vegetable
  stock (see page 459)

750 ml (1¼ pints) water
250 g (9 oz) coarse-ground
  polenta
500 ml (16 fl oz) thick purée
  of roasted squash, such as
  Kabocha (see end of recipe)
50 g (2 oz) fresh white goat's
  cheese

garnish: Parmesan cheese

In a large non-stick pan, cook the chopped onions slowly in the
olive oil and butter, with a generous sprinkle of salt and a pinch of
thyme, until they are very soft and golden brown, about 45 minutes.
Stir them from time to time, and when they are caramelized add
the Marsala, swirling it around quickly to deglaze the pan.

While the onions are browning, combine the vegetable stock,
water, and polenta in a large pot and bring the liquid to a boil,
stirring with a whisk. Reduce the heat to a simmer and cook the
polenta, stirring frequently, for at least 30 minutes, or until it is
very thick. Stir in the caramelized onions, the puréed roasted squash,
and the goat's cheese.

Keep stirring over low heat until the cheese is melted and everything is well blended. Taste and correct the seasoning with a bit of
salt if needed.

Pour the polenta into a big round casserole or shallow bowl and
allow it to cool completely and set. You can refrigerate it, tightly
covered, for a day or so at this point. Unmould the polenta torta
on to a baking sheet, brush it with olive oil, and bake it in a 190°C/
375°F/Gas 5 oven for about 45 minutes.

Transfer the polenta to a large serving platter, surround it with sautéd spinach or roasted vegetables, and cut it in wedges to serve. Pass grated Parmesan cheese.

Serves 8 – 10.

To Roast Winter Squash

Any of the hard winter squashes can be roasted in their skins in a hot oven. If the squash is very large, cut it in half, scrape out the seeds, and place it cut side down in a large baking pan. Very small squashes can be roasted whole – just prick their skins several times with a fork.

Roast squashes at 200°C/400°F/Gas 6 until they are soft enough to collapse easily when pushed with a wooden spoon. The time will vary with the size of the squash, but think in terms of an hour or more.

When the squash is tender, allow it to cool, then scoop out the soft flesh with a spoon. If the squash seems watery, cook it down in a non-stick pan until it has the desired thick texture.

SAUTÉD SPINACH AND GARLIC

This couldn't be simpler, and couldn't be better. Use good, fresh spinach, and do not be afraid of too much garlic.

900 g–1 kg (2–2¼ lb) fresh
  spinach
2–3 tablespoons fruity green
  olive oil
½ head garlic, peeled and
  chopped

salt to taste
dash of rice vinegar or lemon
  juice

Wash the spinach well in several changes of water, until all the mud and grit are gone. Discard any leaves that are yellowed and trim off the heavier stems. Shake the spinach in a kitchen towel or spin it in a salad spinner.

Cook the spinach down in 2 batches: heat half the olive oil in a large non-stick sauté pan and add half the chopped garlic. Stir the garlic around in the hot oil for a minute, then add as much spinach as the pan will hold and start turning it gently as it wilts. Continue adding spinach and turning it over until you've used half of it. Salt it to your taste and keep cooking until there is no excess liquid in the pan.

Remove the sautéd spinach into a bowl and repeat the procedure with the remaining olive oil, garlic, and spinach. When the second batch has cooked down, add back the first batch and sauté all of it together for a few moments until everything is hot. Just before serving, toss the spinach with a little dash of rice vinegar, or some lemon juice if you prefer.

Serves 8 – 10.

ROASTED FENNEL AND RED ONIONS

Fennel and onions both develop a deep, sweet flavour when roasted. They are superb with polenta, and in combination with other vegetables.

6 large bulbs fennel	**2 tablespoons olive oil**
3 large red onions	**salt to taste**

Slice the stalks off the fennel and peel off the top, thick layer. Wash the fennel well, then quarter it lengthwise and trim out the root end. Cut each quarter into halves or thirds.

Peel the onions and cut them into chunks similar in size to the fennel. Combine the vegetables in a large bowl, drizzle with olive oil, and sprinkle generously with salt. Toss them together until everything is evenly, lightly coated with olive oil.

Spread the vegetables out on a large baking sheet with edges. Roast the fennel and onions in a 190°C/375°F/Gas 5 oven for 45 minutes to 1 hour, turning them over after about 20 minutes, and every 10 – 15 minutes after that. The vegetables should be soft through and well browned in spots. Serve hot.

Serves 8 – 10.

STEWED GREEN TOMATOES WITH CHILLIES

The beauty of this easy little stew is the way the sour green tomatoes combine with the sweetness of onions and a little kick of heat from the chillies. It's not a terribly hot dish, just lively. Red chillies look prettier if you can get them.

Serve this with polenta or tamales, add it to quesadillas, or use it as a relish with any mild-flavoured dish that could use some spicing up.

1.4 kg (3 lb) green tomatoes	**2–3 red or green chillies**
3 large onions	**1 small bunch coriander**
2 cloves garlic	**1 teaspoon salt, more to taste**
1 tablespoon olive oil	

Blanch the tomatoes by dropping them into boiling water one by one for about 45 seconds, then retrieve them and slip off their skins. Trim out their cores and cut them in large chunks. Chop the onions and mince the garlic.

Heat the olive oil in a large non-stick sauté pan and stir the onions and garlic into it. Cook them over medium heat, stirring often, until the onions are limp and translucent. Add the green tomatoes.

Trim the chillies and scrape out the seeds if you want a little less heat, then chop them finely. Work carefully (see note, page 89) and wash your hands well afterwards. Remove the coriander leaves from their stems and discard the stems.

Add the chillies, coriander and salt to the tomatoes and continue simmering until the tomatoes are soft and any excess liquid has simmered away. If the mixture dries out too quickly, just add a drop of water. Taste and correct the seasoning if needed.

Makes enough for 8–10 servings.

ROASTED PEARL ONIONS AND GREEN BEANS

700 g (1½ lb) pearl onions
2 tablespoons olive oil
salt to taste

700 g (1½ lb) slender green
beans
6 cloves garlic

Drop the onions into boiling water and let them boil for about 2 minutes, then drain them and let them cool. Peel the onions, trimming them at the stem end and slipping off their skins. Drizzle 1 tablespoon of the olive oil over the onions, sprinkle them with salt, and mix until all the onions are lightly coated with oil.

Spread the onions in a shallow baking pan and roast them in a 190°C/375°F/Gas 5 oven for 45 minutes to 1 hour, depending on their size, and moving them around once or twice during that time.

Meanwhile, wash and trim the green beans. Peel the garlic cloves and slice them in half lengthwise if they are large. In a bowl, toss together the green beans, garlic, the remaining olive oil, and some salt.

Spread the green beans and garlic out on a large, shallow baking pan and roast them in the same oven with the onions for 30–45 minutes. Turn them once or twice during the cooking time, and remove them when they are tender and spotted here and there with dark brown.

Roasting the onions and the green beans in two separate pans allows you to remove each one from the oven when it is done, and not overcook one for the sake of the other. When both the onions and the beans are ready, mix them together, add a dash of salt if needed, and pile them on a serving platter.

Serves 8–10.

CRANBERRY, ORANGE, AND RED WINE SAUCE

Lately there has been a fashion for complicated cranberry sauces full of exotic ingredients. This is understandable, because cranberries are delicious, and if you eat them frequently you want a little variety. However, some of these concoctions stray a little too far from the pure taste of the cranberry for me.

This sauce uses oranges, cinnamon, and red wine to complement the flavour of the berries, without overwhelming them. It's a refreshing relish as part of your meal, but it could also be served as a light dessert with just a touch of sweetened whipped cream.

700 g (1½ lb) fresh cranberries   **90 ml (3 fl oz) dry red wine**
250 ml (8 fl oz) orange juice   **400 g (14 oz) sugar**
120 ml (4 fl oz) water   **½ teaspoon ground cinnamon**
grated zest of 1 orange   **pinch of ground cloves**

Wash the cranberries and pick them over, throwing away any that are too soft or discoloured. Combine all the ingredients in a large non-reactive pot and bring to a boil, stirring with a long-handled wooden spoon. Reduce the heat and simmer for 10 minutes, stirring frequently. The sauce should be thick and glossy.

Allow the sauce to cool, stirring now and then to keep a skin from forming on top, then transfer to a beautiful serving dish.

This makes enough for 8–10 generous servings, or 20 average servings.

GRATIN OF BAKED YAMS WITH PINEAPPLE

Yams and pineapple just go together. It's a natural affinity, I think, like apples and cinnamon, or spinach and cheese. In this dish, the pairing has been stripped down to bare essentials, making a lighter version of a traditional favourite.

1.6 kg (3½ lb) yams	3 tablespoons brown sugar
salt to taste	1 tablespoon butter, plus
350 g (12 oz) crushed	more for the gratin dish
pineapple (fresh or canned	
in juice, not syrup)	

Wash the yams, prick them several times with a fork, and arrange them in a roasting pan. Roast them in a 200°C/400°F/Gas 6 oven for at least an hour, maybe a bit more if they are very large. They should be completely soft and release a syrupy juice when pierced with a fork.

Remove the yams from the oven and allow them to cool until you can easily handle them. Then cut them in half and scoop them out of their skins with a spoon, or peel them, whichever is easier for you. Discard the skins, and mash the pulp with the juices in the roasting pan. Salt the yams to your taste.

Stir the crushed pineapple and brown sugar into the yams. Lightly butter a large, shallow gratin dish, and spoon the yam mixture into it. I like to smooth the top and then score it with a large fork into a pretty pattern. Cut a tablespoon of butter into pea-sized pieces and dot the top of the yams.

Bake the yams again in a 180°C/350°F/Gas 4 oven for about 30 minutes, until they are hot through and browning on top.

Serves 8—12.

BREAD STUFFING WITH APPLES AND WALNUTS
(FOR TURKEY, OR FOR A CASSEROLE)

When my husband roasts a turkey, I usually make this bread stuffing to go with it. It is excellent for stuffing a turkey, but can also be baked separately in a casserole, and thus enjoyed by meat-eaters and vegetarians alike. Greg likes to roast his turkey on a spit, with no stuffing in it, just a handful of herbs and garlic, so that suits him just fine.

Use whatever bread you like. I like a coarse-textured country-style white bread, but you could use a wholemeal bread, sourdough, or some of this and some of that. The bread can be fresh, stale, or perfectly dry – the only difference will be in the amount of stock you use. Trim off the crusts if they are very crusty, or leave them if you want extra texture – anything goes!

175 g (6 oz) butter

2 large onions, chopped

3–4 stalks celery, sliced or chopped

1–2 teaspoons salt

pepper to taste

3 teaspoons dried sage

1 teaspoon dried marjoram

3 teaspoons poultry seasoning

6 tablespoons chopped fresh parsley

2–3 tablespoons cider vinegar

575 g (1¼ lb) bread, cut into 1 cm (½ inch) cubes

900 g (2 lb) green apples, peeled and chopped

250 g (9 oz) raisins

250 g (9 oz) lightly toasted walnuts, finely chopped

500 ml (16 fl oz) vegetable stock (see page 459), or chicken stock, or both

Melt the butter in a large pan and sauté the chopped onion and celery in it until they are soft and just starting to colour. Add about a teaspoon of salt, pepper to your taste, the herbs, and the cider vinegar. Stir well and remove from the heat.

In a very large mixing bowl, combine the bread cubes, chopped apples, raisins, and chopped walnuts. Add the sautéd vegetables and herbs with all their butter, and toss everything together until it is thoroughly combined.

Drizzle on about half the stock, toss again, and test. You are aiming for a mixture that is soft and moist throughout, but not soggy or soupy. Keep adding stock, a little at a time, mixing everything up well after each addition, until you have the consistency you like. The amount of stock used will vary quite a bit, depending on what kind of bread is used and how dry it is.

If you are roasting a turkey, and plan to bake the stuffing separately but want the flavour of the turkey in it, you could add some drippings in place of part of the stock. In that case, however, cut down a little on the butter. If, on the other hand, you plan to stuff a turkey, leave the stuffing just a little on the dry side.

When the texture feels right, taste and correct the seasoning with more salt or pepper if needed.

Spoon the stuffing into two buttered casseroles, or one very large one, cover well, and bake at 180°C/350°F/Gas 4 for about 45 minutes. Or spoon it into a turkey that has been prepared for roasting.

This makes about enough stuffing for a 7.2–8.8 kg (16–20 lb) turkey, or two medium casseroles. It's more than enough for 10 people, but you'll want to have leftovers.

MASHED POTATOES WITH ROASTED GARLIC

1 head garlic	**1 tablespoon butter**
1–2 teaspoons olive oil	**175 ml (6 fl oz) buttermilk**
1.4 kg (3 lb) potatoes	**salt and pepper to taste**

Separate the garlic cloves, but do not peel them. Pile them on a piece of foil, drizzle with olive oil, and fold the foil over them to form a sealed packet. Bake the garlic in a 190°C/375°F/Gas 5 oven for about 45 minutes, or until the cloves are soft.

Peel the potatoes and cut them into 5 cm (2 inch) chunks. If you prefer your mashed potatoes with their skins, just scrub them, trim them, and cut them up. Put the potatoes in a pot with enough well-salted cold water to cover them by 1 cm (½ inch), bring the water to a slow boil, and cook them until they are completely tender. Drain the potatoes, reserving the cooking water. Return the drained potatoes to the pot.

Squeeze the soft garlic out of the cloves and discard the skins. Press the garlic through a strainer and add the pulp to the potatoes, along with the butter, buttermilk, and salt and pepper to your taste. Mash thoroughly with a potato masher while the potatoes are still steaming hot. Add a little of the cooking water if the potatoes seem too dry. (The rest of the water can be saved and used for making bread if you're so inclined.) Taste, and adjust the seasoning.

Serves 6–8.

APPLE PIE

for the pastry
365 g (12½ oz) flour
½ teaspoon salt
150 g (5 oz) cold butter
3–4 tablespoons cold water

for the crumble topping
125 g (4 oz) brown sugar
3 tablespoons softened butter
2 tablespoons flour

for the filling
1.2 kg (2½ lbs) start green
    apples
125 g (4 oz) sugar
1 teaspoon ground cinnamon
pinch of grated nutmeg
2 tablespoons flour
2 tablespoons lemon juice

To make the pastry, put the flour and salt in the container of a food processor, and add the chilled butter, cut in slices. Process until the mixture resembles coarse meal. Add a little cold water at a time, through the feeder tube, as you process, just until the pastry begins to hold together. Remove the pastry, form it into a ball, wrap it well, and chill it.

Peel the apples, cut them in quarters, trim out the cores, and cut the quarters crosswise into thick slices. Mix together the sugar, cinnamon, nutmeg, and flour. Put the apple slices in a bowl, sprinkle the dry mixture over them, and toss until it is evenly distributed. Add the lemon juice and toss again.

Roll the pastry out into a circle about 36 cm (14 inches) across. Line a large, deep pie dish with the pastry, and trim off the excess, leaving about 1 cm (½ inch) hanging over. Fold the extra 1 cm (½ inch) in and crimp it to make a nice, high edge.

Combine the brown sugar, softened butter, and 2 tablespoons of flour in a small bowl and rub it together with your fingers until it forms a crumbly paste.

Fill the prepared pie shell with the apples, and sprinkle the crumble topping over them. Roll and cut leftover pastry into strips and lay a few of them decoratively over the top of the pie.

Bake the pie in a preheated 180°C/350°F/Gas 4 oven for about 1 hour and 15 minutes. Cover it loosely with a piece of foil for the first 45 minutes to keep it from browning too much.

Allow the pie to cool to lukewarm before serving.

Serves 8—10.

PUMPKIN CHEESECAKE
WITH CARAMELIZED WALNUT AND GINGER SAUCE

for the crust
175 g (6 oz) digestive biscuit crumbs
4 tablespoons melted butter
3 tablespoons sugar
1 egg white, lightly beaten

for the filling
700 g (1½ lb) cream cheese
350 g (12 oz) sugar
350 g (12 oz) cooked pumpkin, canned or fresh (see end of recipe)

1 teaspoon ground allspice
2 teaspoons ground cinnamon
¼ teaspoon grated nutmeg
pinch of ground cloves
4 eggs
4 tablespoons double cream
1 recipe Caramelized Walnut and Ginger Sauce (recipe follows)

Prepare the crust by mixing together the biscuit crumbs, melted butter, and sugar, then stirring in the lightly beaten egg white. Press the crust into the bottom and partly up the sides of a 25 cm (10 inch) springform tin. Flatten it evenly with a potato masher, or with your fingers.

Beat the cream cheese with the sugar until it is somewhat fluffy. Remove about 150 g (5 oz) of this mixture and set it aside in the refrigerator in a tightly covered container.

To the remainder of the cream cheese mixture, add the pumpkin and spices and beat thoroughly, then beat in the eggs, one at a time. Pour the filling into the crust and bake in a preheated 180°C/350°F/

Gas 4 oven for 1 hour and 15 minutes. The centre of the cake will still move slightly when shaken.

Remove the cheesecake from the oven and allow it to cool on a rack for 15 minutes, then run a very thin, sharp knife around the sides to loosen it. Let the cake finish cooling, then cover it tightly and chill it for 6 hours, or overnight.

Remove the reserved cream cheese mixture from the refrigerator and allow it to reach room temperature. Whisk in the 4 tablespoons of cream until smooth.

Remove the sides of the cake tin, and spread the cream cheese smoothly over the top of the cheesecake.

Cut the cheesecake in wedges with a very sharp knife, wiping the knife between slices, and spoon Caramelized Walnut and Ginger Sauce over the top of each serving.

Serves 12.

To Cook Fresh Pumpkin

The easiest way to cook fresh pumpkin is to bake it in a hot oven (190°C/375°F/Gas 5) until it is soft throughout. If you are baking an entire pumpkin, prick it in a few places with a fork and put it on a baking sheet to catch any juices. If you're baking a wedge or slice of a large pumpkin, scrape out the seeds, then wrap the piece well in foil and bake until soft. The time will vary with the size of the pumpkin, but count on at least an hour.

When the pumpkin gives easily to slight pressure, it's done. Cut it open, allow it to cool somewhat, then scoop out and discard the seeds. Scrape all the soft flesh off the skin and drain it in a sieve for about 15 minutes, then purée or mash it. You will have a thick pulp which can be used for pies or soups, or for Pumpkin Butter (see page 465).

CARAMELIZED WALNUT AND GINGER SAUCE

75 g (3 oz) sugar
250 ml (8 fl oz) hot water
175 g (6 oz) coarsely chopped
toasted walnuts

40 g (1½ oz) crystallized
ginger, finely chopped

Heat the sugar in a small, heavy-bottomed pot until it melts and turns light golden brown. Add the hot water carefully; the caramel will 'seize up' in contact with the liquid, and there may be some spattering. Lower the heat and simmer the liquid, stirring occasionally, until the caramel completely dissolves into it, making a thin syrup.

Stir the chopped walnuts and ginger into the syrup, remove it from the heat, and allow it to cool somewhat before serving.

Spoon the sauce, in small quantities, over slices of Pumpkin Cheesecake, or over vanilla ice cream.

GREG'S SPIT-ROASTED TURKEY
(Confessions of a Self-Taught Spit-Roaster – GREG NAVA)

At a holiday like Christmas or Thanksgiving, we have a lot of people around the house with different eating habits. So Anna cooks a feast of vegetarian dishes, and my job is cooking the turkey. Everyone is happy, and even the vegetarians usually want to try my great spit-roasted turkey.

Spit-roasting a turkey is an adventure. It is exciting and medieval, and can result in the most delicious turkey you've ever eaten. But if you want everything timed and planned down to the minute, then read no further. An open fire, together with the varying size and construction of birds, can result in wildly differing cooking times.

Use a timetable only to give you a general idea of cooking time, but don't try to spit-roast a turkey according to a timetable; it will only result in disaster. You must use a good meat thermometer and, when the temperature is right, believe that the turkey is ready. Your guests may be eating an hour earlier or an hour later than anticipated, and sometimes it takes sangfroid to pull the turkey off the spit when it cooks quickly, but experience has taught me – believe the thermometer.

So why spit-roast, if it's so unpredictable? Mainly because nothing can compare with the flavour an open charcoal fire imparts. And since the turkey is constantly turning, it is always basting itself, resulting in a moist and succulent roasted turkey. To me, this is the way roasted turkey was meant to taste!

First of all, always use a fresh turkey, with no chemical additives. I can't emphasize this enough. Prepare the turkey as usual for any roasting. Wash it inside and out, and rub the cavity with lemon. Rub the outside of the turkey with a little butter, and salt it.

I think it is better not to stuff the bird. You can bake your stuffing separately in a casserole. It's better for the turkey, and people who don't eat meat can still enjoy the stuffing. I like to go outside and pick handfuls of wild rosemary, and stuff the branches into the cavity, along with several cloves of crushed garlic. I slice more garlic into thin slivers and push it under the skin of the turkey. I sew the cavity closed using string and trussing pins.

Trussing the turkey is extremely important for spit-roasting. The tighter the turkey is held together, the juicier and better the result. I use a free-form approach, tying the legs together first, then looping string around the whole bird and tying it up very tightly.

Putting the turkey on the spit itself is also critical to the success of the whole operation. Spear the turkey so that its weight is balanced as evenly as possible around the spit. Most spit-roasting outfits provide weights to balance the bird. Hand-tighten the forks which hold the turkey on the spit, and then test the turning of the turkey. Adjust the weight until the bird *turns evenly* – or it won't cook evenly. Once the bird is turning evenly, stop and tighten the forks with a pair of pliers so the turkey won't slip.

Now put the charcoal into the rear rack of the spit-roaster and if possible add a little fresh rosemary.

After the first hour of roasting, you will need a pan below the turkey to catch the drippings. You can occasionally baste the bird with these drippings if you want to. In general you will find that there will be far less juice released than with an oven-roasted turkey.

I like to cook up a stock with the giblets and liver to use for the sauce later. Put them in a saucepan along with an onion stuck with a couple of cloves, 1 teaspoon of dried tarragon, 1 clove of garlic, and a sprig of parsley. Cover with water and simmer for a long time. Then skim thoroughly and strain.

Taking the temperature of the turkey is tricky. Plunge the thermometer deep into the turkey without touching the bone. Take the temperature of the white meat at the breast, and the dark meat at the thigh, and do it on both sides of the turkey. No matter how evenly the bird may be turning, parts of it will have been in front of the fire longer than others, and the four temperatures will vary.

White meat is perfectly done between 170°F and 175°F, dark meat between 180°F and 185°F. Now comes the judgement call. With four different temperatures, and with dark and white meat needing different temperatures, when do you call it done?

My experience has shown me that dark meat isn't underdone at 175°F, but white meat is dry at 185°F. I always favour cooking for the white meat, since that's what most people eat first, and the dark meat generally gets reheated. If the white meat is registering 175°F in both breasts, I always pull the turkey. If one breast is reading 172°F and the other breast is reading 180°F, I pull the bird. No matter what, I never let either breast get above 180°F. Nothing is worse than dry white meat.

The turkey should rest between 20 and 30 minutes before being carved. While the bird is resting, I deglaze the drippings in the pan with plenty of Madeira. I add the deglazed juices to the strained giblet stock in a saucepan and reduce it to taste, and that's my delicious brown sauce.

Once you get the hang of it, spit-roasting is easy. Most of the time the turkey is just spinning away and needs little attention, so you have more time to have a drink with your friends.

NEW YEAR'S EVE

caviar and toast triangles

Watercress and Radicchio Salad with Ginger-Sesame Dressing

Timbales of Squash and Pears

Rosemary Sorbet

Wild Mushroom Soup with Cream Cheese Pierogi

Pineapple Meringue Torte

Sometimes a moment comes when you want to serve a meal for gentlemen in black tie and ladies in glittering dresses. This is the one. Chill the Dom Pérignon, and bring up your great wines. This meal is sophisticated in a fun way, with exquisite flavours in unusual combinations, but nothing odd just for the sake of being odd. And if anyone asks why the soup is the last savoury course and not the first, and why there's a sorbet in the middle instead of for dessert, just tell them it's because you're a genius.

The Wild Mushroom Soup is actually one of my own absolutely favourite things to eat. I prepare it every Christmas Eve, and at other times when I can get my hands on some good wild mushrooms. The deep, woodsy flavour of the mushrooms is complemented by little, meltingly tender Cream Cheese Pierogi, with traditional Polish fillings.

The soup certainly merits being the centrepiece of a meal for many reasons, but one of them is that it pairs superbly with the finest red wine, so it makes sense to build up to it in a meal, rather than try to follow it with something. With this menu, you can start with champagne, move on to a lovely Riesling with the timbales, then peak with a great, aged red as companion to the Wild Mushroom Soup.

If you like caviar, then by all means start with caviar and toast triangles with that glass of iced champagne. If not, you'll still get plenty to eat. First there is Watercress and Radicchio Salad. It sets you up for the delicate Timbales of Squash and Pears that follow, a dish that is both savoury and sweet, and perfect with a fruity wine.

Then there is a little surprise – dainty scoops of Rosemary Sorbet are served to clear the palate before the mushroom soup and the rich pierogi. This is a refreshing thing to do, an idea much used in multi-course meals in France, and if you've never tried a palate-clearing sorbet, do try it and see what fun it is.

Now, although you've had some very interesting tastes, you haven't eaten too much yet, so you can really enjoy the splendid combination of the Wild Mushroom Soup with a great Burgundy. Of course, after all that, an elegant dessert seems in order, but nothing too rich. A tart or pastry would be superfluous after the pierogi, but the Pineapple Meringue Torte fits the bill exactly. It's marvellous-looking, tastes sweet and delicious, but is extremely light – and much easier to make than you would think.

I enjoy a meal like this, full of little twists and surprises. It has a genuine celebratory feel and yet does not leave you groaning with a sense of excess afterwards. With a meal like this one, you can see the old year out lavishly, and enjoy the start of the new year the next day.

Leftovers: Don't hesitate to make lots of pierogi. You will enjoy them for several days. And although I think of this as a very grown-up meal, I find that my children actually like a lot of this food, and most of all the pierogi, which they will eat at any time of day and take to school in lunch boxes. Pierogi are best if reheated a bit in the oven, but this is not altogether necessary.

WATERCRESS AND RADICCHIO SALAD WITH
GINGER-SESAME DRESSING

This is a winter salad that works on a combination of pungent, bitter, tart, and sweet tastes. Persimmons are plentiful where I live, and they are available dried starting around Christmas and through the rest of the winter. These dried persimmons are so delicious that people absolutely get addicted to them, so, if you can get your hands on some, do it. However, I know they are not available in most places, and it's fine to substitute raisins, diced prunes, diced dried figs, or the like in their place.

2 large bunches fresh
   watercress
2 small heads radicchio
2 heads Belgian endive
1 fennel bulb

1 large green apple
1 large dried persimmon, or
   125 g (4 oz) other dried fruit
Ginger-Sesame Dressing
(recipe follows)

Break the watercress sprigs off their thick stems and discard the stems. Separate the radicchio leaves and tear them into bite-sized pieces. Wash the watercress and radicchio and spin them dry in a salad spinner or in kitchen towels.

Discard any bruised outer leaves of the endives and slice the endives crosswise. Trim the fennel, quarter it lengthwise, and slice thinly. Cut the apple into wedges, trim out the core, and slice the wedges crosswise. Cut the persimmon, or other dried fruit, into raisin-sized pieces.

Toss everything together in a very large salad bowl, pour the dressing over it, and toss again until all parts of the salad are evenly coated.

Serves 8.

GINGER-SESAME DRESSING

I'm usually a minimalist, happiest with a touch of great olive oil and a few drops of an excellent vinegar. But in this dressing, nine ingredients are combined for refreshing and subtle effect.

about 5 cm (2 inches) fresh ginger root	**2 tablespoons dark sesame oil**
2 tablespoons freshly squeezed lemon juice	**1 tablespoon soy sauce**
	1 tablespoon rice vinegar
	1 tablespoon honey
3 tablespoons freshly squeezed orange juice	**3 tablespoons sesame seeds**
	6 spring onions, thinly sliced

Peel the ginger root and cut it in thin slices, then mince it very finely. You need about 2 tablespoons of minced fresh ginger. Combine the ginger with the lemon juice, orange juice, sesame oil, soy sauce, rice vinegar, and honey in the container of a blender. Process until the mixture is well blended and the ginger nearly puréed.

Dip a lettuce leaf into the dressing to taste it. Correct the seasoning with a little salt or more rice vinegar if you like.

Toast the sesame seeds in a pan, stirring them constantly, until they are a uniform caramel colour; don't let them get dark brown. Set them aside until you're serving the salad.

Just before serving the salad, add the sliced spring onions. Pour the dressing over a very large salad and toss until all the leaves glisten. Sprinkle about a teaspoon of the toasted sesame seeds over each serving.

This makes 150–175 ml (5–6 fl oz) dressing,
enough to dress a salad for 8.

TIMBALES OF SQUASH AND PEARS

450 g (1 lb) peeled, cubed
Kabocha or acorn squash

450 g (1 lb) peeled, cubed
yams

250 ml (8 fl oz) water

½ teaspoon salt

2 large onions

2½ tablespoons butter

3 medium pears, ripe but not
mushy

120 ml (4 fl oz) good white
wine

120 ml (4 fl oz) double cream

5 eggs

white pepper to taste

butter and fine dry
breadcrumbs for the
ramekins

garnish: Sweet Red Pepper Purée (see page 389)

Combine the squash, yams, water, and salt in a heavy-bottomed saucepan, cover, and simmer gently until the squash and yams are completely tender.

Peel and chop the onions. Cook them slowly in 2 tablespoons of butter, stirring often, until they are caramelized – a uniform, deep golden brown.

Meanwhile, peel and core the pears and cut them into even cubes between 0.5 and 1 cm (¼ and ½ inch) in size. When the onions are soft and light brown, remove them from the pan, add the remaining bit of butter, and sauté the pear cubes in it for a few moments. Then add the wine, cover the pan tightly, and simmer the pears on a very low flame for about 15–20 minutes, until they are tender.

Combine the cooked squash and yams, the onions, and the cream, and purée in a blender or food processor until perfectly smooth. Lightly beat the eggs and whisk them into the vegetable purée. Season to taste with salt and white pepper, then stir in the poached pears.

Prepare 8 timbale moulds, ramekins, custard cups, or individual soufflé dishes: butter them thoroughly and coat them with fine dry breadcrumbs. Divide the squash and pear mixture evenly among the ramekins, filling each a little short of the top. Place the ramekins in a baking pan deep enough to hold water at least halfway up the moulds, and bake them that way in a preheated 160°C/325°F/Gas 3 oven for about 50 minutes.

Unmould by sliding a thin knife around the edge of the ramekin and tipping it out on to the serving plate. Surround each unmoulded timbale with a small ribbon of Sweet Red Pepper Purée and serve warm.

Serves 8.

Rosemary Sorbet (see page 390)

WILD MUSHROOM SOUP

1.5–1.7 litres (2½–3 pints) Mushroom Stock (recipe follows)
75 g (3 oz) dried porcini
2 large onions
2½ tablespoons butter
2 cloves garlic, chopped
salt to taste

700 g (1½ lb) fresh wild mushrooms, cleaned and sliced (use porcini if you can get them, morels, chanterelles, or a mix)
3 tablespoons cognac
120 ml (4 fl oz) good red wine
dash of white pepper
pinch of cayenne
90 ml (3 fl oz) double cream

garnish: fresh dill

Make the Mushroom Stock. You can sort through the dried porcini and use any tiny or tough bits for the stock, reserving better pieces for the soup.

Put the dried porcini in a bowl and pour over them 500–700 ml (16–24 fl oz) of boiling water, enough to cover. Leave them to soak for about 30 minutes, then take them out of the water and rinse each one carefully. Strain the soaking water through a paper filter to get rid of all the sediment and reserve it for the stock.

Peel the onions, quarter them lengthwise, and then slice them. Melt 1½ tablespoons of butter in a large non-stick pan and slowly cook the onions and chopped garlic in it, with a bit of salt, until the onions are golden brown.

Slice the soaked porcini into wide strips, chopping any especially tough parts. Thoroughly clean the fresh wild mushrooms and slice them thinly. If you have morels, just cut them in half lengthwise, leaving the tiny ones whole.

Add the remaining butter and all the wild mushrooms to the onions in the pan, turn up the heat, and sauté everything together for a few minutes, stirring. Add the cognac and stir another minute or two, until it is gone.

Add the Mushroom Stock and the soaking liquid from the dried porcini. Simmer everything together for 45 minutes to 1 hour; the flavours should be well developed. Add 120 ml (4 fl oz) of red wine, simmer a few more minutes, and taste. Finish the seasoning with a little more salt if it's needed, a dash of white pepper, a pinch of cayenne, and the cream.

Serve this exquisite soup steaming hot, in wide soup bowls, with a sprinkle of chopped fresh dill on top. Pass a platter of freshly baked pierogi for the full experience.

Serves 10–12.

MUSHROOM STOCK

This is a great stock to use in making mushroom soups, and it could also be used for risotto or pilaf.

25 g (1 oz) dried porcini pieces
2 tablespoons olive oil
1 onion, chopped
1 clove garlic, chopped
1 leek, green part only, chopped
125 g (4 oz) fresh mushrooms, sliced

3 medium carrots, sliced
2 stalks celery, sliced
½ teaspoon dried thyme
6 branches parsley
6 branches coriander
1 teaspoon dried sage
1 teaspoon salt
several peppercorns
3 litres (5 pints) spring water

optional: 2–3 tablespoons sherry

If you are making Wild Mushroom Soup, take all 75 g (3 oz) of dried porcini for that recipe and sort through them. Reserve the nice, big pieces for the soup, and use only the smallest bits for the stock. With good-quality dried mushrooms, you should be able to reserve about three-quarters of them for the soup; it doesn't matter if you have a little less than 25 g (1 oz) for the stock. If you are making the stock for another purpose, use 25 g (1 oz) of dried porcini.

Pour boiling water over the porcini and leave them to soak for a while.

Heat the olive oil in a big pan and cook the onion and garlic in it over medium heat, stirring occasionally, until the onion is golden brown. Add the leeks, fresh mushrooms, carrots, and celery, and cook everything together for a few minutes. Add the herbs, salt, peppercorns, and water.

Drain the porcini, reserving the water. Wash the mushrooms carefully, getting rid of all the grit. Strain the soaking water through a paper filter. Add both the porcini and the filtered soaking water to the stock pot.

Simmer the stock for about an hour. Add a few tablespoons of sherry towards the end if you like. Strain the stock through a fine mesh sieve, taste it, and correct the seasoning if necessary.

You should have about 1.5–1.7 litres (2½–3 pints) of flavourful stock.

CREAM CHEESE PIEROGI

I usually make these once a year, at Christmas, and then I make hundreds, for a big party. When I go to the store with my shopping list in hand, I always feel I should be getting a licence and have a 5-day waiting period before taking home that amount of butter and cream cheese. Well, it's an old-fashioned recipe, but I've been using it for years and years, and it's just too good to change.

425 g (15 oz) flour	1 egg yolk
1 teaspoon salt	1 teaspoon water
225 g (8 oz) butter	Potato Filling and/or Cabbage
225 g (8 oz) cream cheese	Filling (recipes follow)
60 ml (2 fl oz) double cream, chilled	

Put 400 g (14 oz) of flour and the salt into the container of a food processor, and add the butter and cream cheese, cut into chunks. Process briefly, until the mixture has an even texture with no big lumps. Add the chilled cream and process again, until the pastry holds together and forms a ball. Remove the ball of pastry, wrap it, and chill it for at least 30 minutes.

Sprinkle the rest of the flour over a large board and roll out half the dough until it is an even 0.25 cm (⅛ inch) thick. With a cookie cutter or a tin, cut it out in 5 cm (2 inch) rounds.

Whisk the egg yolk with the water. Place a rounded teaspoon of filling in the centre of a pastry round, then brush the edges with the egg-yolk and water mixture, fold it carefully over the filling, and seal. Press the sealed edges together with the tines of a fork, making a pretty, crimped pattern. Pierce the top of the pastry with a fork or a skewer. (When making several kinds of pierogi at once, I create different patterns with the fork tines to identify each type.)

Continue filling and sealing all the pastry rounds, and repeat the procedure with the second half of the pastry. Brush the tops of the pierogi with the remaining egg-yolk and water mixture, and arrange them on lightly buttered baking sheets. Bake the pierogi at 190°C/375°F/Gas 5 for 15–20 minutes, until they are golden brown on top.

These are best eaten warm, just out of the oven, but they are also fine at room temperature and can be prepared several hours ahead of time. I serve them as an accompaniment to Wild Mushroom Soup, a pairing which is almost a meal in itself. They also make a superb finger food to serve with aperitifs or champagne before dinner.

This makes 40–50 pierogi.

POTATO FILLING FOR PIEROGI

This filling is nothing more than seasoned mashed potatoes reduced to the proper thickness, and it is so good.

1.4 kg (3 lb) potatoes	**1 tablespoon butter**
5–6 tablespoons buttermilk, or puréed cottage cheese	**1 medium onion, very finely chopped**
	salt and pepper to taste

Boil the potatoes in their jackets in salted water until they are tender. Drain them, let them cool until you can just handle them, then peel them and cut them into big pieces. You can put them through a ricer if you want to, but it's not strictly necessary. Add the buttermilk or puréed cottage cheese and mash with a potato masher.

Melt the butter in a large sauté pan and cook the chopped onion in it, with a dash of salt, until the onion is soft and just turning golden. Add the potatoes to the pan and continue mashing everything together over medium heat as the excess moisture cooks away and the potatoes become thicker. Taste, and add as much salt and pepper as needed.

When the potatoes are thick enough to hold a stiff shape, put them away in a covered bowl to chill for an hour or two before using.

This makes enough potato filling for 20–25 pierogi. If you are not making another kind of filling, double this to fill a full recipe of pierogi.

CABBAGE FILLING FOR PIEROGI

1 teaspoon olive oil	salt
2½ tablespoons butter	pepper
1 large onion, very finely chopped	1 tablespoon cider vinegar
1 large cabbage, finely shredded	2 hard-boiled eggs
	4 tablespoons chopped fresh dill

Heat the oil and butter in a large non-stick sauté pan and cook the onion in it over medium heat, stirring occasionally, until the onion is golden.

Be sure the cabbage is finely shredded or chopped. I like to use the grating attachment on my food processor for this. Blanch the shredded cabbage for a moment in boiling, salted water, then drain it and squeeze out the excess moisture.

Add the cabbage to the onion, along with a teaspoon of salt and some freshly ground pepper. Cook over medium heat, stirring often, for about 30 minutes. The cabbage should be greatly reduced in volume, and beginning to turn golden brown. Grind on some black pepper, and add the cider vinegar, stirring it in.

Sieve the hard-boiled eggs, and stir them into the cabbage, along with the chopped dill. Taste and correct the seasoning with more salt or pepper if needed. It helps to chill the filling before using it, as it becomes stiffer and easier to work with.

This makes enough cabbage filling for 20–25 pierogi. If you are not making another kind of filling, double this to fill a full recipe of pierogi.

PINEAPPLE MERINGUE TORTE

This beautiful dessert is refreshing and light, perfect for a special-occasion meal when you want to end with something festive but not heavy.

for the meringue layers
175 g (6 oz) blanched almonds
6 large egg whites
¼ teaspoon cream of tartar
225 g (8 oz) icing sugar
½ teaspoon almond extract

for the filling
450 g (1 lb) crushed pineapple
  with its juice (fresh or
  canned in juice, not syrup)
120 ml (4 fl oz) water
60 ml (2 fl oz) fresh lime juice
grated zest of 2 limes
175 g (6 oz) sugar
4 tablespoons cornflour
3 egg yolks

garnish: additional icing sugar

Toast the almonds in a 150°C/300°F/Gas 2 oven for 10–15 minutes, or just until they release their fragrance and begin to turn golden. Do not let them brown. Allow the almonds to cool, then grind them in a food processor.

Line 2 baking sheets with parchment, and draw a 25 cm (10 inch) circle on each sheet.

Beat the egg whites with the cream of tartar until they hold soft peaks, then add the icing sugar and almond extract, and continue beating them until they hold stiff peaks. Fold in the ground almonds.

Spread the beaten whites evenly within the 2 circles, smoothing the tops carefully with a wide knife or spatula. Bake the meringues in a 150°C/300°F/Gas 2 oven for 45 minutes, then lower the heat to 120°C/250°F/Gas ½ and bake another 30 minutes. The meringues should be dry and pale ivory in colour.

Slide the meringues, still on their parchment, carefully on to racks and let them cool completely.

While the meringues bake, prepare the filling. Combine the pine-apple and its juice, the water, lime juice, lime zest, sugar, and cornflour in a medium-sized non-reactive pot and stir until the cornflour is completely dissolved. Bring the mixture to a boil, lower the heat a little, and stir it as it boils gently for 8–10 minutes, or until it becomes completely translucent and thickens.

Remove the filling from the heat, let it cool for a moment, and whisk in the egg yolks, one at a time. Return it to very low heat and whisk for 5 minutes. Do not let it boil. When it thickens again, remove it from the heat, transfer it to a covered bowl, and allow it to cool completely.

To assemble the meringue, first turn over the meringue layers and gently peel the parchment away. Work carefully, as the meringue layers are now at their most fragile, very dry and easy to crack. Later, they will become softer and slightly chewy in the centre.

Place one layer upside down on a large, lovely platter. Stir up the cooled pineapple filling and spread it evenly over the meringue, swirling it right out to the edge. Place the second layer right side up on top of the filling. Cover the torte with clingfilm and chill it in the refrigerator for several hours.

Before serving, sift icing sugar over the top of the torte. Protect the edges of the platter with strips of waxed paper, or dust the excess sugar off the edges of the platter with a pastry brush. The torte can be served just like that, simple and elegant, or it can be decorated with berries and mint sprigs, thin twists of lime zest, or edible flowers.

Serves 8–10.

ABOUT VEGETABLE STOCK

Nothing is as useful to have on hand in the kitchen as a supply of good stock, ready to make a soup or a sauce or to greatly enhance rice and grain dishes. There are many recipes for stock. Some are very basic; others develop specific flavours and are therefore limited to certain dishes. They take a little time to make, but are not nearly as much trouble as you might think. In fact, it only takes a few minutes to rinse and slice some vegetables, and once you get used to the idea of making your own stocks, it becomes easier and easier.

Now, if you happen to have a nice stock on hand, and if you put up tomatoes in the summer when they're great, you can make a fabulous soup in about 5 minutes. You can make a marvellous risotto. You can serve noodles and a few vegetables in a bowl of stock and have a one-dish meal that's ready almost instantly.

In the past, the only way to have this kind of convenience was to make extra amounts of stock and freeze it in small containers. You could get a perfectly usable chicken stock in a can, but the available vegetable stocks were not satisfying. The canned products I tried from health food stores always tasted a little too sweet and carroty for me, and the dissolving cubes and powders were downright nasty.

Now, fortunately, the demand for an acceptable, commercially available vegetable stock has been felt. Good chilled fresh vegetable stock is often available, and it has become a staple item in my pantry or freezer.

Still, home-made is best, and so I think it's good to have a formula for a basic clear vegetable stock, and some variations on the theme. The requirement for a basic stock, which can be used in almost any recipe, is a balance of flavours, neither too sweet nor too bitter, with no single aggressive flavour dominating. It should be delicate, taste nice when sipped from a cup, but better if reduced by a third and lightly salted. This kind of neutrality serves most recipes very well. The idea is to support the other flavours in a dish, not to fight with them.

For some dishes, a stronger-flavoured stock is needed. If you are making a stock with a specific dish in mind – for example, a mushroom soup or a pea soup – you can make a stock strongly flavoured with that element. Clear soups, where the stock is the main thing, are a law unto themselves. Taste and adjust.

It's good to make stock when you're in the kitchen anyway, cooking other things. Then it becomes almost effortless, sort of a calculated by-product. Another way to make life easier is to save those leek tops and chard stems in plastic bags in the crisper, and when they start to add up, set up the stock pot.

After a while, you won't be measuring anything any more, and you'll see that, once you throw a few vegetables and herbs in the pot with some water, the stock really makes itself.

I have included three recipes here: a very basic stock, a darker stock for which a few vegetables are browned in oil first, and a more complex version of that. But the possible combinations are many. Read through the list of vegetables at the end of the basic recipe, think about what you like, and you will be on the way to devising your own favourite stock.

BASIC LIGHT VEGETABLE STOCK

5 large carrots	1 bay leaf
2 large stalks celery	1 teaspoon dried thyme
2 large onions	1 teaspoon black peppercorns
1 head garlic	4 branches flat-leaf parsley
green top of 1 large leek	12 branches coriander
thick peels of 2 small potatoes	1½ teaspoons salt
1 turnip	3 litres (5 pints) water

Wash all the vegetables thoroughly. Scrape the carrots and peel the onions. Thickly peel the potatoes, reserving the inside for another use. Slice or coarsely chop everything except the head of garlic, which can just be sliced crosswise and put in as is.

Combine all the vegetables, herbs, and seasonings with the water in a large pot. The water should just cover everything when you first put it all together. Bring the water to a boil, lower the heat, and let the stock boil gently for about 45 minutes. All the vegetables should be completely soft, and the flavours fully released into the liquid.

Strain the stock through a colander, then through a fine sieve to remove any sediment or cloudiness. Taste, and correct the salt if needed, but bear in mind that it's best to leave a stock undersalted until you know how you're going to use it.

You should have 1.7—2 litres (3—3½ pints) of mild-flavoured,
amber-coloured vegetable broth.

Variations: Many other vegetables can be added to this stock, enriching it and altering its character. Here is a partial list of vegetables I've tried and liked:

chard leaves and stems	**tomatoes**
kale leaves and stems	**broccoli stems**
mushrooms	**spring onions**
fennel	**summer squash**
peeled winter squash	**celery root**
parsnips	

However, it is important to be aware of the individual characteristics of each vegetable, and that some need to be used in moderation.

Chard, kale, and mushrooms all can add an earthy richness to the stock, but none should be allowed to dominate. Mushrooms, especially wild ones, are an excellent addition to stock but have a distinct, woodsy taste, so only add a few unless you want Mushroom Stock.

Fennel, winter squash, and parsnips add sweetness. Fennel has a distinct anise flavour and should be used with care.

Tomatoes will add tartness.

Broccoli stems are nicer than you think, but, again, a little goes a long way.

Spring onions, summer squash, and celery root are terrific and not overwhelming, so throw some in if you have them on hand.

After you've made a few batches of stock, you will have a very good sense of what does what, and you will develop your own favourite combinations.

DARK VEGETABLE STOCK

The flavour of this stock is enhanced by browning some of the vegetables in a little oil before simmering them in water. Use it when you want a deeper, earthier taste in a soup or stew.

2 large onions
8 cloves garlic
5 large carrots
2–3 stalks celery
8 small mushrooms
1 tablespoon olive oil
1 teaspoon salt
pinch of cayenne

2.4 litres (4 pints) water
green top of 1 large leek
1 turnip
thick peel of 1 large potato
4 branches flat-leaf parsley
12 branches coriander
1 bay leaf
1 teaspoon black peppercorns

Peel and coarsely chop the onions and garlic. Scrape and slice the carrots, and slice the celery and mushrooms. Heat the olive oil in a large sauté pan, and add the onions, garlic, carrots, celery, mushrooms, salt, and cayenne. Stir the vegetables frequently over a medium flame for the next 10–15 minutes, until they are well browned. Don't worry about any dark bits that are sticking to the pan.

Add the water. Thoroughly wash the leek top and slice it and the turnip. Add them to the stock, along with the potato peel, parsley, coriander, bay leaf, and peppercorns. Bring the water to a boil, then lower the heat and let it boil gently for about 45 minutes. All the vegetables should be completely soft, and the stock dark brown and fragrant.

Strain the stock through a colander, then through a fine sieve to eliminate any sediment. Taste, and correct the salt if needed.

This makes about 1.5 litres (2½ pints) of stock.

ASSERTIVE VEGETABLE STOCK

This is a stock with a more complex, assertive flavour. It has a slightly sweet-tart edge from the addition of fennel and tomatoes, among other things.

2 large onions	1 turnip
8 cloves garlic	2 parsnips
5 large carrots	3–4 fennel stems, chopped
2–3 large stalks celery	2 medium tomatoes
1 tablespoon olive oil	4 branches parsley
1½ teaspoons salt	12 branches coriander
pinch of cayenne	50 g (2 oz) brown lentils
3 litres (5 pints) water	1 bay leaf
green top of 1 large leek	1 teaspoon dried thyme
thick peel of 1 large potato	1 teaspoon black peppercorns

Peel and coarsely chop the onions and garlic. Scrape and slice the carrots, and slice the celery. Heat the olive oil in a large sauté pan, and add the onions, garlic, carrots, celery, salt, and cayenne. Stir the vegetables frequently over a medium flame for the next 10–15 minutes, until they are well browned. Don't worry about any dark bits that are sticking to the pan.

Add the water. Thoroughly wash the leek top, scrub the potato, turnip, and parsnips, and rinse the fennel stems, tomatoes, and fresh herbs. Slice the leek top, cut the peel off the potato thickly, and slice or coarsely chop the turnip, parsnips, fennel stems, and tomatoes. Add all the remaining ingredients to the water in the pan, and bring it to a boil. Lower the heat and let the liquid boil gently for about 45 minutes. All the vegetables should be completely soft, and the stock quite dark and aromatic.

Strain the stock through a colander, then through a fine sieve to take out the sediment. Taste, and correct the seasoning if needed.

This makes about 1.7–2 litres (3–3½ pints) of stock.

Here are two conserves for the winter. Apple Butter and Pumpkin Butter are both so easy to make, and so rewarding for the effort put in, that I recommend them for a family project. There is no tricky part – nothing needs to set up or jell. In both cases, you only have to cook down the apples or the pumpkins, with sugar and spice to your taste, and when it looks thick enough, it's done.

Though they make welcome home-made gifts for the holidays, don't make the mistake of giving them all away.

APPLE BUTTER

This is what I usually make with my boys before the holidays, and we give away jars and jars of it, wrapped in bright red or green checked tea towels. Every year it comes out different, because we use different combinations of apples, but it's always delicious. Use whatever varieties you like, the best available in your area, but be sure to include some of the tart ones.

The amount of sugar and the amounts of spices are also just as flexible as can be, as it's all a matter of taste. The formula given here was actually used once, and faithfully recorded, but will probably never be precisely duplicated.

7 kg (15 lb) apples, mixed tart and sweet	2 tablespoons ground cinnamon
750 ml (1¼ pints) cider	¾ teaspoon ground cloves
60 ml (2 fl oz) cider vinegar	½ teaspoon ground nutmeg
550 g (18 oz) brown sugar	½ teaspoon ground ginger
	spring water as needed

Peel and core the apples, and combine them in a large, heavy-bottomed kettle with the cider and cider vinegar. Simmer, stirring occasionally with a wooden spoon, for a long, long time – maybe hours. The apples will soften, fall apart, turn to mush, start to thicken.

Add most of the sugar and the spices and continue cooking and stirring for at least another 30 minutes, adding a little spring water only if the mixture becomes so thick that it could scorch. Taste. Correct the seasoning if you like, adding a bit more sugar, more spices, or a touch of vinegar. Simmer for another little while to blend the flavours before tasting again. When it tastes the way you like it, you're done. This is apple butter, after all, not brain surgery.

You can leave it slightly lumpy, or make it beautifully smooth by running it through a blender in batches. Spoon the hot apple butter into sterile jars, screw on scalded lids, and process the jars in a boiling water bath for at least 20 minutes, or according to the manufacturer's instructions. Remove the jars, allow them to cool, and check the seals.

Processed this way, the apple butter will last as long as any sealed preserve. If you haven't the time for the water bath process, you can freeze it in small batches, or simply spoon it into perfectly clean, scalded jars, put on scalded lids, and keep it in the refrigerator for several weeks.

This makes about a dozen 350 g (12 oz) jars.

PUMPKIN BUTTER

If you like pumpkin pie, try this pumpkin butter on your breakfast toast. It's fat-free, and has a wonderfully rich flavour. Sometimes we make a big batch of this to pack into pretty jars and give away for Christmas (instead of apple butter), but we always keep half for ourselves.

The secret is to use a good pumpkin. The giant ones that are grown primarily for use as jack-o'-lanterns don't have a very intense flavour. Smaller pumpkins tend to be much better. Ask for advice at a local farm shop, in the produce department of a good super-market, or from a good gardener, to find out about the best pumpkin available in your area.

4.2–4.4 kg (9½–10 lb)
pumpkin, weighed whole
¾ teaspoon salt
4–5 teaspoons ground
cinnamon
1 teaspoon ground ginger,
more to taste

½ teaspoon grated nutmeg,
more to taste
½ teaspoon ground cloves,
more to taste
4–5 tablespoons cider vinegar
575–700 g (1¼–1½ lb) brown
sugar

optional: 2 tablespoons molasses

Cut the pumpkin in half, scrape out all the seeds, then put the pumpkin halves cut side down in a lightly oiled baking dish. Bake the pumpkin in the oven at 200°C/400°F/Gas 6 for about an hour, or until it feels soft when poked with a wooden spoon.

Remove from the oven and allow to cool slightly, then turn the pumpkin halves over and scoop the soft flesh out of the rind. Be sure not to get pieces of rind into the mix.

Combine the pumpkin in a large, non-reactive, heavy-bottomed pot with the remaining ingredients. Bring the mixture to a simmer and stir over low heat for 20–30 minutes, as the flavours marry and the excess moisture cooks away. Adjust the amounts of vinegar and sugar by tasting. Pumpkins vary a great deal in flavour and sweetness, so you have to play with this a little.

Purée the mixture in batches in a blender, and taste again; correct the seasoning if necessary and cook the purée down a little more if it feels thin – it should hold a soft shape.

Spoon the hot pumpkin butter into sterile jars, screw on new, scalded lids, and process in a boiling water bath for at least 20 minutes, or according to manufacturer's instructions. The pumpkin butter can also be frozen in small batches, or simply kept in tightly covered containers in the refrigerator for several weeks.

This makes about 1.8–2.2 kg (4–5 lb) of thick pumpkin butter. It develops its best flavour after a few days, and I like it served cold, spooned on to toast or a muffin.

BISCOTTI

Biscotti are very popular now, and seem to be everywhere, from supermarkets and bakeries to tiny shops and coffee bars. Most of the biscotti I've bought have been delicious, and I have no objection to 'store-bought', but if they are not easily available where you live, here is a basic recipe, with several variations. It will give you excellent biscotti for a fraction of the price we pay for the fancy packets.

Having a big jar of crisp, almond-studded biscotti on hand is amazingly nice. They can turn an ordinary dish of ice cream or a plate of berries into a fancy dessert, and a cup of coffee into a treat. They keep well, and they're very low in fat – what more could we want?

ALMOND BISCOTTI

2 tablespoons butter
450–575 g (1–1¼ lb) plain
  flour
1 teaspoon baking powder
½ teaspoon bicarbonate of
  soda
¼ teaspoon salt

2 eggs
2 egg whites
225 g (8 oz) sugar
½ teaspoon almond extract
75–175 g (3–6 oz) chopped
  almonds

Melt the butter and let it cool to lukewarm. Sift together 450 g (1 lb) of flour with the baking powder, bicarbonate of soda, and salt.

Beat the eggs and egg whites until foamy. Add the sugar and continue beating until thick and creamy. Beat in the almond extract, the melted butter, and the chopped almonds.

Stir the sifted flour mixture into the beaten eggs, using a wooden spoon – the dough will become too stiff for a beater.

Take half the dough and turn it out on to a well-floured board.

Sprinkle more flour on top and shape it into a smooth log about 4 cm (1½ inches) in diameter and about 36–38 cm (14–15 inches) long. You may have to work in a little extra flour if the dough is too soft to hold a shape – that will depend on the size of the eggs – but don't use any more flour than you need to. You will be able to handle the slightly sticky dough if you just keep it well dredged in flour.

Lift the log carefully on to a large baking sheet that is lined with parchment (or oiled, if you don't have parchment). Form another log with the other half of the dough and place it on the baking sheet, at least 10 cm (4 inches) away from the first one. Pat the logs down gently to flatten them just a little.

Bake the logs at 170°C/325°F/Gas 3 for about 25 minutes, or until they feel firm to the touch. Take them out and let them cool for at least 10–15 minutes. Turn the oven temperature down to 130°C/275°F/Gas 1.

Using a thin, sharp, serrated knife, cut the logs on a diagonal into 1 cm (½ inch) slices. Arrange the slices upright on 2 baking sheets, with space between them for air circulation, and bake them again at 130°C/275°F/Gas 1 for about 40 minutes. Reverse the positions of the baking sheets midway through the baking time to be sure that all the biscotti bake evenly.

Remove the biscotti from the oven and let them cool completely on wire racks. They keep well if packed in airtight tins or jars once they have completely cooled. I've heard that they keep for 3–4 weeks, but I can never keep mine that long.

Makes about 4 dozen biscotti

Anise Biscotti

Add a tablespoon of whole or slightly crushed anise seeds to the beaten egg mixture. You can eliminate the almonds if you want to, or leave them for a nice combination of flavours.

Chocolate-Almond Biscotti

Sift 40 g (1½ oz) of unsweetened pure cocoa powder into the flour mixture.

Gingerbread Biscotti

When sifting the dry ingredients, increase the baking powder to 1½ teaspoons, and add 1½ teaspoons of ground ginger, 2 teaspoons of cinnamon, and a pinch of cloves.

When beating the eggs, use only 1 whole egg, reduce the sugar to 175 g (6 oz), and add 50 g (2 oz) of molasses. Eliminate the almond extract. The chopped almonds are optional.

Chocolate-dipped Biscotti

Melt some excellent bittersweet chocolate carefully in a heavy-bottomed pan, stirring it over very low heat so that it does not scorch.

Dip biscotti into the chocolate, one by one, and lay them on racks or on waxed paper until the chocolate hardens. You can dip them half-way, either lengthwise or vertically, for a nice effect. You can also arrange them on wire racks and drizzle the melted chocolate over them from a spoon, making random patterns or zigzags.

The important thing is to allow the chocolate to cool completely before moving the biscotti. This is a slow process. It can take well over 2 hours. You can speed the process by putting the dipped or drizzled biscotti into the refrigerator, but the chocolate will lose its pretty sheen.

Many Other Variations

Once you've made a few batches of biscotti and have got the hang of it, you will do your own variations. You can add finely grated lemon or orange zest to the batter, or finely chopped dried fruit, or use hazelnuts instead of almonds, and so on.

LIST OF SUPPLIERS

The following will supply chillies by mail order:

The Cool Chile Company
PO Box 5702
London W10 6WE
(tel. 0171 229 9360)

The Cool Chile Company have a wide range of whole and powdered dried chillies, including chipotles, anchos, guajillos and mulatos. They also supply masa harina, and dried corn husks for making tamales.

Masa harina and other specialist ingredients, including chillies. can also be bought at the following:

Wild Oats
210 Westbourne Grove
London W11 2RH
(tel. 0171 229 1063)

Garcia
250 Portobello Road
London W11 1LL
(tel. 0171 221 6119)

Mexicolore
28 Warriner Gardens
London SW11 4EB
(tel. 0171 622 9577)

Street markets can also be a good source of specialist ingredients such as fresh chillies, squashes and (occasionally) nopalitos.

INDEX